Alexander Francis Chamberlain

The Child and Childhood in Folk Thought

(The Child in Primitive Culture)

Alexander Francis Chamberlain

The Child and Childhood in Folk Thought
(The Child in Primitive Culture)

ISBN/EAN: 9783744777414

Printed in Europe, USA, Canada, Australia, Japan

Cover: Foto ©Suzi / pixelio.de

More available books at **www.hansebooks.com**

THE CHILD AND CHILDHOOD
IN FOLK-THOUGHT

(THE CHILD IN PRIMITIVE CULTURE)

ALEXANDER FRANCIS CHAMBERLAIN
M.A., Ph.D.

LECTURER ON ANTHROPOLOGY IN CLARK UNIVERSITY, WORCESTER, MASS.; SOMETIME FELLOW IN
MODERN LANGUAGES IN UNIVERSITY COLLEGE, TORONTO, CANADA; FELLOW OF THE
AMERICAN ASSOCIATION FOR THE ADVANCEMENT OF SCIENCE; MEMBER OF
THE ANTHROPOLOGICAL SOCIETY OF WASHINGTON, OF THE AMERI-
CAN FOLK-LORE SOCIETY, OF THE CANADIAN INSTITUTE,
OF THE AMERICAN ACADEMY OF POLITICAL
AND SOCIAL SCIENCE, ETC.

"A little child shall lead them." — *Isaiah* xi. 6.
"For of such is the Kingdom of Heaven." — *Jesus.*

Norwood Press
J. S. Cushing & Co. — Berwick & Smith
Norwood Mass. U.S.A.

PREFATORY NOTE.

THE present volume is an elaboration and amplification of lectures on "The Child in Folk-Thought," delivered by the writer at the summer school held at Clark University in 1894. In connection with the interesting topic of "Child-Study" which now engages so much the attention of teachers and parents, an attempt is here made to indicate some of the chief child-activities among primitive peoples and to point out in some respects their survivals in the social institutions and culture-movements of to-day. The point of view to be kept in mind is the child and what he has done, or is said to have done, in all ages and among all races of men.

For all statements and citations references are given, and the writer has made every effort to place himself in the position of those whose opinion he records, — receiving and reporting without distortion or alteration.

He begs to return to his colleagues in the University, especially to its distinguished president, the *genius* of the movement for "Child-Study" in America, and to the members of the summer school of 1894, whose kind appreciation of his efforts has mainly led to the publication of this work, his sincerest gratitude for the sympathy and encouragement which they have so often exhibited and expressed with regard to the present and allied subjects of study and investigation in the field of Anthropology, pedagogical and psychological.

A. F. CHAMBERLAIN.

CLARK UNIVERSITY,
WORCESTER, Mass., April, 1895.

CONTENTS.

ix

x   *Contents.*

THE CHILD AND CHILDHOOD IN FOLK–THOUGHT.

——•o𝕏oo——

CHAPTER I.

CHILD-STUDY.

Oneness with Nature is the glory of Childhood; oneness with Childhood is the glory of the Teacher. — *G. Stanley Hall.*

> Homes ont l'estre comme metaulx,
> Vie et augment des vegetaulx,
> Instinct et sens comme les bruts,
> Esprit comme anges en attributs.
> [Man has as attributes: Being like metals,
> Life and growth like plants,
> Instinct and sense like animals,
> Mind like angels.] — *Jehan de Meung.*

> The Child is Father of the Man. — *Wordsworth.*

And he [Jesus] called to him a little child, and set him in the midst of them. — *Matthew* xviii. 2.

IT was an Oriental poet who sang: —

> "On parent knees, a naked, new-born child,
> Weeping thou sat'st, while all around thee smiled;
> So live, that, sinking in thy last, long sleep,
> Calm thou mayst smile, while all around thee weep,"

and not so very long ago even the anthropologist seemed satisfied with the approximation of childhood and old age, — one glance at the babe in the cradle, one look at the graybeard on his death-bed, gave all the knowledge desired or sought for. Man, big, burly, healthy, omniscient, was the subject of all investigation.

B   1

But now a change has come over the face of things. As did that great teacher of old, so, in our day, has one of the ministers of science "called to him a little child and set him in the midst of them,"—greatest in the kingdom of anthropology is assuredly that little child, as we were told centuries ago, by the prophet of Galilee, that he is greatest in the kingdom of heaven. The child, together with woman, who, in so many respects in which the essential human characteristics are concerned, so much resembles him, is now beyond doubt the most prominent figure in individual, as well as in racial, anthropology. Dr. D. G. Brinton, in an appreciative notice of the recent volume on *Man and Woman*, by Havelock Ellis, in which the secondary sexual differences between the male and the female portions of the human race are so well set forth and discussed, remarks: "The child, the infant in fact, alone possesses in their fulness 'the chief distinctive characters of humanity. The highest human types, as represented in men of genius, present a striking approximation to the child-type. In man, from about the third year onward, further growth is to some extent growth in degeneration and senility.' Hence the true tendency of the progressive evolution of the race is to become child-like, to become feminine." (*Psych. Rev.* I. 533.)

As Dr. Brinton notes, in this sense women are leading evolution —Goethe was right: *Das Ewig-weibliche zieht uns hinan.* But here belongs also the child-human, and he was right in very truth who said: "A little child shall lead them." What new meaning flashes into the words of the Christ, who, after declaring that "the kingdom of God cometh not with observation: neither shall they say, Lo, here! or, There! for lo, the kingdom of God is within you," in rebuke of the Pharisees, in rebuke of his own disciples, "called to him a little child and set him in the midst of them, and said, Verily I say unto you, Except ye turn, and become as little children, ye shall in no wise enter into the kingdom of heaven." Even physically, the key to the kingdom of heaven lies in childhood's keeping.

Vast indeed is now the province of him who studies the child. In Somatology,—the science of the physical characteristics and constitution of the body and its members,—he seeks not alone to observe the state and condition of the skeleton and its integuments during life, but also to ascertain their nature and character in the period of prenatal existence, as well as when causes natural, or unnatural, disease, the exhaustion of old age, violence, or the like, have induced the dissolution of death.

In Linguistics and Philology, he endeavours to discover the essence and import of those manifold, inarticulate, or unintelligible sounds, which, with the long flight of time, develop into the splendidly rounded periods of a Webster or a Gladstone, or swell nobly in the rhythmic beauties of a Swinburne or a Tennyson.

In Art and Technology, he would fain fathom the depths of those rude scribblings and quaint efforts at delineation, whence, in the course of ages, have been evolved the wonders of the alphabet and the marvellous creations of a Rubens and an Angelo.

In Psychology, he seeks to trace, in childish prattlings and lore of the nursery, the far-off beginnings of mythology, philosophy, religion. Beside the stories told to children in explanation of the birth of a sister or a brother, and the children's own imaginings concerning the little new-comer, he may place the speculations of sages and theologians of all races and of all ages concerning birth, death, immortality, and the future life, which, growing with the centuries, have ripened into the rich and wholesome dogmas of the church.

Ethnology, with its broad sweep over ages and races of men, its searchings into the origins of nations and of civilizations, illumined by the light of Evolution, suggests that in the growth of the child from helpless infancy to adolescence, and through the strong and trying development of manhood to the idiosyncrasies of disease and senescence, we have an epitome in miniature of the life of the race; that in primitive tribes, and in those members of our civilized communities, whose growth upward and onward has been retarded by inherited tendencies which it has been out of their power to overcome, or by a *milieu* and environment, the control and subjugation of which required faculties and abilities they did not possess, we see, as it were, ethnic children; that in the nursery, the asylum, the jail, the mountain fastnesses of earth, or the desert plains, peopled by races whose ways are not our ways, whose criteria of culture are far below ours, we have a panorama of what has transpired since, alone and face to face with a new existence, the first human beings partook of the fruit of the tree of knowledge and became conscious of the great gulf, which, after millenniums of struggle and fierce competition, had opened between the new, intelligent, speaking anthropoids and their fellows who straggled so far behind.

Wordsworth has said: "The child is father of the man," and a German writer has expanded the same thought: —

> "Die Kindheit von heute
> Ist die Menschheit von morgen,
> Die Kindheit von heute
> Ist die Menschheit von gestern."
> ["The childhood of to-day
> Is the manhood of to-morrow,
> The childhood of to-day
> Is the manhood of yesterday."]

In brief, the child is father of the man and brother of the race. In all ages, and with every people, the arcana of life and death, the mysteries of birth, childhood, puberty, adolescence, maidenhood, womanhood, manhood, motherhood, fatherhood, have called forth the profoundest thought and speculation. From the contemplation of these strange phenomena sprang the esoteric doctrines of Egypt and the East, with their horrible accompaniments of vice and depravity; the same thoughts, low and terrible, hovered before the devotees of Moloch and Cybele, when Carthage sent her innocent boys to the furnace, a sacrifice to the king of gods, and Asia Minor offered up the virginity of her fairest daughters to the first-comer at the altars of the earth-mother. Purified and ennobled by long centuries of development and unfolding, the blossoming of such conceptions is seen in the great sacrifice which the Son of Man made for the children of men, and in the cardinal doctrine of the religion which he founded, — "Ye must be born again," — the regeneration, which alone gave entrance into Paradise.

The Golden Age of the past of which, through the long lapse of years, dreamers have dreamt and poets sung, and the Golden City, glimpses of whose glorious portal have flashed through the prayers and meditations of the rapt enthusiast, seem but one in their foundation, as the Eden of the world's beginning and the heaven that shall open to men's eyes, when time shall be no more, are but closely allied phases, nay, but one and the same phase, rather, of the world-old thought, — the ethnic might have been, the ought to be of all the ages. The imagined, retrospect childhood of the past is twin-born with the ideal, prospective childhood of the world to come. Here the savage and the philosopher, the child and the genius, meet; the wisdom of the first and of the last century of human existence is at one. Childhood is the mirror in which these reflections are cast, — the childhood of the race is depicted with the same colours as the childhood of the individual. We can read a larger thought into the words of Hartley Coleridge : —

"Oh what a wilderness were this sad world,
If man were always man, and never child."

Besides the anthropometric and psycho-physical investigations of the child carried on in the scientific laboratory with exact instruments and unexceptionable methods, there is another field of "Child-Study" well worthy our attention for the light it can shed upon some of the dark places in the wide expanse of pedagogical science and the art of education.

Its laboratory of research has been the whole wide world, the experimenters and recorders the primitive peoples of all races and all centuries, — fathers and mothers whom the wonderland of parenthood encompassed and entranced; the subjects, the children of all the generations of mankind.

The consideration of "The Child in Folk-Thought," — what tribe upon tribe, age after age, has thought about, ascribed to, dreamt of, learned from, taught to, the child, the parent-lore of the human race, in its development through savagery and barbarism to civilization and culture, — can bring to the harvest of pedagogy many a golden sheaf.

The works of Dr. Ploss, *Das kleine Kind, Das Kind,* and *Das Weib,* encyclopædic in character as the two last are, covering a vast field of research relating to the anatomy, physiology, hygiene, dietetics, and ceremonial treatment of child and mother, of girl and boy, all over the world, and forming a huge mine of information concerning child-birth, motherhood, sex-phenomena, and the like, have still left some aspects of the anthropology of childhood practically untouched. In English, the child has, as yet, found no chronicler and historian such as Ploss. The object of the present writer is to treat of the child from a point of view hitherto entirely neglected, to exhibit what the world owes to childhood and the motherhood and the fatherhood which it occasions, to indicate the position of the child in the march of civilization among the various races of men, and to estimate the influence which the child-idea and its accompaniments have had upon sociology, mythology, religion, language; for the touch of the child is upon them all, and the debt of humanity to the little children has not yet been told. They have figured in the world's history and its folk-lore as *magi* and "medicine-men," as priests and oracle-keepers, as physicians and healers, as teachers and judges, as saints, heroes, discoverers, and inventors, as musicians and poets, actors and labourers in many fields of human activity, have been compared to the foolish and to the most wise, have been looked upon as fetiches and as gods, as the fit sacrifice to offended Heaven, and as the saviours and regenerators of mankind. The history of the child in human society and of the human ideas and institutions which have sprung from its consideration can have here only a beginning. This book is written in full sympathy with the thought expressed in the words of the Latin poet Juvenal: *Maxima debetur pueris reverentia,* and in the declaration of Jean Paul: "I love God and every little child."

CHAPTER II.

The Child's Tribute to the Mother.

A good mother is worth a hundred schoolmasters. — *English Proverb.*

The first poet, the first priest, was the first mother.
The first empire was a woman and her children. — *O. T. Mason.*

When society, under the guidance of the "fathers of the church," went almost to destruction in the dark ages, it was the "mothers of the people" who saved it and set it going on the new right path. — *Zmigrodski* (adapted).

The story of civilization is the story of the mother. — *Zmigrodski.*

One mother is more venerable than a thousand fathers. — *Laws of Manu.*

If the world were put into one scale, and my mother into the other, the world would kick the beam. — *Lord Langdale.*

Names of the Mother.

In *A Song of Life,* — a book in which the topic of sex is treated with such delicate skill, — occurs this sentence: "The motherhood of mammalian life is the most sacred thing in physical existence" (120. 92), and Professor Drummond closes his *Lowell Institute Lectures on the Evolution of Man* in the following words: "It is a fact to which too little significance has been given, that the whole work of organic nature culminates in the making of Mothers — that the animal series end with a group which even the naturalist has been forced to call the *Mammalia.* When the savage mother awoke to her first tenderness, a new creative hand was at work in the world" (36. 240). Said Henry Ward Beecher: "When God thought of *Mother,* he must have laughed with satisfaction, and framed it quickly, — so rich, so deep, so divine, so full of soul, power, and beauty, was the conception," and it was unto babes and sucklings that this wisdom was first revealed. From their lips first fell the sound which parents of later ages

7

consecrated and preserved to all time. With motherhood came into the world song, religion, the thought of immortality itself; and the mother and the child, in the course of the ages, invented and preserved most of the arts and the graces of human life and human culture. In language, especially, the mother and the child have exercised a vast influence. In the names for "mother," the various races have recognized the debt they owe to her who is the "fashioner" of the child, its "nourisher" and its "nurse." An examination of the etymologies of the words for "mother" in all known languages is obviously impossible, for the last speakers and interpreters of many of the unwritten tongues of the earth are long since dead and gone. How primitive man — the first man of the race — called his mother, we can but surmise. Still, a number of interesting facts are known, and some of these follow.

The word *mother* is one of the oldest in the language; one of the very few words found among all the great branches of the widely scattered Aryan race, bearing witness, in ages far remote, before the Celt, the Teuton, the Hellene, the Latin, the Slav, and the Indo-Iranian were known, to the existence of the family, with the *mother* occupying a high and honourable place, if not indeed the highest place of all. What the etymological meaning was, of the primitive Aryan word from which our *mother* is descended, is uncertain. It seems, however, to be a noun derived, with the agent-suffix -*t-r*, from the root *ma*, "to measure." Skeat thinks the word meant originally "manager, regulator [of the household]," rejecting, as unsupported by sufficient evidence, a suggested interpretation as the "producer." Kluge, the German lexicographer, hesitates between the "apportioner, measurer," and the "former [of the embryo in the womb]." In the language of the Klamath Indians of Oregon, *p'gishap*, "mother," really signifies the "maker."

The Karankawas of Texas called "mother," *kaninma*, the "suckler," from *kanin*, "the female breast." In Latin *mamma* seems to signify "teat, breast," as well as "mother," but Skeat doubts whether there are not two distinct words here. In Finnish and some other primitive languages a similar resemblance or identity exists between the words for "breast" and "mother." In Lithuanian, *móte* — cognate with our *mother* — signifies "wife," and in the language of the Caddo Indians of Louisiana and Texas *sássin* means both "wife" and "mother." The familiar "mother" of the New England farmer of the "Old Homestead" type, presents, perhaps, a relic of the same thought. The word *dame*, in older English, from being a title of respect for women — there is a close analogy in the history of *sire* — came to signify "mother." Chaucer translates the French of the *Romaunt of the Rose*, "Enfant qui craint ni pere ni mere Ne peut que bien ne le comperre," by "For who that dredeth sire ne dame Shall it abie in bodie or name," and Shakespeare makes poor Caliban declare: "I never saw a woman, But only Sycorax, my dam." Nowadays, the word *dam* is applied only to the female parent of animals, horses especially. The word, which is one with the honourable appellation *dame*, goes back to the Latin *domina*, "mistress, lady," the feminine of *dominus*, "lord, master." In not a few languages, the words for "father" and "mother" are derived from the same root, or one from the other, by simple phonetic change. Thus, in the Sandeh language of Central Africa, "mother" is *n-amu*, "father," *b-amu;* in the Cholona of South America, *pa* is "father," *pa-n*, "mother"; in the Pentlatc of British Columbia, "father" is *māa*, "mother," *tāa*, while in the Songish *măn* is "father" and *tan* "mother" (404. 143).

Certain tongues have different words for "mother," according as it is a male or a female who speaks. Thus in the Okanak·ēn, a Salish dialect of British Columbia, a man or a boy says for "mother," *sk'ōi*, a woman or a girl, *tōm;* in Kalispelm the corresponding terms for "my mother" are *isk'ōi* and *intoop*. This distinction, however, seems not to be so common as in the case of "father."

In a number of languages the words for "mother" are different when the latter is addressed and when she is spoken of or referred to. Thus in the Kwakiutl, Nootka, and Çatlōltq, three British Columbia tongues, the two words for "mother" are respectively *át, abóuk; āt, abᴇmp; niкʜ, tūn*. It is to be noted, apparently, that the word used in address is very often simpler, more primitive, than the other. Even in English we find something similar in the use of *ma* (or *mama*) and *mother*.

In the Gothic alone, of all the great Teutonic dialects, — the language into which Bishop Wulfila translated the Scriptures in the fourth century, — the cognate equivalent of our English *mother* does not appear. The Gothic term is *aithei,* evidently related to *atta,* "father," and belonging to the great series of nursery words, of which our own *ma, mama,* are typical examples. These are either relics of the first articulations of the child and the race, transmitted by hereditary adaptation from generation to generation, or are the coinages of mother and nurse in imitation of the cries of infancy.

These simple words are legion in number and are found over the whole inhabited earth, — in the wigwam of the Redskin, in the tent of the nomad Bedouin, in the homes of cultured Europeans and Americans. Dr. Buschmann studied these "nature-sounds," as he called them, and found that they are chiefly variations and combinations of the syllables *ab, ap, am, an, ad, at, ba, pa, ma, na, da, ta,* etc., and that in one language, not absolutely unrelated to another, the same sound will be used to denote the "mother" that in the second signifies "father," thus evidencing the applicability of these words, in the earliest stages of their existence, to either, or to both, of the parents of the child (166. 85). Pott, while remarking a wonderful resemblance in the names for parents all over the world, seeks to establish the rather doubtful thesis that there is a decided difference in the nature of the words for "father" and those for "mother," the former being "man-like, stronger," the latter "woman-like, mild" (517. 57).

Some languages apparently do not possess a single specialized word for "mother." The Hawaiian, for example, calls "mother and the sisters of the mother" *makua wahine,* "female parent," that being the nearest equivalent of our "mother," while in Tonga, as indeed with us to-day, sometimes the same term is applied to a real mother and to an adopted one (100. 389). In Japan, the paternal aunt and the maternal aunt are called "little mother." Similar terms and appellations are found in other primitive tongues. A somewhat extended discussion of names for "mother," and the questions connected with the subject, will be found in Westermarck (166. 85). Here also will be found notices of the names among various peoples for the nearest relatives of the mother and father. Incidentally it is worth noting that Westermarck controverts Professor Vambéry's opinion that the Turko-

Tartar words for "mother," *ana, ene*, originally meant "nurse" or "woman" (from the root *an, en*), holding that exactly the reverse is the fact, "the terms for *mother* being the primitive words." He is also inclined to think that the Aryan roots *pa*, "to protect, to nourish," and *ma*, "to fashion," came from *pa*, "father," and *ma*, "mother," and not *vice versâ*. Mr. Bridges, the missionary who has studied so well the Yahgans of Tierra del Fuego, states that "the names *imu* and *dabi* — father and mother — have no meaning apart from their application, neither have any of their other very definite and ample list of terms for relatives, except the terms *macu* [cf. *magu*, "parturition"] and *macipa* [cf. *cipa*, "female"], son and daughter." This statement is, however, too sweeping perhaps (166. 88).

According to Colonel Mallery, the Ute Indians indicate "mother" by placing the index finger in the mouth (497 a. 479). Clark describes the common Indian sign as follows: "Bring partially curved and compressed right hand, and strike with two or three gentle taps right or left breast, and make sign for *female;* though in conversation the latter is seldom necessary. Deaf mutes make sign for *female*, and cross hands as in their sign for *baby*, and move them to front and upwards" (420. 262). Somewhat similar is the sign for "father": "Bring the compressed right hand, back nearly outwards, in front of right or left breast, tips of fingers few inches from it; move the hand, mostly by wrist action, and gently tap the breast with tips of fingers two or three times, then make sign for *male*. Some Indians tap right breast for 'father,' and left for 'mother.' Deaf-mutes make sign for *male*, and then holding hands fixed as in their sign for *baby*, but a little higher, move the hands to front and upwards" (420. 167).

Interesting is the following statement of Mr. Codrington, the well-known missionary to the Melanesians: —

"In Mota the word used for 'mother' is the same that is used for the division [tribe?] *veve*, with a plural sign *ra veve*. And it is not that a man's kindred are so called after his mother, but that his mother is called his kindred, as if she were the representative of the division to which he belongs; as if he were not the child of a particular woman, but of the whole kindred for whom she brought him into the world." Moreover, at Mota, in like fashion, " the word for 'consort,' 'husband,' or 'wife,' is in a plural form *ra soai*, the word used for members of a body, or the component parts of a canoe " (25. 307–8).

Mother-Right.

Since the appearance of Bachofen's famous book on the matriarchate, " mother-right," that system of society in which the mother is paramount in the family and the line of inheritance passes through her, has received much attention from students of sociology and primitive history.

Post thus defines the system of mother-right: —

" The matriarchate is a system of relationship according to which the child is related only to his mother and to the persons connected with him through the female line, while he is looked upon as not related to his father and the persons connected with him through the male line. According to this system, therefore, the narrowest family circle consists not, as with us to-day, of father, mother, and child, but of mother, mother's brother, and sister's child, whilst the father is completely wanting, and the mother's brother takes the father's place with the sister's children. The real father is not the father of his own children, but of his nephews and nieces, whilst the brother of his wife is looked upon as father to his children. The brothers and sisters of the mother form with her a social group, to which belong also the children of the sisters, the children of the daughters of the sisters, etc., but not the children of the brothers, the children of the sisters' sons, etc. With every husband the relationship ceases " (127. I. 13–14).

The system of mother-right prevails widely over the whole globe; in some places, however, only in fragmentary condition. It is found amongst nearly all the native tribes of America; the peoples of Malaysia, Melanesia, Australia, Micronesia, and Polynesia, the Dravidian tribes of India; in Africa it is found in the eastern Sahara, the Soudan, the east and west coast, and in the centre of the continent, but not to the exclusion, altogether, of father-right, while in the north the intrusion of Europeans and the followers of Islam has tended to suppress it. Traces of its former existence are discovered among certain of the ancient tribes of Asia Minor, the old Egyptians, Arabs, Greeks, Romans, Teutons, the Aryans of India, the Chinese, Japanese, etc.

Mother-right has been recognized by many sociologists as a system of family relationship, perhaps the most widespread, perhaps the most primitive of all. Dr. Brinton says:—

"The foundation of the gentile system, as of any other family life, is . . . the mutual affection between kindred. In the primitive period this is especially between children of the same mother, not so much because of the doubt of paternity, as because physiologically and obviously, it is the mother in whom is formed, and from whom alone proceeds, the living being" (412. 47).

Professor O. T. Mason, in the course of his interesting address on "Woman's Share in Primitive Culture," remarks (112. 10):—

"Such sociologists as Morgan and McLennan affirm that the primitive society had no family organization at all. They hypothecate a condition in which utter promiscuity prevailed. I see no necessity for this. There is some organization among insects. Birds mate and rear a little family. Many animals set up a kind of patriarchal horde. On the other hand, they err greatly who look among savages for such permanent home life as we enjoy. Marriages are in groups, children are the sons and daughters of these groups; divorces are common. The fathers of the children are not known, and if they were, they would have no authority on that account. The mother never changes her name, the children are named after her, or, at least, are not named after the father. The system of gentes prevails, each gens consisting of a hypothetical female ancestress, and all her descendants through females. These primitive men and women, having no other resort, hit upon this device to hold a band of kin together. Here was the first social tie on earth; the beginning of the state. The first empire was a woman and her children, regardless of paternity. This was the beginning of all the social bonds which unite us. Among our own Indians mother-right was nearly universal. Upon the death of a chief whose office was hereditary, he was succeeded, not by his son, but by the son of a sister, or an aunt, or a niece; all his property that was not buried with him fell to the same parties, could not descend to his children, since a child and the father belonged to different gentes." McLennan has discussed at some length the subject of kinship in ancient Greece (115. 193–246), and maintains that "the system of double kinship, which prevailed in the time of Homer, was preceded by a system of kinship through females only," referring to the cases of Lycaon, Tlepolemus, Helen, Arnæus, Glaucus, and Sarpedon, besides the evidence in the *Orestes* of Euripides, and the *Eumenides* of Æschylus. In the last, " the jury are equally divided on the plea [that Orestes was not of kin to his mother, Clytemnestra, whom he had killed, — " Do you call *me* related by blood to my mother?"], and Orestes gains his cause by the casting vote of Athene." According to tradition, "in Greece, before the time of Cecrops, children always bore the name of their mothers," in marked contrast to tha state of affairs in Sparta, where, according to Philo, "the marriage tie was so loose that men lent their wives to one another, and cared little by whom children were begotten, provided they turned out strong and healthy."

We have preserved for us, by Plutarch and others, some of the opinions of Greek philosophers on the relation of the father and the mother to the child. Plato is represented as calling "mind the conception, idea, model, and *father ;* and matter the mother, *nurse,* or seat and region capable of births." Chrysippus is said to have stated: "The fœtus is nourished in the womb like a plant; but, being born, is refrigerated and hardened by the air, and its spirit being changed it becomes an animal," a view which, as McLennan points out, "constitutes the mother the mere nurse of her child, just as a field is of the seed sown in it."

The view of Apollo, which, in the council of the gods, influenced Athene to decide for Orestes, is this: —

"The bearer of the so-called offspring is not *the mother* of it, but only the nurse of the newly conceived fœtus. It is the male who is the author of its being; while she, as a stranger, for a stranger, preserves the young plant for those for whom the god has not blighted it in the bud. And I will show you a proof of this assertion; one *may* become a father without a mother. There stands by a witness of this in the daughter of Olympian Zeus, who was not even nursed [much less engendered or begotten] in the darkness of the womb" (115. 211). This is akin to the wild discussion in the misogynistic Middle Ages about the possibility of *lucina sine concubitu.* The most recent and most scholarly discussion of all questions involved in "mother-right" will be found

in the *History of Human Marriage* by Edward Westermarck, a
book in which the antiquity of monogamy and the improbability
of anything like promiscuity having ever generally obtained are
clearly shown (106). Mr. Codrington, in his account of *Social
Regulations in Melanesia*, sketches for us the position of the
parent where the mother-descent prevails : —

"To a Melanesian man it may almost be said that all women,
of his own generation at least, are either sisters or wives ; to the
Melanesian woman, that all men are brothers or husbands. An
excellent illustration of this is given in a story from Aurora, in
the New Hebrides, in which Oatu discovers twin boys, children
of his dead sister, and brings them to his wife. 'Are these,' she
asks, 'my children or my husbands?' Oatu answers : 'Your
husbands, to be sure ; they are my sister's children'" (25. 306–7).

Mother-Queen.

Professor Mason has said "the first empire was a woman and
her children," and with not a few primitive tribes women were
chiefs and took large part in the affairs of the nation. Even
among the warlike Iroquois, the back that bore the cradle sustained the burden of the state. The Jesuit Lafiteau declared : —

"There is nothing more real than this superiority of the
women. It is they who constitute the tribe, transmit the nobility
of blood, keep up the genealogical tree and the order of inheritance, and perpetuate the family. They possess all actual authority ; own the land and the fields and their harvests ; they are the
soul of all councils, the arbiters of peace and war ; they have the
care of the public treasury ; slaves are given to them ; they
arrange marriages ; the children belong to them, and to their
blood are confined the lines of descent and the order of inheritance. The men, on the other hand, are wholly isolated and restricted to their personal affairs ; their children are strangers to
them, and when they die, everything comes to an end, and it is
only the women who can keep up and perpetuate the family "
(112. 10).

It was this people who produced men of whom it could be
said : "Physically the stock is most superior, unsurpassed by
any other on the continent, and I may even say by any other

people in the world; for it stands on record that the five companies (five hundred men) recruited from the Iroquois of New York and Canada during our civil war stood first on the list among all the recruits of our army for height, vigour, and corporeal symmetry" (412. 82). And it was this people too who produced Hiawatha, a philosophic legislator and reformer, worthy to rank with Solon and Lycurgus, and the founder of a great league whose object was to put an end to war, and unite all the nations in one bond of brotherhood and peace.

Among the Choctaw-Muskogee tribes, women-chiefs were also known; the Yuchis, Chetimachas, had "Queens"; occasionally we find female rulers elsewhere in America, as among the Winnebagos, the Nah·ane, etc. Scattered examples of gynocracy are to be found in other parts of the world, and in their later development some of the Aryan races have been rather partial to women as monarchs, and striking instances of a like predilection are to be met with among the Semitic tribes, — Boadicea, Dido, Semiramis, Deborah are well-known cases in point, to say nothing of the Christian era and its more enlightened treatment of woman.

The fate of women among those peoples and in those ages where extreme exaltation of the male has been the rule, is sketched by Letourneau in his chapter on *The Condition of Women* (100. 173-185); the contrast between the Australians, to whom "woman is a domestic animal, useful for the purposes of genesic pleasure, for reproduction, and, in case of famine, for food," the Chinese, who can say "a newly-married woman ought to be merely as a shadow and as an echo in the house," the primitive Hindus, who forbade the wife to call her husband by name, but made her term him "master, lord," or even "god," and even some of our modern races in the eye of whose law women are still minors, and the Iroquois, is remarkable. Such great differences in the position and rights of women, existing through centuries, over wide areas of the globe, have made the study of comparative pedagogy a most important branch of human sociology. The mother as teacher has not been, and is not now, the same the world over.

As men holding supreme power have been termed "father," women have in like manner been called "mother." The title of the queen-mother in Ashanti is *nana*, "Grandmother" (438. 259), and to some of the Indian tribes of Canada Queen Victoria is the "Great White Mother," the "Great Mother across the Sea." In Ashanti the "rich, prosperous, and powerful" are termed *oman enna*, "mothers of the tribe," and are expected to make suitably large offerings to the dead, else there will be no child born in the neglectful family for a certain period (438. 228).

With the Romans, *mater* and its derivative *matrona*, came to be applied as titles of honour; and beside the rites of the *parentalia* we find those of the *matronalia* (492. 454).

In the ancient Hebrew chronicles we find mention of Deborah, that "mother in Israel."

With us, off whose tongues "the fathers," "forefathers," "ancestors" (hardly including ancestresses) and the like rolled so glibly, the "Pilgrim Fathers" were glorified long before the "Pilgrim Mothers," and hardly yet has the mother of the "father of his country" received the just remembrance and recognition belonging to her who bore so noble and so illustrious a son. By and by, however, it is to be hoped, we shall be free from the reproach cast upon us by Colonel Higginson, and wake up to the full consciousness that the great men of our land have had mothers, and proceed to re-write our biographical dictionaries and encyclopædias of life-history.

In Latin *mater*, as does *mother* with us, possessed a wide extent of meaning, "mother, parent, producer, nurse, preparer, cause, origin, source," etc. *Mater omnium artium necessitas*, "Necessity is the mother of invention," and similar phrases were in common use, as they are also in the languages of to-day. Connected with *mater* is *materia*, "matter," — *mother*-stuff, perhaps, — and from it is derived *matrimonium*, which testifies concerning primitive Roman sociology, in which the mother-idea must have been prominent, something we cannot say of our word *marriage*, derived ultimately from the Latin *mas*, "a male."

Westermarck notes the Nicaraguans, Dyaks, Minahassers, Andaman Islanders, Pádam, Munda Kols, Santals, Moors of the Western Soudan, Tuaregs, Tedâ, among the more or less primitive peoples with whom woman is held in considerable respect, and sometimes, as among the Munda Kols, bears the proud title "mistress of the house" (166. 500, 501). As Havelock Ellis

c

remarks, women have shown themselves the equals of men as rulers, and most beneficial results have flowed from their exercise of the great political wisdom and adaptation to statecraft which seems to belong especially to the female sex. The household has been a training-school for women in the more extended spheres of human administrative society.

Alma Mater.

The college graduate fondly calls the institution from which he has obtained his degree *Alma Mater,* "nourishing, fostering, cherishing mother," and he is her *alumnus* (foster-child, nourished one). For long years the family of the benign and gracious mother, whose wisdom was lavished upon her children, consisted of sons alone, but now, with the advent of "sweeter manners, purer laws," daughters have come to her also, and the *alumnæ,* "the sweet girl-graduates in their golden hair," share in the best gifts their parent can bestow. To Earth also, the term *Alma Mater* has been applied, and the great nourishing mother of all was indeed the first teacher of man, the first university of the race.

Alma, alumnus, alumna, are all derived from *alo,* "I nourish, support." From the radical *al,* following various trains of thought, have come: *alesco,* "I grow up"; *coalesco,* "I grow together"; *adolesco,* "I grow up," — whence *adolescent,* etc.; *obsolesco,* "I wear out"; *alimentum,* "food"; *alimonium,* "support"; *altor, altrix,* "nourisher"; *altus,* "high, deep" (literally, "grown"); *elementum,* "first principle," etc. Connected with *adolesco* is *adultus,* whence our *adult,* with the radical of which the English word *old (eld)* is cognate. From the root *al,* "to grow, to make to grow, to nourish," spring also the Latin words *prōles,* "offspring," *suboles,* "offspring, sprout," *indōles,* "inborn or native quality."

"Mother's Son."

The familiar expression "every mother's son of us" finds kin in the Modern High German *Muttersohn, Mutterkind,* which, with the even more significant *Muttermensch* (human being), takes us back to the days of "mother-right." Rather different, however, is the idea called up by the corresponding Middle Low German *modersone,* which means "bastard, illegitimate child."

A synonym of *Muttermensch* is *Mutterseele,* for soul and man once meant pretty much the same. The curious expression *mutterseelenallein,* "quite alone; alone by one's self," is given a peculiar interpretation by Lippert, who sees in it a relic of the burial of the dead (soul) beneath the hearth, threshold, or floor of the house; "wessen Mutter im Hause ruht, der kann daheim immer nur mit seiner Mutterseele selbander allein sein." Or, perhaps, it goes back to the time when, as with the Seminoles of Florida, the babe was held over the mouth of the mother, whose death resulted from its birth, in order that her departing spirit might enter the new being.

In German, the "mother-feeling" makes its influence felt in the nomenclature of the lower brute creation. As contrasted with our English female donkey (she-donkey), mare, ewe, ewe-lamb, sow, doe-hare (female hare), queen-bee, etc., we find *Mutteresel,* "mother-donkey"; *Mutterpferd,* "mother-horse"; *Mutterschaf,* "mother-sheep"; *Mutterlamm,* "mother lamb"; *Mutterschwein,* "mother swine"; *Mutterhase,* "mother-hare"; *Mutterbiene,* "mother-bee."

Nor is this feeling absent from the names of plants and things inanimate. We have *Mutterbirke,* "birch"; *Mutterblume,* "seed-flower"; *Mutternelke,* "carnation"; *Mutternägelein* (our "mother-clove"); *Mutterholz.* In English we have "mother of thyme," etc. In Japan a triple arrangement in the display of the flower-vase — a floral trinity — is termed *chichi,* "father"; *haha,* "mother"; *ten,* "heaven" (189. 74).

In the nursery-lore of all peoples, as we can see from the fairy-tales and child-stories in our own and other languages, this attribution of motherhood to all things animate and inanimate is common, as it is in the folk-lore and mythology of the adult members of primitive races now existing.

Mother Poet.

The arts of poetry, music, dancing, according to classic mythology, were presided over by nine goddesses, or Muses, daughters of Mnemosyne, goddess of memory, "Muse-mother," as Mrs. Browning terms her. The history of woman as a poet has yet to be written, but to her in the early ages poetry owed much of its development and its beauty. Mr. Vance has remarked that "among many of the lowest races the only love-dances in vogue are those performed by the women" (545 a. 4069). And Letourneau considers that "there are good grounds for supposing that women may have especially participated in the creation of the lyric of the erotic kind." Professor Mason, in the course of his remarks upon woman's labour in the world in all ages, says (112. 12): —

"The idea of a *maker*, or creator-of-all-things found no congenial soil in the minds of savage men, who manufactured nothing. But, as the first potters, weavers, house-builders were women, the idea of a divine creator as a moulder, designer, and architect originated with her, or was suggested by her. The three Fates, Clotho, who spins the thread of life; Lachesis, who fixes its prolongation; and Atropos, who cuts this thread with remorseless shears, are necessarily derived from woman's work. The mother-goddess of all peoples, culminating in the apotheosis of the Virgin Mary, is an idea, either originated by women, or devised to satisfy their spiritual cravings."

And we have, besides the goddesses of all mythologies, personifying woman's devotion, beauty, love. What shall we say of that art, highest of all human accomplishments, in the exercise of which men have become almost as gods ? The old Greeks called the singer ποιητής, "maker," and perhaps from woman the first poets learned how to worship in noble fashion that great *maker* of all, whose poem is the universe. Religion and poetry have ever gone hand in hand ; Plato was right when he said : "I am persuaded, somehow, that good poets are the inspired interpreters of the gods." Of song, as of religion, it may perhaps be said : *Dux fœmina facti.*

To the mother beside the cradle where lies her tender offspring, song is as natural as speech itself to man. Lullabies are found in every land ; everywhere the joyous mother-heart bursts forth into song. The German proverb is significant: "Wer ein säugendes Kind hat, der hat eine singende Frau," and Fischer, a quaint poet of the sixteenth century, has beautifully expressed a like idea : —

"Wo Honig ist, da sammlen sich die Fliegen,
Wo Kinder sind, da singt man um die Wiegen."

Ploss, in whose book is to be found a choice collection of lullabies from all over the globe, remarks: "The folk-poetry of all
peoples is rich in songs whose texts and melodies the tender
mother herself imagined and composed" (326. II. 128).

The Countess Martinengo-Cesaresco devotes an interesting
chapter of her *Essays in the Study of Folk-Song* to the subject of lullabies. But not cradle-songs alone have sprung from
woman's genius. The world over, dirges and funeral-laments
have received their poetical form from the mother. As name-
giver, too, in many lands, the mother exercised this side of her
imaginative faculty. The mother and the child, from whom
language received its chief inspiration, were also the callers
forth of its choicest and most creative form.

Mother - Wit.

" An ounce o' mother-wit is worth a pound o' clergy," says the
Scotch proverb, and the " mother-wit," *Muttergeist* and *Mutterwitz*,
that instructive common-sense, that saving light that make the
genius and even the fool, in the midst of his folly, wise, appear
in folk-lore and folk-speech everywhere. What the statistics of
genius seem to show that great men owe to their mothers, no less
than fools, is summed up by the folk-mind in the word *mother-wit*.
Jean Paul says: "Die Mütter geben uns von Geiste Wärme und
die Väter Licht," and Goethe, in a familiar passage in his *Auto-
biography,* declares: —

> "Vom Vater hab' ich die Statur,
> Des Lebens ernstes Führen ;
> Vom Mütterchen die Frohnatur,
> Und Lust zu fabulieren."

Shakespeare makes Petruchio tell the shrewish Katherine that
his "goodly speech" is "*extempore* from my mother-wit," and
Emerson calls "mother-wit," the "cure for false theology." Quite
appropriately Spenser, in the *Faerie Queene,* speaks of "all that
Nature by her mother-wit could frame in earth." It is worth
noting that when the ancient Greeks came to name the soul, they
personified it in Psyche, a beautiful female, and that the word
for "soul" is feminine in many European languages.

Among the Teton Indians, according to the Rev. J. Owen Dorsey, the following peculiar custom exists: "Prior to the naming of the infant is the ceremony of the transfer of, character; should the infant be a boy, a brave and good-tempered man, chosen beforehand, takes the infant in his arms and breathes into his mouth, thereby communicating his own disposition to the infant, who will grow up to be a brave and good-natured man. It is thought that such an infant will not cry as much as infants that have not been thus favoured. Should the infant be a girl, it is put into the arms of a good woman, who breathes into its mouth" (433. 482).

Here we have *father*-wit as well as *mother*-wit.

Mother-Tongue.

Where women have no voice whatever in public affairs, and are subordinated to the uttermost in social and family matters, little that is honourable and noble is named for them. In East Central Africa, a Yao woman, asked if the child she is carrying is a boy or a girl, frequently replies: "My child is of the sex that does not speak" (518. XLIII. 249), and with other peoples in higher stages of culture, the "silent woman" lingers yet. *Taceat mulier in ecclesiâ* still rings in our ears to-day, as it has rung for untold centuries. Though the poet has said : —

> "There is a sight all hearts beguiling —
> A youthful mother to her infant smiling,
> Who, with spread arms and dancing feet,
> And cooing voice, returns its answer sweet,"

and mothers alone have understood the first babblings of humanity, they have waited long to be remembered in the worthiest name of the language they have taught their offspring.

The term *mother-tongue*, although Middle English had "birthe-tongue," in the sense of native speech, is not old in our language; the *Century Dictionary* gives no examples of its early use. Even immortal Shakespeare does not know it, for, in *King Richard II.*, he makes Mowbray say : —

> "The language I have learned these forty years
> (My native English) now must I forego."

The German version of the passage has, however, *mein mütter-liches Englisch*.

Cowper, in the *Task*, does use "mother-tongue," in the connection following:—

> "Praise enough
> To fill the ambition of a private man,
> That Chatham's language was his mother-tongue."

Mother-tongue has now become part and parcel of our common speech; a good word, and a noble one.

In Modern High German, the corresponding *Mutterzunge*, found in Sebastian Franck (sixteenth century) has gradually given way to *Muttersprache*, a word whose history is full of interest. In Germany, as in Europe generally, the esteem in which Latin was held in the Middle Ages and the centuries immediately following them, forbade almost entirely the birth or extension of praise-worthy and endearing names for the speech of the common people of the country. So long as men spoke of "hiding the beauties of Latin in homely German words," and a Bacon could think of writing his chief work in Latin, in order that he might be remembered after his death, it were vain to expect aught else.

Hence, it does not surprise us to learn that the word *Mutter-sprache* is not many centuries old in German. Dr. Lübben, who has studied its history, says it is not to be found in Old High German or Middle High German (or Middle Low German), and does not appear even in Luther's works, though, judging from a certain passage in his *Table Talk*, it was perhaps known to him. It was only in the seventeenth century that the word became quite common. Weigand states that it was already in the *Dictionarium latino-germanicum* (Zürich, 1556), and in Maaler's *Die Teutsch Spraach* (Zürich, 1561), in which latter work (S. 262 a) we meet with the expressions *vernacula lingua, patrius sermo, landspraach, muoterliche spraach*, and *muoterspraach* (S. 295 c). Opitz (1624) uses the word, and it is found in Schottel's *Teutsche Haupt-Sprache* (Braunschweig, 1663). Apparently the earliest known citation is the Low German *modersprake*, found in the introduction of Dietrich Engelhus' (of Einbeck) *Deutsche Chronik* (1424).

Nowadays *Muttersprache* is found everywhere in the German book-language, but Dr. Lübben, in 1881, declared that he had never heard it from the mouth of the Low German folk, with whom the word was always *lantsprake, gemene sprake.* Hence, although the word has been immortalized by Klaus Groth, the Low German Burns, in the first poem of his *Quickborn :* —

> "Min Modersprak, so slicht un recht,
> Du ole frame Red !
> Wenn blot en Mund 'min Vader' seggt,
> So klingt mi't as en Bed,"

and by Johann Meyer, in his *Ditmarscher Gedichte :* —

> "Vaderhus un Modersprak !
> Lat mi't nöm'n un lat mi't rop'n ;
> Vaderhus, du helli Sted,
> Modersprak, du frame Red,
> Schönres klingt der Nix tohopen,"

it may be that *modersprak* is not entirely a word of Low German origin ; beautiful though it is, this dialect, so closely akin to our own English, did not directly give it birth. Nor do the corresponding terms in the other Teutonic dialects, — Dutch *moderspraak,* *moedertaal,* Swedish *modersmål,* etc., — seem more original. The Romance languages, however, offer a clue. In French, *langue mère* is a purely scientific term of recent origin, denoting the root-language of a number of dialects, or of a "family of speech," and does not appear as the equivalent of *Muttersprache.* The equivalents of the latter are : French, *langue maternelle ;* Spanish, *lengua materna ;* Italian, *lingua materna,* etc., all of which are modifications or imitations of a Low Latin *lingua materna,* or *lingua maternalis.* The Latin of the classic period seems not to have possessed this term, the locutions in use being *sermo noster,* *patrius sermo,* etc. The Greek had ἡ ἐγχώριος γλῶσσα, ἡ ἰδία γλῶσσα, etc. Direct translations are met with in the *moderlike sprake* of Daniel von Soest, of Westphalia (sixteenth century), and the *muoterliche spraach* of Maaler (1561). It is from an Italian-Latin source that Dr. Lübben supposes that the German prototypes of *modersprak* and *Muttersprache* arose. In the *Bôk der Byen,* a semi-Low German translation (fifteenth century) of the *Liber Apium* of Thomas of Chantimpré, occurs the word *modertale* in the passage "Christus sede to er [the Samaritan woman] mit sachte stemme in erre modertale." A municipal book of Treuenbrietzen informs us that in the year 1361 it was resolved to write in the *ydeoma maternale* — what the equivalent of this was in the common speech is not stated — and in the *Relatio* of Hesso, we find the term *materna lingua* (105 a).

The various dialects have some variants of *Muttersprache,* and in Göttingen we meet with *moimen spraken,* where *moime* (cognate with Modern High German *Muhme,* "aunt"), signifies "mother," and is a child-word.

From the *mother-tongue* to the *mother-land* is but a step. As the speech she taught her babe bears the mother's name, so does also the land her toil won from the wilderness.

Mother-Land.

As we say in English most commonly "native city," so also we say "native land." Even Byron sings: —

> "Adieu, adieu ! my native shore
> Fades o'er the waters blue;
>   *   *   *   *
> My native land — good night ! "

and Fitz-Greene Halleck, in his patriotic poem "Marco Bozzaris," bids strike "For God, and your native land."

Scott's far-famed lines : —

> "Breathes there a man with soul so dead,
> Who never to himself has said,
> This is my own, my native land ! "

and Smith's national hymn, "My country, 'tis of thee," know no *mother-land.*

In the great *Century Dictionary,* the only illustration cited of the use of the word *mother-land* is a very recent one, from the *Century Magazine* (vol. xxix. p. 507).

Shakespeare, however, comes very near it, when, in *King John* (V. ii.), he makes the Bastard speak of "your dear Mother-England," — but this is not quite "mother-land."

In German, though, through the sterner influences which surrounded the Empire in its birth and reorganization, *Vaterland* is now the word, *Mutterland* was used by Kant, Wieland, Goethe, Herder, Uhland, etc. Lippert suggests an ingenious explanation of the origin of the terms *Mutterland, Vaterland,* as well as for the predominance of the latter and younger word. If, in primitive times, man alone could hold property, — women even and children were his chattels, — yet the development of agriculture and horti- culture at the hands of woman created, as it were, a new species of property, property in land, the result of woman's toil and labour ; and this new property, in days when "mother-right" prevailed, came to be called *Mutterland,* as it was essentially " mothers' land." But when men began to go forth to war, and to conquer and acquire land that was not " mothers' land," a new species of landed property, — the "land of the conquering father," — came into existence (and with it a new theory of succession, " father-right "), and from that time forward " Vaterland " has extended its signifi- cation, until it has attained the meaning which it possesses in the German speech of to-day (492. 33, 36).

The inhabitants of the British colonies scattered all over the world speak of Britain as the "mother country," " Mother Eng- land"; and R. H. Stoddard, the American poet, calls her " our Mother's Mother." The French of Canada term France over-sea " la mère patrie " (mother fatherland).

Even Livy, the Roman historian, wrote *terra quam matrem appellamus,* — " the land we call mother," — and Virgil speaks of Apollo's native Delos as *Delum maternum.* But for all this, the proud Roman called his native land, not after his mother, but after his father, *patria;* so also in corresponding terms the Greek, πατρίς, etc. But the latter remembered his mother also, as the word *metropolis,* which we have inherited, shows. Μητρόπολις had the meanings : "mother-state " (whence daughter-colonies went forth) ; " a chief city, a capital, metropolis ; one's mother-city, or mother-country." In English, *metropolis* has been associated with " mother-church," for a *metropolis* or a *metropolitan* city, was long one which was the seat of a bishopric.

Among the ancient Greeks the Cretans were remarkable for saying not πατρίς (father-land), but μητρίς (mother-land), by which name also the Messenians called their native land. Some light upon the loss of " mother-words " in ancient Greece may be shed from the legend which tells that when the question came whether the new town was to be named after Athene or Poseidon, all the women voted for the former, carrying the day by a single vote, whereupon Poseidon, in anger, sent a flood, and the men, determining to punish their wives, deprived them of the power of voting, and decided that thereafter children were not to be named after their mothers (115. 235).

In Gothic, we meet with a curious term for "native land, home," *gabaurths* (from *gabairan* "to bear"), which signifies also "birth." As an exemplification of the idea in the Sophoclean phrase "all-nourishing earth," we find that at an earlier stage in the history of our own English tongue *erd* (cognate with our *earth*) signified "native land," a remembrance of that view of savage and uncivilized peoples in which *earth, land* are "native country," for these are, in the true sense of the term, *Landesleute, homines.*

In the language of the Hervey Islands, in the South Pacific, "the place in which the placenta of an infant is buried is called the *ipukarea*, or *native soil*" (459. 26).

Our English language seems still to prefer "native city, native town, native village," as well as "native land," "mother-city" usually signifying an older town from which younger ones have come forth. In German, though *Vaterstadt* in analogy with *Vaterland* seems to be the favorite, *Mutterstadt* is not unknown.

Besides *Mutterland* and *Mutterstadt*, we find in German the following: —

Mutterboden, "mother-land." Used by the poet Uhland.
Muttergefilde, "the fields of mother-earth." Used by Schlegel.
Muttergrund, "the earth," as productive of all things. Used by Goethe.
Mutterhimmel, "the sky above one's native land." Used by the poet Herder.
Mutterluft, "the air of one's native land."
Mutterhaus, "the source, origin of anything." Uhland even has: —

> "Hier ist des Stromes Mutterhaus,
> Ich trink ihn frisch vom Stein heraus."

More far-reaching, diviner than "mother-land," is "mother-earth."

CHAPTER III.

The Child's Tribute to the Mother (*Continued*).

To the child its mother should be as God. — *G. Stanley Hall.*

A mother is the holiest thing alive. — *Coleridge.*

God pardons like a mother, who kisses the offence into everlasting forgetfulness. — *Henry Ward Beecher.*

When the social world was written in terms of mother-right, the religious world was expressed in terms of mother-god.

There is nothing more charming than to see a mother with a child in her arms, and nothing more venerable than a mother among a number of her children. — *Goethe.*

Mother-Earth.

"Earth, Mother of all," is a world-wide goddess. Professor O. T. Mason says: "The earth is the mother of all mankind. Out of her came they. Her traits, attributes, characteristics, they have so thoroughly inherited and imbibed, that, from any doctrinal point of view regarding the origin of the species, the earth may be said to have been created for men, and men to have been created out of the earth. By her nurture and tuition they grow up and flourish, and, folded in her bosom, they sleep the sleep of death. The idea of the earth-mother is in every cosmogony. Nothing is more beautiful in the range of mythology than the conception of Demeter with Persephone, impersonating the maternal earth, rejoicing in the perpetual return of her daughter in spring, and mourning over her departure in winter to Hades" (389 (1894). 140).

Dr. D. G. Brinton writes in the same strain (409. 238): "Out of the earth rises life, to it it returns. She it is who guards all germs, nourishes all beings. The Aztecs painted her as a woman with countless breasts; the Peruvians called her '*Mama Allpa*,' *mother* Earth; in the Algonkin tongue, the words for earth, mother, father, are from the same root. *Homo, Adam, chamaigenes,* what do all these words mean but earth-born, the son of the soil, repeated in the poetic language of Attica in *anthropos,* he who springs up like a flower?"

Mr. W. J. McGee, treating of "Earth the Home of Man," says (502. 28):—

"In like manner, mankind, offspring of Mother Earth, cradled and nursed through helpless infancy by things earthly, has been brought well towards maturity; and, like the individual man, he is repaying the debt unconsciously assumed at the birth of his kind, by transforming the face of nature, by making all things better than they were before, by aiding the good and destroying the bad among animals and plants, and by protecting the aging earth from the ravages of time and failing strength, even as the child protects his fleshly mother. Such are the relations of earth and man."

The Roman babe had no right to live until the father lifted him up from "mother-earth" upon which he lay; at the baptism of the ancient Mexican child, the mother spoke thus: "Thou Sun, Father of all that live, and thou Earth, our Mother. take ye this child and guard it as your son" (529. 97); and among the Gypsies of northern Hungary, at a baptism, the oldest woman present takes the child out, and, digging a circular trench around the little one, whom she has placed upon the earth, utters the following words: "Like this Earth, be thou strong and great, may thy heart be free from care, be merry as a bird" (392 (1891). 20). All of these practices have their analogues in other parts of the globe.

In another way, infanticide is connected with "mother-earth." In the book of the "Wisdom of Solomon" (xiv. 23) we read: "They slew their children in sacrifices." Infanticide — "murder most foul, as in the best it is, but this most foul, strange, and unnatural" — has been sheltered beneath the cloak of religion. The story is one of the darkest pages in the history of man. A priestly legend of the Khonds of India attributes to child-sacrifice a divine origin:—

"In the beginning was the Earth a formless mass of mud, and could not have borne the dwelling of man, or even his weight; in this liquid and ever-moving slime neither tree nor herb took root.

Then God said: 'Spill human blood before my face!' And they sacrificed a child before Him. . . . Falling upon the soil, the bloody drops stiffened and consolidated it."

But too well have the Khonds obeyed the command: "And by the virtues of the blood shed, the seeds began to sprout, the plants to grow, the animals to propagate. And God commanded that the Earth should be watered with blood every new season, to keep her firm and solid. And this has been done by every generation that has preceded us."

More than once "the mother, with her boys and girls, and perhaps even a little child in her arms, were immolated together," —for sometimes the wretched children, instead of being immediately sacrificed, were allowed to live until they had offspring whose sad fate was determined ere their birth. In the work of Reclus may be read the fearful tale of the cult of "Pennou, the terrible earth-deity, the bride of the great Sun-God" (523. 315).

In Tonga the paleness of the moon is explained by the following legend: Vātea (Day) and Tonga-iti (Night) each claimed the first-born of Papa (Earth) as his own child. After they had quarrelled a great deal, the infant was cut in two, and Vātea, the husband of Papa, "took the upper part as his share, and forthwith squeezed it into a ball and tossed it into the heavens, where it became the sun." But Tonga-iti, in sullen humour, let his half remain on the ground for a day or two. Afterward, however, "seeing the brightness of Vātea's half, he resolved to imitate his example by compressing his share into a ball, and tossing it into the dark sky during the absence of the sun in Avaiki, or netherworld." It became the moon, which is so pale by reason of "the blood having all drained out and decomposition having commenced," before Tonga-iti threw his half up into the sky (458. 45). With other primitive peoples, too, the gods were infanticidal, and many nations like those of Asia Minor, who offered up the virginity of their daughters upon the altars of their deities, hesitated not to slay upon their high places the first innocent pledges of motherhood.

The earth-goddess appears again when the child enters upon manhood, for at Brahman marriages in India, the bridegroom still says to the bride, "I am the sky, thou art the earth, come let us marry" (421. 29).

And last of all, when the ineluctable struggle of death is over, man returns to the "mother-earth"—dust to dust. One of the hymns of the Rig-Veda has these beautiful words, forming part of the funeral ceremonies of the old Hindus:—

> "Approach thou now the lap of Earth, thy mother,
> The wide-extending Earth, the ever-kindly ;
> A maiden soft as wool to him who comes with gifts,
> She shall protect thee from destruction's bosom.

> "Open thyself, O Earth, and press not heavily ;
> Be easy of access and of approach to him,
> As mother with her robe her child,
> So do thou cover him, O Earth !" (421. 31).

The study of the mortuary rites and customs of the primitive peoples of all ages of the world's history (548) reveals many instances of the belief that when men, "the common growth of mother-earth," at last rest their heads upon her lap, they do not wholly die, for the immortality of Earth is theirs. Whether they live again,—as little children are often fabled to do,—when Earth laughs with flowers of spring, or become incarnate in other members of the animate or inanimate creation, whose kinship with man and with God is an article of the great folk-creed, or, in the beautiful words of the burial service of the Episcopal Church, sleep "earth to earth, ashes to ashes, dust to dust, in sure and certain hope of the resurrection," all testifies that man is instinct with the life that throbs in the bosom of Earth, his Mother. As of old, the story ran that man grew into being from the dust, or sprang forth in god-like majesty, so, when death has come, he sinks to dust again, or triumphantly scales the lofty heights where dwell the immortal deities, and becomes "as one of them."

With the idea of the earth-mother are connected the numerous myths of the origin of the first human beings from clay, mould, etc., their provenience from caves, holes in the ground, rocks and mountains, especially those in which the woman is said to have been created first (509. 110). Here belong also not a few ethnic names, for many primitive peoples have seen fit to call themselves "sons of the soil, *terræ filii, Landesleute.*"

Müller and Brinton have much to say of the American earth-goddesses, *Toci,* "our mother," and goddess of childbirth among the ancient Mexicans (509. 494); the Peruvian *Pachamama*, "mother-earth," the mother of men (509. 369); the "earth-mother" of the Caribs, who through earthquakes manifests her animation and cheerfulness to her children, the Indians, who forthwith imitate her in joyous dances (509. 221); the "mother-earth" of the Shawnees, of whom the Indian chief spoke, when he was bidden to regard General Harrison as "Father": "No, the sun yonder is my father, and the earth my mother; upon her bosom will I repose," etc. (509. 117).

Among the earth-goddesses of ancient Greece and Rome are Demeter, Ceres, Tellus, Rhea, Terra, Ops, Cybele, Bona Dea, Bona Mater, Magna Mater, Gæa, Ge, whose attributes and ceremonies are described in the books of classical mythology. Many times they are termed "mother of the gods" and "mother of men"; Cybele is sometimes represented as a woman advanced in pregnancy or as a woman with many breasts; Rhea, or Cybele, as the hill-enthroned protectress of cities, was styled *Mater turrita*.

The ancient Teutons had their *Hertha*, or *Erdemutter*, the *Nertha* of Tacitus, and fragments of the primitive earth-worship linger yet among the folk of kindred stock. The Slavonic peoples had their "earth-mother" also.

The ancient Indian Aryans worshipped Prithîvî-mâtar, "earth-mother," and Dyaus pitar, "sky-father," and in China, Yang, Sky, is regarded as the "father of all things," while Yu, Earth, is the "mother of all things."

Among the ancient Egyptians the "earth-mother," the "parent of all things born," was Isis, the wife of the great Osiris.

The natal ceremonies of the Indians of the Sia Pueblo have been described at great length by Mrs. Stevenson (538. 132–143). Before the mother is delivered of her child the priest repeats in a low tone the following prayer:—

"Here is the child's sand-bed. May the child have good thoughts and know its mother-earth, the giver of food. May it have good thoughts and grow from childhood to manhood. May the child be beautiful and happy. Here is the child's bed; may the child be beautiful and happy. Ashes man, let me make good medicine for the child. We will receive the child into our arms, that it may be happy and contented. May it grow from childhood to manhood. May it know its mother Ût'sĕt [the first created woman], the Ko'pishtaia, and its mother-earth. May the child have good thoughts and grow from childhood to manhood. May it be beautiful and happy" (538. 134).

On the fourth morning after the birth of the child, the doctress in attendance, "stooping until she almost sits on the ground, bares the child's head as she holds it toward the rising sun, and repeats a long prayer, and, addressing the child, she says: 'I bring you to see your Sun-father and Ko'pishtaia, that you may know them and they you'" (538. 141).

Mother-Mountain.

Though we are now accustomed, by reason of their grandeur and sublimity, to personify mountains as masculine, the old fable of Phædrus about the "mountain in labour, that brought forth a mouse," — as Horace has it, *Montes laborabant et parturitur ridiculus mus*, — shows that another concept was not unknown to the ancients. The Armenians call Mount Ararat "Mother of the World" (500. 39), and the Spaniards speak of a chief range of mountains as *Sierra Madre*. In mining we meet with the "mother-lode," *veta madre*, but, curiously enough, the main shaft is called in German *Vaterschacht*.

We know that the Lapps and some other primitive peoples "transferred to stones the domestic relations of father, mother, and child," or regarded them as children of Mother-Earth (529. 64); "eggs of the earth" they are called in the magic songs of the Finns. In Suffolk, England, "conglomerate is called ' mother of stones,' under the idea that pebbles are born of it"; in Germany *Mutterstein*. And in litholatry, in various parts of the globe, we have ideas which spring from like conceptions.

Mother-Night.

Milton speaks of the "wide womb of uncreate night," and some of the ancient classical poets call *Nox* "the mother of all things, of gods as well as men." "The Night is Mother of the Day," says Whittier, and the myth he revives is an old and wide-spread one. "Out of Night is born day, as a child comes forth from the womb of his mother," said the Greek and Roman of

D

old. As Bachofen (6. 16, 219) remarks: "Das Mutterthum verbindet sich mit der Idee der den Tag aus sich gebierenden Nacht, wie das Vaterrecht dem Reiche des Lichts, dem von der Sonne mit der Mutter Nacht gezeugten Tage." Darkness, Night, Earth, Motherhood, seem all akin in the dim light of primitive philosophy. Yet night is not always figured as a woman. James Ferguson, the Scotch poet, tells us how

> "Auld Daddy Darkness creeps frae his hole,
> Black as a blackamoor, blin' as a mole,"

and holds dominion over earth till "Wee Davie Daylicht comes keekin' owre the hill" (230. 73).

An old Anglo-Saxon name for Christmas was *modra-neht*, "mother's night."

Mother-Dawn.

In Sanskrit mythology Ushas, "Dawn," is daughter of Heaven, and poetically she is represented as "a young wife awakening her children and giving them new strength for the toils of the new day."

Sometimes she is termed *gávám gánitrí*, "the mother of the cows," which latter mythologists consider to be either "the clouds which pour water on the fields, or the bright mornings which, like cows, are supposed to step out one by one from the stable of the night" (310. 431).

In an ancient Hindu hymn to Ushas we read: —

"She shines upon us like a young wife, rousing every living being to go to his work. When the fire had to be kindled by men, she made the light by striking down darkness.

"She rose up, spreading far and wide, and moving everywhere. She grew in brightness, wearing her brilliant garment. The mother of the cows, the leader of the days, she shone gold-coloured, lovely to behold" (421. 29).

This daughter of the sky was the "lengthener of life, the love of all, the giver of food, riches, blessings." According to Dr. Brinton, the Quiché Indians of Guatemala speak of Xmucane and Xpiyacoc as being "the great ancestress and the great ancestor" of all things. The former is called *r'atit zih, r'atit zak*, "primal mother of the sun and light" (411. 119).

Mother-Days.

In Russia we meet with the days of the week as "mothers." Perhaps the most remarkable of these is "Mother Friday," a curious product of the mingling of Christian hagiology and Slavonic mythology, of St. Prascovia and the goddess Siwa. On the day sacred to her, "Mother Friday" wanders about the houses of the peasants, avenging herself on such as have been so rash as to sew, spin, weave, etc., on a Friday (520. 206).

In a Wallachian tale appear three supernatural females, — the holy mothers Friday, Wednesday, and Sunday, — who assist the hero in his quest of the heroine, and in another Wallachian story they help a wife to find her lost husband.

"Mother Sunday" is said "to rule the animal world, and can collect her subjects by playing on a magic flute. She is represented as exercising authority over both birds and beasts, and in a Slovak story she bestows on the hero a magic horse" (520. 211). In Bulgaria we even find mother-months, and Miss Garnett has given an account of the superstition of "Mother March" among the women of that country (61. I. 330). William Miller, the poet-laureate of the nursery, sings of *Lady Summer:* —

"Birdie, birdie, weet your whistle !
  Sing a sang to please the wean ;
Let it be o' Lady Summer
  Walking wi' her gallant train !
Sing him how her gaucy mantle,
  Forest-green, trails ower the lea,
Broider'd frae the dewy hem o't
  Wi' the field flowers to the knee !

"How her foot's wi' daisies buskit,
  Kirtle o' the primrose hue,
And her e'e sae like my laddie's,
  Glancing, laughing, loving blue !
How we meet on hill and valley,
  Children sweet as fairest flowers,
Buds and blossoms o' affection,
  Rosy wi' the sunny hours" (230. 161).

Mother-Sun.

In certain languages, as in Modern German, the word for "sun" is feminine, and in mythology the orb of day often appears as a

woman. The German peasant was wont to address the sun and
the moon familiarly as "Frau Sonne" and "Herr Mond," and in
a Russian folk-song a fair maiden sings (520. 184): —

> "My mother is the beauteous Sun,
> And my father, the bright Moon ;
> My brothers are the many Stars,
> And my sisters the white Dawns."

Jean Paul beautifully terms the sun "Sonne, du Mutterauge
der Welt!" and Hölty sings: "Geh aus deinem Gezelt, Mutter
des Tags hervor, und vergülde die wache Welt"; in another
passage the last writer thus apostrophizes the sun: "Heil dir,
Mutter des Lichts!" These terms "mother-eye of the world,"
"mother of day," "mother of light," find analogues in other
tongues. The Andaman Islanders have their *chän·a bô·dô,*
"mother-sun" (498. 96), and certain Indians of Brazil call the
sun *coaraçy,* "mother of the day or earth." In their sacred language the Dakota Indians speak of the sun as "grandmother" and
the moon as "grandfather." The Chiquito Indians "used to call
the sun their mother, and, at every eclipse of the sun, they would
shoot their arrows so as to wound it; they would let loose their
dogs, who, they thought, went instantly to devour the moon"
(100. 289).

The Yuchi Indians called themselves "children of the sun."
Dr. Gatschet tells us: "The Yuchis believe themselves to be the
offspring of the sun, which they consider to be a female. According to one myth, a couple of human beings were born from her
monthly efflux, and from these the Yuchis afterward originated."
Another myth of the same people says: "An unknown mysterious being once came down upon the earth and met people there
who were the ancestors of the Yuchi Indians. To them this
being (*Hi'ki,* or *Ka'la hi'ki*) taught many of the arts of life, and
in matters of religion admonished them to call the sun their
mother as a matter of worship" (389 (1893). 280).

Mother-Moon.

Shelley sings of

> "That orbèd maiden, with white fire laden,
> Whom mortals call the moon,"

and in other languages besides Latin the word for moon is feminine, and the lunar deity a female, often associated with child-
birth. The moon-goddesses of the Orient—Diana (Juno), Astarte,
Anahita, etc.— preside over the beginnings of human life.

Not a few primitive peoples have thought of the moon as mother.
The ancient Peruvians worshipped *Mama-Quilla*, "mother-moon,"
and the Hurons regarded Ataensic, the mother or grandmother of
Jouskeha, the sun, as the "creatress of earth and man," as well as
the goddess of death and of the souls of the departed (509. 363).
The Tarahumari Indians of the Sierra of Chihuahua, Mexico, call
the sun *au-nau-ru-a-mi*, "high father," and the moon, *je-ru-a-mi*,
"high mother." The Tupi Indians of Brazil term the moon *jacy*,
"our mother," and the same name occurs in the Omagua and
other members of this linguistic stock. The Muzo Indians
believe that the sun is their father and the moon their mother
(529. 95).

Horace calls the moon *siderum regina*, and Apuleius, *regina
cœli*, and Milton writes of

> "moonèd Ashtaroth,
> Heaven's queen and mother both."

Froebel's verses, "The Little Girl and the Stars," are stated to
be based upon the exclamation of the child when seeing two large
stars close together in the heavens, "Father-Mother-Star," and a
further instance of like nature is cited where the child applied
the word "mother" to the moon.

Mother-Fire.

An ancient Greek philosopher, Heraclitus of Ephesus, taught
that the world was created from fire, the omnipotent and omniscient essence, and with many savage and barbaric peoples fire-
worship has flourished or still flourishes. The Indic Aryans of
old produced fire by the method of the twirling stick, and in
their symbolism "the turning stick, Pramanta, was the father of
the god of fire; the immovable stick was the mother of the ador-
able and luminous Agni [fire]"—a concept far-reaching in its
mystic and mythological relations (100. 564).

According to Mr. Cushing the Zuñi Indians term fire the
"Grandmother of Men."

In their examination of the burial-places of the ancient Indian population of the Salado River Valley in Arizona, the Hemenway Exploring Expedition found that many children were buried near the kitchen hearths. Mr. Cushing offers the following explanation of this custom, which finds analogies in various parts of the world: "The matriarchal grandmother, or matron of the household deities, is the fire. It is considered the guardian, as it is also, being used for cooking, the principal 'source of life' of the family. The little children being considered unable to care for themselves, were placed, literally, under the protection of the family fire that their soul-life might be nourished, sustained, and increased" (501. 149). Boecler tells us that the Esthonian bride "consecrates her new home and hearth by an offering of money cast into the fire, or laid on the oven, for *Tule-ema*, [the] Fire Mother" (545. II. 285). In a Mongolian wedding-song there is an invocation of "Mother Ut, Queen of Fire," who is said to have come forth "when heaven and earth divided," and to have issued "from the footsteps of Mother-Earth." She is further said to have "a manly son, a beauteous daughter-in-law, bright daughters" (484. 38).

Mother-Water.

The poet Homer and the philosopher Thales of Miletus agreed in regarding water as the primal element, the original of all existences, and their theory has supporters among many primitive peoples. At the baptism festivals of their children, the ancient Mexicans recognized the goddess of the waters. At sunrise the midwife addressed the child, saying, among other things: "Be cleansed with thy mother, Chalchihuitlicue, the goddess of water." Then, placing her dripping finger upon the child's lips, she continued: "Take this, for on it thou must live, grow, become strong, and flourish. Through it we receive all our needs. Take it." And, again, "We are all in the hands of Chalchihuitlicue, our mother"; as she washed the child she uttered the formula: "Bad, whatever thou art, depart, vanish, for the child lives anew and is born again; it is once more cleansed, once more renewed through our mother Chalchihuitlicue." As she lifted the child up into the air, she prayed, "O Goddess, Mother of Water, fill this child with thy power and virtue" (326. I. 263).

In their invocation for the restoration of the spirit to the body, the Nagualists, — a native American mystic sect, — of Mexico and Central America, make appeal to "Mother mine, whose robe is of precious gems," *i.e.* water, regarded as "the universal mother." The "robe of precious stones" refers to "the green or vegetable life" resembling the green of precious stones. Another of her names is the "Green Woman," — a term drawn from "the greenness which follows moisture" (413. 52–54).

The idea of water as the source of all things appears also in the cosmology of the Indic Aryans. In one of the Vedic hymns it is stated that water existed before even the gods came into being, and the Rig-veda tells us that "the waters contained a germ from which everything else sprang forth." This is plainly a myth of the motherhood of the waters, for in the Brâhmanas we are told that from the water arose an egg, from which came forth after a year Pragâpati, the creator (510. 248). Variants of this myth of the cosmic egg are found in other quarters of the globe.

Mother-Ocean.

The Chinchas of Peru looked upon the sea as the chief deity and the mother of all things, and the Peruvians worshipped *Mama-Cocha*, "mother sea" (509. 368), from which had come forth everything, even animals, giants, and the Indians themselves. Associated with *Mama-Cocha* was the god *Vira-Cocha*, "sea-foam." In Peru water was revered everywhere, — rivers and canals, fountains and wells, — and many sacrifices were made to them, especially of certain sea-shells which were thought to be "daughters of the sea, the mother of all waters." The traditions of the Incas point to an origin from Lake Titicaca, and other tribes fabled their descent from fountains and streams (412. 204). Here belong, doubtless, some of the myths of the sea-born deities of classical mythology as well as those of the water-origin of the first of the human race, together with kindred conceits of other primitive peoples.

In the Bengalese tale of "The Boy with the Moon on his Fore-head," recorded by Day, the hero pleads: "O mother Ocean, please make way for me, or else I die" (426. 250), and passes on in safety. The poet Swinburne calls the sea "fair, white mother," "green-girdled mother," "great, sweet mother, mother and lover of men, the sea."

Mother-River.

According to Russian legend "the Dnieper, Volga, and Dvina used once to be living people. The Dnieper was a boy, and the Volga and Dvina his sisters." The Russians call their great river "Mother Volga," and it is said that, in the seventeenth century, a chief of the Don Cossacks, inflamed with wine, sacrificed to the mighty stream a Persian princess, accompanying his action with these words: "O Mother Volga, thou great River! much hast thou given me of gold and of silver, and of all good things; thou hast nursed me and nourished me, and covered me with glory and honor. But I have in no way shown thee my gratitude. Here is somewhat for thee; take it!" (520. 217–220).

In the Mahábhárata, the great Sanskrit epic, King Sántanu is said to have walked by the side of the river one day, where "he met and fell in love with a beautiful girl, who told him that she was the river Ganges, and could only marry him on condition he never questioned her conduct. To this he, with a truly royal gallantry, agreed; and she bore him several children, all of whom she threw into the river as soon as they were born. At last she bore him a boy, Bhíshma; and her husband begged her to spare his life, whereupon she instantly changed into the river Ganges and flowed away" (258. 317). Similar folk-tales are to be met with in other parts of the world, and the list of water-sprites and river-goddesses is almost endless. Greater than "Mother Volga," is "Mother Ganges," to whom countless sacrifices have been made.

In the language of the Caddo Indians, the Mississippi is called *báhat sássin*, "mother of rivers."

Mother-Plant.

The ancient Peruvians had their "Mother Maize," *Mama Cora*, which they worshipped with a sort of harvest-home having, as Andrew Lang points out, something in common with the children's last sheaf, in the north-country (English and Scotch) "kernaby," as well as with the "Demeter of the threshing-floor," of whom Theocritus speaks (484. 18).

An interesting legend of the Indians of the Pueblos of Arizona and New Mexico is recorded by Müller (509. 60). Ages ago there dwelt on the green plains a beautiful woman, who refused all wooers, though they brought many precious gifts. It came to pass that the land was sore distressed by dearth and famine, and when the people appealed to the woman she gave them maize in plenty. One day, she lay asleep naked; a rain-drop falling upon her breast, she conceived and bore a son, from whom are descended the people who built the "Casas Grandes." Dr. Fewkes cites a like myth of the Hopi or Tusayan Indians in which appears *kó-kyan-wüq-ti*, "the spider woman," a character possessing certain attributes of the Earth-Mother. Speaking of certain ceremonies in which *Cá-li-ko*, the corn-goddess, figures, he calls attention to the fact that "in initiations an ear of corn is given to the novice as a symbolic representation of mother. The corn is the mother of all initiated persons of the tribe " (389 (1894). 48).

Mr. Lummis also speaks of "Mother Corn" among the Pueblos Indians: "A flawless ear of pure white corn (type of fertility and motherhood) is decked out with a downy mass of snow-white feathers, and hung with ornaments of silver, coral, and the precious turquoise" (302. 72).

Concerning the Pawnee Indians, Mr. Grinnell tells us that after the separation of the peoples, the boy (medicine-man) who was with the few who still remained at the place from which the others had departed, going their different ways, found in the sacred bundle — the Shekinah of the tribe — an ear of corn. To the people he said: "We are to live by this, this is our Mother." And from "Mother Corn " the Indians learned how to make bows and arrows. When these Indians separated into three bands (according to the legend), the boy broke off the nub of the ear and gave it to the Mandans, the big end he gave to the Pawnees, and the middle to the Rees. This is why, at the present time, the Pawnees have the best and largest corn, the Rees somewhat inferior, and the Mandans the shortest of all — since they planted the pieces originally given them (480 (1893). 125).

The old Mexicans had in Cinteotl a corn-goddess and deity of fertility in whose honour even human sacrifices were made. She was looked upon as "the producer," especially of children, and sometimes represented with a child in her arms (509. 491).

In India there is a regular cult of the holy basil (*Ocymum sanctum*), or *Tulasî*, as it is called, which appears to be a transformation of the goddess Lakshmî. It may be gathered for pious purposes only, and in so doing the following prayer is offered: "Mother *Tulasî*, be thou propitious. If I gather thee with care, be merciful unto me. O *Tulasî*, mother of the world, I beseech thee." This plant is worshipped as a deity, — the wife of Vishnu, whom the breaking of even a little twig grieves and torments, — and "the pious Hindus invoke the divine herb for the protection of every part of the body, for life and for death, and in every action of life; but above all, in its capacity of ensuring children to those who desire to have them." To him who thoughtlessly or wilfully pulls up the plant "no happiness, no health, no children." The *Tulasî* opens the gates of heaven; hence on the breast of the pious dead is placed a leaf of basil, and the Hindu "who has religiously planted and cultivated the *Tulasî*, obtains the privilege of ascending to the palace of Vishnu, surrounded by ten millions of parents" (448. 244).

In Denmark, there is a popular belief that in the elder (*Sambucus*) there lives a spirit or being known as the "elder-mother" (*hylde-moer*), or "elder-woman" (*hilde-qvinde*), and before elder-branches may be cut this petition is uttered: "Elder-mother, elder-mother, allow me to cut thy branches." In Lower Saxony the peasant repeats, on bended knees, with hands folded, three times the words: "Lady Elder, give me some of thy wood; then will I also give thee some of mine, when it grows in the forest" (448. 318–320). In Huntingdonshire, England, the belief in the "elder-mother" is found, and it is thought dangerous to pluck the flowers, while elder-wood, in a room, or used for a cradle, is apt to work evil for children. In some parts of England, it is believed that boys beaten with an elder stick will be retarded in their growth; in Sweden, women who are about to become mothers kiss the elder. In Germany, a somewhat similar personification of the juniper, "Frau Wachholder," exists. And here we come into touch with the dryads and forest-sprites of all ages, familiar to us in the myths of classic antiquity and the tales of the nursery (448. 396).

In a Bengalese tale, the hero, on coming to a forest, cries: "O mother *kachiri*, please make way for me, or else I die," and the wood opens to let him pass through (426. 250).

Perhaps the best and sweetest story of plant mythology under this head is Hans Christian Andersen's beautiful tale of "The Elder-Tree Mother,"—the Dryad whose name is Remembrance (393. 215).

Mother-Thumb.

Our word *thumb* signifies literally "thick or big finger," and the same idea occurs in other languages. With not a few primitive peoples this thought takes another turn, and, as in the speech of the Karankawas, an extinct Indian tribe of Texas, "the *biggest*, or *thickest* finger is called '*father, mother*, or *old*'" (456. 68). The Creek Indians of the Southeastern United States term the "thumb" *ingi itchki*, "the hand its mother," and a like meaning attaches to the Chickasaw *ilbak-ishke*, Hichiti *ilb-iki*, while the Muskogees call the "thumb," the "mother of fingers." It is worthy of note, that, in the Bakaïri language of Brazil, the thumb is called "father," and the little finger, "child," or "little one" (536. 406). In Samoa the "thumb" is named *lima-matua*, "forefather of the hand," and the "first finger" *lima-tama*, "child of the hand." In the Tshi language of Western Africa a finger is known as *ensah-tsia-abbah*, "little child of the hand," and in some other tongues of savage or barbaric peoples "fingers" are simply "children of the hand."

Professor Culin in his notes of "Palmistry in China and Japan," says: "The thumb, called in Japanese, *oya-ubi*, 'parent-finger,' is for parents. The little finger, called in Japanese, *ko-ubi*, 'child-finger,' is for children; the index-finger is for uncle, aunt, and elder brother and elder sister. The third finger is for younger brother and younger sister" (423 a). A short little finger indicates childlessness, and lines on the palm of the hand, below the little finger, children. There are very many nursery-games and rhymes of various sorts based upon the hand and fingers, and in not a few of these the thumb and fingers play the *rôle* of mother and children. Froebel seized upon this thought to teach the child the idea of the family. His verses are well-known:—

> "Das ist die Groszmama,
> Das ist der Groszpapa,
> Das ist der Vater,
> Das ist die Mutter,
> Das ist's kleine Kindchen ja;
> Seht die ganze Familie da."

"Das ist die Mutter lieb und gut,
Das ist der Vater mit frohem Muth;
Das ist der Bruder lang und grosz;
Das ist die Schwester mit Püppchen im Schoosz;
Und dies ist das Kindchen, noch klein und zart,
Und dies die Familie von guter Art."

Referring to Froebel's games, Elizabeth Harrison remarks : —
"In order that this activity, generally first noticed in the use
of the hands, might be trained into right and ennobling habits,
rather than be allowed to degenerate into wrong and often degrad-
ing ones, Froebel arranged his charming set of finger-games for
the mother to teach her babe while he is yet in her arms; thus
establishing the right activity before the wrong one can assert
itself.   In such little songs as the following : —

'This is the mother, good and dear;
This the father, with hearty cheer;
This is the brother, stout and tall;
This is the sister, who plays with her doll;
And this is the baby, the pet of all.
Behold the good family, great and small,'

the child is led to personify his fingers and to regard them as a
small but united family over which he has control" (257 a. 14).

Miss Wiltse, who devotes a chapter of her little volume to
"Finger-songs related to Family Life and the Imaginative Faculty,"
says : —

"The dawning consciousness of the child so turned to the family
relations is surely better than the old nursery method of playing
'This little pig went to market'" (384. 45).

And from the father and mother the step to God is easy.

Dr. Brewer informs us that in the Greek and Roman Church
the Trinity is symbolized by the thumb and first two fingers:
"The thumb, being strong, represents the *Father;* the long, or
second finger, *Jesus Christ;* and the first finger, the *Holy Ghost,*
which proceedeth from the Father and the Son" (*Dict. of Phrase
and Fable*, P. 299).

Mother-God.

The "Motherhood of God" is an expression that still sounds
somewhat strangely to our ears.   We have come to speak readily

enough of the "Fatherhood of God" and the "Brotherhood of Man," but only a still small voice has whispered of the "Motherhood of God" and the "Sisterhood of Woman." Yet there have been in the world, as, indeed, there are now, multitudes to whom the idea of Heaven without a mother is as blank as that of the home without her who makes it. If over the human babe bends the human mother who is its divinity, —

> "The infant lies in blessed ease
>   Upon his mother's breast;
> No storm, no dark, the baby sees
>   Invade his heaven of rest.
> He nothing knows of change or death —
>   Her face his holy skies;
> The air he breathes, his mother's breath —
>   His stars, his mother's eyes," —

so over the infant-race must bend the All-Mother, *das Ewig-weibliche*. Perhaps the greatest service that the Roman Catholic Church has rendered to mankind is the prominence given in its cult of the Virgin Mary to the mother-side of Deity. In the race's final concept of God, the embodiment of all that is pure and holy, there must surely be some overshadowing of a mother's tender love. With the "Father-Heart" of the Almighty must be linked the "Mother-Soul." To some extent, at least, we may expect a harking back to the standpoint of the Buddhist Kalmuck, whose child is taught to pray: "O God, who art my father and my mother."

In all ages and over the whole world peoples of culture less than ours have had their "mother-gods," all the embodiments of motherhood, the joy of the *Magnificat*, the sacrosanct expression of the poet's truth: —

> "Close to the mysteries of God art thou,
>   My brooding mother-heart,"

the recognition of that outlasting secret hope and love, of which the Gospel writer told in the simple words: "Now there stood by the cross of Jesus his mother," and faith in which was strong in the Mesopotamians of old, who prayed to the goddess Istar, "May thy heart be appeased as the heart of a mother who has borne children." The world is at its best when the last, holiest appeal is *ad matrem.* Professor O. T. Mason has eloquently stated the debt of the world's religions to motherhood (112. 12) : —

"The mother-goddess of all peoples, culminating in the apotheosis of the Virgin Mary, is an idea either originated by women, or devised to satisfy their spiritual cravings. So we may go through the pantheons of all peoples, finding counterparts of Rhea, mother-earth, goddess of fertility ; Hera, queen of harvests, feeder of mankind; Hestia, goddess of the hearth and home, of families and states, giving life and warmth; Aphrodite, the beautiful, patron of romantic love and personal charms; Hera, sovereign lady, divine caciquess, embodiment of queenly dignity; Pallas Athene, ideal image of that central inspiring force that we learn at our mother's knee, and that shone in eternal splendour; Isis, the goddess of widowhood, sending forth her son Horus, to avenge the death of his father, Osiris; as moon-goddess, keeping alive the light until the sun rises again to bless the world."

The All-Mother.

In Polynesian mythology we find, dwelling in the lowest depths of Avaiki (the interior of the universe), the "Great Mother," — the originator of all things, *Vari-ma-te-takere,* "the very beginning," — and her pet child, Tu-metua, "Stick by the parent," her last offspring, inseparable from her. All of her children were born of pieces of flesh which she plucked off her own body; the firstborn was the man-fish Vātea, "father of gods and men," whose one eye is the sun, the other the moon; the fifth child was Raka, to whom his mother gave the winds in a basket, and "the children of Raka are the numerous winds and storms which distress mankind. To each child is allotted a hole at the edge of the horizon, through which he blows at pleasure." In the songs the gods are termed "the children of Vātea," and the ocean is sometimes called "the sea of Vātea." Mr. Gill tells us that "the Great Mother approximates nearest to the dignity of creator"; and, curiously enough, the word *Vari,* "beginning," signifies, on the island of Rarotonga, "mud," showing that "these people imagined that once the world was a 'chaos of mud,' out of which some mighty unseen agent, whom they called *Vari,* evolved the present order of things" (458. 3, 21).

Another "All-Mother" is she of whom our own poets have sung, "Nature," the source and sustainer of all.

Mother-Nature.

"So übt Natur die Mutterpflicht," sang the poet Schiller, and "Mother Nature" is the key-word of those modern poets who, in their mystic philosophy, consciously or unconsciously, revive the old mythologies. With primitive peoples the being, growing power of the universe was easily conceived as feminine and as motherly. Nature is the "great parent," the "gracious mother," of us all. In "Mother Nature," woman, the creator of the earliest arts of man, is recognized and personified, and in a wider sense even than the poet dreamt of: "One touch of Nature makes the whole world kin."

Pindar declared that "gods and men are sons of the same mother," and with many savage and barbaric tribes, gods, men, animals, and all other objects, animate and inanimate, are akin (388. 210). As Professor Robertson Smith has said: "The same lack of any sharp distinction between the nature of different kinds of visible beings appears in the old myths in which all kinds of objects, animate and inanimate, organic and inorganic, appear as cognate with one another, with men, and with the gods" (535. 85). Mr. Hartland, speaking of this stage of thought, says: "Sun and moon, the wind and the waters, perform all the functions of living beings; they speak, they eat, they marry and have children" (258. 26). The same idea is brought out by Count D'Alviella: "The highest point of development that polytheism could reach, is found in the conception of a monarchy or divine family, embracing all terrestrial beings, and even the whole universe" (388. 211). Mr. Frank Cushing attributes like beliefs in the kinship of all existences to the Zuñi Indians (388. 66), and Mr. im Thurn to the Indians of Guiana (388. 99).

This feeling of kinship to all that is, is beautifully expressed in the words of the dying Greek Klepht: "Do not say that I am dead, but say that I am married in the sorrowful, strange countries, that I have taken the flat stone for a mother-in-law, the black earth for my wife, and the little pebbles for brothers-in-law." (Lady Verney, *Essays*, II. 39.)

In the Trinity of Upper Egypt the second person was Mut, "Mother Nature." the others being Amun, the chief god, and their son, Khuns.

Among the Slavs, according to Mone, Ziwa is a nature-goddess, and the Wends regard her as "many-breasted Mother Nature," the producing and nourishing power of the earth. Her consort is Zibog, the god of life (125. II. 23).

Curiously reminiscent of the same train of ideas which has given to the *moderson* of Low German the signification of "bastard," is our own equivalent term "natural son."

Poets and orators have not failed to appeal to "Mother Nature" and to sing her panegyrics, but there is perhaps nothing more sweet and noble than the words of Elizabeth Cady Stanton: "Nature, like a loving mother, is ever trying to keep land and sea, mountain and valley, each in its place, to hush the angry winds and waves, balance the extremes of heat and cold, of rain and drought, that peace, harmony, and beauty may reign supreme," and the verses of Longfellow : —

> " And Nature, the old nurse, took
>   The child upon her knee,
> Saying, ' Here is a story-book
>   Thy Father has written for thee.

> " ' Come wander with me,' she said,
>   ' Into regions yet untrod ;
> And read what is still unread,
>   In the manuscripts of God.'

> " And he wandered away and away
>   With Nature, the dear old nurse,
> Who sang to him, night and day,
>   The rhymes of the universe.

> " And whenever the way seemed long,
>   Or his heart began to fail,
> She would sing a more wonderful song,
>   Or tell a more marvellous tale."

Through the long centuries Nature has been the mother, nurse, and teacher of man.

Other Mother-Goddesses.

Among other "mother-goddesses" of ancient Italy we find *Maia Mater, Flora Mater,* both deities of growth and reproduction; *Lua Mater,* "the loosing mother," a goddess of death; *Acca Larentia,* the mother of the Lares (*Acca* perhaps = *Atta,* a child-word for mother, as Lippert suggests); *Mater matuta,* "mother of the dawn," a goddess of child-birth, worshipped especially by married women, and to whom there was erected a temple at Cære.

The mother-goddesses of Germany are quite numerous. Among those minor ones cited by Grimm and Simrock, are: Haulemutter, Mutter Holle, the Klagemütter or Klagemuhmen, Pudelmutter (a name applied to the goddess Berchta), Etelmutter, Kornmutter, Roggenmutter, Mutterkorn, and the interesting Buschgroszmutter, "bush grandmother," as the "Queen of the Wood-Folk" is called. Here the mother-feeling has been so strong as to grant to even the devil a mother and a grandmother, who figure in many proverbs and folk-locutions. When the question is asked a Mecklenburger, concerning a social gathering: "Who was there?" he may answer: "The devil and his mother (*möm*)"; when a whirlwind occurs, the saying is: "The Devil is dancing with his grandmother."

In China the position of woman is very low, and, as Mr. Douglas points out: "It is only when a woman becomes a mother that she receives the respect which is by right due to her, and then the inferiority of her sex disappears before the requirements of filial love, which is the crown and glory of China" (434. 125).

In Chinese cosmogony and mythology motherhood finds recognition. Besides the great Earth-Mother, we meet with Se-wang-moo, the "Western Royal Mother," a goddess of fairy-land, and the "Mother of Lightning," thunder being considered the "father and teacher of all living beings." Lieh-tze, a philosopher of the fifth century B.C., taught: "My body is not my own; I am merely an inhabitant of it for the time being, and shall resign it when I return to the 'Abyss Mother'" (434. 222, 225, 277).

In the Flowery Kingdom there is also a sect "who worship the goddess Pity, in the form of a woman holding a child in her arms."

E

Among the deities and semi-deities of the Andaman Islanders are *chän·a·ē·lewadi*, the "mother of the race,"—Mother E·lewadi; *chän·a·erep, chän·a·chä·riä, chän·a·te·liu, chän·a lĭ·mi, chän·a·jär·a-ngŭd,* all inventors and discoverers of foods and the arts. In the religious system of the Andaman Islanders, *Pŭ·luga-,* the Supreme Being, by whom were created "the world and all objects, animate and inanimate, excepting only the powers of evil," and of whom it is said, "though his appearance is like fire, yet he is (nowadays) invisible," is "believed to live in a large stone house in the sky with a wife whom he created for himself; she is green in appearance, and has two names, *chän·a·äu·lola* (Mother Fresh-water Shrimp) and *chän·a·pä·lak-* (Mother Eel); by her he has a large family, all except the eldest being girls; these last, known as *mô·ro·win-* (sky-spirits or angels), are said to be black in appearance, and, with their mother, amuse themselves from time to time by throwing fish and prawns into the streams and sea for the use of the inhabitants of the world" (498. 90). With these people also the first woman was *chän·a·ē·lewadi* (Mother E·lewadi), the ancestress of the present race of natives. She was drowned, while canoeing, and "became a small crab of a description still named after her *ē·lewadi*" (498. 96).

Quite frequently we find that primitive peoples have ascribed the origin of the arts or of the good things of life to women whom they have canonized as saints or apotheosized into deities.

We may close our consideration of motherhood and what it has given the world with the apt words of Zmigrodzki: —

"The history of the civilization (Kulturgeschichte) of our race, is, so to speak, *the history of the mother-influence.* Our ideas of morality, justice, order, all these are simply *mother-ideas.* The mother began our culture in that epoch in which, like the man, she was *autodidactic.* In the epoch of the Church Fathers, the highly educated mother saved our civilization and gave it a new turn, and only the highly educated mother will save us out of the moral corruption of our age. Taken individually also, we can mark the ennobling, elevating influence which educated mothers have exercised over our great men. Let us strive as much as possible to have highly accomplished mothers, wives, friends, and then the wounds which we receive in the struggle for life will not bleed as they do now" (174. 367).

The history of civilization is the story of the mother, a story that stales not with repetition. Richter, in his *Levana*, makes eloquent appeal: —

"Never, never has one forgotten his pure, right-educating mother! On the blue mountains of our dim childhood, towards which we ever turn and look, stand the mothers who marked out for us from thence our life; the most blessed age must be forgotten ere we can forget the warmest heart. You wish, O woman, to be ardently loved, and forever, even till death. Be, then, the mothers of your children."

Tennyson in *The Foresters* uses these beautiful words: "Every man for the sake of the great blessed Mother in heaven, and for the love of his own little mother on earth, should handle all womankind gently, and hold them in all honour." Herein lies the whole philosophy of life. The ancient Germans were right, who, as Tacitus tells us, saw in woman *sanctum aliquid et providum*, as indeed the Modern German *Weib* (cognate with our *wife*) also declares, the original signification of the word being "the animated, the inspirited."

CHAPTER IV.

The Child's Tribute to the Father.

If the paternal cottage still shuts us in, its roof still screens us; and with a father, we have as yet a prophet, priest, and king, and an obedience that makes us free. — *Carlyle.*

To you your father should be as a god. — *Shakespeare.*

Our Father, who art in Heaven. — *Jesus.*

Father of all! in every age,
In every clime adored,
By saint, by savage, and by sage,
Jehovah, Jove, or Lord. — *Pope.*

Names of the Father.

Father, like *mother,* is a very old word, and goes back, with the cognate terms in Italic, Hellenic, Teutonic, Celtic, Slavonic, and Indo-Aryan speech, to the primitive Indo-European language, and, like *mother,* it is of uncertain etymology.

An English preacher of the twelfth century sought to derive the word from the Anglo-Saxon *fédan,* "to feed," making the "father" to be the "feeder" or "nourisher," and some more modern attempts at explanation are hardly better. This etymology, however incorrect, as it certainly is, in English, does find analogies in the tongues of primitive peoples. In the language of the Klamath Indians, of Oregon, the word for "father" is *t'shishap* (in the Modoc dialect, *p'tishap*), meaning "feeder, nourisher," from a radical *tshi,* which signifies "to give somebody liquid food (as milk, water)." Whether there is any real connection between our word *pap,* — with its cognates in other languages, — which signifies "food for infants," as well as "teat, breast," and the child-word *papa,* "father," is doubtful, and the same may be said of the attempt to find a relation between *teat,*

tit, etc., and the widespread child-words for "father," *tat, dad.*
Wedgewood (Introd. to *Dictionary*), however, maintained that:
"Words formed of the simplest articulations, *ma* and *pa,* are used
to designate the objects in which the infant takes the earliest
interest, — the mother, the father, the mother's breast, the act
of taking or sucking food." Tylor also points out how, in the
language of children of to-day, we may find a key to the origin
of a mass of words for "father, mother, grandmother, aunt, child,
breast, toy, doll," etc. From the limited supply of material at
the disposal of the early speakers of a language, we can readily
understand how the same sound had to serve for the connotation
of different ideas; this is why "*mama* means in one tongue
mother, in another *father,* in a third, *uncle; dada* in one language
father, in a second *nurse,* in another *breast; tata* in one language
father, in another *son,*" etc. The primitive Indo-European *p-tr,*
Skeat takes to be formed, with the agent-suffix *tr,* from the radical *pâ,* "to protect, to guard," — the father having been originally
looked upon as the "protector," or "guarder." Max Müller, who
offers the same derivation, remarks: "The father, as begetter,
was called in Sanskrit *ganitár,* as protector and supporter of his
posterity, however, *pitár.* For this reason, in the Veda both
names together are used in order to give the complete idea of
'father.' In like manner, *mâtar,* 'mother,' is joined with *ganit,*
'genetrix,' and this shows that the word *mâtar* must have soon
lost its etymological signification and come to be a term of respect and caress. With the oldest Indo-Europeans, *mâtar* meant
'maker,' from *mâ,* 'to form.'"

Kluge, however, seems to reject the interpretation "protector,
defender," and to see in the word a derivative from the "nature-
sound" *pa.* So also Westermarck (166. 86–94). In Gothic, pre-
sumably the oldest of the Teutonic dialects, the most common
word for "father" is *atta,* still seen in the name of the far-famed
leader of the Huns, *Attila, i.e.* "little father," and in the *ätti* of
modern Swiss dialects. To the same root attach themselves
Sanskrit *atta,* "mother, elder sister"; Ossetic *ädda,* "little father
(Väterchen)"; Greek *ἄττα,* Latin *atta,* "father"; Old Slavonic
oti-ci, "little father"; Old Irish *aite,* "foster-father." *Atta* belongs to the category of "nature-words" or "nursery-words" of
which our *dad (daddy)* is also a member.

Another member is the widespread *papa, pa.* Our word *papa,* Skeat thinks, is borrowed, through the French, from Latin *papa,* found as a Roman cognomen. This goes back in all probability to ancient Greek, for, in the Odyssey (vi. 57), Nausicaa addresses her father as πάππα φίλε, "dear *papa.*" The *Papa* of German is also borrowed from French, and, according to Kluge, did not secure a firm place in the language until comparatively late in the eighteenth century.

In some of the Semitic languages the word for "father" signifies "maker," and the same thing occurs elsewhere among primitive people (166. 91).

As with "mother," so with "father"; in many languages a man (or a boy) does not employ the same term as a woman (or a girl). In the Haida, Okanāk·ēn, and Kootenay, all Indian languages of British Columbia, the words used by males and by females are, respectively: *kuñ, qāt; lᴇē'u, mistm; tltō, sō.*

In many languages the word for "father," as is also the case with "mother," is different when the parent is addressed from that used when he is spoken of or referred to. In the Tsimshian, Kwakiutl, Nootka, Ntlakyapamuq, four Indian languages of British Columbia, the words for "father," when addressed, are respectively *ā'bō, āts, nō'wē, pāp,* and for "father" in other cases, *nᴇguā'at, āu'mp, nuwē'k·sō, sk·ā'tsa.* Here, again, it will be noticed that the words used in address seem shorter and more primitive in character.

In the Chinantec language of Mexico, *ñuh* signifies at the same time "father" and "man." In Gothic *aba* means both "father" and "husband" (492. 33). Here belongs also perhaps the familiar "father" with which the New England housewife was wont to address her husband.

With many peoples the name "father" is applied to others than the male parent of the child. The following remarks of McLennan, regarding the Tamil and Telugu of India, will stand for not a few other primitive tribes: "All the brothers of a father are usually called fathers, but, in strictness, those who are older than the father are called *great fathers,* and those who are younger, *little fathers.* With the Puharies, all the brothers of a father are equally fathers to his children." In Hawaii, the term "male parent" "applied equally to the father, to the uncles, and even to distant relations." In Japan, the paternal uncle is called "little father" and the maternal uncle "second little father" (100. 389, 391).

A lengthy discussion of these terms, with a wealth of illustration from many primitive languages, will be found in Wester-marck (166. 86–94).

Father-Right.

Of the Roman family it has been said: "It was a community comprising men and things. The members were maintained by adoption as well as by consanguinity. The father was before all things the chief, the general administrator. He was called father even when he had no son; paternity was a question of law, not one of persons. The heir is no more than the continuing line of the deceased person; he was heir in spite of himself for the honour of the defunct, for the lares, the hearth, the manes, and the hereditary sepulchre" (100. 423). In ancient Rome the *pater-familias* and the *patria potestas* are seen in their extreme types. Letourneau remarks further: "Absolute master, both of things and of people, the paterfamilias had the right to kill his wife and to sell his sons. Priest and king in turn, it was he who represented the family in their domestic worship; and when, after his death, he was laid by the side of his ancestors in the common tomb, he was deified, and helped to swell the number of the household gods" (100. 433).

Post thus defines the system of "father-right": —

"In the system of 'father-right' the child is related only to the father and to the persons connected with him through the male line, but not with his mother and the persons connected with him through the female line. The narrowest group organized according to father-right consists of the father and his children. The mother, for the most part, appears in the condition of a slave to the husband. To the patriarchal family in the wider sense belong the children of the sons of the father, but not the children of his daughters; the brothers and sisters of the same father, but not those merely related to the same mother; the children of the brother of the same father, but not the children of the sisters of the same father, etc. With every wife the relationship ceases every time" (127. I. 24).

The system of father-right is found scattered over the whole globe. It is found among the Indo-European peoples (Aryans of Asia, Germans, Slavs, Celts, Romans), the Mongol-Tartar tribes, Chinese, Japanese, and some of the Semitic nations; in northern Africa and scattered through the western part of the continent, among the Kaffirs and Hottentots; among some tribes in Australia and Polynesia and the two Americas (the culture races).

The position of the father among those peoples with whom strict mother-right prevails is thus sketched by Zmigrodski (174. 206) : —

" The only certain thing was motherhood and the maternal side of the family, — mother, daughter, granddaughter, that was the fixed stem continuing with certainty. Father, son, grandson, were only the leaves, which existed only until the autumnal wind of death tore them away, to hurl them into the abyss of oblivion. In that epoch no one said, ' I am the son of such a father and the grandson of such a grandfather,' but ' I am the son of such a mother and the grandson of such a grandmother.' The inheritance went not to the son and grandson, but to the daughter and to the granddaughter, and the sons received a dowry as do the daughters in our society of to-day. In marriage the woman did not assume the name of the man, but *vice versâ.* The husband of a woman, although the father of her children, was considered not so near a relative of them as the wife's brother, their uncle."

Dr. Brinton says, concerning mother-right among the Indians of North America (412. 48) : —

" Her children looked upon her as their parent, but esteemed their father as no relation whatever. An unusually kind and intelligent Kolosch Indian was chided by a missionary for allowing his father to suffer for food. ' Let him go to his own people,' replied the Kolosch, ' they should look after him.' He did not regard a man as in any way related or bound to his paternal parent."

In a certain Polynesian mythological tale, the hero is a young man, " the name of whose father had never been told by his mother," and this has many modern parallels (115. 97). On the Gold Coast of West Africa there is a proverb, " Wise is the son that knows his own father " (127. I. 24), a saying found elsewhere in the world, — indeed, we have it also in English, and Shakespeare presents but another view of it when he tells us: "It is a wise father that knows his own child."

In many myths and folk- and fairy-tales of all peoples the discovery by the child of its parent forms the climax, or at least one of the chief features of the plot; and we have also those stories which tell how parents have been killed unwittingly by their own children, or children have been slain unawares by their parents.

Father-King.

In his interesting study of "Royalty and Divinity" (75), Dr. von Held has pointed out many resemblances between the primitive concepts "King" and "God." Both, it would seem, stand in close connection with "Father." To quote from Dr. von Held: "Fathership (Vaterschaft, *patriarcha*), lordship (Herrentum), and kingship (Königtum) are, therefore (like *rex* and βασιλεύς), ideas not only linguistically, but, to even a greater degree really, cognate, having altogether very close relationship to the word and idea 'God.' Of necessity they involve the existence and idea of a people, and therefore are related not only to the world of faith, but also to that of intellect and of material things."

The Emperor of China is the "father and mother of the empire," his millions of subjects being his "children"; and the ancient Romans had no nobler title for their emperor than *pater patriæ*, the "father of his country," an appellation bestowed in these later days upon the immortal first President of the United States.

In the Yâjnavalkya, one of the old Sanskrit law-books, the king is bidden to be "towards servants and subjects as a father" (75. 122), and even Mirabeau and Grégoire, in the first months of the States-General, termed the king "le père de tous les Français," while Louis XII. and Henry IV. of France, as well as Christian III. of Denmark, had given to them the title "father of the people." The name *pater patriæ* was not borne by the Cæsars alone, for the Roman Senate conferred the title upon Cicero, and offered it to Marius, who refused to accept it. "Father of his Country" was the appellation of Cosmo de' Medici, and the Genoese inscribed the same title upon the base of the statue erected to

Andrea Doria. One of the later Byzantine Emperors, Androni-
cus Palæologus, even went so far as to assume this honoured title.
Nor has the name "Father of the People" been confined to kings,
for it has been given also to Gabriel du Pineau, a French lawyer
of the seventeenth century.

The "divinity that doth hedge a king" and the fatherhood of
the sovereign reach their acme in Peru, where the Inca was king,
father, even god, and the halo of "divine right" has not ceased
even yet to encircle the brows of the absolute monarchs of Europe
and the East.

Landesvater (Vater des Volkes) is the proudest designation of
the German Kaiser. "Little Father" is alike the literal meaning of *Attila*, the name of the far-famed leader of the "Huns,"
in the dark ages of Europe, and of *batyushka*, the affectionate
term by which the peasant of Russia speaks of the Czar.

Nana, "Grandfather," is the title of the king of Ashanti in
Africa, and "Sire" was long in France and England a respectful
form of address to the monarch.

Some of the aboriginal tribes of America have conferred upon
the President of the United States the name of the "Great Father
at Washington," the "Great White Father," and "Father" was
a term they were wont to apply to governors, generals, and other
great men of the whites with whom they came into contact.

The father as head of the family is the basis of the idea of
"father-king." This is seen among the Matchlapis, a Kaffir tribe,
where "those who own a sufficient number of cattle to maintain
a family have the right to the title of chief"; this resembles
the institution of the *pater familias* in ancient Latium (100. 459,
533).

Dr. von Held thus expresses himself upon this point: "The
first, and one may say also the last, naturally necessary society
of man is the family in the manifold forms out of which it has
been historically developed. Its beginning and its apex are,
under given culture-conditions, the man who founds it, the father.
What first brought man experientially to creation as a work of
love was fatherhood. This view is not altered by the fact that
the father, in order to preserve, or, what is the same, to continue
to produce, to bring up, must command, force, punish. If the
family depends on no higher right, it yet appears as the first

state, and then the father appears not only as father, but also as king" (75. 119).

The occurrence to-day of "King" as a surname takes us back to a time when the head of the family enjoyed the proud title, which the Romans conferred upon Cæsar Augustus, *Pater et Princeps*, the natural development from Ovid's *virque paterque gregis*.

The Romans called their senators *patres*, and we now speak of the "city fathers," aldermen, *elder*men, in older English, and the "fathers" of many a primitive people are its rulers and legislators. The term "father" we apply also to those who were monarchs and chiefs in realms of human activity other than that of politics. Following in the footsteps of the Latins, who spoke of Zeno as *Pater stoicorum*, of Herodotus as *Pater historiæ*, and even of the host of an inn as *Pater cenæ*, we speak of "fathering" an idea, a plot, and the like, and denominate "father," the pioneer scientists, inventors, sages, poets, chroniclers of the race.

From *pater* the Romans derived *patrimonium*, patrimony, "what was inherited from the father," an interesting contrast to *matrimonium; patronus*, "patron, defender, master of slaves"; *patria* (*terra*), "fatherland,"—Ovid uses *paterna terra*, and Horace speaks of *paternum flumen; patricius*, "of fatherly dignity, high-born, patrician," etc. Word after word 'in the classic tongues speaks of the exalted position of the father, and many of these have come into our own language through the influence of the peoples of the Mediterranean.

Father-Priest.

Said Henry Ward Beecher: "Look at home, father-priest, mother-priest; your church is a hundred-fold heavier responsibility than mine can be. Your priesthood is from God's own hands." The priesthood of the father is widespread. Mr. Gomme tells us: "Certainly among the Hindus, the Greeks, the Romans, and, so late down as Tacitus, the Germans, the house-father was priest and judge in his own clan" (461. 104). Max Müller speaks to the same effect: "If we trace religion back to the family, the father or head of the family is *ipso facto* the priest. When families grew into clans, and clans into tribes and confederacies, a necessity would arise of delegating to some heads of families the performance of duties which, from having been the spontaneous acts of individuals, had become the traditional acts of families and clans" (510. 183). Africa, Asia, America, furnish us abundant evidence of this. Our own language testifies to it also. We speak of the "Fathers of the Church," — *patres*, as they were called, — and the term "Father" is applied to an ecclesiastic of the Roman Catholic Church, just as in the Romance languages of Europe the descendants of the Latin *pater* (French *père*, Spanish *padre*, Italian *padre*, etc.) are used to denote the same personage. In Russian an endearing term for "priest" is *batyu-shka*, "father dear"; the word for a village-priest, sometimes used disrespectfully, is *pōp*. This latter name is identical with the title of the head of the great Catholic Church, the "Holy Father," at Rome, viz. *papa*, signifying literally "papa, father," given in the early days of Latin Christianity, and the source of our word *Pope* and its cognates in the various tongues of modern Europe. The head of an abbey we call an *abbot*, a name coming, through the Church-Latin *abbas*, from the Syriac *abba*, "father"; here again recurs the correlation of priest and father. It is interesting to note that both the words *papa* and *abba*, which we have just discussed, and which are of such importance in the history of religion, are child-words for "father," bearing evidence of the lasting influence of the child in this sphere of human activity. Among the ancient Romans we find a *pater patratus*, whose duty it was to ratify treaties with the proper religious rites. Dr. von Held is of opinion that, "in the case of a special priesthood, it is not so much the character of its members as spiritual fathers, as their calling of servants of God, of servants of a Father-God, which causes them to be termed fathers, papas" (75. 120).

Father-God.

Shakespeare has aptly said, in the words which Theseus addresses to the fair Hermia : —

> " To you your father should be as a god ;
> One that composed your beauties, yea, and one
> To whom you are but as a form in wax,
> By him imprinted, and within his power
> To leave the figure or disfigure it,"

and widespread indeed, in the childhood of the race, has been the belief in the Fatherhood of God. Concerning the first parents of human kind the ancient Hebrew Scripture declares: "And God created man in His own image," and long centuries afterwards, in his memorable oration to the wise men of Athens upon Mars' Hill, the Apostle Paul quoted with approval the words of the Greek poet, Cleanthes, who had said: "For we are all His offspring." Epictetus, appealing to a master on behalf of his slaves, asked: "Wilt thou not remember over whom thou rulest, that they are thy relations, thy brethren by nature, the offspring of Zeus?" (388. 210).

At the battle of Kadshu, Rameses II., of Egypt, abandoned by his soldiers, as a last appeal, exclaimed: "I will call upon thee, O my father Amon!" (388. 209).

Many prophets and preachers have there been who taught to men the doctrine of "God, the Father," but last and best of all was the "Son of Man," the Christ, who taught his disciples the world-heard prayer: "Our Father, who art in Heaven," who proclaimed that "in my Father's house are many mansions," and whose words in the agony of Gethsemane were: "Abba, Father, all things are possible unto Thee; remove this cup from me: howbeit not what I will, but what Thou wilt."

Between the Buddhist Kalmucks, with whom the newly married couple reverently utter these words: "I incline myself this first time to my Lord God, who is my father and my mother" (518. I. 423), and the deistic philosophers of to-day there is a vast gulf, as there is also between the idea of Deity among the Cakchiquel Indians of Guatemala, where the words for God *alom* and *achalom* signify respectively "begetter of children," and "begetter of sons," and the modern Christian concept of God, the Father, with His only begotten Son, the Saviour of the world.

The society of the gods of human creation has everywhere been modelled upon that of man. He was right who said Olympus was a Greek city and Zeus a Greek father. According to D'Alviella: "The highest point of development that polytheism could reach is found in the conception of a monarchy or divine family, embracing all terrestrial beings, and even the whole universe. The divine monarch or father, however, might still be no more than the first among his peers. For the supreme god to become the Only God, he must rise above all beings, superhuman as well as human, not only in his power, but in his very nature" (388. 211).

Though the mythology of our Teutonic forefathers knew of the "All-Father," — the holy Odin, — it is from those children-loving people, the Hebrews, that our Christian conception of "God the Father," with some modifications, is derived. As Professor Robertson Smith has pointed out, among the Semites we find the idea of the tribal god as father strongly developed: "But in heathen religions the fatherhood of the gods is a physical fatherhood. Among the Greeks, for example, the idea that the gods fashioned men out of clay, as potters fashion images, is relatively modern. The older conception is that the races of men have gods for their ancestors, or are the children of the earth, the common mother of gods and men, so that men are really of the same stock or kin of the gods. That the same conception was familiar to the older Semites appears from the Bible. Jeremiah describes idolaters as saying to a stock, Thou art my father; and to a stone, Thou hast brought me forth. In the ancient poem, Num. xxi. 29, the Moabites are called the sons and daughters of Chemosh, and, at a much more recent date, the prophet Malachi calls a heathen woman, 'the daughter of a strange god'" (535. 41–43).

Professor Smith cites also the evidence furnished by genealogies and personal names: "The father of Solomon's ally, Hiram, King of Tyre, was called *Abibaal*, 'my father is Baal'; Ben-Hadad, of Damascus, is 'the son of the god Hadad'; in Aramæan we find names like *Barlāhā*, 'son of God,' *Barba'shmīn*, 'son of the Lord of Heaven,' *Barate*, 'son of Ate,' etc." We have also that passage in Genesis which tells how the "sons of God saw the daughters of men that were fair; and they took them wives of all which they chose" (vi. 2), while an echo of the same thought dwells with the Polynesians, who term illegitimate children *tamarika na te Atua*, "children of the gods" (458. 121). D'Alviella further remarks: "Presently these family relations of the gods were extended till they embraced the whole creation, and especially mankind. The confusion between the terms for creating and begetting, which still maintained itself in half-developed languages, must have led to a spontaneous fusion of the ideas of creator and father." But there is another aspect of this question. Of the Amazulu Callaway writes: "Speaking generally, the head of each house is worshipped by the children of that house; for they do not know the ancients who are dead, nor their laud-giving names, nor their names. But their father whom they knew is the head by whom they begin and end in their prayer, for they know him best, and his love for his children; they remember his kindness to them whilst he was living; they compare his treatment of them whilst he was living, support themselves by it, and say, 'He will treat us in the same way now he is dead. We do not know why he should regard others beside us; he will regard us only.'" Of these people it is true, as they themselves say : "Our father is a great treasure to us, even when he is dead " (417. 144).

Here we pass over to ancestor worship, seen at its height in China, whose great sage, Confucius, taught: "The great object of marriage is to beget children, and especially sons, who may perform the required sacrifices at the tombs of their parents " (434. 126).

In this connection, the following passage from Max Müller is of interest: " How religious ideas could spring from the perception of something infinite or immortal in our parents, grandparents, and ancestors, we can see even at the present day. Among the Zulus, for instance, *Unkulunkulu* or *Ukulukulu*, which means the great-great-grandfather, has become the name of God. It is true that each family has its own *Unkulunkulu*, and that his name varies accordingly. But there is also an *Unkulunkulu* of all men (*unkulunkulu wabantu bonke*), and he comes very near to being a father of all men. Here also we can watch a very natural process of reasoning. A son would look upon his father as his progenitor; he would remember his father's father, possibly his father's grandfather. But beyond that his own experience could hardly go, and therefore the father of his own great-grandfather, of whom he might have heard, but whom he had never seen, would naturally assume the character of a distant unknown being; and, if the human mind ascended still further, it would almost by necessity be driven to a father of all fathers, that is to a creator of mankind, if not of the world " (510. 156).

Again we reach the "Father" of Pope's "Universal Prayer"—

> " Father of all ! in every age,
> In every clime adored,
> By saint, by savage, and by sage,
> Jehovah, Jove, or Lord,"

having started from the same thought as the Hebrews in the
infancy of their race. An Eastern legend of the child Abraham
has crystallized the idea. It is said that one morning, while with
his mother in the cave in which they were hiding from Nimrod,
he asked his mother, "Who is my God?" and she replied,
"It is I." "And who is thy God?" he inquired farther. "Thy
father" (547. 69). Hence also we derive the declaration of Du Vair,
" Nous devons tenir nos pères comme des dieux en terre," and the
statement of another French writer, of whom Westermarck says:
" Bodin wrote, in the later part of the sixteenth century, that,
though the monarch commands his subjects, the master his disciples, the captain his soldiers, there is none to whom nature has
given any command except the father, ' who is the true image of the
great sovereign God, universal father of all things ' " (166. 238).

Father-Sky.

> "Sweet day, so cool, so calm, so bright,
>   The bridal of the earth and sky,"

sang the poet Herbert, unconsciously renewing an ancient myth.
As many cosmologies tell, Day and Dawn were born of the embraces of Earth and Sky. Ushas, Eos, Aurora, is the daughter of
heaven, and one story of the birth is contained in the Maori myth
of Papa and Rangi. Ushas, Max Müller tells us, " has two parents, heaven and earth, whose lap she fills with light" (510. 431).
From Rangi, "Father-Sky," and Papa, "Mother-Earth," say the
Maoris of New Zealand, sprang all living things; and, in like
manner, the Chinese consider the Sky or Heaven, — Yang, the
masculine, procreative, active element, — to be the "father of all
things," while the Earth, — Yu, the feminine, conceiving, passive
element, — is the "mother of all things." From the union of
these two everything in existence has arisen, and consequently
resembles the one or the other (529. 107).

Among the primitive Aryans, the Sky, or Heaven God, was
called "Father," as shown by the Sanskrit *Dyaus Pitâr*, Greek
Ζεύς πατήρ, Latin *Jupiter*, all of which names signify "sky father."
Dyaus is also called *janitâr*, "producer, father," and Zeus, the
"eternal father of men," the "father of gods and men, the
ruler and preserver of the world." In the Vedic hymns are invo-

cations of Dyaus (Sky), as "our Father," and of Prithivi (Earth), as "our Mother" (388. 210).

Dyaus symbolizes the "bright sky"; from the same primitive Indo-European root come the Latin words *dies* (day), *deus* or *divus* (god); the dark sombre vault of heaven is Varuna, the Greek Οὐρανός, Latin *Uranus*.

Other instances of the bridal of earth and sky, — of "mother earth," and "father sky," — are found among the tribes of the Baltic, the Lapps, the Finns (who have Ukko, "Father Heaven," Akka, "Mother Earth"), and other more barbaric peoples.

In Ashanti, the new deity, which the introduction of Christianity has added to the native pantheon, is called *Nana Nyankupon*, "Grandfather-sky" (438. 24).

The shaman of the Buryats of Alarsk prays to "Father Heaven"; in the Altai Mountains the prayer is to

"Father Yulgen, thrice exalted,
Whom the edge of the moon's axe shuns,
Who uses the hoof of the horse.
Thou, Yulgen, hast created all men,
Who are stirring round about us,
Thou, Yulgen, hast endowed us with all cattle ;
Let us not fall into sorrow !
Grant that we may resist the evil one!" (504. 70, 77).

We too have recollections of that "Father-Sky," whom our far-off ancestors adored, the bright, glad, cheerful sky, the "ancestor of all." Max Müller has summed up the facts of our inheritance in brief terms : —

"Remember that this *Dyaush Pitar* is the same as the Greek Ζεὺς Πατήρ, and the Latin *Jupiter*, and you will see how this one word shows us the easy, the natural, the almost inevitable transition from the conception of the active sky as a purely physical fact, to the *Father-Sky* with all his mythological accidents, and lastly to that Father in heaven whom Æschylus meant when he burst out in his majestic prayer to Zeus, *whosoever he is*" (510. 410).

Unnumbered centuries have passed, but the "witchery of the soft blue sky" has still firm hold upon the race, and we are, as of old, children of "our Father, who art in Heaven."

F

Father-Sea.

Montesinos tells us that Viracocha, " sea-foam," the Peruvian god of the sea, was regarded as the source of all life and the origin of all things, — world-tiller, world-animator, he was called (509. 316). Xenophanes of Kolophon, a Greek philosopher of the sixth century B.C., taught that "the mighty sea is the father of clouds and winds and rivers." In Greek mythology Oceanus is said to be the father of the principal rivers of earth. Neptune, the god of the sea, — "Father Neptune," he is sometimes called, — had his analogue in a deity whom the Libyans looked upon as "the first and greatest of the gods." To Neptune, as the "Father of Streams," the Romans erected a temple in the Campus Martius and held games and feasts in his honour. The sea was also spoken of as *pater æquoreus.*

Father-River.

The name "Father of Waters" is assigned, incorrectly perhaps, to certain American Indian languages, as an appellation of the Mississippi. From Macaulay's "Lay of Horatius," we all know

> "O Tiber, Father Tiber,
> To whom the Romans pray,"

and "Father Thames" is a favourite epithet of the great English river.

Father-Frost.

In our English nursery-lore the frost is personified as a mischievous boy, "Jack Frost," to whose pranks its vagaries are due. In old Norse mythology we read of the terrible "Frost Giants," offspring of Ymir, born of the ice of Niflheim, which the warmth exhaled from the sun-lit land of Muspelheim caused to drop off into the great Ginnunga-gap, the void that once was where earth is now. In his "Frost Spirit" Whittier has preserved something of the ancient grimness.

We speak commonly of the "Frost-King," whose fetters bind the earth in winter.

In Russia the frost is called "Father Frost," and is personified as a white old man, or "a mighty smith who forges strong chains

with which to bind the earth and the waters," and on Christmas
Eve "the oldest man in each family takes a spoonful of kissel (a
sort of pudding), and then, having put his head through the window, cries: 'Frost, Frost, come and eat kissel! Frost, Frost,
do not kill our oats! Drive our flax and hemp deep into the
ground'" (520. 223–230).

Quite different is the idea contained in Grimm's tale of "Old
Mother Frost," — the old woman, the shaking of whose bed in
the making causes the feathers to fly, and "then it snows on
earth."

Father-Fire.

Fire has received worship and apotheosis in many parts of the
globe. The Muskogee Indians of the southeastern United States
"gave to fire the highest Indian title of honour, *grandfather*, and
their priests were called 'fire-makers'" (529. 68). The ancient
Aztecs called the god of fire "the oldest of the gods, *Huehueteotl*,
and also 'our Father,' *Tota*, as it was believed that from him all
things were derived." He was supposed "to govern the genera-
tive proclivities and the sexual relations," and he was sometimes
called *Xiuhtecutli*, "'God of the Green Leaf,' that is, of vegetable
fecundity and productiveness." He was worshipped as "the life-
giver, the active generator of animate existence," — the "primal
element and the immediate source of life" (413). These old
Americans were in accord with the philosopher, Heraclitus of
Ephesus, who held that "fire is the element, and all things were
produced in exchange for fire"; and Heraclitus, in the fragments
in which he speaks of "God," the "one wise," that which "knows
all things," means "Fire." In the rites of the Nagualists occurs
a "baptism by fire," which was "celebrated on the fourth day
after the birth of the child, during which time it was deemed
essential to keep the fire burning in the house, but not to permit
any of it to be carried out, as that would bring bad luck to the
child," and, in the work of one of the Spanish priests, a protest
is made: "Nor must the lying-in women and their assistants be
permitted to speak of Fire as the father and mother of all things,
and the author of nature; because it is a common saying with
them that Fire is present at the birth and death of every creature." It appears also that the Indians who followed this strange

cult were wont to speak of "what the Fire said and how the Fire wept" (413. 45–46).

Among various other peoples, fire is regarded as auspicious to children; its sacred character is widely recognized. In the Zend-Avesta, the Bible of the ancient Persians, whose religion survives in the cult of the Parsees, now chiefly resident in Bombay and its environs, we read of Ahura-Mazdâ, the "Wise Lord," the "Father of the pure world," the "best thing of all, the source of light for the world." Purest and most sacred of all created things was fire, light (421. 32). In the Sar Dar, one of the Parsee sacred books, the people are bidden to "keep a continual fire in the house during a woman's pregnancy, and, after the child is born, to burn a lamp [or, better, a fire] for three nights and days, so that the demons and fiends may not be able to do any damage and harm." It is said that when Zoroaster, the founder of the ancient religion of Persia, was born, "a demon came at the head of a hundred and fifty other demons, every night for three nights, to slay him, but they were put to flight by seeing the fire, and were consequently unable to hurt him" (258. 96).

In ancient Rome, among the Lithuanians on the shores of the Baltic, in Ireland, in England, Denmark, Germany, "while a child remained unbaptized," it was, or is, necessary "to burn a light in the chamber." And in the island of Lewis, off the northwestern coast of Scotland, "fire used to be carried round women before they were churched, and children before they were christened, both night and morning; and this was held effectual to preserve both mother and infant from evil spirits, and (in the case of the infant) from being changed."

In the Gypsy mountain villages of Upper Hungary, during the baptism of a child, the women kindle in the hut a little fire, over which the mother with the baptized infant must step, in order that milk may not fail her while the child is being suckled (392. II. 21).

In the East Indies, the mother with her new-born child is made to pass between two fires.

Somewhat similar customs are known to have existed in northern and western Europe; in Ireland and Scotland especially, where children were made to pass through or leap over the fire.

To Moloch ("King"), their god of fire, the Phœnicians used to sacrifice the first-born of their noblest families. A later development of this cult seems to have consisted in making the child pass between two fires, or over or through a fire. This "baptism of fire" or "purification by fire," was in practice among the ancient Aztecs of Mexico. To the second water-baptism was added the fire-baptism, in which the child was drawn through the fire four times (509. 653).

Among the Tarahumari Indians of the Mexican Sierra Madre, the medicine-man "cures" the infant, "so that it may become strong and healthy, and live a long life." The ceremony is thus described by Lumholtz: "A big fire of corn-cobs, or of the branches of the mountain-cedar, is made near the cross [outside the house], and the baby is carried over the smoke three times towards each cardinal-point, and also three times backward. The motion is first toward the east, then toward the west, then south, then north. The smoke of the corn-cobs assures him of success in agriculture. With a fire-brand the medicine-man makes three crosses on the child's forehead, if it is a boy, and four, if a girl" (107. 298).

Among certain South American tribes the child and the mother are "smoked" with tobacco (326. II. 194).

With marriage, too, fire is associated. In Yucatan, at the betrothal, the priest held the little fingers of bridegroom and bride to the fire (509. 504), and in Germany, the maiden, on Christmas night, looks into the hearth-fire to discover there the features of her future husband (392. IV. 82). Rademacher (130 a) has called attention to the great importance of the hearth and the fireplace in family life. In the Black Forest the stove is invoked in these terms: "Dear oven, I beseech thee, if thou hast a wife, I would have a man" (130 a. 60). Among the White Russians, before the wedding, the house of the bridegroom and that of the bride are "cleansed from evil spirits," by burning a heap of straw in the middle of the living-room, and at the beginning of the ceremonies, after they have been elevated upon a cask, as "Prince" and "Princess," the guests, with the wedding cake and two tapers in their hands, go round the cask three times, and with the tapers held crosswise burn them a little on the neck, the forehead, and the temples, so that the hair is singed away somewhat. At church the wax tapers are of importance: if they burn brightly and clearly, the young couple will have a happy, merry married life; if feeble, their life will be a quiet one; if they flicker, there will be strife and quarrels between them (392 (1891). 161).

Writing of Manabozho, or Michabo, the great divinity of the Algonkian tribes of the Great Lakes, Dr. D. G. Brinton says: "Michabo, giver of life and light, creator and preserver, is no apotheosis of a prudent chieftain, still less the fabrication of an idle fancy, or a designing priestcraft, but, in origin, deeds, and name, the not unworthy personification of the purest conceptions they possessed concerning the Father of All" (409. 469).

To Agni, fire, light, "in whom are all the gods," the ancient Hindu prayed: "Be unto us easy of access, as a father to his son" (388. 210), and later generations of men have seen in light the embodiment of God. As Max Müller says, "We ourselves also, though we may no longer use the name of Morning-Light for the Infinite, the Beyond, the Divine, still find no better expression than *Light* when we speak of the manifestations of God, whether in nature or in our mind" (510. 434).

In the Christian churches of to-day hymns of praise are sung to God as "Father of Light and Life," and their neophytes are bidden, as of old, to "walk as Children of Light."

Father-Sun.

At the naming of the new-born infant in ancient Mexico, the mother thus addressed the Sun and the Earth: "Thou Sun, Father of all that live, and thou Earth, our Mother, take ye this child, and guard it as your son." A common affirmation with them was: "By the life of the Sun, and of our Lady, the Earth" (529. 97).

Many primitive tribes have the custom of holding the new-born child up to the sun.

Not a few races and peoples have called themselves "children of the sun." The first of the Incas of Peru — a male and a female — were children of the Sun "our Father," who, "seeing the pitiable condition of mankind, was moved to compassion, and sent to them, from Heaven, two of his children, a son and a daughter, to teach them how to do him honour, and pay him divine

worship "; they were also instructed by the sun in all the needful arts of life, which they taught to men (529. 102). When the
"children of the Sun" died, they were said to be "called to the
home of the Sun, their Father" (100. 479).

The Comanche Indians, who worship the sun with dances and
other rites, call him *taab-apa*, "Father Sun," and the Sarcees
speak of the sun as "Our Father," and of the earth as "Our
Mother" (412. 122, 72).

With the Piute Indians "the sun is the father and ruler of
the heavens. He is the big chief. The moon is his wife, and the
stars are their children. The sun eats his children whenever he
can catch them. They fall before him, and are all the time
afraid when he is passing through the heavens. When he (their
father) appears in the morning, you see all the stars, his children, fly out of sight, — go away back into the blue of the above,
— and they do not wake to be seen again until he, their father,
is about going to his bed" (485. I. 130).

Dr. Eastman says of the Sioux Indians: "The sun was regarded as the father, and the earth as the mother, of all things
that live and grow; but, as they had been married a long time
and had become the parents of many generations, they were
called the great-grandparents" (518 (1894). 89).

Widespread over the earth has been, and still is, the worship
of the sun; some mythologists, indeed, would go too far and
explain almost every feature of savage and barbarous religion as
a sun-myth or as smacking of heliolatry.

Imagery and figurative language borrowed from the consideration of the aspect and functions of the great orb of day have
found their way into and beautified the religious thought of every
modern Christian community. The words of the poet Thomson:

> "Prime cheerer light!
> Of all material beings first and best!
> Efflux divine! Nature's resplendent robe!
> Without whose vesting beauty all were wrapt
> In unessential gloom; and thou, O Sun!
> Soul of surrounding worlds! in whom best seen
> Shines out thy Maker!"

find briefer expression in the simple speech of the dying Turner:
"The sun is God."

Father-Earth.

Though in nearly every portion of the globe the apotheosis of earth is as a woman, we find in America some evidences of a cult of the terrestrial Father-God. Concerning the cave-worship of the Mexican aborigines, Dr. Brinton says (413. 38, 50) : " The intimate meaning of this cave-cult was the worship of the Earth. The Cave-God, the Heart of the Hills, really typified the Earth, the Soil, from whose dark recesses flow the limpid streams and spring the tender shoots of the food-plants as well as the great trees. To the native Mexican the Earth was the provider of food and drink, the common Father of All; so that, to this day, when he would take a solemn oath, he stoops to the earth, touches it with his hand, and repeats the solemn formula: ' *Cuix amo nechitla in toteotzin ?* Does not our Great God see me ? ' "

Father-Wind.

Dr. Berendt, when travelling through the forests of Yucatan, heard his Maya Indian guide exclaim in awe-struck tones, as the roar of a tornado made itself heard in the distance: *He catul nohoch yikal nohoch tat,* "Here comes the mighty wind of the Great Father." As Dr. Brinton points out, this belief has analogues all over the world, in the notion of the wind-bird, the master of breath, and the spirit, who is father of all the race, for we learn also that "the whistling of the wind is called, or attributed to, *tat acmo,* words which mean 'Father Strong-Bird' " (411. 175).

The cartography of the Middle Ages and the epochs of the great maritime discoveries has made us familiar with the wind-children, offspring of the wind-father, from whose mouths came the breezes and the storms, and old Boreas, of whom the sailors sing, has traces of the fatherhood about him. More than one people has believed that God, the Father, is Spirit, breath, wind.

Other Father-Gods.

The ancient Romans applied the term *Pater* to many of their gods beside the great Jove. Vulcan was called *Lemnus Pater,* the "Lemnian Father"; Bacchus, *Pater Lenœus;* Janus, the

"early god of business," is termed by Horace, *Matutinus Pater,*
"Early-morning Father"; Mars is *Mars Pater,* etc. The Guarayo
Indians, of South America, prayed for rain and bountiful harvests to "Tamoï, the grandfather, the old god in heaven, who
was their first ancestor and had taught them agriculture" (100.
288).

The Abipones, of Paraguay, called the Pleiades their "Grandfather" and "Creator." When the constellation was invisible,
they said: "Our Grandfather, Keebet, is ill" (509. 274, 284).

In his account of the folk-lore of Yucatan, Dr. Brinton tells us
that the giant-beings known as *Hbalamob,* or *balams,* are sometimes "affectionately referred to as *yum balam,* or 'Father Balam.'"
The term *yum* is practically the equivalent of the Latin *pater,* and
of the "*father,*" employed by many primitive peoples in addressing, or speaking of, their great male divinities (411. 176).

In his acute exposition of the philosophy of the Zuñi Indians,
Mr. Cushing tells us (424. 11) that "all beings, whether deistic
and supernatural, or animistic and mortal, are regarded as belonging to one system; and that they are likewise believed to be
related by blood seems to be indicated by the fact that human
beings are spoken of as the 'children of men,' while *all* other
beings are referred to as 'the Fathers,' the 'All-Fathers (Á-tä-
tchu),' and 'Our Fathers.'" The "Priest of the Bow," when
travelling alone through a dangerous country, offers up a prayer,
which begins: "Si! This day, My Fathers, ye Animal Beings,
although this country be filled with enemies, render me precious"
(424. 41). The hunter, in the ceremonial of the "Deer Medicine," prays: "Si! This day, My Father, thou Game Animal, even
though thy trail one day and one night hast (been made) round
about; however, grant unto me one step of my earth-mother.
Wanting thy life-blood, wanting that flesh, hence I address to
thee good fortune, address to thee treasure," etc. When he has
stricken down the animal, "before the 'breath of life' has left
the fallen deer (if it be such), he places its fore feet back of its
horns, and, grasping its mouth, holds it firmly, closely, while he
applies his lips to its nostrils and breathes as much wind into
them as possible, again inhaling from the lungs of the dying
animal into his own. Then, letting go, he exclaims: 'Ah!
Thanks, my father, my child. Grant unto me the seeds of

earth ('daily bread') and the gift of water.   Grant unto me
the light of thy favour, do" (424. 36).

Something of a like nature, perhaps, attaches to the bear-
ceremonials among the Ainu and other primitive peoples of
northeastern Asia, with whom that animal is held in great
respect and reverence, approaching to deification.

Of Pó-shai-an-k'ia, "the God (Father) of the Medicine Societies, or sacred esoteric orders of the Zuñis," Mr. Cushing tells us:
"He is supposed to have appeared in human form, poorly clad,
and therefore reviled by men; to have taught the ancestors of
the Zuñi, Taos, Oraibi, and Coçonino Indians their agricultural
and other arts; their systems of worship by means of plumed
and painted prayer-sticks; to have organized their medicine societies, and then to have disappeared toward his home in Shi-pä-
pu-li-ma (from *shi-pa-a* = mist, vapour; *u-lin*, surrounding; and
i-mo-na = sitting-place of; 'The mist-enveloped city'), and to have
vanished beneath the world, whence he is said to have departed
for the home of the Sun.   He is still the conscious auditor of the
prayers of his children, the invisible ruler of the spiritual Shi-pä-
pu-li-ma, and of the lesser gods of the medicine orders, the principal 'Finisher of the Paths of our Lives.'   He is, so far as any
identity can be established, the 'Montezuma' of popular and
usually erroneous Mexican tradition" (424. 16).   Both on the
lowest steps of civilization and on the highest, we meet with this
passing over of the Father into the Son, this participation of God
in the affairs and struggles of men.

CHAPTER V.

The Name Child.

Liebe Kinder haben viele Namen
[Dear children have many names]. — *German Proverb.*

Child or boy, my darling, which you will. — *Swinburne.*

Men ever had, and ever will have, leave
To coin new words well-suited to the age.
Words are like leaves, some wither every year,
And every year a younger race succeeds. — *Roscommon.*

Child and its Synonyms.

Our word *child* — the good old English term; for both *babe* and *infant* are borrowed — simply means the " product of the womb " (compare Gothic *kilthei*, " womb "). The Lowland-Scotch dialect still preserves an old word for " child " in *bairn*, cognate with Anglo-Saxon *bearn*, Icelandic, Swedish, Danish, and Gothic *barn* (the Gothic had a diminutive *barnilo*, " baby "), Sanskrit *bharna*, which signifies " the borne one," " that which is born," from the primitive Indo-European root *bhr*, " to bear, to carry in the womb," whence our " to *bear* " and the German " ge-*bären.*" *Son*, which finds its cognates in all the principal Aryan dialects, except Latin, and perhaps Celtic, — the Greek *vios* is for *συιος*, and is the same word, — a widespread term for " male child, or descendant," originally meant, as the Old Irish *suth*, " birth, fruit," and the Sanskrit *sû*, " to bear, to give birth to," indicate, " the fruit of the womb, the begotten " — an expression which meets us time and again in the pages of the Hebrew Bible. The words *offspring, issue, seed*, used in higher diction, explain themselves and find analogues all over the world. To a like category belong Sanskrit *gárbha*, " brood of birds, child, shoot"; Pali *gabbha*, " womb, embryo, child"; Old High German *chilburra*, "female lamb"; Gothic

75

kalbô, "female lamb one year old"; German *Kalb;* English *calf;* Greek δελφύς, "womb"; whence ἀδελφός, "brother," literally "born of the same womb." Here we see, in the words for their young, the idea of the kinship of men and animals in which the primitive races believed. The "brought forth" or "born" is also the signification of the Niskwalli Indian *ba'-ba-ad*, "infant"; *de-bād-da*, "infant, son"; Maya *al*, "son or daughter of a woman"; Cakchiquel *4ahol*, "son," and like terms in many other tongues. Both the words in our language employed to denote the child before birth are borrowed. *Embryo*, with its cognates in the modern tongues of Europe, comes from the Greek ἔμβρυον, "the fruit of the womb before delivery; birth; the embryo, fœtus; a lamb newly born, a kid." The word is derived from ἐν, "within"; and βρύω, "I am full of anything, I swell or teem with"; in a transitive sense, "I break forth." The radical idea is clearly "swelling," and cognates are found in Greek βρύον, "moss"; and German *Kraut*, "plant, vegetable." *Fœtus* comes to us from Latin, where it meant "a bearing, offspring, fruit; bearing, dropping, hatching, — of animals, plants, etc.; fruit, produce, offspring, progeny, brood." The immediate derivation of the word is from *fēto*, "I breed," whence also *effētus*, "having brought forth young, worn out by bearing, effete." *Fēto* itself is from an old verb *feuere*, "to generate, to produce," possibly related to *fui* and our *be*. The radical signification of *fœtus* then is "that which is bred, or brought to be"; and from the same root *fē* are derived *fēles*, "cat" (the fruitful animal); *fē-num*, "hay"; *fē-cundus*, "fertile"; *fē-lix*, "happy" (fruitful). The corresponding verb in Greek is φύειν, "to grow, to spring forth, to come into being," whence the following: φύσις, "a creature, birth, nature," — nature is "all that has had birth"; φυτόν, "something grown, plant, tree, creature, child"; φῦλή, φῖλον, "race, clan, tribe," — the "aggregate of those born in a certain way or place"; φύς, "son"; φύσας, "father," etc.

In English, we formerly had the phrase "to look *babies* in the eyes," and we still speak of the *pupil* of the eye, the old folk-belief having been able to assert itself in the every-day speech of the race, — the thought that the soul looked out of the windows of the eyes. In Latin, *pūpilla pūpila*, "girl, pupil of the eye," is a diminutive of *pūpa* (*puppa*), "girl, damsel, doll, puppet";

other related words are *pŭpulus*, "little boy"; *pŭpillus*, "orphan, ward," our *pupil; pŭpulus*, "little child, boy"; *pŭpus*, "child, boy." The radical of all these is *pu*, "to beget"; whence are derived also the following: *pŭer*, "child, boy"; *pŭella* (for *puerula*), a diminutive of *puer*, "girl"; *pūsus*, "boy"; *pūsio*, "little boy," *pŭsillus*; "a very little boy"; *pŭtus*, "boy"; *pŭtillus*, "little boy"; *pŭtilla*, "little girl,"—here belongs also *pusillanimus*, "small-minded, boy-minded"; *pūbis*, "ripe, adult"; *pŭbertas*, "puberty, maturity"; *pullus*, "a young animal, a fowl," whence our *pullet*. In Greek we find the cognate words πῶλος, "a young animal," related to our *foal, filly;* πωλιόν, "pony," and, as some, perhaps too venturesome, have suggested, παῖς, "child," with its numerous derivatives in the scientifical nomenclature and phraseology of to-day. In Sanskrit we have *putra*, "son," a word familiar as a suffix in river-names, — *Brahmaputra*, "son of Brahma," — *pota*, "the young of an animal," etc. Skeat thinks that our word *boy*, borrowed from Low German and probably related to the Modern High German *Bube*, whence the familiar "bub" of American colloquial speech, is cognate with Latin *pŭpus*.

To this stock of words our *babe*, with its diminutive *baby*, seems not akin. Skeat, rejecting the theory that it is a reduplicative child-word, like *papa*, sees in it merely a modification (infantine, perhaps) of the Celtic *maban*, diminutive of *mab*, "son," and hence related to *maid*, the particular etymology of which is discussed elsewhere.

Infant, also, is a loan-word in English. In Latin, *infans* was the coinage of some primitive student of children, of some prehistoric anthropologist, who had a clear conception of "infancy" as "the period of inability to speak," — for *infans* signifies neither more nor less than "not speaking, unable to speak." The word, like our "childish," assumed also the meanings "child, young, fresh, new, silly," with a diminutive *infantulus*. The Latin word *infans* has its representatives in French and other Romance languages, and has given rise to *enfanter*, "to give birth to a child," *enfantement*, "labour," two of the few words relating to child-birth in which the child is directly remembered. The history of the words *infantry*, "foot-soldiers," and *Infanta*, "a princess of the blood royal" in Spain (even though she be married), illustrates a curious development of thought.

Our word *daughter,* which finds cognates in Teutonic, Slavonic, Armenian, Zend, Sanskrit, and Greek, Skeat would derive from the root *dugh,* "to milk," the "daughter" being primitively the "milker," — the "milkmaid," — which would remove the term from the list of names for "child" in the proper sense of the word. Kluge, however, with justice perhaps, considers this etymology improbable.

A familiar phrase in English is "babes and sucklings," the last term of which, cognate with German *Säugling,* meets with analogues far and wide among the peoples of the earth. The Latin words for children in relation to their parents are *filius* (diminutive *filiolus*), "son," and *filia* (diminutive *filiola*), "daughter," which have a long list of descendants in the modern Neo-Latin or Romance languages, — French *fils, fille, filleul,* etc.; Italian *figlio, figlia,* etc. According to Skeat, *filius* signified originally "infant," perhaps "suckling," from *fēlare,* "to suck," the radical of which, *fē* (Indo-European *dhē*), appears also in *fēmina,* "woman," and *fēmella,* "female," the "sucklers" *par excellence.* In Greek the cognate words are τίτθη, "nurse," θῆλυς, "female," θηλή, "teat," etc.; in Lithuanian, *dēls,* "son." With *nonagan,* "teat, breast," are cognate in the Delaware Indian language *nonoshelluan,* "to suckle," *nonetschik,* "suckling," and other primitive tongues have similar series.

The Modern High German word for child is *Kind,* which, as a substantive, finds representatives neither in Gothic nor in early English, but has cognates in the Old Norse *kunde,* "son," Gothic *-kunds,* Anglo-Saxon *-kund,* a suffix signifying "coming from, originating from." The ultimate radical of the word is the Indo-European root *gen* (Teutonic *ken*), "to bear, to produce," whence have proceeded also *kin,* Gothic *kuni; queen,* Gothic *qvêns,* "woman"; *king,* Modern High German *König,* originally signifying perhaps "one of high origin"; Greek γένος and its derivatives; Latin *genus, gens, gigno;* Lithuanian *gentis,* "relative"; Sanskrit *janas,* "kin, stock," *janús,* "creature, kin, birth," *jantú,* "child, being, stock," *játá,* "son." *Kind,* therefore, while not the same word as our *child,* has the same primitive meaning, "the produced one," and finds further cognates in *kid* and *colt,* names applied to the young of certain animals, and the first of which, in the slang of to-day, is applied to children also. In some parts of

Germany and Switzerland *Kind* has the sense of *boy;* in Thuringia, for example, people speak of *zwei Kinder und ein Mädchen,* "two boys and a girl." From the same radical sprang the Modern High German *Knabe,* Old High German *chnabo,* "boy, youth, young fellow, servant," and its cognates, including our English *knave,* with its changed meaning, and possibly also German *Knecht* and English *knight,* of somewhat similar import originally.

To the same original source we trace back Greek γενέτηρ, Latin *genitor,* "parent," and their cognates, in all of which the idea of *genesis* is prominent. Here belong, in Greek: γένεσις, "origin, birth, beginning"; γυνή, "woman"; γενεά, "family, race"; γείνομαι, "I beget, produce, bring forth, am born"; γίγνομαι, "I come into a new state of being, become, am born." In Latin: *gigno,* "I beget, bring forth"; *gens,* "clan, race, nation," — those born in a certain way; *ingens,* "vast, huge, great," — "not *gens,*" *i.e.* "born beyond or out of its kind"; *gentilis,* "belonging to the same clan, race, tribe, nation," then, with various turns of meaning, "national, foreign," whence our *gentile, genteel, gentle, gentry,* etc.; *genus,* "birth, race, sort, kind"; *ingenium,* "innate quality, natural disposition"; *ingeniosus,* "of good natural abilities, born well-endowed," hence *ingenious; ingenuus,* "native, free-born, worthy of a free man," hence "frank, *ingenuous*"; *progenies,* "descent, descendants, offspring, progeny"; *gener,* "son-in-law"; *genius,* "innate superior nature, tutelary deity, the god born to a place," hence the *genius,* who is "born," not "made"; *genuinus,* "innate, born-in, *genuine*"; *indigena,* "native, born-there, indigenous"; *generosus,* "of high, noble birth," hence "noble-minded, *generous*"; *genero,* "I beget, produce, engender, create, procreate," and its derivatives *degenero, regenero,* etc., with the many words springing from them. From the same radical *gen* comes the Latin (*g*)*nascor,* "I am born," whose stem (*g*)*na* is seen also in *natio,* "the collection of those born," or "the birth," and *natura,* "the world of birth," — like Greek φύσις, — for "nations" and "nature" have both "sprung into being." The Latin *germen* (our *germ*), which signified "sprig, offshoot, young bud, sprout, fruit, embryo," probably meant originally simply "growth," from the root *ker,* "to make to grow." From the same Indo-European radical have come the Latin *creare,* "to create, make, produce," with its derivatives *procreare* and *creator,* which we now apply to the Supreme Being, as the "maker" or "producer" of all things. Akin are also *crescere*, "to come forth, to arise, to appear, to increase, to grow, to spring, to be born," and *Ceres*, the name of the goddess of agriculture (growth and creation), whence our word *cereal;* and in Greek Κρόνος, the son of Uranus (Heaven) and Gæa (Earth), κράτος, "strength," and its derivatives ("democracy," etc.).

Another interesting Latin word is *pario*, "I bring forth, produce," whence *parens*, "producer, parent," *partus*, " birth, bearing, bringing forth; young, offspring, fœtus, embryo of any creature," *parturio*, *parturitio*, etc. *Pario* is used alike of human beings, animals, birds, fish, while *parturio* is applied to women and animals, and, by Virgil, even to trees, — *parturit arbos*, "the tree is budding forth," — and by other writers to objects even less animate.

In the Latin *ēnītor*, "I bring forth or bear children or young,"— properly, "I struggle, strive, make efforts," — we meet with the idea of "labour," now so commonly associated with child-bearing, and deriving from the old comparison of the tillage of the soil and the bearing of the young. This association existed in Hebrew also, and Cain, the first-born of Adam, was the first agriculturist. We still say the tree *bears* fruit, the land *bears* crops, is *fertile*, and the most characteristic word in English belonging to the category in question is "to *bear*" children, cognate with Modern High German *ge-bären*, Gothic *gabairan*, Latin *ferre* (whence *fertilis*), Greek φέρειν, Sanskrit *bhri*, etc., all from the Indo-European root *bher*, "to carry" — compare the use of *tragen* in Modern High German : *sie trägt ein Kind unter dem Herzen*. The passive verb is "to be *born*," literally, "to be borne, to be carried, produced," and the noun corresponding, *birth*, cognate with German *Geburt*, and Old Norse *burthr*, which meant "embryo" as well. Related ideas are seen in *burden*, and in the Latin, *fors*, *fortuna*, for "fortune" is but that which is "borne" or "produced, brought forth," just as the Modern High German *Heil*, "fortune, luck," is probably connected with the Indo-European radical *gen*, "to produce."

Corresponding to the Latin *parentes*, in meaning, we have the Gothic *berusjös*, "the bearers," or "parents"; we still use in English, "forbears," in the sense of ancestors. The good old

English phrase "with child," which finds its analogues in many other languages, has, through false modesty, been almost driven out of literature, as it has been out of conversational language, by *pregnant,* which comes to us from the Latins, who also used *gravidus,* — a word we now apply only to animals, especially dogs and ants, — and *enceinte,* borrowed from French, and referring to the ancient custom of girding a woman who was with child. Similarly barren of direct reference to the child are *accouchement,* which we have borrowed from French, and the German *Entbindung.*

In German, Grimm enumerates, among other phrases relating to child-birth, the following, the particular meanings and uses of which are explained in his great dictionary: *Schwanger, gross zum Kinde, zum Kinde gehen, zum Kinde arbeiten, um's Kind kommen, mit Kinde, ein Kind tragen, Kindesgrosz, Kindes schwer, Kinder haben, Kinder bekommen, Kinder kriegen, niederkommen, entbinden,* and the quaint and beautiful *eines Kindes genesen,* — all used of the mother. Applied to both parents we find *Kinder machen, Kinder bekommen* (now used more of the mother), *Kinder erzeugen* (more recently, of the father only), *Kinder erzielen.*

Our English word *girl* is really a diminutive (from a stem *gir,* seen in Old Low German *gör,* "a child") from some Low German dialect, and, though it now signifies only "a female child, a young woman," in Middle English *gerl* (*girl, gurl*) was applied to a young person of either sex. In the Swiss dialects to-day *gurre,* or *gurrli,* is a name given to a "girl" in a depreciatory sense, like our own "girl-boy." In many primitive tongues there do not appear to be special words for "son" and "daughter," or for "boy" and "girl," as distinguished from each other, these terms being rendered "male-child (man-child)," and "female-child (woman-child)" respectively. The "man-child" of the King James' version of the Scriptures belongs in this category. In not a few languages, the words for "son" and "daughter" and for "boy" and "girl" mean really "little man," and "little woman" — a survival of which thought meets us in the "little man" with which his elders are even now wont to denominate "the small boy." In the Nahuatl language of Mexico, "woman" is *ciuatl,* "girl" *ciuatontli;* in the Niskwalli, of the State of Washington, "man" is *stobsh,* "boy" *stótomish,* "woman" *sldne,*

G

"girl" *cháchas* (*i.e.* "small") *sláne;* in the Tacana, of South
America, "man" is *dreja,* "boy" *drejave,* "woman" *epuna,*
"girl" *epunave.* And but too often the "boys" and "girls"
even as mere children are "little men and women" in more
respects than that of name.

In some languages the words for "son," "boy," "girl" are
from the same root. Thus, in the Mazatec language, of Mexico,
we find *indidi* "boy," *tzadi* "girl," *indi* "son," and in the
Cholona, of Peru, *nun-pullup* "boy," *ila-pullup* "girl," *pul* "son,"
— where *ila* means "female," and *nun* "male."

In some others, as was the case with the Latin *puella,* from
puer, the word for "girl" seems derived from that for "boy."
Thus, we have in Maya, *mehen* "son," *ix-mehen* "daughter," —
-ix is a feminine prefix; and in the Jívaro, of Ecuador, *vila*
"son," *vilalu,* "daughter."

Among very many primitive peoples, the words for "babe, infant,
child," signify really "small," "little one," like the Latin *parvus,*
the Scotch *wean* (for *wee ane,* "wee one"), etc. In Hawaiian,
for example, the "child" is called *keiki,* "the little one," and in
certain Indian languages of the Western Pacific slope, the Wiyot
kusha'ma "child," Yuke *únsil* "infant," Wintun *cru-tut* "infant,"
Niskwalli *chá chesh* "child (boy)," all signify literally "small,"
"little one."

Some languages, again, have diminutives of the word for
"child," often formed by reduplication, like the *wee wean* of
Lowland Scotch, and the *pilpil,* "infant" of the Nahuatl of
Mexico.

In the Snanaimuq language, of Vancouver Island, the words
k·ä'ela, "male infant," and *k·ä'k·ela,* "female infant," mean simply "the weak one." In the Modoc, of Oregon, a "baby" is
literally, "what is carried on one's self." In the Tsimshian, of
British Columbia, the word *wok·ä'üts,* "female infant," signifies
really "without labrets," indicating that the creature is yet too
young for the lip ornaments. In Latin, *liberi,* one of the words
for "children," shows on its face that it meant only "children,
as opposed to the slaves of the house, *servi*"; for *liberi* really
denotes "the free ones." In "the Galibi language of Brazil,
tigami signifies 'young brother, son, and little child,' indis-
criminately."

The following passage from Westermarck recalls the "my son," etc., of our higher conversational or even officious style (166. 93):—

"Mr. George Bridgman states that, among the Mackay blacks of Queensland, the word for 'daughter' is used by a man for any young woman belonging to the class to which his daughter would belong if he had one. And, speaking of the Australians, Eyre says, 'In their intercourse with each other, natives of different tribes are exceedingly punctilious and polite; . . . almost everything that is said is prefaced by the appellation of father, son, brother, mother, sister, or some other similar term, corresponding to that degree of relationship which would have been most in accordance with their relative ages and circumstances."

Similar phenomena meet us in the language of the criminal classes, and the slang of the wilder youth of the country.

Among the Andaman Islanders : "Parents, when addressing or referring to their children, and not using names, employ distinct terms, the father calling his son *dar ō·dire, i.e.* 'he that has been begotten by me,' and his daughter, *dar ō·dire-pail-;* while the mother makes use of the word *dab ē·tire, i.e.* 'he whom I have borne,' for the former, and *dab ē·tire pail-* for the latter; similarly, friends, in speaking of children to their parents, say respectively, *ngar ō·dire,* or *ngab ē·tire* (your son), *ngar ō·dire-pail-,* or *ngab ē·tire-pail-* (your daughter)" (498. 59).

In the Tonkawé Indian language of Texas, "to be born" is *nikaman yekéwa,* literally, "to become bones," and in the Klâmath, of Oregon, "to give birth," is *nkákgi,* from *nkák,* "the top of the head," and *gi,* "to make," or perhaps from *kák'gi,* "to produce bones," from the idea that the seat of life is in the bones. In the Nipissing dialect of the Algonkian tongue, *ni kanis,* "my brother," signifies literally, "my little bone," an etymology which, in the light of the expressions cited above, reminds one of the Greek ἀδελφός, and the familiar "bone of my bone," etc. A very interesting word for "child" is Sanskrit *toka,* Greek τέκνον, from the Indo-European radical *tek,* "to prepare, make, produce, generate." To the same root belong Latin *texere,* "to weave," Greek τέχνη, "art"; so that the child and art have their names from the same primitive source — the mother was the former of the child as she was of the chief arts of life.

"*Flower-Names.*"

The people who seem to have gone farthest in the way of words for "child" are the Andaman Islanders, who have an elaborate system of nomenclature from the first year to the twelfth or fifteenth, when childhood may be said to end. There are also in use a profusion of "flower-names" and complimentary terms. The "flower-names" are confined to girls and young women who are not mothers. The following list shows the peculiarity of the name-giving : —

1. Proper name chosen before birth of child : .*dô·ra.*
2. If child turns out to be a boy, he is called : .*dô·ra-ô·ta ;* if a girl, .*dô·ra-kâ·ta ;* these names (*ô·ta* and *kâ·ta* refer to the genital organs of the two sexes) are used during the first two or three years only.
3. Until he reaches puberty, the boy is called : .*dô·ra dâ·la,* and the girl, .*dô·ra-pō·il·ola.*
4. When she reaches maturity, the girl is said to be *ûn-lâ-wi,* or *â·kâ-lâ-wi,* and receives a "flower-name" chosen from the one of "the eighteen prescribed trees which blossom in succession" happening to be in season when she attains womanhood.
5. If this should occur in the middle of August, when the *Pterocarpus dalbergoides,* called *châ·langa,* is in flower, ".*dô·ra-pō·ilola* would become ·*châ·gara dô·ra,* and this double name would cling to the girl until she married and was a mother, then the 'flower' name would give way to the more dignified term *chän·a* (madam or mother) .*dô·ra ;* if childless, a woman has to pass a few years of married life before she is called *chän·a,* after which no further change is made in her name."

Much other interesting information about name-giving may be found in the pages of Mr. Man's excellent treatise on this primitive people (498. 59–61 ; 201–208).

Sign Language.

Interesting details about signs and symbols for "child" may be found in the elaborate article of Colonel Mallery on "Sign Language among North American Indians" (497a), and the book of Mr. W. P. Clark on *Indian Sign Language* (420).

Colonel Mallery tells us that "the Egyptian hieroglyphists, notably in the designation of Horus, their dawn-god, used the finger in or on the lips for 'child.' It has been conjectured in the last instance that the gesture implied, not the mode of taking nourishment, but inability to speak, *in-fans.*" This conjecture, however, the author rejects (497a. 304). Among the Arapaho Indians "the sign for *child, baby,* is the forefinger in the mouth, *i.e.* a nursing child, and a natural sign of a deaf-mute is the same;" related seem also the ancient Chinese forms for "son" and "birth," as well as the symbol for the latter among the Dakota Indians (494 a. 356). Clark describes the symbol for "child," which is based upon those for "parturition" and "height," thus: "Bring the right hand, back outwards, in front of centre of body, and close to it, fingers extended, touching, pointing outwards and downwards; move the hands on a curve downwards and outwards; then carry the right hand, back outwards, well out to front and right of body, fingers extended and pointing upwards, hand resting at supposed height of child; the hand is swept into last position at the completion of first gesture. In speaking of children generally, and, in fact, unless it is desired to indicate height or age of the child, the first sign is all that is used or is necessary. This sign also means the young of any animal. In speaking of children generally, sometimes the signs for different heights are only made. Deaf-mutes make the combined sign for male and female, and then denote the height with right hand held horizontally" (420. 109).

For "baby," deaf-mutes "hold extended left hand back down, in front of body, forearm about horizontal and pointing to right and front; then lay the back of partially compressed right hand on left forearm near wrist" (420. 57).

Names.

The interesting and extensive field of personal onomatology — the study of personal names — cannot be entered upon exhaustively here. Shakespeare has said: —

> "What's in a name? That which we call a rose
> By any other name would smell as sweet," —

and the same remark might be made of the children of some primitive peoples. Not infrequently the child is named before it is born. Of the Central Eskimo we read that often before the birth of the child, "some relative or friend lays his hand upon the mother's stomach, and decides what the infant is to be called; and, as the name serves for either sex, it is of no consequence whether it be a girl or a boy" (402. 612, 590). Polle has a good deal to say of the deep significance of the name with certain peoples — "to be" and "to be named" appearing sometimes as synonymous (517. 99). "Hallowed be Thy name" expresses the ideas of many generations of men. With the giving of a name the soul and being of a former bearer of it were supposed to enter into and possess the child or youth upon whom it was conferred. Rink says of the Eskimo of East Greenland, that "they seemed to consider man as consisting of three independent parts, — soul, body, name" (517. 122). One can easily understand the mysterious associations of the name, the taboos of its utterance or pronunciation so common among primitive peoples — the reluctance to speak the name of a dead person, as well as the desire to confer the name of such a one upon a new-born child, spring both from the same source.

The folk-lore and ceremonial of name-giving are discussed at length in Ploss, and the special treatises on popular customs. In several parts of Germany, it is held to be ominous for misfortune or harm to the child, if the name chosen for it should be made known before baptism. Sometimes, the child is hardly recognized as existing until he has been given a name. In Gerbstädt in Mansfeld, Germany, the child before it receives its name is known as "dovedung," and, curiously enough, in far-off Samoa, the corresponding appellation is "excrement of the family-god" (517. 103).

The following statement, regarding one of the American Indian tribes, will stand for many other primitive peoples: "The proper names of the Dakotas are words, simple and compounded, which are in common use in the language. They are usually given to children by the father, grandfather, or some other influential relative. When young men have distinguished themselves in battle, they frequently take to themselves new names, as the names of distinguished ancestors of warriors now dead. The son of a chief when he comes to the chieftainship, generally takes the name of his father or grandfather, so that the same names, as in other more powerful dynasties, are handed down along the royal lines" (524. 44–45).

Of the same people we are also told: "The Dakotas have no family or surnames. But the children of a family have particular names which belong to them, in the order of their birth up to the fifth child. These names are for boys, Caské, Hepán, Hepí, Catán, and Haké. For girls they are, Winóna, Hápan, Hápistinna, Wánské, and Wiháké."

Terms applied to Children.

An interesting study might be made of the words we apply to children in respect of size, *little, small, wee, tiny,* etc., very many of which, in their etymology, have no reference to childhood, or indeed to smallness. The derivation of *little* is uncertain, but the word is reasonably thought to have meant "little" in the sense of "deceitful, mean," from the radical *lut,* "to stoop" (hence "to creep, to sneak"). Curiously enough, the German *klein* has lost its original meaning, — partly seen in our *clean,* — "bright, clear." *Small* also belongs in the same category, as the German *schmal,* "narrow, slim," indicates, though perhaps the original signification may have been "small" as we now understand it; a cognate word is the Latin *macer,* "thin, lean," which has lost an *s* at the beginning. Even *wee,* as the phrase "a little wee bit" hints, is thought (by Skeat) to be nothing more than a Scandinavian form of the same word which appears in our English *way.* Skeat also tells us that "a little teeny boy," meant at first "a little fractious (peevish) boy," being derived from an old word *teen,* "anger, peevishness." Analogous to *tiny* is *pettish,* which is derived from *pet,* "mama's pet," "a spoiled child." Endless would the list of words of this class be, if we had at our disposal the projected English dialect dictionary; many other illustrations might be drawn from the numerous German dialect dictionaries and the great Swiss lexicon of Tobler.

Still more interesting, perhaps, would be the discussion of the special words used to denote the actions and movements of children of all ages, and the names and appellatives of the child derived from considerations of age, constitution, habits, actions, speech, etc., which are especially numerous in Low German dialects and such forms of English speech as the Lowland Scotch.

Worthy of careful attention are the synonyms of child, the comparisons in which the child figures in the speech of civilized and uncivilized man; the slang terms also, which, like the common expression of to-day, *kid*, often go back to a very primitive state of mind, when "children" and "kids" were really looked upon as being more akin than now.   Beside the terms of contempt and sarcasm, — *goose, loon, pig, calf, donkey,* etc., — those figures of speech which, the world over, express the sentiment of the writer of the *Wisdom of Solomon* regarding the foolishness of babes, — we, like the ancient Mexicans and many another lower race, have terms of praise and endearment, — "a jewel of a babe," and the like, — legions of caressives and diminutives in the use of which some of the Low German dialects are more lavish even than Lowland Scotch.

In Grimm's great *Deutsches Wörterbuch,* the synonymy of the word *Kind* and its semasiology are treated at great length, with a multitude of examples and explanations, useful to students of English, whose dictionaries lag behind in these respects.   The child in language is a fertile subject for the linguist and the psychologist, and the field is as yet almost entirely unexplored.

CHAPTER VI.

THE CHILD IN THE PRIMITIVE LABORATORY.

As if no mother had made you look nice. — *Proverbial Saying of Songish Indians.*

Spare the rod and spoil the child. — *Hebrew Proverb.*

Thou art weighed in the balance and found wanting. — *Daniel v. 27.*

He has lost his measure. — *German Saying.*

"Licking into Shape."

Pope, in the *Dunciad,* has the well-known lines: —

> "So watchful Bruin forms, with plastic care,
> Each growing lump, and brings it to a bear,"

a conceit found in Burton, Montaigne, Byron, and other writers, and based upon an old folk-belief that the cubs are born a formless lump which the mother-bear has to "lick into shape." The same idea gave rise to the "ours mal léché" of French, and our own colloquial expression "an ill-licked cub." In an Alemanian lullaby sung while washing and combing the child, occurs the following curious passage: —

> "I bin e chleine Pumpernickel,
> I bin e chleine Bär,
> Und wie mi Gott erschaffe hät,
> So wagglen ich derher,"
> ["I am a little Pumpernickel,
> I am a little bear,
> And just as God has fashioned me
> I wiggle about,"]

which, perhaps, contains the same thought. In a recent article, Professor E. W. Fay offers an etymology of the word "livid" which facilitates the passage from animal to man: "*Lividus*

meant 'licked.' The word derives from an animal's licking hurts
and sores on the young. A mother of the human species still
kisses (licks) a child's hurt to make it well" (*Mod. Lang.
Notes*, IX. 263). Who has not had his mother say: "Does it
hurt? Come and let me kiss it, and make it well."

Moreover, Reclus tells us, "There are Esquimaux who go
further in their demonstrations of affection, and carrying their
complaisance as far as Mamma Puss and Mamma Bruin, lick
their babies to clean them, lick them well over from head to foot"
(523. 38). Nor is it always the mother who thus acts. Mantegazza observes: "I even know a very affectionate child, who, without having learnt it from any one, licks the people to whom he
wishes to show friendship" (499. 144).

Massage.

Che nasce bella nasce maritata, — "the girl born pretty is born
married," — says the Italian proverb, and many devices there are
among primitive races to ensure the beauty which custom demands, but which nature has failed to provide.

Among the Songish Indians of British Columbia, there is a
saying: *Tōu ō'wuna täns ksɛtctcā'ai,* — "as if no mother had made
you look nice." Doctor Boas describes the "making the child
look nice" as follows (404. 20): —

"As soon as it is born, the mother rubs it from the mouth
towards the ears, so as to press the cheek-bones somewhat upward. The outer corners of the eyes are pulled outward that
they may not become round, which is considered ill-looking. The
calves of the legs are pressed backward and upward, the knees
are tied together to prevent the feet from turning inward, the
forehead is pressed down." Among the Nootka Indians, according to the same authority: "Immediately after birth, the eyebrows of the babe are pressed upward, its belly is pressed forward,
and the calves of the legs are squeezed from the ankles upward.
All these manipulations are believed to improve the appearance
of the child. It is believed that the pressing of the eyebrows
will give them the peculiar shape that may be noticed in all
carvings of the Indians of the North Pacific Coast. The squeez-
ing of the legs is intended to produce slim ankles" (404. 39).

The subject of the human physiognomy and physical characteristics in folk-lore and folk-speech is a very entertaining one, and the practices in vogue for beautifying these are legion and found all over the world (204).

Face-Games.

Some recollection of such procedure as that of the Songish Indians seems to linger, perhaps, in the game, which Sicilian nurses play on the baby's features. It consists in "lightly touching nose, mouth, eyes, etc., giving a caress or slap to the chin," and repeating at the same time the verses:—

> " Varvaruttedu
> Vucca d'aneddu,
> Nasu affilatu,
> Occhi di stiddi
> Frunti quatrata
> E te 'ccà 'na timpulata."

In French we have corresponding to this:—

> " Beau front
> Petits yeux,
> Nez can can,
> Bouche d'argent,
> Menton fleuri,
> Chichirichi."

In Scotch:—

> " Chin cherry,
> Moo merry,
> Nose nappie,
> Ee winkie,
> Broo brinkie,
> Cock-up jinkie."

In English:—

> " Eye winker,
> Tom Tinker,
> Nose dropper,
> Mouth eater.
> Chin chopper."

And cognate practices exist all over the globe (204. 21).

Primitive Weighing.

"Worth his weight in gold" is an expression which has behind it a long history of folk-thought. Professor Gaidoz, in his essay on *Ransom by Weight* (236), and Haberlandt, in his paper on the *Tulâpurusha, Man-Weighing* (248) of India, have shown to what extent has prevailed in Europe and Asia the giving of one's weight in gold or other precious substances by prisoners to their captors, in order to secure their liberty, by devotees to the church, or to some saint, as a cure for, or a preventitive of disease, or as an act of charity or of gratitude for favours received.

The expression used of Belshazzar in Daniel v. 27, "Thou art weighed in the balance, and found wanting" (and the analogue in Job xxxi. 6), has been taken quite literally, and in Brittany, according to the Abbot of Soissons, there was a Chapel of the Balances, "in which persons who came to be cured miraculously, were weighed, to ascertain whether their weight diminished when prayer was made by the monks in their behalf." Brewer informs us that "Rohese, the mother of Thomas Becket, used to weigh her boy every year on his birthday, against the money, clothes, and provisions which she gave to the poor" (191. 41). From Gregory of Tours we learn that Charicus, King of the Suevi, when his son was ill, "hearing of the miraculous power of the bones of St. Martin, had his son weighed against gold and silver, and sent the amount to his sepulchre and sanctuary at Tours" (236. 60).

Weighing of infants is looked upon with favour in some portions of western Europe, and to the same source we may ultimately trace the modern baby's card with the weight of the newcomer properly inscribed upon it, — a fashion which bids fair to be a valuable anthropometric adjunct. "Hefting the baby" has now taken on a more scientific aspect than it had of yore.

The following curious custom of the eastern Eskimo is perhaps to be mentioned here, a practice connected with their treatment of the sick. "A stone weighing three or four pounds, according to the gravity of the sickness, is placed by a matron under the pillow. Every morning she weighs it, pronouncing meanwhile words of mystery. Thus she informs herself of the state of the patient and his chances of recovery. If the stone grows constantly heavier, it is because the sick man cannot escape, and his days are numbered" (523. 39).

It is a far cry from Greenland to England, but there are connecting links in respect of folk-practice. Mr. Dyer informs us that in the parish church of Wingrove, near Ailesbury, as late as 1759, a certain Mrs. Hammokes was accused of witchcraft, and her husband demanded the "trial by the church Bible." So "she was solemnly conducted to the parish church, where she was stript of all her clothes to her shift, and weighed against the great parish Bible in the presence of all her neighbours. The result was that, to the no small mortification of her accuser, she outweighed the Bible, and was triumphantly acquitted of the charge" (436. 307, 308).

How often has not woman, looked upon in the light of a child, been subjected to the same practices and ceremonies!

Primitive Measurements.

The etymology and original significance of our common English words, *span, hand, foot, cubit, fathom,* and their cognates and equivalents in other languages, to say nothing of the self-explanatory *finger's breadth, arm's length, knee-high, ankle-deep,* etc., go back to the same rude anthropometry of prehistoric and primitive times, from which the classic peoples of antiquity obtained their canons of proportion and symmetry of the human body and its members. Among not a few primitive races it is the child rather than the man that is measured, and we there meet with a rude sort of anthropometric laboratory. From Ploss, who devotes a single paragraph to "Measurements of the Body," we learn that these crude measurements are of great importance in folk-medicine: —

"In Bohemia, the new-born child is usually measured by an old woman, who measures all the limbs with a ribbon, and compares them with one another; the hand, *e.g.*, must be as long as the face. If the right relations do not subsist, prayers and various superstitious practices are resorted to in order to prevent the devil from injuring the child, and the evil spirits are driven out of the house by means of fumigation. In the case of sick children in Bohemia the measuring is resorted to as a sympathetic cure. In other parts of Germany, on the other hand, in Schleswig-Holstein, Thuringia, Oldenburg, it is thought that measuring and weighing the new-born child may interfere with its thriving and growth" (326. I. 302).

Sibree states that in Madagascar, at circumcision, the child is measured and sprinkled with water (214. 6), and Ellis, in his history of that island, gives the following details of the ceremony (*History of Madagascar*, Vol. I. p. 182): —

"The children on whom the rite is to be performed are next led across the blood of the animal just killed, to which some idea of sacredness is attached. They are then placed on the west side of the house, and, as they stand erect, a man holding a light cane in his hand, measures the first child to the crown of the head, and at one stroke cuts off a piece of the cane measured to that height, having first carefully dipped the knife in the blood of the slaughtered sheep. The knife is again dipped in the blood, and the child measured to the waist, when the cane is cut to that height. He is afterwards measured to the knee with similar results. The same ceremony is performed on all the children successively. The meaning of this, if indeed any meaning can be attached to it, seems to be the symbolical removal of all evils to which the children might be exposed, — first from the head to the waist, then from the waist to the knees, and finally, from the knees to the sole of the foot."

The general question of the measurement of sick persons (not especially children), and of the payment of an image or a rod of precious metal of the height of a given person, or the height of his waist, shoulders, knee, etc., of the person, in recompense for some insult or injury, has been treated of by Grimm, Gaidoz, and Haberlandt. Gaidoz remarks (236. 74): "It is well known that in Catholic countries it is customary to present the saints with votive offerings in wax, which are representative of the sicknesses for which the saints are invoked; a wax limb, or a wax eye, for instance, are representative of a sore limb or of a sore eye, the cure of which is expected from the saint. Wax bodies were offered in the same way, as we learn from a ludicrous story told by Henri Estienne, a French writer of the sixteenth century. The story is about a clever monk who made credulous parents believe he had saved their child by his prayers, and he says to the father, 'Now your son is safe, thanks to God; one hour ago I should not have thought you would have kept him alive. But do you know what you are to do? You ought to have a wax effigy of his own size made for the glory of God, and put it before the image of the holy Ambrose, at whose intercession our Lord did this favour to you.'" Even poorer people were in the habit of offering wax candles of the height or of the weight of the sick person.

In 1888, M. Letourneau (299) called attention to the measurement of the neck as a test of puberty, and even of the virginity of maidens. In Brittany, "According to popular opinion, there is a close relation between the volume of the neck and puberty, sometimes even the virginity of girls. It is a common sight to see three young girls of uncertain age measure in sport the circumference of the neck of one of them with a thread. The two ends of this thread are placed between the teeth of the subject, and the endeavour is made to make the loop of the thread pass over the head. If the operation succeeds, the young girl is declared 'bonne à marier.'" MM. Hanoteau and Letourneau state that among the Kabyles of Algeria a similar measurement is made of the male sex. In Kabylia, where the attainment of the virile state brings on the necessity of paying taxes and bearing arms, families not infrequently endeavour to conceal the puberty of their young men. If such deceit is suspected, recourse is had to the test of neck-measurement. Here again, as in Brittany, if the loop formed by the thread whose two ends are held in the teeth passes over the head, the young man is declared of age, and enrolled among the citizens, whilst his family is punished by a fine. M. Manouvrier also notes that the same test is also employed to discover whether an adolescent is to be compelled to keep the fast of Rhamadan.

Measurements of Limbs and Body.

M. Mahoudeau cites from Tillaux's *Anatomie topographique*, and MM. Perdrizet and Gaidoz in *Mélusine* for 1893, quote from the *Secrets merveilleux de la magie naturelle et cabalistique du Petit Albert* (1743) extracts relating to this custom, which is also referred to by the Roman writers C. Valerius, Catullus, Vossius, and Scaliger. The subject is an interesting one, and merits further investigation. Ellis (42. 233) has something to say on the matter from a scientific point of view. Grimm has called attention to the very ancient custom of measuring a patient, "partly by way of cure, partly to ascertain if the malady were growing or abating." This practice is frequently mentioned in the German poems and medical books of the fourteenth and fifteenth centuries. In one case a woman says of her husband, "I measured him till he forgot everything," and another, desirous of persuading hers that he was not of sound mind, took the measure of his length and across his head. In a Zürich Ms. of 1393, "measuring" is included among the unchristian and forbidden things of sorcery. In the region about Trèves, a malady known as night-grip (*Nachtgriff*) is ascertained to be present by the following procedure: "Draw the sick man's belt about his naked body lengthwise and breadthwise, then take it off and hang it on a nail with the words 'O God, I pray thee, by the three virgins, Margarita, Maria Magdalena, and Ursula, be pleased to vouchsafe a sign upon the sick man, if he have the night-grip or no'; then measure again, and if the belt be shorter than before, it is a sign of the said sickness." In the Liegnitz country, in 1798, we are told there was hardly a village without its *messerin* (measuress), an old woman, whose *modus operandi* was this: "When she is asked to say whether a person is in danger from consumption, she takes a thread and measures the patient, first from head to heel, then from tip to tip of the outspread arms; if his length be less than his breadth then he is consumptive; the less the thread will measure his arms, the farther has the disease advanced; if it reaches only to the elbow, there is no hope for him. The measuring is repeated from time to time; if the thread stretches and reaches its due length again, the danger is removed. The wise woman must never ask money for her trouble, but take what is given." In another part of Germany, "a woman is stript naked and measured with a piece of red yarn spun on a Sunday." Sembrzycki tells us that in the Elbing district, and elsewhere in that portion of Prussia, the country people are firmly possessed by the idea that a decrease in the measure of the body is the source of all sorts of maladies. With an increase of sickness the hands and feet are believed to lose more and more their just proportional relations one with another, and it is believed that one can determine how much measure is yet to be lost, how long the patient has yet to live. This belief has given rise to the proverbial phrase *das Maas ver-lieren* — " to lose one's measure " (462. III. 1163–5).

Not upon adults alone, however, were these measurements carried out, but upon infants, children, and youths as well. Even in the New World, among the more conservative of the population of Aryan origin, these customs still flourish, as we learn from comparatively recent descriptions of trustworthy investigators. Professor J. Howard Gore, in the course of an interesting article on "The Go-Backs," belief in which is current among the dwellers in the mountain regions of the State of Virginia, tells us that when some one has suggested that "the baby has the 'go-backs,'" the following process is gone through: "The mother then must go alone with the babe to some old lady duly instructed in the art or science of curing this blighting disease. She, taking the infant, divests it of its clothing and places it on its back. Then, with a yarn string, she measures its length or height from the crown of the head to the sole of the heel, cutting off a piece which exactly represents this length. This she applies to the foot, measuring off length by length, to see if the piece of yarn contains the length of the foot an exact number of times. This operation is watched by the mother with the greatest anxiety, for on this coincidence of measure depends the child's weal or woe. If the length of the string is an exact multiple of the length of the foot, nothing is wrong, but if there is a remainder, however small, the baby has the go-backs, and the extent of the malady is proportional to this remainder. Of course in this measuring, the elasticity of the yarn is not regarded, nor repetitions tried as a test of accuracy" (244. 108). Moreover, "the string with which the determination was made must be hung on the hinge of a gate on the premises of the infant's parents, and as the string by gradual decay passes away, so passes away the 'go-backs.' But if the string should be lost, the ailment will linger until a new test is made and the string once more hung out to decay. Sometimes the cure is hastened by fixing the string so that wear will come upon it."

Professor Gore aptly refers to the Latin proverb *ex pede Her-*

culem, which arose from the calculation of Pythagoras, who from the *stadium* of 6000 feet laid out by Hercules for the Olympian games, by using his own foot as the unit, obtained the length of the foot of the mighty hero, whence he also deduced his height. We are not told, however, as the author remarks, whether or not Hercules had the "go-backs."

Among the white settlers of the Alleghanies between south-western Georgia and the Pennsylvania line, according to Mr. J. Hampden Porter, the following custom is in vogue: "Measuring an infant, whose growth has been arrested, with an elastic cord that requires to be stretched in order to equal the child's length, will set it right again. If the spell be a wasting one, take three strings of similar or unlike colours, tie them to the front door or gate in such a manner that whenever either are opened there is some wear and tear of the cords. As use begins to tell upon them, vigour will recommence" (480. VII. 116). Similar practices are reported from Central Europe by Sartori (392 (1895). 88), whose article deals with the folk-lore of counting, weighing, and measuring.

Tests of Physical Efficiency.

That certain rude tests of physical efficiency, bodily strength, and power of endurance have been and are in use among primitive peoples, especially at the birth of children, or soon after, or just before, at, or after, puberty, is a well-known fact, further testified to by the occurrence of these practices in folk-tales and fairy-stories. Lifting stones, jumping over obstacles, throwing stones, spears, and the like, crawling or creeping through holes in stones, rocks, or trees, have all been in vogue, and some of them survive even to-day in England and in other parts of Europe as popular tests of puberty and virginity. Mr. Dyer, in his *Church Lore Gleanings,* mentions the "louping," or "petting" stone at Belford, in Northumberland (England), a stone "placed in the path outside the church porch, over which the bridal pair with their attendants must leap"—the belief is that "the bride must leave all her pets and humours behind her when she crosses it." At High-Coquetdale, according to Mr. Henderson, in 1868, a bride was made to jump over a stick held by two groomsmen at the church door (436. 125). Another very curious practice

is connected with St. Wilfrid's "needle" at Ripon Cathedral —
said to be an imitation of the Basilican transenna. Through this
passage maidens who were accused of unchastity crept in order
to prove their innocence. If they could not pass through, their
guilt was presumed. It is also believed that "poor palsied folk
crept through in the expectation of being healed." At Boxley
Church in Kent, there was a "small figure of St. Rumbold, which
only those could lift who had never sinned in thought or deed"
(436. 312, 313).

At a marriage among the Nootka Indians of Vancouver Island,
the groom's party essay feats like these: "Heavy weights are
lifted; they try who is the best jumper. A blanket with a hole
in the centre is hung up, and men walk up to it blindfolded from
a distance of about twenty steps. When they get near it they
must point with their fingers towards the blanket, and try to hit
the hole. They also climb a pole, on top of which an eagle's nest,
or something representing an eagle's nest, is placed. The winner
of each game receives a number of blankets from the girl's
father. When the games are at an end, the groom's father dis-
tributes blankets among the other party" (404. 43). This reminds us of the games at picnics and social gatherings of our own
people.

In the *Gentleman's Magazine* for January, 1895, S. O. Addy,
in an article entitled "English Surnames and Heredity," points
out how the etymologies give us some indications of the physical
characteristics of the persons on whom the names were conferred.
In primitive times and among the lower races names are even of
more importance in this respect.

Clark says: "I have seen a baby not two days old snugly tied
up in one of these little sacks; the rope tied to the pommel of the
saddle, the sack hanging down alongside of the pony, and mother
and child comfortably jogging along, making a good day's march
in bitter cold winter weather, easily keeping up with a column of
cavalry which was after hostile Indians. After being carefully
and firmly tied in the cradle, the child, as a rule, is only taken
out to be cleaned in the morning, and again in the evening just
before the inmates of a lodge go to sleep; sometimes also in the
middle of the day, but on the march only morning and evening"
(420. 57).

In his account of the habits of the Tarahumari Indians, Lumholtz observes: " Heat never seems to trouble them.   I have seen young babies sleeping with uncovered heads on the backs of their mothers, exposed to the fierce heat of the summer sun."   The same writer tells us that once he pulled six hairs at once from a sleeping child, " without causing the least disturbance," and only when twenty-three had been extracted at once did the child take notice, and then only scratched its head and slept on (107. 297).

Colonel Dodge notes the following practice in vogue among the wild Indians of the West: —

" While the child, either boy or girl, is very young, the mother has entire charge, control, and management of it.   It is soon taught not to cry by a very summary process.   When it attempts to ' set up a yell,' the mother covers its mouth with the palm of her hand, grasps its nose between her thumb and forefinger, and holds on until the little one is nearly suffocated.   It is then let go, to be seized and smothered again at the first attempt to cry.   The baby very soon comprehends that silence is the best policy " (432. 187).

Of the Indians of Lower California, who learn to stand and walk before they are a year old, we are told on the authority of the missionary Baegert: " When they are born they are cradled in the shell of a turtle or on the ground.   As soon as the child is a few months old, the mother places it perfectly naked astraddle on her shoulders, its legs hanging down on both sides in front.   In this guise the mother roves about all day, exposing her helpless charge to the hot rays of the sun and the chilly winds that sweep over the inhospitable country " (306. 185).

Sleep.

Curious indeed are some of the methods in use among primitive peoples to induce sleep.   According to Mr. Fraser, the natives of a village near the banks of the Girree, in the Himalayan region of India, had the following custom (*Quart. Rev.* XXIV. 109): —

" The mother, seizing the infant with both arms and aided by the knees, gives it a violent whirling motion, that would seem rather calculated to shake the child in pieces than to produce the effect of soft slumber; but the result was unerring, and in a few seconds the child was fast asleep."

Somewhat akin to this procedure is the practice our modern mothers and nurses have of swinging the baby through a sort of semicircle in their arms, accompanying it with the familiar song, —

"This way,
And that way," etc.

This song and action, their dolls doing duty as children, have been introduced into the kindergarten, and even figure now in "doll-drills" on the stage, and at church festivals and society entertainments.

Of the same village the author goes on to say:—

"Several straw sheds are constructed on a bank, above which a cold clear stream is led to water their fields, and a small portion of this, probably of three fingers' breadth, is brought into the shed by a hollow stick or piece of bark, and falls from this spout into a small drain, which carries it off about two feet below. The women bring their children to these huts in the heat of the day, and having lulled them to sleep and wrapt their bodies and feet warm in a blanket, they place them on a small bench or tray horizontally, in such a way that the water shall fall upon the crown of the head, just keeping the whole top wet with its stream. We saw two under this operation, and several others came in while we remained, to place their children in a similar way. Males and females are equally used thus, and their sleep seemed sound and unruffled."

"*Heroic Treatment.*"

The Andamanese baby "within a few hours of its birth has its head shaved and painted with *kòi·ob-* (an ochre-mixture), while its diminutive face and body are adorned with a design in *tá·la-ŏg-* (white clay); this latter, as may be supposed, is soon obliterated, and requires therefore to be constantly renewed." We are further informed that before shaving an infant, "the mother usually moistens the head with milk which she presses from her breast," while with older children and adults water serves for this purpose (498. 114).

The "heroic treatment," meted out by primitive peoples to children, as they approach puberty, has been discussed in detail

by Ploss, Kulischer, Daniels. Religion and the desire to attract
the affection or attention of the other sex seem to lie very close
to the fundamental reasons for many of these practices, as
Westermarck points out in his chapter on the "Means of
Attraction" (166. 165–212). A divine origin is often ascribed
to these strange mutilations. "The Australian Dieyerie, on
being asked why he knocks out two front teeth of the upper
jaw of his children, can answer only that, when they were created,
the Muramura, a good spirit, thus disfigured the first child, and,
pleased at the sight, commanded that the like should be done to
every male or female child for ever after. The Pelew Islanders
believe that the perforation of the septum of the nose is necessary for winning eternal bliss; and the Nicaraguans say that
their ancestors were instructed by the gods to flatten their children's heads. Again, in Fiji it is supposed that the custom of
tattooing is in conformity with the appointment of the god
Dengei, and that its neglect is punished after death. A similar
idea prevails among the Kingsmill Islanders and Ainos; and
the Greenlanders formerly believed that the heads of those girls
who had not been deformed by long stitches made with a needle
and black thread between the eyes, on the forehead, and upon the
chin, would be turned into train tubs and placed under the lamps
in heaven, in the land of souls" (165. 170, 171).

Were all the details of the fairy-tales true, which abound in
every land, the cruelty meted out to the child suspected of being
a changeling would surpass human belief. Hartland enumerates
the following procedures as having been in use, according to
legend, to determine the justice of the suspicion: Flinging the
child on a dung-heap; putting in the oven; holding a red-hot
shovel before the child's face; heating a poker red-hot to mark
a cross on its forehead; heating the tongs red-hot to seize it by
the nose; throwing on, or into, the fire; suspending over the fire
in a pot; throwing the child naked on the glowing embers at midnight; throwing into lake, river, or sea (258. 120–123). These
and many more figure in story, and not a few of them seem to
have been actually practised upon the helpless creatures, who,
like the heathen, were not supposed to call for pity or love. Mr.
Hartland cites a case of actual attempt to treat a supposed
changeling in a summary manner, which occurred no later than

May 17, 1884, in the town of Clonmel, Ireland. In the absence of the mother of a three-year-old child (fancied by the neighbours to be a changeling), two women "entered her house and placed the child naked on a hot shovel, 'under the impression that it would break the charm,'" — the only result being, of course, that the infant was very severely burned (258. 121).

On the other hand, children of true Christian origin, infants who afterwards become saints, are subject to all sorts of torment at the hands of Satan and his angels, at times, but come forth, like the "children" of the fiery furnace in the time of Daniel, in imitation of whose story many of the hagiological legends have doubtless been put forth, unscathed from fire, boiling water, roaring torrents, and other perilous or deadly situations (191. 9, 122).

CHAPTER VII.

The Bright Side of Child-Life: Parental Affection.

> These are my jewels. — *Cornelia (mother of the Gracchi).*

> A simple child
> That lightly draws its breath,
> And feels its life in every limb,
> What should it know of death? — *Wordsworth.*

> Children always turn towards the light. — *Hare.*

> That I could bask in Childhood's sun
> And dance o'er Childhood's roses! — *Praed.*

> Grief fills the room up of my absent child. — *Shakespeare.*

Parental Love.

In his essay on *The Pleasures of Home*, Sir John Lubbock makes the following statement (494. 102): —

"In the *Origin of Civilization*, I have given many cases showing how small a part family affection plays in savage life. Here I will only mention one case in illustration. The Algonquin (North America) language contained no word for 'to love,' so that when the missionaries translated the Bible into it they were obliged to invent one. What a life, and what a language, without love!"

How unfortunately inaccurate, how entirely unjustifiable, such a declaration is, may be seen from the study of the words for love in two of the Algonkian dialects, — Cree and Chippeway, — which Dr. Brinton has made in one of his essays, *The Conception of Love in some American Languages.* Let us quote the *ipsissima verba* (411. 415): —

(1) "In both of them the ordinary words for love and friendship are derived from the same monosyllabic root, *sak.* On this, accord-

104

ing to the inflectional laws of the dialects, are built up the terms for the love of man to woman, a lover, love in the abstract, a friend, friendship, and the like. It is also occasionally used by the missionaries for the love of man to God and of God to man."

(2) "The Cree has several words which are confined to parental and filial love, and to that which the gods have for men."

(3) "In the Chippeway there is a series of expressions for family love and friendship which in their origin carry us back to the same psychological process which developed the Latin *amare* from the Sanscrit *sam.*"

(4) "The highest form of love, however, that which embraces all men and all beings, that whose conception is conveyed in the Greek ἀγάπη, we find expressed in both the dialects by derivatives from a root different from any I have mentioned. It is in its dialectic forms *kis, keche,* or *kiji,* and in its origin it is an intensive interjectional expression of pleasure, indicative of what gives joy. Concretely, it signifies what is completed, permanent, powerful, perfected, perfect. As friendship and love yield the most exalted pleasure, from this root the natives drew a fund of words to express fondness, attachment, hospitality, charity; and from the same worthy source they selected that adjective [*kije, kise*], which they applied to the greatest and most benevolent divinity."

Surely this people cannot be charged with a lack of words for love, whose language enables them so well to express its every shade of meaning. Nay, they have even seen from afar that "God is Love," as their concept of Michabo tells us they had already perceived that He was "Light."

Motherhood and Fatherhood.

The nobility and the sanctity of motherhood have found recognition among the most primitive of human races. A Mussulman legend of Adam and Eve represents the angel Gabriel as saying to the mother of mankind after the expulsion from Paradise: "Thou shalt be rewarded for all the pains of motherhood, and the death of a woman in child-bed shall be accounted as martyrdom" (547. 38). The natives of the Highlands of Borneo hold that to a special hereafter, known as "Long Julan," go those who have suffered a violent death (been killed in battle, or by

the falling of a tree, or some like accident), and women who die
in child-birth; which latter become the wives of those who have
died in battle. In this Paradise everybody is rich, with no need
for labour, as all wants are supplied without work (475. 199).

Somewhat similar beliefs prevailed in ancient Mexico and
among the Eskimo.

Even so with the father. Zoroaster said in the book of the
law: "I name the married before the unmarried, him who has
a household before him who has none, the father of a family
before him who is childless" (125. I. 108). Dr. Winternitz
observes of the Jews: "To possess children was always the greatest good-fortune that could befall a Jew. It was deemed the duty
of every man to beget a son; the Rabbis, indeed, considered a
childless man as dead. To the Cabbalists of the Middle Ages,
the man who left no posterity behind him seemed one who had
not fulfilled his mission in this world, and they believed that he
had to return once more to earth and complete it" (385. 5).

Ploss (125. I. 108) and Lallemand (286. 21) speak in like terms
of this children-loving people. The Talmud ranks among the
dead "the poor, the leprous, the blind, and those who have no
children," and the wives of the patriarchs of old cheerfully
adopted as their own the children born to their husband by slave
or concubine. To be the father of a large family, the king of a
numerous people, was the ideal of the true Israelite. So, also,
was it in India and China.

Ploss and Haberlandt have a good deal to say of the ridicule
lavished upon old maids and bachelors among the various peoples
and races, and Rink has recorded not a few tales on this head
from the various tribes of the Eskimo — in these stories, which
are of a more or less trifling and *outré* character, bachelors are
unmercifully derided (525. 465).

With the Chippeways, also, the bachelor is a butt for wit and
sarcasm. A tale of the Mississagas of Skūgog represents a
bachelor as "having gone off to a certain spot and built a lot of
little 'camps.' He built fires, etc., and passed his time trying to
make people believe he was not alone. He used to laugh and
talk, and pretend that he had people living there." Even the
culture-heroes Glūskap and Nāniboju are derided in some of the
tales for not being married (166. 376).

According to Barbosa (67. 161), a writer of the early part of the sixteenth century, the Nairs, a Dravidian people of the Malabar coast (523. 159), believed that "a maiden who refused to marry and remained a virgin would be shut out of Paradise." The Fijians excluded from Paradise all bachelors; they were smashed to pieces by the god Nangganangga (166. 137).

In the early chronicles and mythic lore of many peoples there are tales of childless couples, who, in their quaint fashion, praying to the gods, have been blest with the desired offspring. There is, however, no story more pathetic, or more touching, than the Russian folk-tale cited by Ralston, in which we read concerning an old childless couple (520. 176): "At last the husband went into the forest, felled wood, and made a cradle. Into this his wife laid one of the logs he had cut, and began swinging it, crooning the while a tune beginning: —

'Swing, blockie dear, swing.'

After a little time, behold! the block already had legs. The old woman rejoiced greatly, and began swinging anew, and went on swinging until the block became a babe."

The rude prayers and uncouth aspirations of barbarous and savage peoples, these crude ideas of the uncivilized races of men, when sounded in their deepest depths, are the folk-expression of the sacredness of the complete family, the forerunners of the poet's prayer: —

"Seigneur! préservez-moi, préservez ceux que j'aime,
Frères, parents, amis, et ennemis même
Dans le mal triomphants,
De jamais voir, Seigneur! l'été sans fleurs vermeilles,
La cage sans oiseaux, la ruche sans abeilles,
La maison sans enfants."

The affection of the ancient Egyptians for their children is noted by Erman. The child is called "mine," "the only one," and is "loved as the eyes of its parents"; it is their "beauty," or "wealth." The son is the "fair-come" or "welcome"; at his birth "wealth comes." At the birth of a girl it is said "beauty comes," and she is called "the lady of her father" (441. 216–230). Interesting details of Egyptian child-life and education may be read in the recently edited text of Amélineau (179), where many maxims of conduct and behaviour are given. Indeed, in the naming of children we have some evidence of motherly and fatherly affection, some indication of the gentle ennobling influence of this emotion over language and linguistic expression. True is it all over the world: —

> Liebe Kinder haben viele Namen.
> [Dear children have many names.]

The Dead Child.

Parental affection is nowhere more strongly brought out than in the lamentations for the dead among some of the lowest tribes of Californian Indians. Of the Yokaia, Mr. Powers tells us (519. 166): —

"It is their custom to 'feed the spirits of the dead' for the space of one year, by going daily to places which they were accustomed to frequent while living, where they sprinkle piñole upon the ground. A Yokaia mother who has lost her babe goes every day for a year to some place where her little one played while alive, or to the spot where its body was burned, and milks her breasts into the air. This is accompanied by plaintive mourning and weeping and piteous calling upon her little one to return, and sometimes she sings a hoarse and melancholy chant, and dances with a wild, ecstatic swaying of the body."

Of the Miwok the same authority says: —

"The squaws wander off into the forest, wringing their arms piteously, beating the air, with eyes upturned, and adjuring the departed one, whom they tenderly call 'dear child,' or 'dear cousin' (whether a relative or not), to return."

Of the Niskwalli Indians, of the State of Washington, Dr. Gibbs observes (457. 205): —

"They go out alone to some place a little distant from the lodge or camp, and in a loud, sobbing voice, repeat a sort of stereotyped formula, as, for instance, a mother on the loss of her child: —

> '*Ah seahb! shed-da bud-dah ah-ta-bud! ad-de-dah!*
> Ah chief   my   child   dead !   alas ! '

When in dreams they see any of their deceased friends this lamentation is renewed."

Very beautiful and touching in the extreme is the conduct of the Kabinapek of California : —

" A peculiarity of this tribe is the intense sorrow with which they mourn for their children when dead. Their grief is immeasurable. They not only burn up everything that the baby ever touched, but everything that they possess, so that they absolutely begin life over again — naked as they were born, without an article of property left " (519. 206).

Besides the custom of " feeding the spirits of the dead," just noticed, there exists also among certain of the Californian Indians the practice of " whispering a message into the ear of the dead." Mr. Powers has preserved for us the following most beautiful speech, which, he tells us, was whispered into the ear of a child by a woman of the Karok ere the first shovelful of earth was cast upon it (519. 34): " O, darling, my dear one, good-bye ! Never more shall your little hands softly clasp these old withered cheeks, and your pretty feet shall print the moist earth around my cabin never more. You are going on a long journey in the spirit-land, and you must go alone, for none of us can go with you. Listen then to the words which I speak to you and heed them well, for I speak the truth. In the spirit-land there are two roads. One of them is a path of roses, and it leads to the Happy Western Land beyond the great water, where you shall see your dear mother. The other is a path strewn with thorns and briars, and leads, I know not whither, to an evil and dark land, full of deadly serpents, where you wander forever. O, dear child, choose you the path of roses, which leads to the Happy Western Land, a fair and sunny land, beautiful as the morning. And may the great Kareya [the Christ of these aborigines] help you to walk in it to the end, for your little tender feet must walk alone. O, darling, my dear one, good-bye !'

This whispering to the dead is found in other parts of the world. Mr. Hose, describing the funeral of a boy, which he witnessed in Borneo, says (475. 198) : —

"As the lid of the coffin was being closed, an old man came out on the verandah of the house with a large gong (Tetawak) and solemnly beat it for several seconds. The chief, who was sitting near, informed me that this was done always before clos-

ing the lid, that the relations of the deceased might know that
the spirit was coming to join them; and upon his arrival in
Apo Leggan [Hades] they would probably greet him in such
terms as these: 'O grandchild, it was for you the gong was
beating, which we heard just now; what have you brought?
How are they all up above? Have they sent any messages?'"
The new arrival then delivers the messages entrusted to him, and
gives the cigarettes — which, rolled up in a banana-leaf, have
been placed in his hand — as proof of the truth of what he says.
These cigarettes retain the smell of the hand that made them,
which the dead relations are thought to be able to recognize.

Motherhood and Infanticide.

The intimate relationship recognized as existing between the
infant and its mother has been among many primitive peoples a
frequent cause of infanticide, or has been held at least to excuse
and justify that crime. Of the natives of Ashanti, Ellis says: —
"Should the mother die in childbirth, and the child itself be
born alive, it is customary to bury it with the mother. . . . The
idea seems to be that the child belongs to the mother, and is sent
to accompany her to *Srahmanadzi* [ghost-land], so that her *srah-
man* [ghost] may not grieve for it" (438. 234). Post states that
in Unyóro, when the mother dies in childbirth, the infant is
killed; among the Hottentots it was exposed (if the mother died
during the time of suckling, the child was buried alive with her);
among the Damara, "when poor women die and leave children
behind them, they are often buried with the mother" (127. I.
287).

According to Collins and Barrington, among certain native
tribes of Australia, "when the mother of a suckling dies, if no
adoptive parents can be found, the child is placed alive in the
arms of the corpse and buried together with it" (125. II. 589).
Of the Banians of Bombay, Niebuhr tells us that children under
eighteen months old are buried when the mother dies, the corpse
of the latter being burned at ebb tide on the shore of the sea, so
that the next tide may wash away the ashes (125. II. 581). In
certain parts of Borneo: "If a mother died in childbirth, it was
the former practice to strap the living babe to its dead mother,

and bury them both together. 'Why should it live?' say they. 'It has been the death of its mother; now she is gone, who will suckle it?'" (481 (1893). 133).

In certain parts of Australia, "children who have caused their mother great pain in birth are put to death" (127. I. 288), and among the Sakalavas of Madagascar, the child of a woman dying in childbed is buried alive with her, the reason given being "that the child may thus be punished for causing the death of its mother" (125. II. 590).

As has been noted elsewhere, not a few primitive peoples have considered that death, in consequence of giving birth to a child, gained for the mother entrance into Paradise. But with some more or less barbarous tribes quite a different idea prevails. Among the Ewe negroes of the slave coast of West Africa, women dying in childbirth become blood-seeking demons; so also in certain parts of Borneo, and on the Sumatran island of Nias, where they torment the living, plague women who are with child, and kill the embryo in the womb, thus causing abortion; in Java, they make women in labour crazy; in Amboina, the Uliase and Kei Islands, and Gilolo, they become evil spirits, torturing women in labour, and seeking to prevent their successful delivery; in Giloo, the Kei group, and Celebes, they even torment men, seeking to emasculate them, in revenge for the misfortune which has overtaken them (397. 19).

Of the Doracho Indians of Central America, the following statement is made: "When a mother, who is still suckling her child, dies, the latter is placed alive upon her breast and burned with her, so that in the future life she may continue to suckle it with her own milk" (125. II. 589). Powers remarks concerning the Karusi (Patwin) Indians of California (519. 222): "When a woman died, leaving her infant very young, the friends shook it to death in a skin or blanket. This was done even with a half-breed child." Of the Nishinam Indians, the same authority informs us: "When a mother dies, leaving a very young infant, custom allows the relatives to destroy it. This is generally done by the grandmother, aunt, or other near relative, who holds the poor innocent in her arms, and, while it is seeking the maternal fountain presses it to her breast until it is smothered. We must not judge them too harshly for this. They knew nothing of bottle nurture, patent nipples, or any kind of milk whatever, other than the human " (519. 328).

Among the Wintūn, also, young infants are known to have been buried when the mother had died shortly after confinement (519. 232).

The Eskimo, Letourneau informs us, were wont to bury the little child with its dead mother, for they believed that unless this were done, the mother herself would call from *Killo*, the other world, for the child she had borne (100. 147, 148).

The Dead Mother.

To none of the saintly dead, to none of our race who have entered upon the life beyond the grave, is it more meet to pray than to the mother; folk-faith is strong in her power to aid and bless those left behind on earth. That sympathetic relation existing between mother and child when both are living, is often believed to exist when one has departed into the other world. By the name *wa-hdé ċa-pi*, the Dakota Indians call the feeling the (living) mother has for her absent (living) child, and they assert that " mothers feel peculiar pain in their breasts when anytling of importance happens to their absent children, or when about to hear from them. This feeling is regarded as an omen." That the mother, after death, should feel the same longing, and should return to help or to nourish her child, is an idea common to the folk-belief of many lands, as Ploss (125. II. 589) and Zmigrodzki have noted.

" Amid the song of the angels," says Zmigrodzki (174 142), "the plaint of her child on earth reaches the mother's ear, and pierces her heart like a knife. Descend to earth she must and does." In Brittany she is said to go to God Himself and obtain permission to visit earth. Her flight will be all the easier, if, before burial, her relatives have loosed her hair. In various parts of Germany and Switzerland, the belief is that for six weeks the dead mother will come at night to suckle her child, and a pair of slippers or shoes are always put into the coffin with the corpse, for the mother has to travel over thistles, thorns, and sharp stones to reach her child. Widespread over Europe is this belief in the return of the mother, who has died in giving life to her little one. Till cock-crow in the morning she may suckle it, wash it, fondle it; the doors open of themselves for her. If the child is being well treated by its relatives, the mother rejoices, and soon departs; but if it has been neglected, she attends to it, and waits till the last moment, making audible her unwillingness to depart. If the neglect continues, the mother descends to earth once more, and, taking the child with her, returns to heaven for good. And when the mother with her offspring approaches the celestial gates, they fly wide open to receive them. Never, in the folk-faith, was entrance readier granted, never was Milton's concept more completely realized, when

> " Heaven open'd wide
> Her ever-during gates, harmonious sound,
> On golden hinges moving."

In a modern Greek folk-song three youths plot to escape from Hades, and a young mother, eager to return to earth to suckle her infant child, persuades them to allow her to accompany them. Charon, however, suddenly appears upon the scene and seizes them just as they are about to flee. The beautiful young woman then appeals to him : " Let go of my hair, Charon, and take me by the hand. If thou wilt but give my child to drink, I will never try to escape from thee again " (125. II. 589).

The watchful solicitude of the mother in heaven over her children on earth appears also in the Basque country (505. 73), and Ralston, noting its occurrence in Russia, observes (520. 265) : —

"Appeals for aid to a dead parent are of frequent occurrence in the songs still sung by the Russian peasantry at funerals or over graves; especially in those in which orphans express their grief, calling upon the grave to open, and the dead to appear and listen and help. So in the Indian story of Punchkin, the seven hungry, stepmother-persecuted princesses go out every day and sit by their dead mother's tomb, and cry, and say, ' Oh, mother, mother, cannot you see your poor children, how unhappy we are,' etc., until a tree grows up out of the grave laden with fruits for their relief. So, in the German tale, Cinderella is aided by the white bird, which dwells in the hazel-tree growing out of her mother's grave."

Crude and savage, but born of a like faith in the power of the

ɪ

dead mother, is the inhuman practice of the people of the Congo, where, it is said, "the son often kills his mother, in order to secure the assistance of her soul, now a formidable spirit" (388. 81).

Heavy upon her offspring weighs the curse of a mother. Ralston, speaking of the Russian folk-tales, says (520. 363) : —

" Great stress is laid in the skazkas and legends upon the terrible power of a parent's curse. The ' hasty word ' of a father or a mother will condemn even an innocent child to slavery among devils, and, when it has once been uttered, it is irrevocable." The same authority states, however, that "infants which have been cursed by their mothers before their birth, or which are suffocated during their sleep, or which die from any causes unchristened or christened by a drunken priest, become the prey of demons," and in order to rescue the soul of such a babe from the powers of evil "its mother must spend three nights in a church, standing within a circle traced by the hand of a priest; when the cocks crow on the third morning the demons will give her back her dead child."

Fatherly Affection.

That the father, as well as the mother, feels for his child after death, and appears to him, is an idea found in fairy-story and legend, but nowhere so sweetly expressed as in the beautiful Italian belief that "the kind, dear spirits of the dead relatives and parents come out of the tombs to bring presents to the children of the family, — whatever their little hearts most desire." The proverb, — common at Aci, — *Veni mè patri? — Appressu,* " Is my father coming ? — By and by," used " when an expected friend makes himself long waited for," is said to have the following origin: —

" There was once a little orphan boy, who, in his anxiety to see his dead father once again, went out into the night when the kind spirits walk, and, in spite of all the fearful beating of his little heart, asked of every one whom he met: *Veni mè patri?* and each one answered: *Appressu.* As he had the courage to hold out to the end, he finally had the consolation of seeing his father and having from him caresses and sweetmeats " (449. 327).

Rev. Mr. Gill speaks highly of the affection for children of the
Polynesians. Following is the translation of a song composed
and sung by Rakoia, a warrior and chief of Mangaia, in the
Hervey Archipelago, on the death of his eldest daughter Enuatau-
rere, by drowning, at the age of fifteen (459. 32) : —

> " My first-born ; where art thou ?
> Oh that my wild grief for thee,
> Pet daughter, could be assuaged !
> Snatched away in time of peace.
>
> Thy delight was to swim,
> Thy head encircled with flowers,
> Interwoven with fragrant laurel
> And the spotted-leaved jessamine.
>
> Whither is my pet gone —
> She who absorbed all my love —
> She whom I had hoped
> To fill with ancestral wisdom ?
>
> Red and yellow pandanus drupes
> Were sought out in thy morning rambles,
> Nor was the sweet-scented myrtle forgotten.
>
> Sometimes thou didst seek out
> Fugitives perishing in rocks and caves.
>
> Perchance one said to thee,
> ' Be mine, be mine, forever ;
> For my love to thee is great.'
>
> Happy the parent of such a child !
> Alas for Enuataurere ! Alas for Enuataurere !
>
> Thou wert lovely as a fairy !
> A husband for Enuataurere !
>
> Each envious youth exclaims :
> ' Would that she were mine ! '
>
> Enuataurere now trips o'er the ruddy ocean.
> Thy path is the foaming crest of the billow.
>
> Weep for Enuataurere —
> For Enuataurere."

This song, though published in 1892, seems to have been composed about the year 1815, at a *fête* in honour of the deceased. Mr. Gill justly calls attention to the beauty of the last stanza but one, where "the spirit of the girl is believed to follow the sun, tripping lightly over the crest of the billows, and sinking with the sun into the underworld (Avaiki), the home of disembodied spirits."

Among others of the lower races of men, we find the father, expressing his grief at the loss of a child, as tenderly and as sincerely as, if less poetically than, the Polynesian chief, though often the daughter is not so well honoured in death as is the son. Our American Indian tribes furnish not a few instances of such affectionate lamentation.

Much too little has been made of the bright side of child-life among the lower races. But from even the most primitive of tribes all traces of the golden age of childhood are not absent. Powers, speaking of the Yurok Indians of California, notes "the happy cackle of brown babies tumbling on their heads with the puppies" (519. 51), and of the Wintūn, in the wild-clover season, "their little ones frolicked and tumbled on their heads in the soft sunshine, or cropped the clover on all-fours like a tender calf" (519. 231). Of the Pawnee Indians, Irving says (478. 214): "In the farther part of the building about a dozen naked children, with faces almost hid by their tangled hair, were rolling and wrestling upon the floor, occasionally causing the lodge to re-echo with their childish glee." Mr. im Thurn, while among the Indians of Guiana, had his attention "especially attracted by one merry little fellow of about five years old, whom I first saw squatting, as on the top of a hill, on top of a turtle-shell twice as big as himself, with his knees drawn up to his chin, and solemnly smoking a long bark cigarette" (477. 39). Of the wild Indians of the West, Colonel Dodge tells us: "The little children are much petted and spoiled; tumbling and climbing, unreproved, over the father and his visitors in the lodge, and never seem to be an annoyance or in the way" (432. 189). Mr. Mac-Cauley, who visited the Seminole Indians of Florida, says: "I remember seeing, one day, one jolly little fellow, lolling and rollicking on his mother's back, kicking her and tugging away at the strings of beads which hung temptingly between her shoulders, while the mother, hand-free, bore on one shoulder a log, which, a moment afterwards, still keeping her baby on her back as she did so, she chopped into small wood for the camp-fire" (496. 498).

There is a Zuñi story of a young maiden, "who, strolling along, saw a beautiful little baby boy bathing in the waters of a spring; she was so pleased with his beauty that she took him home, and told her mother that she had found a lovely little boy" (358. 544). Unfortunately, it turned out to be a serpent in the end.

Kissing.

As Darwin and other authorities have remarked, there are races of men upon the face of the earth, in America, in Africa, in Asia, and in the Island world, who, when first seen of white discoverers, knew not what it meant to kiss (499. 139). The following statement will serve for others than the people to whom it refers: "The only kiss of which the Annamite woman is cognizant is to place her nose against the man's cheek, and to rub it gently up and down, with a kind of canine sniff."

Mantegazza tells us that Raden-Saleh, a "noble and intelligent" Javanese painter, told him that, "like all Malays, he considered there was more tenderness in the contact of the noses than of the lips," and even the Japanese, the English of the extreme Orient, were once ignorant of the art of kissing (499. 139).

Great indeed is the gulf between the Javanese artist and the American, Benjamin West, who said: "A kiss from my mother made me a painter." To a kiss from the Virgin Mother of Christ, legend says, St. Chrysostom owed his "golden mouth." The story runs thus: "St. Chrysostom was a dull boy at school, and so disturbed was he by the ridicule of his fellows, that he went into a church to pray for help to the Virgin. A voice came from the image: 'Kiss me on the mouth, and thou shalt be endowed with all learning.' He did this, and when he returned to his schoolfellows they saw a golden circle about his mouth, and his eloquence and brilliancy astounded them" (347. 621).

Among the natives of the Andaman Islands, Mr. Man informs us, "Kisses are considered indicative of affection, but are only bestowed upon infants" (498. 79).

Tears.

"Tears, idle tears, I know not what they mean,
'Tears from the depths of some divine despair,
Rise in the heart and gather to the eyes,
In looking at the happy autumn fields,
And thinking of the days that are no more."

Thus sang the great English laureate, and to the simple folk — the treasure-keepers of the lore of the ages — his words mean much.

Pliny, the Elder, in his *Natural History*, makes this statement: "Man alone at the very moment of his birth, cast naked upon the naked earth, does she [Nature] abandon to cries and lamentations;" the writer of the *Wisdom of Solomon*, in the Apocrypha, expresses himself in like manner: "When I was born, I drew in the common air, and fell upon the earth, which is of like nature, and the first voice I uttered was crying, as all others do." Burton, in his *Anatomy of Melancholy*, bluntly resumes both: "He is born naked, and falls a-whining at the first."

The Spaniards have a proverb, brusque and cynical: —

"Des que nací lloré, y cada dia nace porqué.
[I wept as soon as I was born, and every day explains why.]"

A quaint legend of the Jewish Rabbis, however, accounts for children's tears in this fashion: —

"Beside the child unborn stand two angels, who not only teach it the whole Tora [the traditional interpretation of the Mosaic law], but also let it see all the joys of Paradise and all the torments of Hell. But, since it may not be that a child should come into the world endowed with such knowledge, ere it is born into the life of men an angel strikes it on the upper lip, and all wisdom vanishes. The dimple on the upper lip is the mark of the stroke, and this is why new-born babes cry and weep" (385. 6).

Curiously enough, as if to emphasize the relativity of folk-explanations, a Mussulman legend states that it is "the touch of Satan" that renders the child "susceptible of sin from its birth," and that is the reason why "all children cry aloud when they are born" (547. 249).

Henderson tells us that in the north and south of England

"nurses think it lucky for the child to cry at its baptism; they say that otherwise the baby shows that it is too good to live." But there are those also who believe that "this cry betokens the pangs of the new birth," while others hold that it is "the voice of the Evil Spirit as he is driven out by the baptismal water" (469. 16).

Among the untaught peasantry of Sicily, the sweet story goes that "Mary sends an angel from Heaven one day every week to play with the souls of the unbaptized children [in hell]; and when he goes away, he takes with him, in a golden chalice, all the tears which the little innocents have shed all through the week, and pours them into the sea, where they become pearls" (449. 326).

Here again we have a borrowing from an older myth. An Eastern legend has it that when Eden was lost, Eve, the mother of all men, wept bitterly, and "her tears, which flowed into the ocean, were changed into costly pearls, while those which fell on the earth brought forth all beautiful flowers" (547. 34). In the classic myth, the pearl is said to have been born of the tears of Venus, just as a Greek legend makes ἤλεκτρον come from the tears of the sisters of Phaëthon, the daughters of the sun, and Teutonic story turns the tears of the goddess Freyja into drops of gold (462. III. 1218).

In the *Kalevala* we read how, after the wonderful harping of Wäinämöinen, the great Finnish hero, which enchanted beasts, birds, and even fishes, was over, the musician shed tears of gratitude, and these, trickling down his body and through his many garments, were transmuted into pearls of the sea.

Shakespeare, in *King Henry V.*, makes Exeter say to the King,—

> "But all my mother came into mine eyes,
> And gave me up to tears," —

and the tears of the mother-god figures in the folk-lore of many lands. The vervain, or verbena, was known as the "Tears of Isis," as well as the "Tears of Juno," — a name given also to an East Indian grass (*Coix lacryma*). The lily of the valley, in various parts of Europe, is called "The Virgin's Tears," "Tears of Our Lady," "Tears of St. Mary." Zmigrodzki notes the following belief as current in Germany: "If the mother weeps too much, her dead child comes to her at night, naked and trembling, with its little shirt in its hand, and says: 'Ah, dearest mother, do not weep! See! I have no rest in the grave; I cannot put on my little shirt, it is all wet with your tears.'" In Cracow, the common saying is, "God forbid that the tears of the mother should fall upon the corpse of her child." In Brittany the folk-belief is that "the dead child has to carry water up a hill in a little bucket, and the tears of the mother increase its weight" (174. 141).

The Greeks fabled Eos, the dawn-goddess, to have been so disconsolate at the death of Memnon, her son, that she wept for him every morning, and her tears are the dewdrops found upon the earth. In the mythology of the Samoans of the Pacific, the Heaven-god, father of all things, and the Earth-goddess, mother of all things, once held each other in firm embrace, but were separated in the long ago. Heaven, however, retains his love for earth, and, mourning for her through the long nights, he drops many tears upon her bosom, — these, men call dewdrops. The natives of Tahiti have a like explanation for the thick-falling rain-drops that dimple the surface of the ocean, heralding an approaching storm, — they are tears of the heaven-god. The saying is: —

> "Thickly falls the small rain on the face of the sea,
> They are not drops of rain, but they are tears of Oro."
>
> (Tylor, *Early Hist. of Mankind*, p. 334.)

An Indian tribe of California believe that "the rain is the falling tears of Indians sick in heaven," and they say that it was "the tears of all mankind, weeping for the loss of a good young Indian," that caused the deluge, in which all were drowned save a single couple (440. 488).

Oriental legend relates, that, in his utter loneliness after the expulsion from Paradise, "Adam shed such an abundance of tears that all beasts and birds satisfied their thirst therewith; but some of them sunk into the earth, and, as they still contained some of the juices of his food in Paradise, produced the most fragrant trees and spices." We are further told that "the tears flowed at last in such torrents from Adam's eyes, that those of his right started the Euphrates, while those of his left set the Tigris in motion" (547. 34).

These are some of the answers of the folk to the question of Shakespeare : —

> " What's the matter,
> That this distempered messenger of wet,
> The many-coloured Iris, rounds thine eye ? "

And many more are there that run along the lines of Scott's epigrammatic summation : —

> " A child will weep a bramble's smart,
> A maid to see her sparrow part,
> A stripling for a woman's heart:
> But woe betide a country, when
> She sees the tears of bearded men."

Cradles.

According to Mr. Powers : "The conspicuous painstaking which the Modok squaw expends upon her baby-basket is an index of her maternal love. And indeed the Modok are strongly attached to their offspring, — a fact abundantly attested by many sad and mournful spectacles witnessed in the closing scenes of the war of 1873. On the other hand, a California squaw often carelessly sets her baby in a deep, conical basket, the same in which she carries her household effects, leaving him loose and liable to fall out. If she makes a baby-basket, it is totally devoid of ornament; and one tribe, the Miwok, contemptuously call it 'the dog's nest.' It is among Indians like these that we hear of infanticide " (519. 257).

The subject of children's cradles, baby-baskets, baby-boards, and the methods of manipulating and carrying the infant in connection therewith, have been treated of in great detail by Ploss (325), Pokrovski, and Mason (306), the second of whom has written especially of the cradles in use among the various peoples of European and Asiatic Russia, with a general view of those employed by other races, the last with particular reference to the American aborigines. The work is illustrated, as is also that of Ploss, with many engravings. Professor Mason thus briefly sums up the various purposes which the different species of cradle subserve (306. 161–162) : —

" (1) It is a mere nest for the helpless infant.

" (2) It is a bed so constructed and manipulated as to enable the child to sleep either in a vertical or a horizontal position.

" (3) It is a vehicle in which the child is to be transported, chiefly on the mother's back by means of a strap over the forehead, but frequently dangling like a bundle at the saddle-bow. This function, of course, always modifies the structure of the cradle, and, indeed, may have determined its very existence among nomadic tribes.

" (4) It is indeed a cradle, to be hung upon the limbs to rock, answering literally to the nursery-rhyme : —

> ' Rock-a-bye baby upon the tree-top,
> When the wind blows the cradle will rock,
> When the bough bends, the cradle will fall,
> Down will come baby, and cradle, and all.'

" (5) It is also a playhouse and baby-jumper. On many — nearly all — specimens may be seen dangling objects to evoke the senses, foot-rests by means of which the little one may exercise its legs, besides other conveniences anticipatory of the child's needs.

" (6) The last set of functions to which the frame is devoted are those relating to what we may call the graduation of infancy, when the papoose crawls out of its chrysalis little by little, and then abandons it altogether. The child is next seen standing partly on the mother's cincture and partly hanging to her neck, or resting like a pig in a poke within the folds of her blanket."

Professor Mason sees in the cradle-board or frame " the child of geography and of meteorology," and in its use "a beautiful illustration of Bastian's theory of 'great areas.' " In the frozen North, for example, "the Eskimo mother carries her infant in the hood of her parka whenever it is necessary to take it abroad. If she used a board or a frame, the child would perish with the cold."

The varieties of cradles are almost endless. We have the " hood" (sometimes the "boot") of the Eskimo ; the birch-bark cradle (or hammock) of several of the northern tribes (as in Alaska, or Cape Breton); the "moss-bag" of the eastern Tinné, the use of which has now extended to the employés of the Hudson's Bay Company ; the "trough-cradle" of the Bilqula;

the Chinook cradle, with its apparatus for head-flattening; the trowel-shaped cradle of the Oregon coast; the wicker-cradle of the Hupas; the Klamath cradle of wicker and rushes; the Pomo cradle of willow rods and wicker-work, with rounded portion for the child to sit in; the Mohave cradle, with ladder-frame, having a bed of shredded bark for the child to lie upon; the Yaqui cradle of canes, with soft bosses for pillows; the Nez Percé cradle-board with buckskin sides, and the Sahaptian, Ute, and Kootenay cradles which resemble it; the Moki cradle-frame of coarse wicker, with an awning; the Navajo cradle, with wooden hood and awning of dressed buckskin; the rude Comanche cradle, made of a single stiff piece of black-bear skin; the Blackfoot cradle of lattice-work and leather; the shoe-shaped Sioux cradle, richly adorned with coloured bead-work; the Iroquois cradle (now somewhat modernized), with "the back carved in flowers and birds, and painted blue, red, green, and yellow." Among the Araucanians of Chili we meet with a cradle which "seems to be nothing more than a short ladder, with cross-bars," to which the child is lashed. In the tropical regions and in South America we find the habit of "carrying the children in the shawl or sash, and bedding them in the hammock." Often, as in various parts of Africa, the woman herself forms the cradle, the child clinging astride her neck or hips, with no bands or attachments whatever. Of woman as carrier much may be read in the entertaining and instructive volume of Professor Mason (113). The primitive cradle, bed, and carrier, was the mother.

Father and Child.

With many of the more primitive races, the idea so tritely expressed in our familiar saying, " He is a chip of the old block," — *patris est filius*, "he is the son of his father," — and so beautifully wrought out by Shakespeare, —

> " Behold, my lords,
> Although the print be little, the whole matter
> And copy of the father: eye, nose, lip,
> The trick of his frown, his forehead; nay, the valley,
> The pretty dimples of his chin and cheek; his smiles,
> The very mould and frame of hand, nail, finger,"

has a strong hold, making itself felt in a thousand ways and fashions. The many rites and ceremonies, ablutions, fastings, abstentions from certain foods and drinks, which the husband has to undergo and submit to among certain more or less uncivilized peoples, shortly before, or after, or upon, the occasion of the birth of a child, or while his wife is pregnant, arise, in part at least, from a firm belief in the influence of parent upon child and the intimate sympathy between them even while the latter is yet unborn. Of the Indians of British Guiana, Mr. im Thurn says, they believe that if the father should eat the flesh of the capybara, the child would have large protruding teeth like that animal, while if he should eat that of the labba, the child's skin would be spotted. "Apparently there is also some idea that for the father to eat strong food, to wash, to smoke, to handle weapons, would have the same result as if the new-born baby ate such food, washed, smoked, or played with edged tools." The connection between the father and the child, the author thinks, is thought by these Indians to be much closer than that existing between the mother and her offspring (477. 218). Much has been written about, and many explanations suggested for, this ancient and widespread custom. The investigations of recent travellers seem to have cast some light upon this difficult problem in ethnology.

Dr. Karl von den Steinen (536. 331–337) tells us that the native tribes of Central Brazil not only believe that the child is "the son of the father," but that it *is* the father. To quote his own significant words: "The father is the patient in so far as he feels himself one with the new-born child. It is not very difficult to see how he arrives at this conclusion. Of the human egg-cell and the Graafian follicle the aborigine is not likely to know anything, nor can he know that the mother lodges the thing corresponding to the eggs of birds. For him the man is the bearer of the eggs, which, to speak plainly and clearly, lays in the mother, and which she hatches during the period of pregnancy. In the linguistic material at hand we see how this very natural attempt to explain generation finds expression in the words for 'father,' 'testicle,' and 'egg.' In Guarani *tub* means 'father, spawn, eggs,' *tupid* 'eggs,' and even *tup-i*, the name of the people (the *-i* is diminutive) really signifies 'little father,' or 'eggs,' or 'children,' as you please; the 'father' is 'egg,' and

the 'child' is 'the little father.' Even the language declares that
the 'child' is nothing else than the 'father.' Among the Tupi the
father was also accustomed to take a new name after the birth of
each new son; to explain this, it is in no way necessary to assume
that the 'soul' of the father proceeds each time into the son.
In Karaïbi we find exactly the same idea; *imu* is 'egg,' or 'testicles,' or 'child.'"

Among other cognate tribes we find the same thoughts:—

In the Ipurucoto language *imu* signifies "egg."

In the Bakaïrí language *imu* signifies "testicles."

In the Tamanako language *imu* signifies "father."

In the Makusi language *imu* signifies "semen."

In several dialects *imu-ru* signifies "child."

Dr. von den Steinen further observes: "Among the Bakaïrí
'child' and 'small' are both *iméri*, 'the child of the chief,'
pîma iméri; we can translate as we please, either 'the child of
the chief,' or 'the little chief,' and in the case of the latter form,
which we can use more in jest of the son, we are not aware that
to the Indian the child is really nothing more than the little
chief, the miniature of the big one. Strange and hardly intelligible to us is this idea when it is a girl that is in question. For
the girl, too, is 'the little *father*,' and not 'the little *mother*';
it is only the father who has made her. In Bakaïrí there are
no special words for 'son' and 'daughter,' but a sex-suffix is
added to the word for child when a distinction is necessary;
pîma iméri may signify either the son or the daughter of the
chief. The only daughter of the chief is the inheritrix of possession and rank, both of which pass over with her own possession to the husband." The whole question of the "Couvade"
and like practices finds its solution in these words of the author:
"The behaviour of the mother, according as she is regarded as
more or less suffering, may differ much with the various tribes,
while the conduct of the father is practically the same with all.
She goes about her business, if she feels strong enough, suckles
her child, etc. Between the father and the child there is no
mysterious correlation; the child is a multiplication of him; the
father is duplicated, and in order that no harm may come to the
helpless, irrational creature, a miniature of himself, he must de-
mean himself as a child" (536. 338).

The close relationship between father and child appears also in folk-medicine, where children (or often adults) are preserved from, or cured of, certain ailments and diseases by the application of blood drawn from the father.

In Bavaria a popular remedy against cramps consisted in "the father pricking himself in the finger and giving the child in its mouth three drops of blood out of the wound," and at Rackow, in Neu Stettin, to cure epilepsy in little children, "the father gives the child three drops of blood out of the first joint of his ring-finger" (361. 19). In Annam, when a physician cures a small-pox patient, it is thought that the pocks pass over to his children, and among the Dieyerie of South Australia, when a child has met with an accident, "all the relatives are beaten with sticks or boomerangs on the head till the blood flows over their faces. This is believed to lessen the pain of the child" (397. 60, 205).

Among some savage and uncivilized peoples, the father is associated closely with the child from the earliest days of its existence. With the Mincopies of the Andaman Islands, it is the father who, "from the day of its birth onwards presses the skull and body of the child to give them the proper form," and among the Macusi Indians of Guiana, the father "in early youth, pierces the ear-lobe, the lower lip, and the septum of the nose," while with the Pampas Indians of the Argentine, in the third year of the child's life, the child's ears are pierced by the father in the following fashion: "A horse has its feet tied together, is thrown to the ground, and held fast. The child is then brought out and placed on the horse, while the father bores its ears with a needle" (326. I. 296, 301).

With some primitive peoples the father evinces great affection for his child. Concerning the natives of Australia whom he visited, Lumholtz observes: "The father may also be good to the child, and he frequently carries it, takes it in his lap, pats it, searches its hair, plays with it, and makes little boomerangs which he teaches it to throw. He, however, prefers boys to girls, and does not pay much attention to the latter" (495. 193). Speaking of another region of the world where infanticide prevailed, — the Solomon Islands, — Mr. Guppy cites not a few instances of parental regard and affection. On one occasion "the chief's son, a little shapeless mass of flesh, a few months old, was handed about from man to man with as much care as if he had been composed of something brittle." Of chief Gorai and his wife, whose child was blind, the author says: "I was much struck with the tenderness displayed in the manner of both the parents towards their little son, who, seated in his mother's lap, placed his hand in that of his father, when he was directed to raise his eyes towards the light for my inspection" (466. 47).

Of the Patwin Indians of California, who are said to rank among the lowest of the race, Mr. Powers tells us: "Parents are very easygoing with their children, and never systematically punish them, though they sometimes strike them in momentary anger. On the Sacramento they teach them how to swim when a few weeks old by holding them on their hands in the water. I have seen a father coddle and teeter his baby in an attack of crossness for an hour with the greatest patience, then carry him down to the river, laughing good-naturedly, gently dip the little brown smooth-skinned nugget in the waves clear under, and then lay him on the moist, warm sand. The treatment was no less effectual than harmless, for it stopped the perverse, persistent squalling at once" (519. 222). Such demonstrations of tenderness have been supposed to be rare among the Indians, but the same authority says again: "Many is the Indian I have seen tending the baby with far more patience and good-nature than a civilized father would display" (519. 23). Concerning the Eskimo, Reclus observes: "All over Esquimaux Land fathers and mothers vie with one another in spoiling their offspring, never strike, and rarely rebuke them" (523. 37).

Among the Indians of British Guiana, according to Mr. im Thurn, both mother and father are "very affectionate towards the young child." The mother "almost always, even when working, carries it against her hip, slung in a small hammock from her neck or shoulder," while the father, "when he returns from hunting, brings it strange seeds to play with, and makes it necklaces and other ornaments." The young children themselves "seem fully to reciprocate the affection of their parents; but as they grow older, the affection on both sides seems to cool, though, in reality, it perhaps only becomes less demonstrative" (477. 219).

Everywhere we find evidence of parental affection and love for children, shining sometimes from the depths of savagery and filling with sunshine at least a few hours of days that seem so sombre and full of gloom when viewed afar off.

Mr. Scudder has treated at considerable length the subject of "Childhood in Literature and Art" (350), dealing with it as found in Greek, Roman, Hebrew, Early Christian, English, French, German, American, literature, in mediæval art, and in Hans Christian Andersen's fairy tales. Of Greek the author observes: "There is scarcely a child's voice to be heard in the whole range of Greek poetic art. The conception is universally of the child, not as acting, far less as speaking, but as a passive member of the social order. It is not its individual so much as its related life which is contemplated." The silent presence of children in the rôles of the Greek drama is very impressive (350. 21). At Rome, though childhood is more of a "vital force" than in Greece, yet "it is not contemplated as a fine revelation of nature." Sometimes, in its brutal aspects, "children are reckoned as scarcely more than cubs," yet with refinement they "come to represent the more spiritual side of the family life." The folktale of Romulus and Remus and Catullus' picture of the young Torquatus represent these two poles (350. 32). The scant appearances of children in the Old Testament, the constant prominence given to the male succession, are followed later on by the promise which buds and flowers in the world-child Jesus, and the childhood which is the new-birth, the golden age of which Jewish seers and prophets had dreamt. In early Christianity, it would appear that, with the exception of the representation in art of the child, the infant Christ, "childhood as an image had largely faded out of art and literature" (350. 80). The Renaissance "turned its face toward childhood, and looked into that image for the profoundest realization of its hopes and dreams" (350. 102), and since then Christianity has followed that path. And the folk were walking in these various ages and among these different peoples humbly along the same road, which their geniuses travelled. Of the great modern writers and poets, the author notes especially Wordsworth, through whom the child was really born in our literature, the linker together of the child and the race; Rousseau, who told of childhood as "refuge from present evil, a mournful reminiscence of a lost Paradise, who (like St. Pierre) preached a return to nature, and left his own offspring to the tender mercy of a foundling asylum"; Luther, the great religious reformer, who was ever "a father among his children"; Goethe, who represents German intellectualism, yet a great child-artist; Froebel, the patron saint of the kindergarten; Hans Andersen, the "inventor" of fairy-tales, and the transformer of folk-stories, that rival the genuine, untouched, inedited article; Hawthorne, the child-artist of America.

K

CHAPTER VIII.

CHILDHOOD THE GOLDEN AGE.

Heaven lies about us in our infancy. — *Wordsworth.*

Die Kindheit ist ein Augenblick Gottes. — *Achim v. Arnim.*

Wahre dir den Kindersinn,
Kindheit blüht in Liebe hin,
Kinderzeit ist heil'ge Zeit,
Heidenkindheit — Christenheit. — *B. Goltz.*

Happy those early days, when I
Shined in my angel infancy. — *Henry Vaughan.*

Childhood shall be all divine. — *B. W. Proctor.*

But Heaven is kind, and therefore all possess,
Once in their life, fair Eden's simpleness. — *H. Coleridge.*

But to the couch where childhood lies,
    A more delicious trance is given,
Lit up by rays from seraph eyes,
    And glimpses of remembered heaven. — *W. M. Praed.*

O for boyhood's time of June,
Crowding years in one brief moon ! — *Whittier.*

Golden Age.

THE English word *world*, as the Anglo-Saxon *weorold*, Icelandic *veröld*, and Old High German *weralt* indicate, signified originally "age of man," or "course of man's life," and in the mind of the folk the life of the world and the life of man have run about the same course. By common consent the golden age of both was at the beginning, *ab ovo*. With Wordsworth, unlettered thousands have thought : —

"Bliss was it in that dawn to be alive,
But to be young was very heaven !"

Die Kindheit ist ein Augenblick Gottes, "childhood is a moment of God," said Achim von Arnim, and Hartley Coleridge expresses the same idea in other words: —

> " But Heaven is kind, and therefore all possess,
> Once in their life, fair Eden's simpleness."

This belief in the golden age of childhood, — *die heilige Kinderzeit,* the heaven of infancy, — is ancient and modern, world-wide, shared in alike by primitive savage and nineteenth-century philosopher. The peasant of Brittany thinks that children preserve their primal purity up to the seventh year of their age, and, if they die before then, go straight to heaven (174. 141), and the great Chinese philosopher, linking together, as others have done since his time, the genius and the child, declared that a man is great only as he preserves the pure ideas of his childhood, while Coleridge, in like fashion tells us: "Genius is the power of carrying the feelings of childhood into the power of manhood."

Everywhere we hear the same refrain: —

> " Aus der Jugendzeit, aus der Jugendzeit,
> Klingt ein Lied immerdar;
> O wie liegt so weit, o wie liegt so weit,
> Was mein einst war!"

The Paradise that man lost, the Eden from which he has been driven, is not the God-planted Garden by the banks of Euphrates, but the "happy days of angel infancy," and "boyhood's time of June," the childhood out of which in the fierce struggle for existence the race has rudely grown, and back to which, for its true salvation, it must learn to make its way again. As he, who was at once genius and child, said, nearly twenty centuries ago: "Except ye turn and become as little children, ye shall in no wise enter the kingdom of heaven."

When we speak of "the halcyon days of childhood," we recall an ancient myth, telling how, in an age when even more than now "all Nature loved a lover," even the gods watched over the loves of Ceyx and Halcyone. Ever since the kingfisher has been regarded as the emblem of lasting fidelity in love. As Ebers aptly puts it: "Is there anywhere a sweeter legend than that of the Halcyons, the ice-birds who love each other so tenderly that, when the male becomes enfeebled by age, his mate carries him on her outspread wings whithersoever he wills; and the gods desiring to reward such faithful love cause the sun to shine more kindly, and still the winds and waves on the 'Halcyon Days' during which these birds are building their nests and brooding over their young" (390. II. 269).

Of a special paradise for infants, something has been said elsewhere. Of Srahmanadzi, the other world, the natives of Ashanti say: "There an old man becomes young, a young man a boy, and a boy an infant. They grow and become old. But age does not carry with it any diminution of strength or wasting of body. When they reach the prime of life, they remain so, and never change more" (438. 157).

The Kalmucks believe that some time in the future "each child will speak immediately after its birth, and the next day be capable of undertaking its own management" (518. I. 427). But that blissful day is far off, and the infant human still needs the overshadowing of the gods to usher him into the real world of life.

Guardian Angels and Deities.

Christ, speaking his memorable words about little children to those who had inquired who was greatest in the kingdom of heaven, uttered the warning: "See that ye despise not one of these little ones; for I say unto you, that in heaven their angels do always behold the face of my Father which is in heaven." In the hagiology of the Christian churches, and in the folk-lore of modern Europe, the idea contained in our familiar expression "guardian angel" has a firm hold; by celestial watchers and protectors the steps of the infant are upheld, and his mind guided, until he reaches maturity, and even then the guardian spirit often lingers to guide the favoured being through all the years of his life (191. 8). The natives of Ashanti believe that special spirits watch over girls until they are married, and in China there is a special mother-goddess who guards and protects childhood.

Walter Savage Landor has said: —

> "Around the child bend all the three
> Sweet Graces, — Faith, Hope, Charity,"

and the "three Fates" of classic antiquity, the three Norns of Scandinavian mythology, the three Sudiêcky or fate-goddesses of the Czechs of Bohemia, the three fate- and birth-goddesses of the other Slavonic peoples, the three Μοῖραι of Modern Greece, the three Phatite of Albania, the three white ladies, three virgins, three Mary's, etc., of German legend of to-day, have woven about them a wealth of quaint and curious lore (326. I. 42–47).

The survival of the old heathen belief alongside the Christian is often seen, as, *e.g.*, at Palermo, in Sicily, where "the mother, when she lifts the child out of the cradle, says aloud: '*Nuome di Dio*, In God's name,' but quickly adds sotto voce: '*Cu licenzi, signuri mui*, By your leave, Ladies.'" The reference is to the "three strange ladies," representing the three Fates, who preside over the destiny of human beings.

Ploss has discussed at length the goddesses of child-birth and infancy, and exhibited their relations to the growing, fertilizing, regenerative powers of nature, especially the earth, sun, moon, etc.; the Hindu *Bhavani* (moon-goddess); the Persian *Anahita;* the Assyrian *Belit*, the spouse of *Bel;* the Phœnician *Astarte;* the Egyptian *Isis;* the Etruscan *Mater matuta;* the Greek *Hera, Eileithyia, Artemis;* the Roman *Diana, Lucina, Juno;* the Phrygian *Cybele;* the Germanic *Freia, Holla, Gude, Harke;* the Slavonic *Siwa, Libussa, Zlata Baba* ("the golden woman"); the ancient Mexican *Itzcuinam, Yohmaltcitl, Tezistecatl;* the Chibchan rainbow-goddess *Cuchavira;* the Japanese *Kojasi Kwanon*, and hundreds more.

The number of gods and goddesses presiding over motherhood and childhood is legion; in every land divine beings hover about the infant human to protect it and assure the perpetuity of the race. In ancient Rome, besides the divinities who were connected with generation, the embryo, etc., we find, among others, the following tutelary deities of childhood : —

Parca or *Partula*, the goddess of child-birth; *Diespiter*, the god who brings the infant to the light of day; *Opis*, the divinity who takes the infant from within the bosom of mother-earth; *Vaticanus*, the god who opens the child's mouth in crying; *Cunina*, the protectress of the cradle and its contents; *Rumina*, the goddess of the teat or breast; *Ossipaga*, the goddess who hardens and solidifies the bones of little children; *Carna*, the goddess who strengthens the flesh of little children; *Diva potina*, the goddess of the drink of children; *Diva edusa*, the goddess of the food of children; *Cuba*, the goddess of the sleep of the child; *Levana*, the goddess who lifts the child from the earth; *Statanus*, the god, and *Dea Statina*, the goddess, of the child's standing; *Fabulinus*, the god of the child's speech; *Abeona* and *Adiona*, the protectresses of the child in its goings out and its comings in; *Deus catus pater*, the father-god who "sharpens" the wits of children; *Dea mens*, the goddess of the child's mind; *Minerva*, the goddess who is the giver of memory to the child; *Numeria*, the goddess who teaches the child to count; *Voleta*, the goddess, and *Volumnus* the god, of will or wishing; *Venilia*, the goddess of hope, of "things to come"; *Deus conus*, the god of counsel, the counsel-giver; *Peragenor* or *Agenona*, the deity of the child's action; *Camœna*, the goddess who teaches the child to sing, etc. (398. 188).

Here the child is overshadowed, watched over, taught and instructed by the heavenly powers : —

> "But to the couch where childhood lies
> A more delicious trance is given,
> Lit up by rays from seraph eyes,
> And glimpses of remembered heaven."

In line with the poet's thought, though of a ruder mould, is the belief of the Iroquois Indians recorded by Mrs. Smith: "When a living nursing child is taken out at night, the mother takes a pinch of white ashes and rubs it on the face of the child so that the spirits will not trouble, because they say that a child still continues to hold intercourse with the spirit-world whence it so recently came" (534. 69).

Birth-Myths.

President Hall has treated of "The Contents of Children's Minds on Entering School" (252), but we yet lack a like elaborate and suggestive study of "The Contents of Parents' Minds on Entering the Nursery." We owe to the excellent investigation carried on by Principal Russell and his colleagues at the State Normal School in Worcester, Mass., "Some Records of the Thoughts and Reasonings of Children" (194), and President Hall has written about "Children's Lies" (252a), but we are still without a correspondingly accurate and extensive compilation of "The Thoughts and Reasonings of Parents," and a plain, unbiassed register of the "white lies" and equivoques, the fictions and epigrammatic myths, with which parents are wont to answer, or attempt to answer, the manifold questions of their tender offspring. From time immemorial the communication between parent (and nurse) and child, between the old of both sexes and little children, far from being yea and nay, has been cast in the mould of the advice given in the German quatrain:—

> " Ja haltet die Aequivocabula nur fest,
> Sind sie doch das einzige Mittel,
> Dem Kind die Wahrheit zu bergen und doch
> Zu brauchen den richtigen Titel."
> [" Hold fast to the words that we equivoques call;
> For they are indeed the only safe way
> To keep from the children the truth away,
> Yet use the right name after all."]

Around the birth of man centres a great cycle of fiction and myth. The folk-lore respecting the provenience of children may be divided into two categories. The first is represented by our "the doctor brought it," "God sent it," and the "van Moor" of the peasantry of North Friesland, which may signify either "from the moor," or "from mother." The second consists of renascent myths of bygone ages, distorted, sometimes, it is true, and recast. As men, in the dim, prehistoric past, ascribed to their first progenitors a celestial, a terrestrial, a subterranean, a subaqueous origin, a coming into being from animals, birds, insects, trees, plants, rocks, stones, etc.,—for all were then akin,—so, after long centuries have rolled by, father, mother, nurse, older brother or sister, speaking of the little one in whom they see their stock renewed, or their kinship widened, resurrect and regild the old fables and rejuvenate and reanimate the lore that lay sunk beneath the threshold of racial consciousness. Once more "the child is father of the man"; his course begins from that same spring whence the first races of men had their remotest origins. George Macdonald, in the first lines of his poem on "Baby" (337. 182):—

> "Where did you come from, baby dear?
> Out of the *everywhere* into here,"

has expressed a truth of folk-lore, for there is scarcely a place in the "everywhere" whence the children have not been fabled to come. Children are said to come from heaven (Germany, England, America, etc.); from the sea (Denmark); from lakes, ponds, rivers (Germany, Austria, Japan); from moors and sand-hills (northeastern Germany); from gardens (China); from under the cabbage-leaves (Brittany, Alsace), or the parsley-bed (England); from sacred or hollow trees, such as the ash, linden, beech, oak, etc. (Germany, Austria); from inside or from underneath rocks and stones (northeastern Germany, Switzerland, Bohemia, etc.). It is worthy of note how the topography of the country, its physiographic character, affects these beliefs, which change with hill and plain, with moor and meadow, seashore and inland district. The details of these birth-myths may be read in Ploss (326. I. 2), Schell (343), Sundermann (366). Specially interesting are the *Kindersee* ("child-lake"), *Kinderbaum* ("child-tree"), and *Kinderbrunnen* ("child-fountain") of the Teutonic lands, — offering analogies with the "Tree of Life" and the "Fountain of Eternal Youth" of other ages and peoples; the *Titistein*, or "little children's stone," and the *Kindertruog* ("child's trough") of Switzerland, and the "stork-stones" of North Germany.

Dr. Haas, in his interesting little volume of folk-lore from the island of Rügen, in the Baltic, records some curious tales about the birth of children. The following practice of the children in that portion of Germany is significant: "Little white and black smooth stones, found on the shore, are called 'stork-stones.' These the children are wont to throw backwards over their heads, asking, at the same time, the stork to bring them a little brother or sister" (466 a. 144). This recalls vividly the old Greek deluge-myth, in which we are told, that, after the Flood, Deucalion was ordered to cast behind him the "bones of his mother." This he interpreted to mean the "stones," which seemed, as it were, the "bones" of "mother-earth." So he and his wife Pyrrha picked up some stones from the ground and cast them over their shoulders, whereupon those thrown by Deucalion became men, those thrown by Pyrrha, women. Here belongs, also, perhaps, the Wallachian custom, mentioned by Mr. Sessions (who thinks it was "probably to keep evil spirits away"), in accordance with which "when a child is born every one present throws a stone behind him."

On the island of Rügen erratic blocks on the seashore are called *Adeborsteine*, "stork-stones," and on such a rock or boulder near Wrek in Wittow, Dr. Haas says "the stork is said to dry the little children, after he has fetched them out of the sea, before he brings them to the mothers. The latter point out these blocks to their little sons and daughters, telling them how once they were laid upon them by the stork to get dry." The great blocks of granite that lie scattered on the coast of Jasmund are termed *Schwansteine*, "swan-stones," and, according to nursery-legend, the children to be born are shut up in them. When a sister or brother asks: "Where did the little *swan-child*"—for so babies are called—"come from?" the mother replies: "From the swan-stone. It was opened with a key, and a little swan-child taken out." The term "swan-child" is general in this region, and Dr. Haas is inclined to think that the swan-myth is older than the stork-myth (466 a. 143, 144).

Curious indeed is the belief of the Hidatsa Indians, as reported by Dr. Matthews, in the "Makadistati, or house of infants." This is described as "a cavern near Knife River, which, they supposed, extended far into the earth, but whose entrance was only a span wide. It was resorted to by the childless husband or the barren wife. There are those among them who imagine that in some way or other their children come from the Makadistati; and marks of contusion on an infant, arising from tight swaddling or other causes, are gravely attributed to kicks received from his former comrades when he was ejected from his subterranean home" (433. 516).

In Hesse, Germany, there is a children's song (326. I. 9):—

> Bimbam, Glöckchen,
> Da unten steht ein Stöckchen,
> Da oben steht ein golden Haus,
> Da gucken viele schöne Kinder raus.

The current belief in that part of Europe is that "unborn children live in a very beautiful dwelling, for so long as children are no year old and have not yet looked into a mirror, everything that comes before their eyes appears to be gold." Here folk-thought makes the beginnings of human life a real golden age. They are Midases of the eye, not of the touch.

Children's Questions and Parents' Answers.

Another interesting class of "parents' lies" consists in the replies to, or comments upon, the questionings and remarks of children about the ordinary affairs of life. The following examples, selected from Dirksen's studies of East-Frisian Proverbs, will serve to indicate the general nature and extent of these.

1. When a little child says, "I am hungry," the mother sometimes answers, "Eat some salt, and then you will be thirsty, too."

2. When a child, seeing its mother drink tea or coffee, says, "I'm thirsty," the answer may be, "If you're thirsty, go to Jack ter Host; there's a cow in the stall, go sit under it and drink." Some of the variants of this locution are expressed in very coarse language (431. I. 22).

3. If a child asks, when it sees that its parent is going out, "Am I not going, too?" the answer is, "You are going along, where nobody has gone, to Poodle's wedding," or "You are going along on Stay-here's cart." A third locution is, "You are going along to the Kükendell fair" (Kükendell being a part of Meiderich, where a fair has never been held). In Oldenburg the answer is: "You shall go along on Jack-stay-at-home's (Janblievtohûs) cart." Sometimes the child is quieted by being told, "I'll bring you back a little silver nothing (enn silwer Nickske)" (431. I. 33).

4. If, when he is given a slice of bread, he asks for a thinner one, the mother may remark, "Thick pieces make fat bodies" (431. I. 35).

5. When some one says in the hearing of the father or mother of a child that it ought not to have a certain apple, a certain article of clothing, or the like, the answer is, "That is no illegitimate child." The locution is based upon the fact that illegitimate children do not enjoy the same rights and privileges as those born in wedlock (431. I. 42).

6. Of children's toys and playthings it is sometimes said, when they are very fragile, "They will last from twelve o'clock till midday" (431. I. 43).

7. When any one praises her child in the presence of the mother, the latter says, "It's a good child when asleep" (431. I. 51).

8. In the winter-time, when the child asks its mother for an apple, the latter may reply, "the apples are piping in the tree," meaning that there are no longer any apples on the tree, but the sparrows are sitting there, crying and lamenting. In Meiderich the locution is "Apples have golden stems," *i.e.* they are rare and dear in winter-time (431. I. 75).

9. When the child says, "I can't sit down," the mother may remark, "Come and sit on my thumb; nobody has ever fallen off it" (*i.e.* because no one has ever tried to sit on it) (431. I. 92).

10. When a lazy child, about to be sent out upon an errand, protests that it does not know where the person to whom the message is to be sent lives, and consequently cannot do the errand, the mother remarks threateningly, "I'll show where Abraham ground the mustard," *i.e.* "I give you a good thrashing, till the tears come into your eyes (as when grinding mustard)" (431. I. 105).

11. When a child complains that a sister or brother has done something to hurt him, the mother's answer is, "Look out! He shall have water in the cabbage, and go barefoot to bed" (431. I. 106).

12. Sometimes their parents or elders turn to children and ask them "if they would like to be shown the Bremen geese." If the child says yes, he is seized by the ears and head with both hands and lifted off the ground. In some parts of Germany this is called "showing Rome," and there are variants of the practice in other lands (431. II. 14).

13. When a child complains of a sore in its eye, or on its neck, the answer is: "That will get well before you are a great-grandmother" (431. II. 50).

14. When one child asks for one thing and another for something else, the mother exclaims petulantly, "One calls out 'lime,' the other 'stones.'" The reference is to the confusion of tongues at Babel, which is assumed to have been of such a nature that one man would call out "lime," and another "stones" (431. II. 53).

15. When a child asks for half a slice of bread instead of a whole one, the mother may say, "Who doesn't like a whole, doesn't like a half either" (431. II. 43).

16. When a child says, "That is my place, I sat there," the

reply is, " You have no place; your place is in the churchyard " (*i.e.* a grave) (431. II. 76).

When the child says "I will," the mother says threateningly, "Your ' will ' is in your mother's pocket." It is in her pocket that she carries the rope for whipping the child. Another locution is, "Your will is in the corner" (*i.e.* the corner of the room in which stands the broomstick) (431. II. 81).

These specimens of the interchange of courtesies between the child and its parent or nurse might be paralleled from our own language; indeed, many of the correspondences will suggest themselves at once. The deceits practised in the Golden Age of childhood resemble those practised by the gods in the Golden Age of the world, when divine beings walked the earth and had intercourse with the sons and daughters of men.

"*Painted Devils.*"

Even as the serpent marred the Eden of which the sacred legends of the Semites tell, so in the folk-thought does some evil sprite or phantom ever and anon intrude itself in the Paradise of childhood and seek its ruin.

Shakespeare has well said: —

> " 'Tis the eye of childhood
> That fears a painted devil,"

and the chronicle of the "painted devils," bogies, scarecrows, *et id genus omne*, is a long one, whose many chapters may be read in Ploss, Hartland, Henderson, Gregor, etc. Some of the "devils" are mild and almost gentlemen, like their lord and master at times; others are fierce, cruel, and bloodthirsty; their number is almost infinite, and they have the forms of women as well as of men.

Over a large portion of western Europe is found the nursery story of the " Sand-Man," who causes children to become drowsy and sleepy; " the sand-man is coming, the sand-man has put dust in your eyes," are some of the sayings in use. By and by the child gets " so fast asleep that one eye does not see the other," as the Frisian proverb puts it. When, on a cold winter day, her little boy would go out without his warm mittens on, the East

Frisian mother says, warningly: *De Fingerbiter is buten*, "the Finger-biter is outside."

Among the formidable evil spirits who war against or torment the child and its mother are the Hebrew Lilith, the long-haired night-flier; the Greek *Strigalai*, old and ugly owl-women; the Roman *Caprimulgus*, the nightly goat-milker and child-killer, and the wood-god Silvanus; the Coptic *Berselia;* the Hungarian "water-man," or "water-woman," who changes children for cripples or demons; the Moravian *Vestice*, or "wild woman," able to take the form of any animal, who steals away children at the breast, and substitutes changelings for them; the Bohemian *Polednice*, or "noon-lady," who roams around only at noon, and substitutes changelings for real children; the Lithuanian and Old Prussian *Laume*, a child-stealer, whose breast is the thunderbolt, and whose girdle is the rainbow; the Servian *Wjeschtitza*, or witches, who take on the form of an insect, and eat up children at night; the Russian "midnight spirit," who robs children of rest and sleep; the Wendish "Old mountain-woman"; the German (Brunswick) "corn-woman," who makes off with little children looking for flowers in the fields; the *Röggenmuhme* ("rye-aunt"), the *Tremsemutter*, who walks about in the cornfields; the *Katzenveil*, a wood spirit, and a score of bogies called *Popel, Popelmann, Popanz, Butz*, etc.; the Scotch "Boo Man," "Bogie Man," "Jenny wi' the Airn Teeth," "Jenny wi' the lang Pock"; the English and American bogies, goblins, ogres, ogresses, witches, and the like; besides, common to all peoples, a host of werwolves and vampires, giants and dwarfs, witches, ogres, ogresses, fairies, evil spirits of air, water, land, inimical to childhood and destructive of its peace and enjoyment. The names, lineage, and exploits of these may be read in Ploss, Grimm, Hartland, etc.

In the time of the Crusades, Richard Cœur de Lion, the hero-king of England, became so renowned among the Saracens that (Gibbon informs us) his name was used by mothers and nurses to quiet their infants, and other historical characters before and after him served to like purpose. To the children of Rome in her later days, Attila, the great Hun, was such a bogy, as was Narses, the Byzantian general (d. 568 A.D.), to the Assyrian children. Bogies also were Matthias Corvinus (d. 1490 A.D.), the Hungarian king and general, to the Turks; Tamerlane (Timur),

the great Mongolian conqueror (d. 1405 A.D.), to the Persians;
and Bonaparte, at the close of the eighteenth and the beginning
of the nineteenth century, in various parts of the continent of
Europe. These, and other historical characters have, in part,
taken the place of the giants and bogies of old, some of whom,
however, linger, even yet, in the highest civilizations, together
with fabulous animals (reminiscent of stern reality in primitive
times), with which, less seriously than in the lands of the eastern
world, childhood is threatened and cowed into submission.

The Ponka Indian mothers tell their children that if they do
not behave themselves the Indaciñga (a hairy monster shaped
like a human being, that hoots like an owl) will get them; the
Omaha bogy is Icibajĭ; a Dakota child-stealer and bogy is
Añungite or "Two Faces" (433. 386, 473). With the Kootenay
Indians, of south-eastern British Columbia, the owl is the bogy
with which children are frightened into good behaviour, the
common saying of mothers, when their children are troublesome,
being, "If you are not quiet, I'll give you to the owl" (203).
Longfellow, in his *Hiawatha,* speaks of one of the bogies of the
eastern Indians: —

> " Thus the wrinkled old Nokomis
> Nursed the little Hiawatha,
> Rocked him in his linden cradle,
> Stilled his fretful wail by saying,
> ' Hush ! the naked bear will get thee ! ' "

Among the Nipissing Algonkian Indians, *koko* is a child-word
for any terrible being; the mothers say to their children, "beware
of the *koko.*" Champlain and Lescarbot, the early chroniclers of
Canada, mention a terrible creature (concerning which tales were
told to frighten children) called *gougou,* supposed to dwell on an
island in the Baie des Chaleurs (200. 239). Among the bogies
of the Mayas of Yucatan, Dr. Brinton mentions: the *balams*
(giant beings of the night), who carry off children; the *culcalkin,*
or "neckless priest"; besides giants and witches galore (411.
174, 177).

Among the Gualala Indians of California, we find the " devil-
dance," which Powers compares to the *haberfeldtreiben* of the
Bavarian peasants, — an institution got up for the purpose of

frightening the women and children, and keeping them in order. While the ordinary dances are going on, there suddenly stalks forth " an ugly apparition in the shape of a man, wearing a feather mantle on his back, reaching from the arm-pits down to the mid-thighs, zebra-painted on his breast and legs with black stripes, bear-skin shako on his head, and his arms stretched out at full length along a staff passing behind his neck. Accoutred in this harlequin rig, he dashes at the squaws, capering, dancing, whooping; and they and the children flee for life, keeping several hundred yards between him and themselves." It is believed that, if they were even to touch his stick, their children would die (519. 194).

Among the Patwin, Nishinam, and Pomo Indians, somewhat similar practices are in vogue (519. 157, 160, 225). From the golden age of childhood, with its divinities and its demons, we may now pass to the consideration of more special topics concerning the young of the races of men.

CHAPTER IX.

CHILDREN'S FOOD.

Der Mensch ist, was er isst. — *Feuerbach.*

For he on honey-dew hath fed,
And drunk the milk of Paradise. — *Coleridge.*

Man did eat angels' food. — *Psalm* lxxviii. 25.

Honey.

Der Mensch ist, was er isst, — "man is what he eats," — says Feuerbach, and there were food-philosophies long before his time. Among primitive peoples, the food of the child often smacks of the Golden Age. Tennyson, in *Eleanore,* sings : —

> "Or, the yellow-banded bees,
> Through half-open lattices
> Coming in the scented breeze,
> Fed thee, a child lying alone,
> With white honey, in fairy gardens cull'd —
> A glorious child dreaming alone,
> In silk-soft folds, upon yielding down,
> With the hum of swarming bees
> Into dreamful slumber lull'd."

This recalls the story of Cretan Zeus, fed, when an infant, by the nymphs in a cave on Mount Ida with the milk of the goat Amalthæa and honey brought by the bees of the mountain.

In the sacred books of the ancient Hindus we read : "The father puts his mouth to the right ear of the new-born babe, and murmurs three times, 'Speech! Speech!' Then he gives it a name. Then he mixes clotted milk, honey, and butter, and feeds the babe with it out of pure gold" (460. 129). Among the ancient Frisians and some other Germanic tribes, the father had the right

144

to put to death or expose his child so long as it had not taken food; but "so soon as the infant had drunk milk and eaten honey he could not be put to death by his parents" (286. 69). The custom of giving the new-born child honey to taste is referred to in German counting-out rhymes, and the ancient Germans used to rub honey in the mouth of the new-born child. The heathen Czechs used to drop honey upon the child's lips, and in the Eastern Church it was formerly the custom to give the baptized child milk and honey to taste (392. II. 35). When the Jewish child, in the Middle Ages, first went to school, one of the ceremonial observances was to have him lick a slate which had been smeared with honey, and upon which the alphabet, two Bible verses, and the words "The Tora shall be my calling" were written; this custom is interestingly explanative of the passage in Ezekiel (iii. 3) where we read "Then I did eat it [the roll of a book given the prophet by God]; and it was in my mouth as honey for sweetness." There were also given to the child sweet cakes upon which Bible verses were written. Among the Jews of Galicia, before a babe is placed in the cradle for the first time, it is customary to strew into the latter little pieces of honey-comb. Among the Wotjaks we find the curious belief that those who, in eating honey, do not smear their mouth and hands with it, will die. With children of an older growth, — the second Golden Age, — honey and cakes again appear. Magyar maidens at the new moon steal honey and cakes, cook them, and mix a part in the food of the youth of their desires; among the White Russians, the bridal couple are fed honey with a spoon. Even with us "the first sweet month of matrimony," after the "bless you, my children" has been spoken by parents, church, and state, is called the "honey-moon," for our Teutonic ancestors were in the habit of drinking honey-wine or mead for the space of thirty days after marriage (392. IV. 118, 211). In wedding-feasts the honey appears again, and, as Westermarck observes, the meal partaken of by the bride and bridegroom practically constitutes the marriage-ceremony among the Navajos, Santal, Malays, Hovas, and other primitive peoples (166. 419).

In Iceland, in ancient times, "the food of sucklings was sweetened by honey," and "in the mouths of weakly children a slice of meat was placed at which they sucked." Among other inter-

L

esting items from Scandinavia, Ploss (326. II. 182) gives the following: "In Iceland, if the child has been suckled eight (at most, fourteen) days, it is henceforth placed upon the ground; near it is put a vessel with luke-warm whey, in which a reed or a quill is stuck, and a little bread placed before it. If the child should wake and show signs of hunger, he is turned towards the vessel, and the reed is placed in his mouth. When the child is nine months old, it must eat of the same food as its parents do."

In Shropshire, England, the first food given a child is a spoonful of sugar and butter, and, in the Highlands of Scotland, "at the birth of an infant the nurse takes a green stick of ash, one end of which she puts into the fire, and, while it is burning, receives in a spoon the sap that oozes from the other, which she administers to the child as its first food." This recalls the sap of the sacred ash of Scandinavian mythology. Solinus states that the ancient Irish mother "put the first food of her new-born son on the sword of her husband, and, lightly introducing it into his mouth, expressed a wish that he might never meet death otherwise than in war and amid arms," and a like custom is said "to have been kept up, prior to the union, in Annandale and other places along the Scottish border" (460. 129, 131).

Salt.

Among the Negritos of the Philippine Islands, when a child is born, one of the other children immediately gives it to eat some salt on the point of a knife (326. I. 258). The virtues of salt are recognized among many peoples. In the Middle Ages, when mothers abandoned their infants, they used to place beside them a little salt in token that they were unbaptized (326. I. 284); in Scotland, where the new-born babe is "bathed in salted water, and made to taste it three times, because the water was strengthening and also obnoxious to a person with the evil eye," the lady of the house first visited by the mother and child must, with the recital of a charm, put some salt in the little one's mouth. In Brabant, during the baptismal ceremony, the priest consecrates salt, given him by the father, and then puts a grain into the child's mouth, the rest being carefully kept by the father. The great importance of salt in the ceremonies of the Zuñi and related Indians of the Pueblos has been pointed out by Mr. Cushing.

Salt appears also at modern European wedding-feasts and pre-nuptial rites, as do also rice and meal, which are also among the first foods of some primitive races. Among the Badagas of the Nilgiri Hills, when the child is named (from twenty to thirty days after birth), the maternal uncle places three small bits of rice in its mouth (326. I. 284).

Folk-Medicine.

Among the Tlingit Indians, of Alaska, the new-born infant " is not given the breast until all the contents of its stomach (which are considered the cause of disease) are removed by vomiting, which is promoted by pressing the stomach" (403. 40), and among the Hare Indians, "the infant is not allowed food until four days after birth, in order to accustom it to fasting in the next world" (396. I. 121). The Songish Indians do not give the child anything to eat on the first day (404. 20); the Kolosh Indians, of Alaska, after ten to thirty months "accustom their children to the taste of a sea-animal," and, among the Arctic Eskimo, Kane found "children, who could not yet speak, devouring with horrible greediness, great lumps of walrus fat and flesh." Klutschak tells us how, during a famine, the Eskimo of Hudson's Bay melted and boiled for the children the blood-soaked snow from the spot where a walrus had been killed and cut up (326. II. 181).

In Culdaff, in the county of Donegal, Ireland, "an infant at its birth is forced to swallow spirits, and is immediately afterwards [strange anticipation of Dr. Robinson] suspended by the upper jaw on the nurse's forefinger. Whiskey is here the representative of the Hindu sôma, the sacred juice of the ash, etc., and the administration of alcoholic liquors to children of a tender age in sickness and disease so common everywhere but a few years ago, founded itself perhaps more upon this ancient belief than upon anything else (401. 180).

The study of the food of sick children is an interesting one, and much of value may be read of it in Zanetti (173), Black (401), and other writers who have treated of folk-medicine. The decoctions of plants and herbs, the preparations of insects, reptiles, the flesh, blood, and ordure of all sorts of beasts (and of man), which the doctrines of signatures and sympathies, the craze of *similia similibus*, forced down the throat of the child, in the way of food and medicine, are legion in number, and must be read in Folkard and the herbalists, in Bourke (407), Strack, etc.

In some parts of the United States even snail-water and snail-soup are not unknown; in New England, as Mrs. Earle informs us (221. 6), much was once thought of "the admirable and most famous snail-water."

Milk and Honey.

As we have abundantly seen, the first food of the child is the "food of the gods," for so were honey and milk esteemed among the ancient Germans, Greeks, Slavs, Hindus, etc., and of the Paradise where dwelt the Gods, and into which it was fabled children were born, we have some recollection, as Ploss suggests, in the familiar "land flowing with milk and honey," into the possession of which the children of Israel entered after their long wandering in the wilderness (462. II. 696). Of the ancient Hindu god Agni, Letourneau (100. 315) observes: "After being for a long time fed upon melted butter and the alcoholic liquor from the acid asclepias, the sacred Sôma, he first became a glorious child, then a metaphysical divinity, a mediator living in the fathers and living again in the sons." It was the divine *Sôma* that, like the nectar of the Greeks, the elixirs of the Scandinavians, conferred youth and immortality upon those who drank it.

According to Moslem legend, after his birth, Abraham "remained concealed in a cave during fifteen months, and his mother visited him sometimes to nurse him. But he had no need of her food, for Allah commanded water to flow from one of Abraham's fingers, milk from another, honey from the third, the juice of dates from the fourth, and butter from the fifth" (547. 69).

Poison.

In the *Gesta Romanorum* (Cap. XI.) we read of the "Queen of the North," who "nourished her daughter from the cradle upon a certain kind of deadly poison; and when she grew up, she was considered so beautiful, that the sight of her alone affected one with madness." Moreover, her whole nature had become so imbued with poisons that "she herself had become the deadliest poison in existence. Poison was her element of life. With that rich perfume of her breath she blasted the very air. Her love would have been poison, her embrace death." Hawthorne's story of "Rappaccini's Daughter," — "who ever since infancy had grown and blossomed with the plants whose fatal properties she had imbibed with the air she breathed," — comes from the same original source (390. II. 172). Here we are taken back again to the Golden Age, when even poisons could be eaten without harm.

Priest and Food.

With the giving of the child's food the priest is often associated. In the Fiji Islands, at Vitilevu, on the day when the navel-string falls off, a festival is held, and the food of the child is blest by the priest with prayers for his life and prosperity. In Upper Egypt, a feast is held at the house of the father and the child consecrated by the cadi or a priest, to whom is brought a plate with sugar-candy. The priest chews the candy and lets the sweet juice fall out of his mouth into that of the child, and thus "gives him his name out of his mouth" (326. I. 284).

The over-indulgence of children in food finds parallels at a later period of life, when, as with the people of southern Nubia and the Sahara between Talifet and Timbuktu, men fatten girls before marriage, making them consume huge quantities of milk, butter, etc.

For children, among many primitive peoples, there are numerous *taboos* of certain classes and kinds of food, from religious or superstitious motives. This *taboo*-system has not lost all its force even to-day, as no other excuse can reasonably be offered for the refusal of certain harmless food to the young.

Tobacco.

Concerning certain Australian tribes, Lumholtz remarks: "Before the children are big enough to hold a pipe in their mouth they are permitted to smoke, and the mother will share her pipe with the nursing babe" (495. 193). In like manner, among the natives of the Solomon Islands, Mr. Guppy witnessed displays of precocity in this regard: "Bright-looking lads, eight or nine years of age, stood smoking their pipes as gravely as Haununo [a chief] himself; and even the smallest babe in its father's arms caught hold of his pipe and began to suck instinctively" (466. 42). With the Jívaro Indians of Ecuador, according to Simson, the child, when three or four years old, is initiated into the mysteries of tobacco-smoking, amid great festivities and ceremonies (533. 388).

Drink of Immortality.

Feeding the dead has been in practice among many primitive peoples. The mother, with some of the Indian tribes of New Mexico, used to drop milk from her breast on the lips of her dead babe; and in many parts of the world we meet with the custom of placing food near the grave, so that the spirits may not hunger, or of placing it in the grave or coffin, so that on its way to the spirit-land the soul of the deceased may partake of some refreshment. Among the ancient natives of Venezuela, "infants who died a few days after their birth, were seated around the Tree of Milk, or Celestial Tree, that distilled milk from the extremity of its branches"; and kindred beliefs are found elsewhere (448. 297).

We have also the tree associated beautifully with the new-born child, as Reclus records concerning the Todas of the Nilgiri Hills, in India: "Immediately the deliverance has taken place — it always happens in the open air — three leaves of the afore-mentioned tree [under which the mother and father have passed the night] are presented to the father, who, making cups of them, pours a few drops of water into the first, wherewith he moistens his lips; the remainder he decants into the two other leaves; the mother drinks her share, and causes the baby to swallow his. Thus, father, mother, and child, earliest of Trinities, celebrate their first communion, and drink the living water, more sacred than wine, from the leaves of the Tree of Life" (523. 201).

The sacred books of the Hebrews tell us that the race of man in its infancy became like the gods by eating of the fruit of the tree of knowledge, and in the legends of other peoples immortality came to the great heroes by drinking of the divine sap of the sacred tree, or partaking of some of its fruit. The ancient Egyptians believed that milk from the breast of the divine mother Isis conferred divinity and immortality upon him who drank of it or imbibed it from the sacred source. Wiedemann aptly compares with this the Greek story of the infancy of Hercules. The great child-hero was the son of the god Jupiter and Alcmena, daughter of Electryon, King of Argos. He was exposed by his mother, but the goddess Athene persuaded Hera to give him her breast (another version says Hermes placed Hercules on the breast of Hera, while she slept) and the infant Hercules drew so lustily of the milk that he caused pain to the goddess, who snatched him away. But Hercules had drunk of the milk of a goddess and had become immortal, and as one of the gods (167. 266).

CHAPTER X.

CHILDREN'S SOULS.

The soul that rises with us, our life's star,
Hath elsewhere its setting,
And cometh from afar. — *Wordsworth.*

And rest at last where souls unbodied dwell
In ever-flowing meads of Asphodel.
—*Homer (Pope's Transl.).*

Baptism.

WITH certain Hindu castes, the new-born child is sprinkled with cold water, "in order that the soul, which, since its last existence, has remained in a condition of dreamy contemplation, may be brought to the consciousness that it has to go through a new period of trial in this corporeal world" (326. II. 13). Perhaps, among the myriad rites and ceremonies of immersion and sprinkling to which the infant is submitted with other primitive peoples, some traces of similar beliefs may be found.

When the new world-religion was winning its way among the gentiles, baptism was the great barrier erected between the babe and the power of ill, spirits of air, earth, and water, survivals of old heathenism antagonistic to Christianity. Before that holy rite was performed, the child lay exposed to all their machinations. Baptism was the armour of the infant against the assaults of Satan and his angels, against the cunning of the wanderers from elfin-land, the fairy-sprites, with their changelings and their impish tricks.

Hence, the souls of still-born and unbaptized children came into the power of these evil ones and were metamorphosed into insects, birds, beasts, and the like, whose peculiar notes and voices betray them as having once been little children, or were

152

compelled to join the train of the wild huntsman, or mingle in
the retinue of some other outcast, wandering sprite or devil; or,
again, as some deceitful star, or will-o'-the-wisp, mislead and
torment the traveller on moor and in bog and swamp, and guide
him to an untimely death amid desert solitudes. Ploss, Henderson, and Swainson have a good deal to say on the subject of Frau
Berctha and her train, the Wild Huntsman, the "Gabble Ketchet,"
"Yeth Hounds," etc. Mr. Henderson tells us that, "in North
Devon the local name is 'yeth hounds,' *heath* and *heathen* being
both 'yeth' in the North Devon dialect. Unbaptized infants
are there buried in a part of the churchyard set apart for the
purpose called 'Chrycimers,' *i.e.* Christianless, hill, and the
belief seems to be that their spirits, having no admittance into
Paradise, unite in a pack of 'Heathen' or 'yeth' hounds, and
hunt the Evil One, to whom they ascribe their unhappy condition" (469. 131, 132). The prejudice against unbaptized children
lingers yet elsewhere, as the following extract from a newspaper
published in the year 1882 seems to indicate (230. 272) : —

"There is in the island of Mull a little burial-ground entirely
devoted to unbaptized children, who were thus severed in the
grave from those who had been interred in the hope of resurrection to life. Only one adult lies with the little babes — an old
Christian woman — whose last dying request it was that she
should be buried with the unbaptized children." The Rev. Mr.
Thom has given the facts poetic form and made immortal that
mother-heart whose love made holy — if hallowed it needed to
be — the lonely burial-ground where rest the infant outcasts : —

> "A spot that seems to bear a ban,
>   As if by curse defiled :
> No mother lies there with her babe,
>   No father by his child."

Among primitive peoples we find a like prejudice against still-
born children and children who die very young. The natives of
the Highlands of Borneo think that still-born infants go to a
special spirit-land called *Tenyn lallu*, and "the spirits of these
children are believed to be very brave and to require no weapon
other than a stick to defend themselves against their enemies.
The reason given for this idea is, that the child has never felt

pain in this world and is therefore very daring in the other"
(475. 199). In Annam the spirits of children still-born and of
those dying in infancy are held in great fear. These spirits,
called *Con Ranh*, or *Con Lôn* (from *lôn*, "to enter into life"),
are ever seeking "to incorporate themselves in the bodies of
others, though, after so doing, they are incapable of life." Moreover, "their names are not mentioned in the presence of women,
for it is feared they might take to these, and a newly-married
woman is in like manner afraid to take anything from a woman,
or to wear any of the clothing of one, who has had such a child.
Special measures are necessary to get rid of the *Con Ranh*"
(397. 18–19). The Alfurus, of the Moluccas, "bury children
up to their waists and expose them to all the tortures of thirst
until they wrench from them the promise to hurl themselves
upon the enemies of the village. Then they take them out, but
only to kill them on the spot, imagining that the spirits of the
victims will respect their last promise" (388. 81). On the other
hand, Callaway informs us that the Zulu diviner may divine by
the *Amatongo* (spirit) of infants, "supposed to be mild and benefi-
cent" (417. 176).

Transmigration.

Wordsworth, in that immortal poem, which belongs to the
jewels of the treasure-house of childhood, has sung of the birth
of man : —

> "Our birth is but a sleep and a forgetting;
>   The soul that rises with us, our life's star,
>   Hath had elsewhere its setting,
>   And cometh from afar.
>   Not in entire forgetfulness,
>   And not in utter nakedness,
>   But, trailing clouds of glory, do we come
>   From God, who is our home:
>   Heaven lies about us in our infancy," —

and the humbler bards of many an age, whose names have per-
ished with the races that produced them, have thought and sung
of soul-incarnation, metempsychosis, transmigration, and kindred
concepts, in a thousand different ways. In their strangely poetical language, the Tupi Indians, of Brazil, term a child *pitanga*,
"suck soul," from *piter*, "to suck," *anga*, "soul." The Seminole

Indians, of Florida, "held the baby over the face of the woman dying in child-birth, so that it might receive her parting spirit" (409. 271). A similar practice (with the father) is reported from Polynesia. In a recently published work on "Souls," by Mrs. Mary Alling Aber, we read : —

"Two-thirds of all the babies that are born in civilized lands to-day have no souls attached to them. These babies are emanations from their parents, — not true entities; and, unless a soul attaches itself, no ordinary efforts can carry one of them to the twentieth year. Souls do attach themselves to babies after birth sometimes so late as the third year. On the other hand, babies who have souls at birth sometimes lose them because the soul finds a better place, or is drawn away by a stronger influence; but this rarely occurs after the third year."

This somewhat *outré* declaration of modern spiritualism finds kindred in some of the beliefs of primitive peoples, concerning which there is much in Ploss, Frazer, Bastian, etc.

In one of the Mussulman stories of King Solomon, the Angel of Death descends in human form to take the soul of an aged man, whose wish was to die when he had met the mightiest prophet. He dies talking to the wise Hebrew king. Afterwards the Angel says to Solomon : —

"He [the angel, whose head reaches ten thousand years beyond the seventh heaven, whose feet are five hundred years below the earth, and upon whose shoulders stands the Angel of Death] it is who points out to me when and how I must take a soul. His gaze is fixed on the tree Sidrat Almuntaha, which bears as many leaves inscribed with names as there are men living on the earth.

"At each new birth a new leaf, bearing the name of the newly-born, bursts forth; and when any one has reached the end of his life, his leaf withers and falls off, and at the same instant I am with him to receive his soul. . . .

"As often as a believer dies, Gabriel attends me, and wraps his soul in a green silken sheet, and then breathes it into a green bird, which feeds in Paradise until the day of the resurrection. But the soul of the sinner I take alone, and, having wrapped it in a coarse, pitch-covered, woollen cloth, carry it to the gates of Hell, where it wanders among abominable vapours until the last day" (547. 213, 214).

According to the belief of the Miao-tse, an aboriginal tribe of the province of Canton, in China, the souls of unborn children are kept in the garden of two deities called "Flower-Grandfather" and "Flower-Grandmother," and when to these have been made by a priest sacrifices of hens or swine, the children are let out and thus appear among men. As a charm against barrenness, these people put white paper into a basket and have the priest make an invocation. The white paper represents the deities, and the ceremony is called *kau fa; i.e.* "Flower Invocation."

In Japan, a certain Lake Fakone, owing its origin to an earthquake, and now surrounded by many temples, is looked upon as the abode of the souls of children about to be born (326. I. 3).

Certain Californian Indians, near Monterey, thought that "the dead retreated to verdant islands in the West, while awaiting the birth of the infants whose souls they were to form" (396. III. 525).

In Calabria, Italy, when a butterfly flits around a baby's cradle, it is believed to be either an angel or a baby's soul, and a like belief prevails in other parts of the world; and we have the classic personification of Psyche, the soul, as a butterfly.

Among the uneducated peasantry of Ireland, the pure white butterfly is thought to be the soul of the sinless and forgiven dead on the way to Paradise, whilst the spotted ones are the embodiments of spirits condemned to spend their time of purgatory upon earth, the number of the sins corresponding with the number of spots on the wings of the insect (418. 192).

In early Christian art and folk-lore, the soul is often figured as a dove, and in some heathen mythologies of Europe as a mouse, weasel, lizard, etc.

In various parts of the world we find that children, at death, go to special limbos, purgatories, or heavens, and the folk-lore of the subject must be read at length in the mythological treatises.

The Andaman Islanders "believe that every child which is conceived has had a prior existence, but only as an infant. If a woman who has lost a baby is again about to become a mother, the name borne by the deceased is bestowed on the fœtus, in the expectation that it will prove to be the same child born again. Should it be found at birth that the babe is of the same sex as the one who died, the identity is considered to be sufficiently established; but, if otherwise, the deceased one is said to be

under the *ràu-* (*Ficus laccifera*), in *·chà·itàn-* (Hades)." Under
this tree, upon the fruit of which they live, also dwell "the
spirits and souls of all children who die before they cease to be
entirely dependent on their parents (*i.e.* under six years of age)"
(498. 86, 93). There was a somewhat similar myth in Venezuela
(448. 297).

Mr. Codrington gives some interesting illustrations of this
belief from Melanesia (25. 311) : —

"In the island of Aurora, Maewo, in the New Hebrides, women
sometimes have a notion that the origin, beginning, of one of
their children is a cocoanut or a bread-fruit, or something of that
kind ; and they believe, therefore, that it would be injurious to
the child to eat that food. It is a fancy of the woman, before the
birth of the child, that the infant will be the *nunu*, which may be
translated the echo, of such an object. Women also fancy that
a child is the *nunu* of some dead person. It is not a notion
of metempsychosis, as if the soul of the dead person returned in
the new-born child ; but it is thought that there is so close a connection that the infant takes the place of the deceased. At Mota,
also, in the Banks Islands, there was the belief that each person
had a source of his being, his origin, in some animate or inanimate thing, which might, under some circumstances, become
known to him." As Mr. Codrington suggests, such beliefs throw
light upon the probable origin of totemism and its development.

Spirit-World.

Mrs. Stevenson informs us that "although the Sia do not
believe in a return of the spirits of their dead when they have
once entered Shipapo [the lower world], there was once an exception to this." The priestly tale, as told to Mrs. Stevenson, is
as follows (538. 143) : —

"When the years were new, and this village had been built
perhaps three years, all the spirits of our dead came here for a
great feast. They had bodies such as they had before death ;
wives recognized husbands, husbands wives, children parents, and
parents children. Just after sundown the spirits began arriving,
only a few passing over the road by daylight, but after dark they
came in great crowds and remained until near dawn. They tar-

ried but one night; husbands and wives did not sleep together; had they done so, the living would have surely died. When the hour of separation came, there was much weeping, not only among the living, but the dead. The living insisted upon going with the dead, but the dead declared they must wait, — that they could not pass through the entrance to the other world; they must first die or grow old and again become little children to be able to pass through the door of the world for the departed. It was then that the Sia first learned all about their future home. They learned that the fields were vast, the pastures beautiful, the mountains high, the lakes and rivers clear like crystal, and the wheat and cornfields flourishing. During the day the spirits sleep, and at night they work industriously in the fields. The moon is father to the dead as the sun is father to the living, the dead resting when the sun travels, for at this time they see nothing; it is when the sun returns to his home at night that the departed spirits work and pass about in their world below. The home of the departed spirits is in the world first inhabited by the Sia."

We learn further: "It is the aim of the Sia to first reach the intermediate state at the time the body ceases to develop, and then return gradually back to the first condition of infancy; at such periods one does not die, but sleeps to awake in the spirit-world as a little child. Many stories have come to the Sia by those who have died only for a time; the heart becomes still and the lips cold, and the spirit passes to the entrance of the other world and looks in, but does not enter, and yet it sees all, and in a short time returns to inhabit its earthly body. Great alarm is felt when one returns in this way to life, but much faith is put in the stories afterwards told by the one who has passed over the road of death."

In the belief of these Indians of North America we see some foreshadowing of the declaration of Jesus, a rude expression of the fundamental thought underlying his words: —

"Suffer little children to come unto me, and forbid them not; for of such is the kingdom of God. Verily I say unto you, whosoever shall not receive the kingdom of God as a little child, he shall in nowise enter therein."

Certain Siouan Indians think: "The stars are all deceased

men. When a child is born, a star descends and appears on earth in human form; after death it reascends and appears as a star in heaven" (433. 508). How like this is the poet's thought: —

> " Our birth is but a sleep and a forgetting:
> The soul that rises with us, our life's star,
> Hath had elsewhere its setting,
> And cometh from afar."

CHAPTER XI.

CHILDREN'S FLOWERS, PLANTS, AND TREES.

As for man, his days are as grass; as a flower of the field so he flourishes.
—*Psalm* ciii. 15.

> A child at play in meadows green,
> Plucking the fragrant flowers,
> Chasing the white-winged butterflies,—
> So sweet are childhood's hours.

> We meet wi' blythesome and kythesome cheerie weans,
> Daffin' and laughin' far adoon the leafy lanes,
> Wi' gowans and buttercups buskin' the thorny wands—
> Sweetly singin' wi' the flower-branch wavin' in their hands.
> — *William Miller.*

Many savage nations worship trees, and I really think my first feeling would be one of delight and interest rather than of surprise, if some day when I am alone in a wood, one of the trees were to speak to me. — *Sir John Lubbock.*

> O who can tell
> The hidden power of herbs, and might of magic spell? — *Spenser.*

Plant Life and Human Life.

FLOWERS, plants, and trees have ever been interwoven with the fate of man in the minds of poets and folk-thinkers. The great Hebrew psalmist declared: "As for man, his days are as grass; as a flower of the field so he flourisheth," and the old Greeks said beautifully, οἵηπερ φύλλων γενεή, τοιήδε καὶ ἀνδρῶν, "as is the generation of leaves, so is also that of men"; or, to quote the words of Homer (*Iliad*, vi. 146):—

"Like as the generation of leaves, so also is that of men;
For the wind strews the leaves on the ground; but the forest,
Putting forth fresh buds, grows on, and spring will presently return.
Thus with the generation of men; the one blooms, the other fades away."

magaths is a derivative from *magus,* " son, boy, servant," cognate
with Old Irish *mac,* " boy, son, youth," *mog (mug),* " slave," Old
Norse *mǫgr,* " son," Anglo-Saxon *mago,* " son, youth, servant,
man," the radical of all these terms being *mag,* " to have power,
to increase, to grow," — the Gothic *magus* was properly " a growing (boy)," a " maid " is " a growing (girl)." The same idea
underlies the month-name *May,* for, to the Romans, this was
" the month of growth," — flowery, bounteous May, — and dedicated to *Maia,* " the increaser," but curiously, as Ovid tells us,
the common people considered it unlucky to marry in May, for
then the rites of Bona Dea, the goddess of chastity, and the feasts
of the dead, were celebrated.

Plant-Lore.

The study of dendanthropology and human florigeny would
lead us wide afield. The ancient Semitic peoples of Asia Minor
had their " Tree of Life," which later religions have spiritualized,
and more than one race has ascribed its origin to trees. The
Carib Indians believed that mankind — woman especially — were
first created from two trees (509. 109). According to a myth of
the Siouan Indians, the first two human beings stood rooted as
trees in the ground for many ages, until a great snake gnawed at
the roots, so that they got loose and became the first Indians.
In the old Norse cosmogony, two human beings — man and
woman — were created from two trees — ash and elm — that
stood on the sea-shore ; while Tacitus states that the holy grove
of the Semnones was held to be the cradle of the nation, and in
Saxony, men are said to have grown from trees. The Maya
Indians called themselves " sons of the trees " (509. 180, 264).

Doctor Beauchamp reports a legend of the Iroquois Indians,
according to which a god came to earth and sowed five handfuls
of seed, and these, changing to worms, were taken possession of
by spirits, changed to children, and became the ancestors of the
Five Nations (480. IV. 297).

Classical mythology, along with dryads and tree-nymphs of all
sorts, furnishes us with a multitude of myths of the metamorphosis of human beings into trees, plants, and flowers. Among
the most familiar stories are those of Adonis, Crocus, Phyllis,

Narcissus, Leucothea, Hyacinthus, Syrinx, Clytie, Daphne, Orchis, Lotis, Philemon and Baucis, Atys, etc. All over the world we find myths of like import.

A typical example is the Algonkian Indian legend of the transformation of Mishosha, the magician, into the sugar-maple, — the name *aninatik* or *ininatik* is interpreted by folk-etymology as "man-tree," the sap being the life-blood of Mishosha. Glūskap, the culture-hero of the Micmacs, once changed "a mighty man" into the cedar-tree.

Many of the peculiarities of trees and plants are explained by the folk as resulting from their having once been human creatures.

Grimm and Ploss have called attention to the widespread custom of planting trees on the occasion of the birth of a child, the idea being that some sort of connection between the plant and the human existed and would show itself sympathetically. In Switzerland, where the belief is that the child thrives with the tree, or *vice versâ*, apple-trees are planted for boys and pear- or nut-trees for girls. Among the Jews, a cedar was planted for a boy and a pine for a girl, while for the wedding canopy, branches were cut from both these trees (385. 6). From this thought the orators and psalmists of old Israel drew many a noble and inspiring figure, such as that used by David: "The righteous shall flourish like the palm-tree: he shall grow like a cedar in Lebanon." Here belong also "flourishing like a green bay-tree," and the remark of the Captain in Shakespeare's *King Richard Second :* —

> "'Tis thought the king is dead. We will not stay ;
> The bay-trees in our country are all withered."

Child-Flowers and -Plants.

The planting of trees for the hero or the heroine and the belief that these wither when a death is near, blossom when a happy event approaches, and in many ways react to the fate and fortune of their human fellows, occur very frequently in fairy-tales and legends.

There is a sweet Tyrolian legend of "a poor idiot boy, who lived alone in the forest and was never heard to say any words but 'Ave Maria.' After his death a lily sprang up on his grave, on whose petals 'Ave Maria' might be distinctly read" (416. 216).

An old Greek myth relates that the Crocus "sprang from the blood of the infant Crocus, who was accidentally struck by a metal disc thrown by Mercury, whilst playing a game" (448. 299). In Ossianic story, "Malvina, weeping beside the tomb of Fingal, for Oscar and his infant son, is comforted by the maids of Morven, who narrate how they have seen the innocent infant borne on a light mist, pouring upon the fields a fresh harvest of flowers, amongst which rises one with golden disc, encircled with rays of silver, tipped with a delicate tint of crimson." Such, according to this Celtic legend, was the origin of the daisy (448. 308).

The peasants of Brittany believe that little children, when they die, go straight to Paradise and are changed into beautiful flowers in the garden of heaven (174. 141). Similar beliefs are found in other parts of the world, and a like imagery is met with among our poets. Well known is Longfellow's little poem "The Reaper and the Flowers," in which death, as a reaper, reaps not alone the "bearded grain," but also "the flowers [children] that grow between," for : —

> "'My Lord has need of these flowerets gay,'
> The reaper said, and smiled ;
> 'Dear tokens of the earth are they,
> Where he was once a child.'"

And so : —

> "The mother gave, in tears and pain,
> The flowers she most did love ;
> She knew she should find them all again
> In the field of light above."

According to a myth of the Chippeway Indians, a star once came down from heaven to dwell among men. Upon consulting with a young man in a dream as to where it should live, it was told to choose a place for itself, and, "at first, it dwelt in the white rose of the mountains ; but there it was so buried that it could not be seen. It went to the prairie ; but it feared the hoof of the buffalo. It next sought the rocky cliff ; but there it was so high that the children whom it loved most could not see it." It decided at last to dwell where it could always be seen, and so one morning the Indians awoke to find the surface of river, lake, and pond covered with thousands of white flowers. Thus came into existence the beautiful water-lilies (410. 68–70).

Perhaps the most beautiful belief regarding children's flowers is that embodied in Hans Christian Andersen's tale *The Angel*, where the Danish prose-poet tells us: "Whenever a child dies, an angel from heaven comes down to earth and takes the dead child in his arms, spreads out his great white wings, and flies away over all the places the child has loved and picks quite a handful of flowers, which he carries up to the Almighty, that they may bloom in heaven more brightly than on earth. And the Father presses all the flowers to His heart; but He kisses the flower that pleases Him best, and the flower is then endowed with a voice and can join in the great chorus of praise" (393. 341).

Star-Flowers.

Beside this, however, we may perhaps place the following quaint story of "The Devils on the Meadows of Heaven," of which a translation from the German of Rudolph Baumbach, by "C. F. P.," appears in the *Association Record* (October, 1892), published by the Young Women's Christian Association of Worcester, Mass. : —

"As you know, good children, when they die, come to Heaven and become angels. But if you perhaps think they do nothing the sweet, long day but fly about and play hide-and-seek behind the clouds, you are mistaken. The angel-children are obliged to go to school like the boys and girls on the earth, and on week days must be in the angel-school three hours in the forenoon and two in the afternoon. There they write with golden pens on silver slates, and instead of ABC-books they have story-books with gay-coloured pictures. They do not learn geography, for of what use in Heaven is earth-knowledge; and in eternity one doesn't know the multiplication table at all. Dr. Faust is the angel-school teacher. On earth he was an A.M., and on account of a certain event which does not belong here, he is obliged to keep school in Heaven three thousand years more before the long vacation begins for him. Wednesday and Saturday afternoons the little angels have holiday; then they are taken to walk on the Milky Way by Dr. Faust.   But Sunday they are allowed to play on the great meadow in front of the gate of Heaven, and that they joyfully anticipate during the whole week.

" The meadow is not green, but blue, and on it grow thousands and thousands of silver and golden flowers.   They shine in the night and we men call them stars.

" When the angels are sporting about before the gate of Heaven, Dr. Faust is not present, for on Sunday he must recover from the toil of the past week.   St. Peter, who keeps watch at the Heavenly gate, then takes charge.   He usually sees to it that the play goes on properly, and that no one goes astray or flies away; but if one ever gets too far away from the gate, then he whistles on his golden key, which means ' Back ! '

" Once — it was really very hot in Heaven — St. Peter fell asleep.   When the angels noticed this, they ceased swarming hither and thither and scattered over the whole meadow.   But the most enterprising of them went out on a trip of discovery, and came at last to the place where the world is surrounded by a board fence.   First they tried to find a crack somewhere through which they might peep, but as they found no gap, they climbed up the board fence and hung dangling and looking over.

" Yonder, on the other side, was hell, and before its gate a crowd of little devils were just running about.   They were coal-black, and had horns on their heads and long tails behind.   One of them chanced to look up and noticed the angels, and immediately begged imploringly that they would let them into Heaven for a little while; they would behave quite nice and properly. This moved the angels to pity, and because they liked the little black fellows, they thought they might perhaps allow the poor imps this innocent pleasure.

" One of them knew the whereabouts of Jacob's ladder.   This they dragged to the place from the lumber-room (St. Peter had, luckily, not waked up), lifted it over the fence of boards, and let it down into hell.   Immediately the tailed fellows clambered up its rounds like monkeys, the angels gave them their hands, and thus came the devils upon Heaven's meadows.

" At first they behaved themselves in a quite orderly manner. Modestly they stepped along and carried their tails on their arms like trains, as the devil grandmother, who sets great value on propriety, had taught them. But it did not last long; they became frolicsome, turned wheels and somersaults, and shrieked at the same time like real imps. The beautiful moon, who was looking kindly out of a window in Heaven, they derided, thrust out their tongues and made faces (German: long noses) at her, and finally began to pluck up the flowers which grew on the meadow and throw them down on the earth. Now the angels grew frightened and bitterly repented letting their evil guests into Heaven. They begged and threatened, but the devils cared for nothing, and kept on in their frolic more madly. Then, in terror, the angels waked up St. Peter and penitently confessed to him what they had done. He smote his hands together over his head when he saw the mischief which the imps had wrought. 'March in!' thundered he, and the little ones, with drooping wings, crept through the gate into Heaven. Then St. Peter called a few sturdy angels. They collected the imps and took them where they belonged.

"The little angels did not escape punishment. Three Sundays in succession they were not allowed in front of Heaven's gate, and, if they were taken to walk, they were obliged to first unbuckle their wings and lay aside their halos; and it is a great disgrace for an angel to go about without wings and halo.

"But the affair resulted in some good, after all. The flowers which the devils had torn up and thrown upon the earth took root and increased from year to year. To be sure, the star-flower lost much of its heavenly beauty, but it is still always lovely to look at, with its golden-yellow disk, and its silvery white crown of rays.

"And because of its Heavenly origin, a quite remarkable power resides in it. If a maiden, whose mind harbours a doubt, pulls off, one by one, the white petals of the flower-star, whispering meanwhile a certain sentence at the fall of the last little petal, she is quite sure of what she desires to know."

The very name *Aster* is suggestive of star-origin and recalls the lines of Longfellow: —

> " Spake full well, in language quaint and olden,
>   One who dwelleth by the castled Rhine,
> When he called the flowers, so blue and golden,
>   Stars, that in earth's firmament do shine."

The reference seems to be to Friedrich Wilhelm Carové, of Coblentz, in whose *Märchen ohne Ende*, a forget-me-not is spoken of as "twinkling as brightly as a blue star on the green firmament of earth" (390. II. 149).

Another contribution to floral astrology is the brief poem of H. M. Sweeny in the *Catholic World* for November, 1892: —

> "The Milky Way is the foot-path
>   Of the martyrs gone to God;
> Its stars are the flaming jewels
>   To show us the way they trod.

> "The flowers are stars dropped lower,
>   Our daily path to light,
> In daylight to lead us upward
>   As those jewels do at night."

Flower-oracles are discussed in another section, and the "language of flowers" of which the poet tells, —

> "In Eastern lands they talk in flowers,
>   And they tell in a garland their loves and cares;
> Each blossom that blooms in their garden bower
>   On its leaves a mystic language bears,"

must be studied in Dyer, Friend, and Folkard, or in the various booklets which treat of this entertaining subject.

Though in Bohemia it is believed that "seven-year-old children will become beautiful by dancing in the flax," and in some parts of Germany "when an infant seems weakly and thrives slowly, it is placed naked upon the turf on Midsummer Day, and flax-seed is sprinkled over it; the idea being, that, as the flax-seed grows, so the child will gradually grow stronger" (435. 278, 279); flowers and plants are sometimes associated with ill-luck and death. In Westphalia and Thuringia the superstition prevails that "any child less than a year old, who is permitted to wreathe himself with flowers, will soon die." In the region about Cockermouth, in the county of Cumberland, England, the red campion (*Lychnis diurna*) is known as "mother-die," the belief being that, if children gather it, some misfortune is sure to happen to the parents. Dyer records also the following: "In West Cumberland, the herb-robert (*Geranium robertianum*) is called 'death come quickly,' from a like reason, while in parts of Yorkshire, the belief is that the mother of a child who has gathered the germander speedwell (*Veronica chamœdrys*) will die ere the year is out" (435. 276)

Children's Plant-Names.

Mr. H. C. Mercer, discussing the question of the presence of Indian corn in Italy and Europe in early times, remarks (*Amer. Naturalist*, Vol. XXVIII., 1894, p. 974) : —

"An etymology has been suggested for the name *Grano Turco* [Turkish grain], in the antics of boys when bearded and moustached with maize silk, they mimic the fierce looks of Turks in the high 'corn.' We cannot think that the Italian lad does not smoke the mock tobacco that must tempt him upon each ear. If he does, he apes a habit no less American in its origin than the maize itself. So the American lad playing with a 'shoe-string bow' or a 'corn-stalk fiddle' would turn to Italy for his inspiration."

In the interesting lists of popular American plant-names, published by Mrs. Fanny D. Bergen (400), are found the following in which the child is remembered : —

Babies' breath, *Galium Mollugo.* In Eastern Massachusetts.
Babies' breath, *Muscari botryoides.* In Eastern Massachusetts.
Babies' feet, *Polygala paucifolia.* In New Hampshire.
Babies' slippers, *Polygala paucifolia.* In Western Massachusetts.
Babies' toes, *Polygala paucifolia.* In Hubbardston, Mass.
Baby blue-eyes, *Nemophila insignis.* In Sta. Barbara, Cal.
Blue-eyed babies, *Houstonia cœrulea.* In Springfield, Mass.
Boys and girls, *Dicentra cucullaria.* In New York.
Boys' love, *Artemisia absinthium.* In Wellfleet, Mass.
Death-baby, *Phallus sp.* (?). In Salem, Mass.
Girls and boys, *Dicentra cucullaria.* In Vermont.
Little boy's breeches, *Dicentra cucullaria.* In Central Iowa.

"Blue-eyed babies" is certainly an improvement upon "Quaker ladies," the name by which the *Houstonia* is known in some parts of New England; "death-baby" is a term that is given, Mrs Bergen tells us, "from the fancy that they foretell death in the family near whose house they spring up. I have known of intelligent people rushing out in terror and beating down a colony of these as soon as they appeared in the yard."

The parents have not been entirely forgotten, as the following names show : —

Mother's beauties, *Calandrina Menziesii*.   In Sta. Barbara, Cal.
Mother of thousands, *Tradescantia crassifolia* (?).   In Boston, Mass.
Daddy-nuts, *Tilia sp.* (?).   In Madison, Wis.

At La Crosse, Wis., the *Lonicera talarica* is called "twin sisters," a name which finds many analogues.

As we have seen, the consideration of children as flowers, plants, trees, traverses many walks of life.   Floral imagery has appealed to many primitive peoples, perhaps to none more than to the ancient Mexicans, with whom children were often called flowers, and the Nagualists termed Mother-Earth "the flower that contains everything," and "the flower that eats everything" — being at once the source and end of life (413. 54).

A sweet old German legend has it that the laughter of little children produced roses, and the sweetest and briefest of the "good-night songs" of the German mothers is this : —

> " Guten Abend, gute Nacht !
> Mit Rosen bedacht,
> Mit Näglein besteckt ;
> Morgen früh, wenn's Gott will,
> Wirst du wieder geweckt."

CHAPTER XII.

CHILDREN'S ANIMALS, BIRDS, ETC.

My brother, the hare, . . . my sisters, the doves. — *St. Francis of Assisi.*

Love of animals is inborn. The child that has had no pets is to be pitied.
— *G. Stanley Hall.*

For what are the voices of birds —
Aye, and of beasts, — but words, our words,
Only so much more sweet ? — *Browning.*

I know not, little Ella, what the flowers
    Said to you then, to make your cheek so pale ;
And why the blackbird in our laurel bowers
    Spoke to you, only: and the poor pink snail
Fear'd less your steps than those of the May-shower
    It was not strange those creatures loved you so,
    And told you all. 'Twas not so long ago
You were yourself a bird, or else a flower.
— *Lord Lytton (Owen Meredith).*

Children and Young Animals.

THE comparisons sometimes made of children with various of the lower animals, such as monkeys, bears, pigs, etc., come more naturally to some primitive peoples, who, as Ploss has pointed out, suckle at the breast the young of certain animals simultaneously with their own offspring. In this way, the infant in the Society Islands comes early into association with puppies, as he does also among several of the native tribes of Australia and America; so was it likewise in ancient Rome, and the custom may yet be found among the tent-gypsies of Transylvania, in Persia, and even within the present century has been met with in Naples and Göttingen. The Maori mother, in like manner, suckles young pigs, the Arawak Indian of Guiana young monkeys

171

(as also do the Siamese), the natives of Kamtschatka young
bears. An old legend of the city of Breslau has it that the
fashion certain ladies have of carrying dogs around with them
originated in the fact that Duke Boleslau, in the last quarter of
the eleventh century, punished the women of Breslau, for some
connubial unfaithfulness, by taking away their suckling children and making them carry instead puppies at the breast (392.
I. 61).

Of the Arekuna of Guiana, Schomburgk tells us: —

"They bring up children and monkeys together. The monkeys
are members of the family, eat with the other members, are
suckled by the women, and have great affection for their human
nurses. Oftentimes a woman is to be seen with a child and
a monkey at the breast, the two nurselings quarrelling" (529.
13).

The young children of the less nomadic tribes grow up in close
association with the few domestic animals possessed by their
parents, tumbling about with the puppies on the wigwam-floor or
racing with them around the camp-stead.

The history of totemism· and fetichism, primitive medicine,
and the arts connected therewith, their panaceas, talismans, and
amulets, show early association of the child with animals. In
the village of Issapoo, on the island of Fernando Po, in Western
Africa, there is fastened to a pole in the market-place a snake-
skin, to touch which all infants born the preceding year are
brought by their mothers during an annual festival (529. 32). In
various parts of the world, novices and neophytes are put to
dream or fast in seclusion until they see some animal which
becomes their tutelary genius, and whose form is often tattooed
upon their body.

Sir John Maundeville, the veracious mediæval chronicler, reported that in Sicily serpents were used to test the legitimacy of
children; "if the children be illegitimate, the serpents bite and
kill them." Hartland cites, on the authority of Thiele, " a story
in which a wild stallion colt is brought in to smell two babes,
one of which is a changeling. Every time he smells one he is
quiet and licks it; but, on smelling the other, he is invariably
restive and strives to kick it. The latter, therefore, is the
changeling" (258. 111).

Animal Nurses.

Akin to these practices are many of the forms of exposure and abandonment all over the world. Shakespeare, in *The Winter's Tale*, makes Antigonus say:—

> "Come on (poor Babe).
> Some powerful Spirit instruct the Kites and Ravens
> To be thy Nurses. Wolves and Bears, they say
> (Casting their savageness aside), have done
> Like offices of pity."

An old Egyptian painting represents a child and a calf being suckled by the same cow, and in Palestine and the Canary Islands, goats are used to suckle children, especially if the mother of the little one has died (125. II. 393). The story of Psammetichus and the legend of Romulus and Remus find parallels in many lands. Gods, heroes, saints, are suckled and cared for in their infancy by grateful beasts.

Wild Children.

Doctor Tylor has discussed at some length the subject of "wild men and beast children" (376), citing examples from many different parts of the globe. Procopius, the chronicler of the Gothic invasion of Italy, states (with the additional information that he saw the child in question himself), that, after the barbarians had ravaged the country, "an infant, left by its mother, was found by a she-goat, which suckled and took care of it. When the survivors came back to their deserted homes, they found the child living with its adopted mother, and called it Ægisthus." Doctor Tylor calls attention to the prevalence of similar stories in Germany after the destruction and devastation of the Napoleonic wars; there appears to be record of several children wild or animal-reared having, during this period, been received into Count von Recke's asylum at Overdyke. Many of these tales we need not hesitate to dismiss as purely fabulous, though there may be truth in some of the rest. Among the best-known cases (some of which are evidently nothing more than idiots, or poor wandering children) are: Peter, the "Wild Boy" of Hameln (in 1724); the child reported in the Hessian Chronicle as having been found by some hunters living with wolves in 1341; the child reported

by Bernard Connor as living with she-bears, and the child found
with bears at Grodno in Poland; the wolf-child of the Ardennes,
mentioned by Koenig, in his treatise on the subject; the Irish boy
said to feed on grass and hay, found living among the wild sheep;
the girl found living wild in Holland in 1717; the two goat-like
boys of the Pyrenees (in 1719); the amphibious wild girl of
Châlons sur Marne (in 1731); the wild boy of Bamberg, who lowed
like an ox; and, the most renowned of all, Kaspar Hauser. This
celebrated "wild boy" has recently been made the subject of a
monograph by the Duchess of Cleveland (208), of which the first
words are these: "The story of Kaspar Hauser is both curious
and instructive. It shows on how commonplace and unpromis-
ing a foundation a myth of European celebrity may rest." Sir
William Sleeman has something to say of "beast-children" in
the Kingdom of Oude (183), and Mr. Ball, who writes of wolf-
reared children in India, calls attention to the fact that in that
country there seems to have been no instance of a wolf-reared
girl (183. 474).

In the *Kathá sarit ságara* ("Ocean of the River of Story"), a
work belonging to the twelfth century, there is the story of the
immoral union of a *yaksha*, or *jin*, and the daughter of a holy
man, who was bathing in the Ganges. The relatives of the girl
by magic changed the two guilty persons into a lion and a lion-
ess. The latter soon died, but gave birth to a human child, which
the lion-father made the other lionesses suckle. The baby grew
up and became "the world-ruling king, Satavahana" (376. 29).

Another Hindu story tells how the daughter of a Brahman,
giving birth to a child while on a journey, was forced to leave it
in a wood, where it was suckled and nursed by female jackals
until rescued by merchants who happened to pass by.

Herodotus repeats the tales that Cyrus was nursed and suckled
by a bitch; Zeus figures as suckled by a goat; Romulus and
Remus, the founders of Rome according to the ancient legend,
were nursed by a she-wolf; and others of the heroes and gods of
old were suckled by animals whose primitive kinship with the
race of man the folk had not forgotten.

Professor Rauber of Dorpat, in his essay on "Homo Sapiens
Ferus" (335), discusses in detail sixteen cases of wild children
(including most of those treated by Tylor) as follows: the two

Hessian wolf-children, boys (1341–1344); the Bamberg boy, who grew up among the cattle (at the close of the sixteenth century); Hans of Liège; the Irish boy brought up by sheep; the three Lithuanian bear-boys (1657, 1669, 1694); the girl of Oranienburg (1717); the two Pyrenæan boys (1719); Peter, the wild boy of Hameln (1724); the girl of Songi in Champagne (1731); the Hungarian bear-girl (1767); the wild man of Cronstadt (end of eighteenth century); the boy of Aveyron (1795). It will be noticed that in this list of sixteen cases but two girls figure.

As a result of his studies Professor Rauber concludes: "What we are wont to call reason does not belong to man as such; in himself he is without it. The appellation *Homo sapiens* does not then refer to man as such, but to the ability under certain conditions of becoming possessed of reason. It is the same with language and culture of every sort. The title *Homo sapiens ferus* (Linnæus) is in a strict sense unjustifiable and a contradiction in itself." To prehistoric man these wild children are like, but they are not the same as he; they resemble him, but cannot be looked upon as one and the same with him. From the standpoint of pedagogy, Professor Rauber, from the consideration of these children, feels compelled to declare that "the ABC-school must be replaced by the culture-school." In other words: "The ABC is not, as so many believe, the beginning of all wisdom. In order to be able to admeasure this sufficiently, prehistoric studies are advisable, nay, necessary. Writing is a very late acquisition of man. In the arrangement of a curriculum for the first years of the culture-school, reading and writing are to be placed at the end of the second school year, but never are they to begin the course. . . . Manual training ought also to be taken up in the schools; it is demanded by considerations of culture-history " (335. 133).

Animal Stories.

Professor W. H. Brewer of New Haven, discussing the "instinctive interest of children in bear and wolf stories," observes (192): "The children of European races take more interest in bear and wolf stories than in stories relating to any other wild animals. Their interest in bears is greater than that in wolves, and in the plays of children bears have a much more conspicu-

ous part. There is a sort of fascination in everything relating
to these animals that attracts the child's attention from a very
early age, and 'Tell me a bear story' is a common request long
before it learns to read." After rejecting, as unsatisfactory, the
theory that would make it a matter of education with each
child, — "the conservative traditions of children have preserved
more stories about bears and wolves, parents and nurses talk
more about them, these animals have a larger place in the literature for children; hence the special interest," — Professor Brewer
expresses his own belief that "the special interest our children
show towards these two animals is instinctive, and it is of the
nature of an inherited memory, vague, to be sure, yet strong
enough to give a bend to the natural inclinations." He points out
that the bear and the wolf are the two animals "which have been
and still are the most destructive to human life (and particularly
to children) in our latitude and climate," and that "several of the
large breeds of dogs, — the wolf-hound proper, the mastiff (particularly the Spanish mastiff), and even the St. Bernard, — were
originally evolved as wolf-dogs for the protection of sheep and
children." His general conclusion is: "The fear inspired by
these animals during the long ages of the childhood of our civilization, and the education of the many successive generations
of our ancestors in this fear, descends to us as an inherited memory, or, in other words, an instinct. While not strong, it is of
sufficient force to create that kind of fascination which stories of
bears and wolves have in children before the instincts are covered
up and obscured by intellectual education. The great shaggy bear
appeals more strongly to the imagination of children, hence its
superior value to play 'boo' with."

Rabbit and Hare.

The rabbit and the hare figure in many mythologies, and around
them, both in the Old World and the New, has grown up a vast
amount of folk-lore. The rabbit and the child are associated in
the old nursery-rhyme: —

> "Bye, bye, Baby Bunting,
> Papa's gone a-hunting,
> To get a rabbit-skin,
> To wrap Baby Bunting in,"

which reminds us at once of the Chinook Indians and the Flat Heads of the Columbia, with whom "the child is wrapped in rabbit-skins and placed in this little coffin-like cradle, from which it is not in some instances taken out for several weeks" (306. 174).

An Irish belief explains hare-lip as having been caused, before the birth of the child, by the mother seeing a hare. The Chinese think that "a hare or a rabbit sits at the foot of the cassia-tree in the moon, pounding the drugs out of which the elixir of immortality is compounded" (401. 155).

The Ungava Eskimo, according to Turner, have a legend that the hare was once a little child, abused by its elders; it ran away to dwell by itself. The hare has no tail, because as a child he had none; and he lays back his ears, when he hears a shout, because he thinks people are talking about him" (544. 263).

In a myth of the Menomoni Indians, reported by Dr. W. J. Hoffman, we read that Manabush [the great culture-hero] and a twin brother were born the sons of the virgin daughter of an old woman named Nokómis. His brother and mother died. Nokómis wrapped Manabush in dry, soft grass, and placed a wooden bowl over him. After four days a noise proceeded from the bowl, and, upon removing it, she saw "a little white rabbit with quivering ears." Afterwards, when grown up, and mourning for the death of his brother, Manabush is said to have hid himself in a large rock near Mackinaw, where he was visited by the people for many years. When he did not wish to see them in his human form, he appeared to them as "a little white rabbit with trembling ears" (389. (1890) 246). Of the white rabbit, the Great Hare, Manabush, Näniboju, etc., more must be read in the mythological essays of Dr. Brinton.

Among the tales of the Ainu of Yezo, Japan, recorded by Professor B. H. Chamberlain, is the following concerning the Hare-god: —

"Suddenly there was a large house on top of a hill, wherein were six persons beautifully arrayed, but constantly quarrelling. Whence they came was not known. Thereupon [the god] Okikurumi came, and said: 'Oh, you bad hares! you wicked hares! Who should not know your origin? The children in the sky were pelting each other with snowballs, and the snowballs fell into this world of men. As it would have been a pity to waste heaven's snow, the snowballs were turned into hares, and those hares are you. You who live in this world of mine, this world of human beings, must be quiet. What is it that you are brawling about?' With these words, Okikurumi seized a fire-brand, and beat each of the six with it in turn. Thereupon all the hares ran away. This is the origin of the hare-god, and for this reason the body of the hare is white, because made of snow, while its ears, which are the part which was charred by the fire, are black" (471. 486).

The Mayas of Yucatan have a legend of a town of hares under the earth (411. 179).

In Germany we meet with the "Easter-Hare" (Oster-Hase). In many parts of that country the custom prevails at or about Easter-tide of hiding in the garden, or in the house, eggs, which, the children are told, have been laid by the "Easter-hare." Another curious term met with in northeastern Germany is "hare-bread" (Hasenbrod). In Quedlinburg this name is given to bread (previously placed there intentionally by the parents) picked up by children when out walking with their parents or elders. In Lüneburg it is applied to dry bread given a hungry child with an exhortation to patience. In the first case, the little one is told that the hare has lost it, and in the second, that it has been taken away from him. The name "hare-bread" is also given to bread brought home by the parents or elders, when returning from a journey, the children being told that it has been taken away from the hare.

In the shadow-pictures made on the wall for the amusement of children the rabbit again appears, and the hare figures also in children's games.

Squirrel.

According to the belief of certain Indians of Vancouver Island, there once lived "a monstrous old woman with wolfish teeth, and finger-nails like claws." She used to entice away little children whom she afterwards ate up. One day a mother, who was about to lose her child thus, cried out to the spirits to save her child in any way or form. Her prayer was answered, and "The Great Good Father, looking down upon the Red Mother, pities her; lo! the child's soft brown skin turns to fur, and there slides from the ogress's grip, no child, but the happiest, liveliest, merriest little squirrel of all the West, — but bearing, as its descendants still bear, those four dark lines along the back that show where the cruel claws ploughed into it escaping" (396. III. 52–54).

Elsewhere, also, the squirrel is associated with childhood. Familiar is the passage in Longfellow's *Hiawatha*, where the hero speaks to the squirrel, who has helped him out of a great difficulty : —

> " Take the thanks of Hiawatha,
> And the name which now he gives you ;
> For hereafter, and forever,
> Boys shall call you *adjidaumo*,
> *Tail in air* the boys shall call you."

Seals.

Those noble and indefatigable missionaries, the Moravians, have more than once been harshly criticised in certain quarters, because, in their versions of the Bible, in the Eskimo language, they saw fit to substitute for some of the figurative expressions employed in our rendering, others more intelligible to the aborigines. In the New Testament Christ is termed the " Lamb of God," but since, in the Arctic home of the Innuit, shepherds and sheep are alike unknown, the translators, by a most felicitous turn of language, rendered the phrase by " little seal of God," a figure that appealed at once to every Eskimo, young and old, men and women ; for what sheep were to the dwellers on the Palestinian hillsides, seals are to this northernmost of human races. Rink tells us that the Eskimo mother " reserves the finest furs for her new-born infant," while the father keeps for it "the daintiest morsels from the chase," and, to make its eyes beautiful, limpid, and bright, he gives it seal's eyes to eat " (523. 37).

Fish.

Mrs. Bramhall tells us how in Japan the little children, playing about the temples, feed the pet fishes of the priests in the temple-lake. At the temple of the Mikado, at Kioto, she saw " six or eight little boys and girls . . . lying at full length on the bank of the pretty lake." The fishes were called up by whistling, and the children fed them by holding over the water their open hands full of crumbs (189. 65). Other inhabitants of the sea and the waters of the earth are brought into early relation with children.

Crabs and Crawfishes.

Among the Yeddavanad, of the Congo, a mother tells her children concerning three kinds of crabs: "Eat *kallali*, and you will become a clever man; eat *hullali*, and you will become as brave as a tiger; eat *mandalli*, and you will become master of the house" (449. 297).

In the Chippeway tale of the "Raccoon and the Crawfish," after the former, by pretending to be dead, has first attracted to him and then eaten all the crawfish, we are told: —

"While he was engaged with the broken limbs, a little female crawfish, carrying her infant sister on her back, came up seeking her relations. Finding they had all been devoured by the raccoon, she resolved not to survive the destruction of her kindred, but went boldly up to the enemy, and said: 'Here, Aissibun (Raccoon), you behold me and my little sister. We are all alone. You have eaten up our parents and all our friends. Eat us, too!' And she continued to say: 'Eat us, too! *Aissibun amoon, Aissibun amoon!*' The raccoon was ashamed. 'No!' said he, 'I have banqueted on the largest and fattest; 1 will not dishonour myself with such little prey.' At this moment, Manabozho [the culture-hero or demi-god of these Indians] happened to pass by. ' *Tyau,*' said he to the raccoon, 'thou art a thief and an unmerciful dog. Get thee up into trees, lest I change thee into one of these same worm-fish; for thou wast thyself a shell-fish originally, and 1 transformed thee.' Manabozho then took up the little supplicant crawfish and her infant sister, and cast them into the stream. 'There,' said he, 'you may dwell. Hide yourselves under the stones; and hereafter you shall be playthings for little children'" (440. 411, 412).

Games.

The imitation of animals, their movements, habits, and peculiarities in games and dances, also makes the child acquainted at an early age with these creatures.

In the section on "Bird and Beast," appropriately headed by the words of the good St. Francis of Assisi — "My brother, the hare, . . . my sisters, the doves," — Mr. Newell notices some of the children's games in which the actions, cries, etc., of animals are imitated. Such are "My Household," "Frog-Pond," "Bloody Tom," "Blue-birds and Yellow-birds," "Ducks Fly" (313. 115).

Doves.

Not at Dodona and in Arcadia alone has the dove been associated with religion, its oracles, its mysteries, and its symbolism. In the childhood of the world, according to the great Hebrew cosmologist, "the Spirit of God moved upon the face of the waters," and a later bard and seer of our own race reanimated the ancient figure of his predecessor in all its pristine strength, when in the story of Paradise lost and found again, he told how, at the beginning, the creative spirit

"Dove-like sat brooding o'er the vast abyss."

In the childhood of the race, it was a dove that bore to the few survivors of the great flood the branch of olive, token that the anger of Jahveh was abated, and that the waters no longer covered the whole earth. In the childhood of Christianity, when its founder was baptized of John in the river Jordan, "Lo, the heavens were opened unto Him, and the Spirit of God descended like a dove, and lighted on Him," — and the "Heavenly Dove" still beautifies the imagery of oratory and song, the art and symbolism of the great churches, its inheritors. In the childhood of man the individual, the dove has also found warm welcome. At the moment of the birth of St. Austrebertha (630–704 A.D.), as the quaint legend tells, "the chamber was filled with a heavenly odour, and a white dove, which hovered awhile above the house, flew into the chamber and settled on the head of the infant," and when Catherine of Racconigi (1486–1547 A.D.) was only five years old "a dove, white as snow, flew into her chamber and lighted on her shoulder"; strange to relate, however, the infant first took the bird for a tool of Satan, not a messenger of God. When St. Briocus of Cardigan, a Welsh saint of the sixth century, "was receiving the communion for the first time, a dove, white as

snow, settled on his head, and the abbot knew that the young boy
was a chosen vessel of honour" (191. 107, 108).

In a Swedish mother's hymn occurs the following beautiful
thought : —

> " There sitteth a dove so white and fair,
>   All on the lily spray,
> And she listeneth how to Jesus Christ
>   The little children pray.

> " Lightly she spreads her friendly wings,
>   And to Heaven's gate hath sped,
> And unto the Father in Heaven she bears
>   The prayers which the children have said.

> " And back she comes from Heaven's gate,
>   And brings, that dove so mild,
> From the Father in Heaven, who hears her speak,
>   A blessing on every child.

> " Then, children, lift up a pious prayer !
>   It hears whatever you say ;
> That heavenly dove so white and fair,
>   All on the lily spray " (379. 255).

The bird-messenger of childhood finds its analogue in the beliefs
of some primitive tribes that certain birds have access to the
spirit-land, and are the bearers of tidings from the departed.   Into
the same category fall the ancient practice of releasing a dove (or
some other winged creature) at the moment of death of a human
being, as a means of transport of his soul to the Elysian fields,
and the belief that the soul itself took its flight in the form and
semblance of a dove (509. 257).

The Haida Indians, of British Columbia, think that, " in the
land of light, children often transform themselves into bears,
seals, and birds," and wonderful tales are told of their adventures.

Hartley Coleridge found for the guardian angel of infancy, no
apter figure than that of the dove : —

> " Sweet infant, whom thy brooding parents love
> For what thou art, and what they hope to see thee,
> Unhallow'd sprites, and earth-born phantoms flee thee ;
> Thy soft simplicity, a hovering dove,

"That still keeps watch from blight and bane to free thee,
With its weak wings, in peaceful care outspread,
Fanning invisibly thy pillow'd head,
Strikes evil powers with reverential dread,
Beyond the sulphurous bolts of fabled Jove,
Or whatsoe'er of amulet or charm
Fond ignorance devised to save poor souls from harm."

Perhaps the sweetest touch of childhood in all Latin literature is that charming passage in Horace (*Carm.* Lib. III. 4) : —

" Me fabulosæ Vulture in Apulo,
Nutrices extra limen Apuliæ,
Ludo fatigatoque somno
Fronde nova puerum palumbes
Texere,"

which Milman thus translates : —

" The vagrant infant on Mount Vultur's side,
Beyond my childhood's nurse, Apulia's bounds,
By play fatigued and sleep,
Did the poetic doves
With young leaves cover."

The amativeness of the dove has lent much to the figurative language of that second golden age, that other Eden where love is over all. Shenstone, in his beautiful pastoral, says : —

" I have found out a gift for my fair ;
I have found where the wood-pigeons breed,"

and the "love of the turtle," "billing and cooing," are now transferred to human affection. Venus, the goddess of love, and the boy-god Cupid ride in a chariot drawn by doves, which birds were sacred to the sea-born child of Uranus. In the springtime, when "the voice of the turtle is heard in the land," then "a young man's fancy lightly turns to thoughts of love." If, from the sacred oaks of Dodona, to the first Greeks, the doves disclosed the oracles of Jove, so has "the moan of doves in immemorial elms" divulged to generation after generation of lovers the mission of his son of the bow and quiver.

Robin.

What the wood-pigeon was to Horace, the robin-redbreast has been to the children of old England. In the celebrated ballad of the "Children in the Wood," we are told that, after their murder by the cruel uncle,—

> "No burial these pretty babes
> Of any man receives,
> Till Robin Redbreast piously
> Did cover them with leaves."

The poet Thomson speaks of "the redbreast sacred to the household gods," and Gray, in a stanza which, since the edition of 1753, has been omitted from the *Elegy*, wrote:—

> "There scattered oft, the earliest of the year,
> By hands unseen are frequent violets found;
> The robin loves to build and warble there,
> And little footsteps lightly print the ground."

Dr. Robert Fletcher (447) has shown to what extent the redbreast figures in early English poetry, and the belief in his pious care for the dead and for children is found in Germany, Brittany, and other parts of the continent of Europe. In England the robin is the children's favourite bird, and rhymes and stories in his honour abound,—most famous is the nursery song, "Who killed Cock Robin?"

A sweet legend of the Greek Church tells us that "Our Lord used to feed the robins round his mother's door, when a boy; moreover, that the robin never left the sepulchre till the Resurrection, and, at the Ascension, joined in the angels' song." The popular imagination, before which the robin appears as "the pious bird with the scarlet breast," found no difficulty in assigning a cause for the colour of its plumage. One legend, current amongst Catholic peoples, has it that "the robin was commissioned by the Deity to carry a drop of water to the souls of unbaptized infants in hell, and its breast was singed in piercing the flames." In his poem *The Robin*, Whittier has versified the story from a Welsh source. An old Welsh lady thus reproves her grandson, who had tossed a stone at the robin hopping about in the apple-tree:—

" ' Nay ! ' said the grandmother ; ' have you not heard,
　My poor, bad boy ! of the fiery pit,
And how, drop by drop, this merciful bird
　Carries the water that quenches it ?

" ' He brings cool dew in his little bill,
　And lets it fall on the souls of sin ;
You can see the mark on his red breast still
　Of fires that scorch as he drops it in.' "

Another popular story, however, relates that when Christ was
on His way to Calvary, toiling beneath the burden of the cross,
the robin, in its kindness, plucked a thorn from the crown that
oppressed His brow, and the blood of the divine martyr dyed the
breast of the bird, which ever since has borne the insignia of its
charity. A variant of the same legend makes the thorn wound
the bird itself and its own blood dye its breast.

According to a curious legend of the Chippeway Indians, a stern
father once made his young son undergo the fasting necessary to
obtain a powerful guardian spirit. After bravely holding out for
nine days, he appealed to his father to allow him to give up, but
the latter would not hear of it, and by the eleventh day the boy
lay as one dead. At dawn the next morning, the father came
with the promised food. Looking through a hole in the lodge,
he saw that his son had painted his breast and shoulders as far
as he could reach with his hands. When he went into the lodge,
he saw him change into a beautiful bird and fly away. Such was
the origin of the first robin-redbreast (440. 210). Whittier, in
his poem, *How the Robin Came,* has turned the tale of the Red
Men into song. As the father gazed about him, he saw that on
the lodge-top —

" Sat a bird, unknown before,
　And, as if with human tongue,
　' Mourn me not,' it said, or sung ;
' I, a bird, am still your son,
　Happier than if hunter fleet,
　Or a brave before your feet
　Laying scalps in battle won.
　Friend of man, my song shall cheer
　Lodge and corn-land ; hovering near,
　To each wigwam I shall bring
　Tidings of the coming spring ;

Every child my voice shall know
In the moon of melting snow
When the maple's red bud swells,
And the wind-flower lifts its bells.
As their fond companion
Men shall henceforth own your son,
And my song shall testify
That of human kin am I.' "

Stork.

The *Lieblingsvogel* of German children is the stork, who, as
parents say, brings them their little brothers and sisters, and who
is remembered in countless folk and children's rhymes. The
mass of child-literature in which the stork figures is enormous.
Ploss has a good deal to say of this famous bird, and Carstens
has made it the subject of a brief special study, — "The
Stork as a Sacred Bird in Folk-Speech and Child-Song" (198).
The latter says: "It is with a sort of awe (*Ehrfurcht*) that
the child looks upon this sacred bird, when, returning with the
spring he settles down on the roof, throwing back his beak
and greeting the new home with a flap of his wings; or when,
standing now on one foot, now on the other, he looks so solemnly at things, that one would think he was devoutly medi-
tating over something or other; or, again, when, on his long
stilt-like legs, he gravely strides over the meadows. With great
attention we listened as children to the strange tales and songs
which related to this sacred bird, as our mother told them to us
and then added with solemn mien, 'where he keeps himself during
the winter is not really known,' or, 'he flies away over the *Leber-
meer,* whither no human being can follow.' 'Storks are enchanted
(*verwünscht*) men,' my mother used to say, and in corroboration
told the following story: 'Once upon a time a stork broke a leg.
The owner of the house upon which the stork had its nest, inter-
ested himself in the unfortunate creature, took care of it and
attended to it, and soon the broken leg was well again. Some
years later, it happened that the kind-hearted man, who was a
mariner, was riding at anchor near the North Sea Coast, and the
anchor stuck fast to the bottom, so that nothing remained but for
the sailor to dive into the depths of the sea. This he did, and

lo! he found the anchor clinging to a sunken church-steeple. He set it free, but, out of curiosity, went down still deeper, and far down below came to a magnificent place, the inhabitants of which made him heartily welcome. An old man addressed him and informed him that he had been the stork whose leg the sailor had once made well, and that the latter was now in the real home of the storks.'" Carstens compares this story with that of Frau Holle, whose servant the stork, who brings the little children out of the child-fountain of the Götterburg, would seem to be. In North Germany generally the storks are believed to be human beings in magical metamorphosis, and hence no harm must be done them. Between the household, upon whose roof the stork takes up his abode, and the family of the bird, a close relation is thought to subsist. If his young ones die, so will the children of the house; if no eggs are laid, no children will be born that year; if a stork is seen to light upon a house, it is regarded by the Wends of Lusatia as an indication that a child will be born there the same year; in Switzerland the peasant woman about to give birth to a child chants a brief appeal to the stork for aid. A great variety of domestic, meteorological, and other superstitions are connected with the bird, its actions, and mode of life. The common Low German name of the stork, *Adebar*, is said to mean "luck-bringer"; in Dutch, he is called *ole vaer*, "old father." After him the wood-anemone is called in Low German *Hannoterblume*, "stork's-flower." An interesting tale is "The Storks," in Hans Christian Andersen.

Bird-Language.

In the Golden Age, as the story runs, men were able to hold converse with the birds of the air and the beasts of the field, nor had a diversity of dialects yet sprung up among them. In Eden of old the whole world was of one tongue and one speech; nay more, men talked with the gods and with God. Many legends of primitive peoples there are telling how confusion first arose, — every continent has its Babel-myth, — and how men came at last to be unable to comprehend each other's speech. The Indians of Nova Scotia say that this occurred when Glūskap, the culture-hero of the Micmacs, after giving a parting banquet to all creatures of earth, sea, and air, "entered his canoe in the Basin of Minas, and, sailing westward in the moonlight, disappeared. Then the wolves, bears, and beavers, who had before been brothers, lost the gift of common language, and birds and beasts, hating one another, fled into the distant forests, where, to this day, the wolf howls and the loon utters its sad notes of woe" (418. 185).

The Mexican legend of the deluge states that the vessel in which were Coxcox, — the Mexican Noah, — and his wife, Xochiquetzal, stranded on a peak of Colhuacan. To them were born fifteen sons, who, however, all came into the world dumb, but a dove gave them fifteen tongues, and thence are descended the fifteen languages and tribes of Anahuac (509. 517).

In later ages, among other peoples, the knowledge of the forgotten speech of the lower creation was possessed by priests and seers alone, or ascribed to innocent little children, — some of the power and wisdom of the bygone Golden Age of the race is held yet to linger with the golden age of childhood. In the beautiful lines, —

> "O du Kindermund, o du Kindermund,
> Unbewuszter Weisheit froh,
> Vogelsprachekund, vogelsprachekund,
> Wie Salamo!"

the poet Rückert attributes to the child that knowledge of the language of birds, which the popular belief of the East made part of the lore of the wise King Solomon. Weil (547. 191) gives the Mussulman version of the original legend : —

"In him [Solomon] David placed implicit confidence, and was guided by him in the most difficult questions, for he had heard, in the night of his [Solomon's] birth, the angel Gabriel exclaim, 'Satan's dominion is drawing to its close, for this night a child is born, to whom Iblis and all his hosts, together with all his descendants, shall be subject. The earth, air, and water with all the creatures that live therein, shall be his servants. He shall be gifted with nine-tenths of all the wisdom and knowledge which Allah has granted to mankind, and understand not only the languages of men, but those also of beasts and birds.'" Some recollection of this appears in Ecclesiastes (x. 20), where we read, "For a bird of the air shall carry the voice, and that which hath wings shall tell the matter," and in our own familiar saying "a little bird told me," as well as in the Bulbul-hezar or talking bird of the *Arabian Nights*, and its imitation "the little green bird who tells everything," in the *Fairy Tales* of the Comtesse d'Aunoy. The interpretation of the cries of birds and animals into human speech has also some light thrown upon it from this source. Various aspects of this subject have been considered by Hopf (474), Swainson (539), Treichel (372), Brunk, Grimm (462). The use of certain birds as oracles by children is well known. A classical example is the question of the Low German child: —

> " Kukuk van Hewen,
>   Wi lank sall ik lewen ? '
> [" Cuckoo of Heaven,
>   How long am I to live ? "]

Of King Solomon we are told: "He conversed longest with the birds, both on account of their delicious language, which he knew as well as his own, as also for the beautiful proverbs that are current among them." The interpretation of the songs of the various birds is given as follows: —

The cock : " Ye thoughtless men, remember your Creator."
The dove: " All things pass away; Allah alone is eternal."
The eagle: "Let our life be ever so long, yet it must end in death."
The hoopoo : " He that shows no mercy, shall not obtain mercy."
The kata: " Whosoever can keep silence goes through life most securely."
The nightingale : " Contentment is the greatest happiness."
The peacock : " As thou judgest, so shalt thou be judged."
The pelican : " Blessed be Allah in Heaven and Earth."
The raven : " The farther from mankind, the pleasanter."
The swallow : " Do good, for you shall be rewarded hereafter.
The syrdak: " Turn to Allah, O ye sinners."
The turtle-dove : " It were better for many a creature had it never been born."

The King, it appears, chose the hoopoo and the cock for his companions, and appointed the doves to dwell in the temple which he was to erect (547. 200, 201). In fairy-tale and folk-lore bird-speech constantly appears. A good example is the story " Wat man warrn kann, wenn man blot de Vageln richti verstan deit," included by Klaus Groth in his *Quickborn*.

In the Micmac legend of the *Animal Tamers*, by collecting the "horns" of the various animals a youthful hero comes to understand their language (521. 347).

Longfellow, in his account of "Hiawatha's Childhood," has not forgotten to make use of the Indian tradition of the lore of language of bird and of beast possessed by the child : —

> "Then the little Hiawatha
> Learned of every bird its language,
> Learned their names and all their secrets,
> How they built their nests in summer,
> Where they hid themselves in winter,
> Talked with them whene'er he met them,
> Called them 'Hiawatha's Chickens.'

> "Of all the beasts he learned the language,
> Learned their names and all their secrets,
> How the beavers built their lodges,
> Where the squirrels hid their acorns,
> How the reindeer ran so swiftly,
> Why the rabbit was so timid,
> Talked with them whene'er he met them,
> Called them 'Hiawatha's Brothers.'"

In the Middle Ages the understanding of the language of birds, their *Latin*, as it was called, ranked as the highest achievement of human learning, the goal of wisdom and knowledge, and the thousand rhyming questions asked of birds by children to-day are evidence of a time when communication with them was deemed possible. Some remembrance of this also lingers in not a few of the lullabies and nursery-songs of a type corresponding to the following from Schleswig-Holstein : —

> "Hör mal, lütje Kind
> Wo düt lütje Vagel singt
> Baben in de Hai!
> Loop, lüt Kind, un hal mi dat lüt Ei."

Among the child-loving Eskimo we find many tales in which children and animals are associated; very common are stories of children metamorphosed into birds and beasts. Turner has obtained several legends of this sort from the Eskimo of the Ungava district in Labrador. In one of these, wolves are the gaunt and hungry children of a woman who had not wherewithal to feed her numerous progeny, and so they were turned into ravening beasts of prey; in another the raven and the loon were children, whom their father sought to paint, and the loon's spots are evidence of the attempt to this day; in a third the sea-pigeons or guillemots are children who were changed into these birds for having scared away some seals. The prettiest story, however, is that of the origin of the swallows: Once there were some children who were wonderfully wise, so wise indeed that they came to be called *zulugagnak*, "like the raven," a bird that knows the past and the future. One day they were playing on the edge of a cliff near the village, and building toy-houses, when they were changed into birds. They did not forget their childish occupation, however, and, even to this day, the swallows come to the cliff to build their nests or houses of mud, — " even the raven does not molest them, and Eskimo children love to watch them " (544. 262, 263). From time immemorial have the life and actions of the brute creation been associated with the first steps of education and learning in the child.

CHAPTER XIII.

CHILD-LIFE AND EDUCATION IN GENERAL.

The mother's heart is the child's school-room. — *Henry Ward Beecher.*

The father is known from the child. — *German Proverb.*

> Learn young, learn fair,
> Learn auld, learn mair. — *Scotch Proverb.*

We bend the tree when it is young. — *Bulgarian Proverb.*

Fools and bairns should na see things half done. — *Scotch Proverb.*

No one is born master. — *Italian Proverb.*

Mother as Teacher.

Nihil est in intellectu quod non prius in sensu is a favourite dictum of philosophy; primitive peoples might, perhaps, be credited with a somewhat different crystallization of thought: *nihil est in puero quod non prius in parenti*, "nothing is in the child which was not before in the parent," for belief in prenatal influence of parent upon child is widely prevalent. The following remarks, which were written of the semi-civilized peoples of Annam and Tonquin, may stand, with suitable change of terms, for very many barbarous and savage races: —

"The education of the children begins even before they come into the world. The prospective mother is at once submitted to a kind of material and moral *régime* sanctioned by custom. Gross viands are removed from her table, and her slightest movements are regarded that they may be regular and majestic. She is expected to listen to the reading of good authors, to music and moral chants, and to attend learned societies, in order that she may fortify her mind by amusements of an elevated character. And she endeavours, by such discipline, to assure to the child

192

whom she is about to bring into the world, intelligence, docility, and fitness for the duties imposed by social life" (518. XXXI. 629).

Among primitive peoples these ceremonies, dietings, doctorings, tabooings, number legion, as may be read in Ploss and Zmigrodzki.

The influence of the mother upon her child, beginning long before birth, continued in some parts of the world until long after puberty. The Spartan mothers even preserved "a power over their sons when arrived at manhood," and at the puberty-dance, by which the Australian leaves childhood behind to enter upon man's estate, his significant cry is: "My mother sees me no more!" (398. 153). Among the Chinese, "at the ceremony of going out of childhood, the passage from boyhood into manhood, the goddess of children 'Mother,' ceases to have the superintendence of the boy or girl, and the individual comes under the government of the gods in general."

That women are teachers born, even the most uncultured of human races have not failed to recognize, and the folk-faith in their ministrations is world-wide and world-old; for, as Mrs. Browning tells us:—

> " Women know
> The way to rear up children (to be just);
> They know a simple, merry, tender knack
> Of tying sashes, fitting baby-shoes,
> And stringing pretty words that make no sense,
> And kissing full sense into empty words;
> Which things are corals to cut life upon,
> Although such trifles."

Intellectually, as well as physically,—as the etymology of the name seems to indicate,—the mother is the "former" of her child. As Henry Ward Beecher has well said, "the mother's heart is the child's school-room." Well might the Egyptian mother-goddess say (167. 261): "I am the mother who shaped thy beauties, who suckled thee with milk; I give thee with my milk festal things, that penetrate thy limbs with life, strength, and youth; I make thee to become the great ruler of Egypt, lord of the space which the sun circles round." In the land of the Pharaohs they knew in some dim fashion that "the hand that rocks the cradle is the hand that rules the world."

The extensive *rôle* of the mother, as a teacher of the practical

o

arts of life, may be seen from the book of Professor Mason (113). Language, religion, the social arts, house-building, skin-dressing, weaving, spinning, animal-domestication, agriculture, are, with divers primitive peoples, since they have in great part originated with her, or been promoted chiefly by her efforts, left to woman as teacher and instructor, and well has the mother done her work all over the globe.

The function of the mother as priestess — for woman has been the preserver, as, to so large an extent, she has been the creator, of religion — has been exercised age after age, and among people after people. Henry Ward Beecher has said: "Every mother is a priestess ordained by God Himself," and Professor Mason enlarges the same thought: "Scarcely has the infant mind begun to think, ere this perpetual priestess lights the fires of reverence and keeps them ever burning, like a faithful vestal" (112. 12).

Though women and mothers have often been excluded from the public or the secret ceremonials and observations of religion, the household in primitive and in modern times has been the temple, of whose *penetralia* they alone have been the ministers.

Imitation.

Tarde, in his monograph on the "Laws of Imitation," has shown the great influence exerted among peoples of all races, of all grades and forms of culture, by imitation, conscious or unconscious, — a factor of the highest importance even at the present day and among those communities of men most advanced and progressive. Speaking a little too broadly, perhaps, he says (541. 15): —

"All the resemblances, of social origin, noticed in the social world are the direct or indirect result of imitation in all its forms, — custom, fashion, sympathy, obedience, instruction, education, naïve or deliberate imitation. Hence the excellence of that modern method which explains doctrines or institutions by their history. This tendency can only be generalized. Great inventors and great geniuses do sometimes stumble upon the same thing together, but these coincidences are very rare. And when they do really occur, they always have their origin in a fund of common instruction upon which, independent of one another, the two authors of the same invention have drawn; and this fund consists of a mass of traditions of the past, of experiments, rude or more or less arranged, and transmitted imitatively by language, the great vehicle of all imitations."

In her interesting article on "Imitation in Children," Miss Haskell observes: "That the imitative faculty is what makes the human being educable, that it is what has made progressive civilization possible, has always been known by philosophical educators. The energy of the child must pass from potentiality to actuality, and it does so by the path of *imitation* because this path offers the least resistance or the greatest attraction, or perhaps because there is no other road. Whatever new and striking things he sees in the movements or condition of objects about him, provided he already has the experience necessary to apperceive this particular thing, he imitates" (260. 31).

In the pedagogy of primitive peoples imitation has an extensive *rôle* to play. Of the Twana Indians, of the State of Washington, Rev. Mr. Eells observes: "Children are taught continually, from youth until grown, to mimic the occupations of their elders." They have games of ball, jumping and running races, and formerly "the boys played at shooting with bows and arrows at a mark, and with spears, throwing at a mark, with an equal number of children on each side, and sometimes the older ones joined in." Now, however, "the boys mimic their seniors in the noise and singing and gambling, but without the gambling." The girls play with dolls, and sometimes "the girls and boys both play in canoes, and stand on half of a small log, six feet long and a foot wide, and paddle around in the water with a small stick an inch in thickness; and, in fact, play at most things which they see their seniors do, both whites and Indians" (437. 90, 91).

Concerning the Seminoles of Florida, we are told: "The baby, well into the world, learns very quickly that he is to make his own way through it as best he may. His mother is prompt to nourish him, and solicitous in her care for him if he falls ill; but, as far as possible, she goes her own way and leaves the little fellow to go his." Very early in life the child learns to help and to imitate its elders. "No small amount," Mr. MacCauley tells us, "of the labour in a Seminole household is done by children, even as young as four years of age. They can stir the soup while it is boiling; they can aid in kneading the dough for bread; they can wash the 'koonti' root, and even pound it; they can watch and replenish the fire; they contribute in this and many other small ways to the necessary work of the home" (496. 497, 498).

Of the Indians of British Guiana, Mr. im Thurn reports: " As soon as the children can run about, they are left almost to themselves; or, rather, they begin to mimic their parents. As with the adults, so with the children. Just as the grown-up woman works incessantly, while the men alternately idle and hunt, so the boys run wild, playing not such concerted games as in other parts of the world more usually form child's play, but only with mimic bows and arrows; but the girls, as soon as they can walk, begin to help the older women. Even the youngest girl can peel a few cassava roots, watch a pot on the fire, or collect and carry home a few sticks of firewood. The games of the boy are all such as train him to fish and hunt when he grows up; the girl's occupations teach her woman's work " (477. 219). The children imitate their elders in other ways also, for in nearly every Indian house are to be seen toy vessels of clay ; for " while the Indian women of Guiana are shaping the clay, their children, imitating them, make small pots and goglets " (477. 298). And in like manner have been born, no doubt, among other peoples, some of the strange freaks of art which puzzle the *connoisseurs* in the museums of Europe and America.

Mr. Powers, speaking of the domestic economy of the Achomâwi Indians of California, says: " An Achomâwi mother seldom teaches her daughters any of the arts of barbaric housekeeping before their marriage. They learn them by imitation and experiment after they grow old enough to perceive the necessity thereof" (519. 271). This peculiar neglect, however, is not entirely absent from our modern civilization, for until very recently no subject has been so utterly overlooked as the proper training of young girls for their future duties as mothers and housekeepers. The Achomâwi, curiously enough, have the following custom, which helps, no doubt, the wife whose education has been so imperfect: " The parents are expected to establish a young couple in their lodge, provide them with the needful basketry, and furnish them with cooked food for some months, which indulgent parents sometimes continue for a year or even longer; so that the young people have a more real honeymoon than is vouchsafed to most civilized people."

Among the Battas of Sumatra, " It is one of the morning duties of women and girls, even down to children of four and five years old, to bring drinking-water in the *gargitis*, a water-vessel made of a thick stalk of bamboo. The size and strength of growing girls are generally measured by the number of *gargitis* they can carry " (518. XXII. 110).

Of the Kaffir children Theal informs us : " At a very early age they commence trials of skill against each other in throwing knobbed sticks and imitation assegais. They may often be seen enjoying this exercise in little groups, those of the same age keeping together, for there is no greater tyrant in the world than a big Kaffir boy over his younger fellows; when above nine or ten years old they practise sham-fighting with sticks; an imitation hunt is another of their boyish diversions " (543. 220).

Among the Apaches, as we learn from Reclus: " The child remains with its mother until it can pluck certain fruits for itself, and has caught a rat by its own unaided efforts. After this exploit, it goes and comes as it lists, is free and independent, master of its civil and political rights, and soon lost in the main body of the horde" (523. 131).

On the Andaman Islands, " little boys hunt out swarms of bees in the woods and drive them away by fire. They are also expected regularly to collect wood." From their tenth year they are " accustomed to use little bows and arrows, and often attain great skill in shooting." The girls " seek among the coral-reefs and in the swamps to catch little fish in hand-nets." The Solomon Islands boy, as soon as he can walk a little, goes along with his elders to hunt and fish (326. I. 6). Among the Somali, of northeastern Africa, the boys are given small spears when ten or twelve years old and are out guarding the milk-camels (481 (1891). 163).

Of the Eskimo of Baffin Land, Dr. Boas tells us that the children, " when about twelve years old, begin to help their parents; the girls sewing and preparing skins, the boys accompanying their fathers in hunting expeditions " (402. 566). Mr. Powers records that he has seen a Wailakki Indian boy of four-

teen "run a rabbit to cover in ten minutes, split a stick fine at
one end, thrust it down the hole, twist it into its scut, and pull
it out alive" (519. 118).

Among the games and amusements of the Andamanese children, of whom he says "though not borrowed from aliens, their
pastimes, in many instances, bear close resemblance to those in
vogue among children in this and other lands; notably is this the
case with regard to those known to us as blind-man's buff, leap-
frog, and hide-and-seek," — Mr. Man enumerates the following:
mock pig-hunting (played after dark); *mock turtle-catching* (played
in the sea); going after the Evil Spirit of the Woods; swinging
by means of long stout creepers; swimming-races (sometimes
canoe-races); pushing their way with rapidity through the jungle;
throwing objects upwards, or skimming through the air; playing
at "duck-and-drakes"; shooting at moving objects; wrestling on
the sand; hunting small crabs and fish and indulging in sham
banquets, comparable to the "doll's feast" with us; making miniature canoes and floating them about in the water (498. 165).

Education of Boys and Girls.

With the Dakota Indians, according to Mr. Riggs, the grandfather and grandmother are often the principal teachers of the
child. Under the care of the father and grandfather the boy
learns to shoot, hunt, and fish, is told tales of war and daring
exploits, and "when he is fifteen or sixteen joins the first war-
party and comes back with an eagle feather in his head, if he is
not killed and scalped by the enemy." Among the amusements
he indulges in are foot-races, horse-racing, ball-playing, etc. Another branch of his education is thus described: "In the long
winter evenings, while the fire burns brightly in the centre of
the lodge, and the men are gathered in to smoke, he hears the
folk-lore and legends of his people from the lips of the older
men. He learns to sing the love-songs and the war-songs of the
generations gone by. There is no new path for him to tread, but
he follows in the old ways. He becomes a Dakota of the Dakota.
His armour is consecrated by sacrifices and offerings and vows.
He sacrifices and prays to the stone god, and learns to hold up
the pipe to the so-called Great Spirit. He is killed and made

alive again, and thus is initiated into the mysteries and promises of the Mystery Dance. He becomes a successful hunter and warrior, and what he does not know is not worth knowing for a Dakota. His education is finished. If he has not already done it, he can now demand the hand of one of the beautiful maidens of the village" (524. 209, 210).

Under the care and oversight of the mother and grandmother the girl is taught the elements of household economy, industrial art, and agriculture. Mr. Riggs thus outlines the early education of woman among these Indians: "She plays with her 'made child,' or doll, just as children in other lands do. Very soon she learns to take care of the baby; to watch over it in the lodge, or carry it on her back while the mother is away for wood or dressing buffalo-robes. Little girl as she is, she is sent to the brook or lake for water. She has her little work-bag with awl and sinew, and learns to make small moccasins as her mother makes large ones. Sometimes she goes with her mother to the wood and brings home her little bundle of sticks. When the camp moves, she has her small pack as her mother carries the large one, and this pack is sure to grow larger as her years increase. When the corn is planting, the little girl has her part to perform. If she cannot use the hoe yet, she can at least gather off the old corn-stalks. Then the garden is to be watched while the god-given maize is growing. And when the harvesting comes, the little girl is glad for the corn-roasting." And so her young life runs on. She learns bead-work and ornamenting with porcupine quills, embroidering with ribbons, painting, and all the arts of personal adornment, which serve as attractions to the other sex. When she marries, her lot and her life (Mr. Riggs says) are hard, for woman is much less than man with these Dakotas (524. 210).

More details of girl-life among savage and primitive peoples are to be found in the pages of Professor Mason (113. 207–211). In America, the education varied from what the little girl could pick up at her mother's side between her third and thirteenth years, to the more elaborate system of instruction in ancient Mexico, where, "annexed to the temples were large buildings used as seminaries for girls, a sort of aboriginal Wellesley or Vassar" (113 208).

Games and Plays.

In the multifarious games of children, echoes, imitations, re-renderings of the sober life of their elders and of their ancestors of the long ago, recur again and again. The numerous love games, which Mr. Newell (313. 39–62) and Miss Gomme (243) enumerate, such as "Knights of Spain," "Three kings," "Here comes a Duke a-roving," "Tread, tread the Green Grass," "I'll give to you a Paper of Pins," "There she stands a lovely Creature," "Green Grow the Rushes, O!" "The Widow with Daughters to marry," "Philander's March," "Marriage," etc., corresponding to many others all over the globe, evidence the social instincts of childhood as well as the imitative tendencies of youth.

Under "Playing at Work" (313. 80–92), Mr. Newell has classed a large number of children's games and songs, some of which now find their representatives in the kindergarten, this education of the child by itself having been so modified as to form part of the infantile curriculum of study. Among such games are: "Threading the Needle," "Draw a Bucket of Water," "Here I Brew and here I Bake," "Here we come gathering Nuts of May," "When I was a Shoemaker," "Do, do, pity my Case," "As we go round the Mulberry Bush," "Who'll be the Binder?" "Oats, Pease, Beans, and Barley grows." Mr. Newell includes in this category, also, that well-known dance, the "Virginia Reel," which he interprets as an imitation of weaving, something akin to the "Hemp-dressers' Dance," of the time of George III., in England.

In a recent interesting and valuable essay, "Education by Plays and Games," by Mr. G. E. Johnson, of Clark University, — an effort "to present somewhat more correctly than has been done before, the educational value of play, and to suggest some practical applications to the work of education in the grades above the kindergarten," — we have presented to us a list of some five hundred games, classified according to their value for advancing mental or physical education, for cultivating and strengthening the various faculties of mind and body. These games have also been arranged by Mr. Johnson, into such classes and divisions as might be held to correspond to the needs and necessities of the pupils in each of the eight grades above the kindergarten. Of the educational value of play and of "playing at work," there can be no doubt in the mind of any one at all acquainted with the history of the individual and the history of the race. As Mr. Johnson justly observes (269. 100): "The field of the study of play is very wide; the plays are well-nigh infinite, and as varied as life itself. No one can estimate the value of them. Given right toys and surroundings, the young child has an almost perfect school. It is marvellous how well he learns. Preyer does not overestimate the facts when he says the child in the first three or four years of his life learns as much as the student in his entire university course. In the making of mud pies and doll dresses, sand-pile farms and miniature roads, tiny dams and water-wheels, whittled-out boats, sleds, dog-harnesses, and a thousand and one other things, the child receives an accumulation of facts, a skill of hand, a trueness of eye, a power of attention and quickness of perception; and in flying kites, catching trout, in pressing leaves and gathering stones, in collecting stamps, and eggs, and butterflies, a culture also, seldom appreciated by the parent or teacher."

Upon the banner of the youthful hosts might well be inscribed *in hoc ludo vincemus.* Yet there is danger that the play-theory may be carried to excess. Mr. James L. Hughes, discussing "The Educational Value of Play and the Recent Play-Movement in Germany," remarks: "The Germans had the philosophy of play, the English had an intuitive love of play, and love is a greater impelling force than philosophy. English young men never played in order to expand their lungs, to increase their circulation, to develop their muscles in power and agility, to improve their figures, to add grace to their bearing, to awaken and refine their intellectual powers, or to make them manly, courageous, and chivalrous. They played enthusiastically for the mere love of play, and all these, and other advantages resulted from their play" (265. 328).

Swimming is an art soon learned by the children of some primitive races. Mr. Man says of the Andaman Islanders: "With the exception of some of the *ē·rem-tá·ga-* (inlanders), a knowledge of the art of swimming is common to members of both sexes; the *children* even, learning almost as soon as they can run, speedily acquire great proficiency" (498. 47).

Language.

With some primitive peoples the ideas as to language-study are pretty much on a par with those prevalent in Europe at a date not so very remote from the present. Of the Káto Pomo Indians of California, Mr. Powers remarks: "Like the Kai Pomo, their northern neighbours, they forbid their squaws from studying languages — which is about the only accomplishment possible to them save dancing — principally, it is believed, in order to prevent them from gadding about and forming acquaintances in neighbouring valleys, for there is small virtue among the unmarried of either sex. But the men pay considerable attention to linguistic studies, and there is seldom one who cannot speak most of the Pomo dialects within a day's journey of his ancestral valley. The chiefs, especially, devote no little care to the training of their sons as polyglot diplomatists; and Robert White affirms that they frequently send them to reside several months with the chiefs of contiguous valleys to acquire the dialects there in vogue" (519. 150).

Nevertheless, as Professor Mason observes, among primitive races, woman's share in the "invention, dissemination, conservation, and metamorphosis of language" has been very great, and she has been *par excellence* the teacher of language, as indeed she is to-day in our schools when expression and *savoir faire* in speech, rather than deep philological learning and dry grammatical analysis, have been the object of instruction.

Geography.

Much has been said and written about the wonderful knowledge of geography and topography possessed by the Indian of America, and by other primitive peoples as well. The following passage from Mr. Powers' account of the natives of California serves to explain some of this (519. 109): —

"Besides the coyote-stories with which gifted squaws amuse their children, and which are common throughout this region, there prevails among the Mattoal a custom which might almost be dignified with the name of geographical study. In the first place, it is necessary to premise that the boundaries of all the tribes on Humboldt Bay, Eel River, Van Dusen's Fork, and in fact everywhere, are marked with the greatest precision, being defined by certain creeks, cañons, bowlders, conspicuous trees, springs, etc., each one of which objects has its own individual name. It is perilous for an Indian to be found outside of his tribal boundaries, wherefore it stands him well in hand to make himself acquainted with the same early in life. Accordingly, the squaws teach these things to their children in a kind of sing-song not greatly unlike that which was the national *furore* some time ago in rural singing-schools, wherein they melodiously chanted such pleasing items of information as this: 'California, Sacramento, on the Sacramento River.' Over and over, time and again, they rehearse all these bowlders, etc., describing each minutely and by name, with its surroundings. Then when the children are old enough, they take them around to beat the bounds like Bumble the Beadle; and so wonderful is the Indian memory naturally, and so faithful has been their instruction, that the little shavers generally recognize the objects from the descriptions of them previously given by their mothers. If an Indian knows but little of this great world more than pertains to boundary bush and bowlder, he knows his own small fighting-ground infinitely better than any topographical engineer can learn it."

Mr. Powers' reference to "beating the bounds like Bumble the Beadle" is an apt one. Mr. Frederick Sessions has selected as one of his *Folk-Lore Topics* the subject of "Beating the Bounds" (352), and in his little pamphlet gives us much interesting information concerning the part played by children in these performances. The author tells us: "One of the earliest of my childish pleasures was seeing the Mayor and Corporation, preceded by Sword-bearer, Beadles, and Blue Coat School boys, going in procession from one city boundary-stone to another, across the meadows and the river, or over hedges and gardens, or anything else to which the perambulated border-line took them. They were followed along the route by throngs of holiday makers. Many of the crowd, and all the Blue boys, were provided with willow-wands, *peeled*, if I remember rightly, with which each boundary mark was well flogged. The youngest boys were bumped against the 'city stones.'" In the little town of Charlbury in Oxfordshire, "the perambulations seem to have been performed mostly by boys, accompanied by one or more of their seniors." At Houghton, a village near St. Ives in Huntingdonshire: "The bounds are still beaten triennially. They are here marked by holes in some places, and by stones or trees in others. The procession starts at one of the holes. Each new villager present is instructed in the position of this corner of the boundary by having his head forcibly thrust into the hole, while he has to repeat a sort of mumbo-jumbo prayer, and receives three whacks with a shovel. He pays a shilling for his 'footing' (boys only pay sixpence), and then the forty or fifty villagers march off to the opposite corner and repeat the process, except the monetary part, and regale themselves with bread and cheese and beer, paid for by the farmers who now occupy any portion of the old common lands."

In Russia, before the modern system of land-registration came into vogue, "all the boys of adjoining Cossack village communes were 'collected and driven like flocks of sheep to the frontier, whipped at each boundary-stone, and if, in after years two whipped lads, grown into men, disputed as to the precise spot at which they had been castigated, then the oldest inhabitant carrying a sacred picture from the church, led the perambulations, and acted as arbitrator."

Here also ought to be mentioned perhaps, as somewhat akin and reminiscent of like practices among primitive peoples, "the *blason populaire* (as it is neatly called in French), in which the inhabitants of each district or city are nicely ticketed off and distinguished by means of certain abnormalities of feature or form, or certain mental peculiarities attributed to them" (204. 19). In parts of Hungary and Transylvania a somewhat similar practice is in vogue (392 (1892). 128).

Story-Telling.

Some Indian children have almost the advantages of the modern home in the way of story-telling. Clark informs us (420. 109) : —

"Some tribes have regular story-tellers, men who have devoted a great deal of time to learning the myths and stories of their people, and who possess, in addition to a good memory, a vivid imagination. The mother sends for one of these, and, having prepared a feast for him, she and her little 'brood,' who are curled up near her, await the fairy stories of the dreamer, who, after his feast and smoke, entertains them for hours. Many of these fanciful sketches or visions are interesting and beautiful in their rich imagery, and have been at times given erroneous positions in ethnological data."

Knortz refers in glowing terms to the *adisoke-winini*, or " storyteller" of the Chippeway Indians, those gifted men, who entertain their fellows with the tales and legends of the race, and who are not mere reciters, but often poets and transformers as well (*Skizzen*, 294).

So, too, among the Andaman Islanders, " certain mythic legends are related to the young by *ôkopai·ads* [shamans], parents, and others, which refer to the supposed adventures or history of remote ancestors, and though the recital not unfrequently evokes much mirth, they are none the less accepted as veracious " (498. 95).

Morals.

Among some of the native tribes of California we meet with *i-wa-mūsp*, or " men-women" (519. 132). Among the Yuki, for example, there were men who dressed and acted like women, and " devoted themselves to the instruction of the young by the narration of legends and moral tales." Some of these, Mr. Powers informs us, " have been known to shut themselves up in the assembly-hall for the space of a month, with brief intermissions, living the life of a hermit, and spending the whole time in rehearsing the tribal-history in a sing-song monotone to all who chose to listen."

Somewhat similar, without the hermit-life, appear to be the functions of the orators and " prophets " of the Miwok and the peace-chiefs, or " shell-men," of the Pomo (519. 157, 352).

Of the Indians of the Pueblo of Tehua, Mr. Lummis, in his entertaining volume of fairy-tales, says: " There is no duty to which a Pueblo child is trained in which he has to be content with the bare command, 'Do thus'; for each he learns a fairytale designed to explain how people first came to know that it was right to do thus, and detailing the sad results which befell those who did otherwise." The old men appear to be the story-tellers, and their tales are told in a sort of blank verse (302. 5).

Mr. Grinnell, in his excellent book about the Blackfeet, — one of the best books ever written about the Indians, — gives some interesting details of child-life. Children are never whipped, and "are instructed in manners as well as in other more general and more important matters." Among other methods of instruction we find that "men would make long speeches to groups of boys playing in the camps, telling them what they ought to do to be successful in life," etc. (464. 188–191).

Of the Delaware Indians we are told that "when a mere boy the Indian lad would be permitted to sit in the village council-house, and hear the assembled wisdom of the village or his tribe discuss the affairs of state and expound the meaning of the *keekq'* (beads composing the wampum belts). . . . In this way he early acquired maturity of thought, and was taught the traditions of his people, and the course of conduct calculated to win him the praise of his fellows" (516. 43). This reminds us of the Roman senator who had his child set upon his knee during the session of that great legislative and deliberative body.

Playthings and Dolls.

As Professor Mason has pointed out, the cradle is often the "play-house" of the child, and is decked out to that end in a hundred ways (306. 162). Of the Sioux cradle, Catlin says : —

"A broad hoop of elastic wood passes around in front of the child's face to protect it in case of a fall, from the front of which is suspended a little toy of exquisite embroidery for the child to handle and amuse itself with. To this and other little trinkets hanging in front of it, there are attached many little tinselled and tinkling things of the brightest colours to amuse both the eyes and the ears of the child. While travelling on horseback, the arms of the child are fastened under the bandages, so as not to be endangered if the cradle falls, and when at rest they are generally taken out, allowing the infant to reach and amuse itself with the little toys and trinkets that are placed before it and within its reach" (306. 202). In like manner are "playthings of various kinds" hung to the awning of the birch-bark cradles found in the Yukon region of Alaska. Of the Nez Percé, we read: "To the hood are attached medicine-bags, bits of shell, haliotis perhaps, and the whole artistic genius of the mother is in play to adorn her offspring." The old chronicler Lafiteau observed of the Indians of New France: "They put over that half-circle [at the top of the cradle] little bracelets of porcelain and other little trifles that the Latins call *crepundia*, which serve as an ornament and as playthings to divert the child" (306. 167, 187, 207).

And so is it elsewhere in the world. Some of the beginnings of art in the race are due to the mother's instinctive attempts to please the eyes and busy the hands of her tender offspring. The children of primitive peoples have their dolls and playthings as do those of higher races. In an article descriptive of the games and amusements of the Ute Indians, we read: "The boy remains under maternal care until he is old enough to learn to shoot and engage in manly sports and enjoyments. Indian children play, laugh, cry, and act like white children, and make their own play-things from which they derive as much enjoyment as white children" (480. IV. 238).

Of the Seminole Indians of Florida, Mr. MacCauley says that among the children's games are skipping and dancing, leap-frog, teetotums, building a merry-go-round, carrying a small make-believe rifle of stick, etc. They also "sit around a small piece of land, and, sticking blades of grass into the ground, name it a 'corn-field,'" and "the boys kill small birds in the bush with their bows and arrows, and call it 'turkey-hunting.'" Moreover, they "have also dolls (bundles of rags, sticks with bits of cloth wrapped around them, etc.), and build houses for them which they call 'camps'" (496. 506).

Of the Indians of the western plains, Colonel Dodge says: "The little girls are very fond of dolls, which their mothers make and dress with considerable skill and taste. Their baby houses are miniature teepees, and they spend as much time and take as much pleasure in such play as white girls" (432. 190).

Dr. Boas tells us concerning the Eskimo of Baffin Land: "Young children are always carried in their mothers' hoods, but when about a year and a half old they are allowed to play on the bed, and are only carried by their mothers when they get too mis-

chievous." The same authority also says: "Young children play
with toys, sledges, kayaks, boats, bow and arrows, and dolls.
The last are made in the same way by all the tribes, a wooden
body being clothed with scraps of deerskin cut in the same way
as the clothing of the men" (402. 568, 571). Mr. Murdoch has
described at some length the dolls and toys of the Point Barrow
Eskimo. He remarks that "though several dolls and various
suits of miniature clothing were made and brought over for sale,
they do not appear to be popular with the little girls." He did
not see a single girl playing with a doll, and thinks the articles
collected may have been made rather for sale than otherwise.
Of the boys, Mr. Murdoch says: "As soon as a boy is able to
walk, his father makes him a little bow suited to his strength,
with blunt arrows, with which he plays with the other boys,
shooting at marks — for instance the fetal reindeer brought home
from the spring hunt — till he is old enough to shoot small birds
and lemmings" (514. 380, 383).

   In a recent extensive and elaborately illustrated article, Dr.
J. W. Fewkes has described the dolls of the Tusayan Indians
(one of the Pueblo tribes). Of the *tihus*, or carved wooden dolls,
the author says (226. 45): "These images are commonly men
tioned by American visitors to the Tusayan Pueblos as idols, but
there is abundant evidence to show that they are at present used
simply as children's playthings, which are made for that purpose
and given to the girls with that thought in mind." Attention is
called to the difficulty of drawing the line between a doll and an
idol among primitive peoples, the connection of dolls with religion, psychological evidence of which lingers with us to-day in the
persistent folk-etymology which connects *doll* with *idol*. The following remarks of Dr. Fewkes are significant: "These figurines
[generally images of deities or mythological personages carved
in true archaic fashion] are generally made by participants in
the *Ni-mán-kā-tci-nā*, and are presented to the children in July
or August at the time of the celebration of the farewell of the
Kā-tci'-nas [supernatural intercessors between men and gods].
It is not rare to see the little girls after the presentation carrying
the dolls about on their backs wrapped in their blankets in the
same manner in which babies are carried by their mothers or
sisters. Those dolls which are more elaborately made are gen-

erally hung up as ornaments in the rooms, but never, so far as I have investigated the subject, are they worshipped. The readiness with which they are sold for a proper remuneration shows that they are not regarded as objects of reverence." But, as Dr. Fewkes himself adds, "It by no means follows that they may not be copies of images which have been worshipped, although they now have come to have a strictly secular use." Among some peoples, perhaps, the dolls, images of deities of the past, or even of the present, may have been used to impart the fundamentals of theology and miracle-story, and the play-house of the children may have been at times a sort of religious kindergarten of a primitive type. Worthy of note in this connection is the statement of Castrén that "the Finns manufacture a kind of dolls, or *paras*, out of a child's cap filled with tow and stuck at the end of a rod. The fetich thus made is carried nine times round the church, with the cry 'synny para' (Para be born) repeated every time to induce a *hal'tia* — that is to say, a spirit — to enter into it" (388. 108).

A glance into *St. Nicholas,* or at the returns to the syllabus on dolls sent out by President Hall, is sufficient to indicate the far-reaching associations of the subject, while the doll-congress of St. Petersburg has had its imitators both in Europe and America. A bibliography of doll-poems, doll-descriptions, doll-parties, doll-funerals, and the like would be a welcome addition to the literature of dolls, while a doll-museum of extended scope would be at once entertaining and of great scientific value.

The familiar phrase " to cry for the moon " corresponds to the French "prendre la lune avec ses dents." In illustration of this proverbial expression, which Rabelais used in the form *Je ne suis point clerc pour prendre la lune avec les dents*, Loubens tells the amusing story of a servant who, when upbraided by the parents for not giving to a child what it wanted and for which it had been long crying, answered: " You must give it him yourself. A quarter-of-an-hour ago, he saw the moon at the bottom of a bucket of water, and wants me to give it him. That's all." (*Prov. et locut. franç.*, p. 225.)

To-day children cry for the moon in vain, but 'twas not ever thus. In payment for the church, which King Olaf wanted to have built, — a task impossible, the saint thought, — the giant

P

demanded "the sun and moon, or St. Olaf himself." Soon the building was almost completed, and St. Olaf was in great perplexity at the unexpected progress of the work. As he was wandering about "he heard a child cry inside a mountain, and a giant-woman hush it with these words: 'Hush! hush! to-morrow comes thy father Wind-and-Weather home, bringing both sun and moon, or saintly Olaf's self.'" Had not the king overheard this, and, by learning the giant's name, been enabled to crush him, the child could have had his playthings the next day.

In the course of an incarnation-myth of the raven among the Haida Indians of the Queen Charlotte Islands, Mr. Mackenzie tells us (497. 53): —

"In time the woman bore a son, a remarkably small child. This child incessantly cried for the moon to play with, thus — *Koong-ah-ah, Koong-ah-ah* ('the moon, the moon'). The spirit-chief, in order to quiet the child, after carefully closing all apertures of the house, produced the moon, and gave it to the child to play with." The result was that the raven (the child) ran off with the moon, and the people in consequence were put to no little inconvenience. But by and by the raven broke the original moon in two, threw half up into the sky, which became the sun, while of the other half he made the moon, and of the little bits, which were left in the breaking, all the stars.

In the golden age of the gods, the far-off *juventus mundi*, the parts of the universe were the playthings, the *Spielzeug* of the divine infants, just as peasants and human infants figure in the folk-tales as the toys of giants and Brobdingnagians. Indeed, some of the phenomena of nature and their peculiarities are explained by barbarous or semi-barbarous peoples as the result of the games and sports of celestial and spiritual children.

With barbarous or semi-civilized peoples possessing flocks and herds of domesticated animals the child is early made acquainted with their habits and uses. Regarding the Kaffirs of South Africa Theal says that it is the duty of the young boys to attend to the calves in the kraal, and "a good deal of time is passed in training them to run and to obey signals made by whistling. The boys mount them when they are eighteen months or two years old, and race about upon their backs" (543. 220). In many parts of the world the child has played an important *rôle* as shepherd

and watcher of flocks and herds, and the shepherd-boy has often
been called to high places in the state, and has even ascended
the thrones of great cities and empires, ecclesiastical as well as
political.

Dress.

In his little book on the philosophy of clothing Dr. Schurtz
has given us an interesting account of the development and variation of external ornamentation and dress among the various races,
especially the negro peoples of Africa. The author points out
that with not a few primitive tribes only married persons wear
clothes, girls and boys, young women and men even, going about
in puris naturalibus (530. 13). Everywhere the woman is better
clothed than the girl, and in some parts of Africa, as the ring is
with us, so are clothes a symbol of marriage. Among the
Balanta, for example, in Portuguese Senegambia, when a man
marries he gives his wife a dress, and so long as this remains
whole, the marriage-union continues in force. On the coast of
Sierra Leone, the expression " he gave her a dress," intimates that
the groom has married a young girl (530. 14, 43–49).

Often, with many races the access of puberty leads to the adoption of clothing and to a refinement of dress and personal adornment. A relic of this remains, as Dr. Schurtz points out, in the
leaving off of knickerbockers and the adoption of "long dresses,"
by the young people in our civilized communities of to-day
(530. 13).

With others the clothing of the young is of the most primitive
type, and children in very many cases go about absolutely naked.
That the development of the sex-feeling, and entrance upon
marriage, have with very many peoples been the chief incite-
ments to dress and personal ornamentation, has been pointed out
by Schurtz and others (530. 14).

Not alone this, but, sometimes, as among the Buru Negroes of
the upper Blue Nile region, the advent of her child brings with it
a modification in the dress of the mother. With these people,
young girls wear an apron in front, married women one in front
and one behind, but women who have already had a child wear
two in front, one over the other. A similar remark applies to
tattooing and kindred ornamentations of the body and its mem-

bers. Among the women of the Bajansi on the middle Congo, for example, a certain form of tattoo indicated that the woman had borne a child (530. 78).

Schurtz points out that the kangaroo-skin breast-covering of the Tasmanian women, the shoulder and arm strips worn by the women of the Monbuttu in Africa, the skin mantles of the Marutse, the thick hip-girdle of the Tupende, and other articles of clothing of a like nature, seem to be really survivals of devices for carrying children, and not to have been originally intended as dress *per se* (530. 110, 111). Thus early does childhood become a social factor.

CHAPTER XIV.

The Child as Member and Builder of Society.

In great states, children are always trying to remain children, and the parents wanting to make men and women of them. In vile states, the children are always wanting to be men and women, and the parents to keep them children. — *Ruskin.*

Children generally hate to be idle; all the care is then that their busy humour should be constantly employed in something of use to them. — *Locke.*

> Look into our childish faces;
>   See you not our willing hearts?
> Only love us — only lead us;
> Only let us know you need us,
>   And we all will do our parts. — *Mary Howitt.*

᾿Ανθρωπος φύσει ζώον πολιτικόν [Man is by nature a political (social) animal]. — *Aristotle.*

Never till now did young men, and almost children, take such a command in human affairs. — *Carlyle.*

Predestination and Caste.

> " Who can tell for what high cause
>   This darling of the Gods was born ? "

asks the poet Marvell. But with some peoples the task of answering the question is an easy one; for fate, or its human side, caste, has settled the matter long before the infant comes into the world. The Chinese philosopher, Han Wăn-Kung, is cited by Legge as saying: "When Shuh-yu was born, his mother knew, as soon as she looked at him, that he would fall a victim to his love of bribes. When Yang sze-go was born, the mother of Shuh-hĕ-ang knew, as soon as she heard him cry, that he would cause the destruction of all his kindred. When Yueh-tsĕaou was born, Tzewăn considered it was a great calamity, knowing that through

213

him all the ghosts of the Johgaou family would be famished"
(487. 89).

In India, we meet with the Bidhata-Purusha, a "deity that
predestines all the events of the life of man or woman, and writes
on the forehead of the child, on the sixth day of its birth, a brief
précis of them" (426. 9). India is *par excellence* the land of caste,
but other lands know the system that makes the man follow in
his father's footsteps, and often ignores the woman altogether,
not even counting her in the census of the people, as was formerly the case even in Japan and China, where a girl was not
worthy to be counted beside the son. Of ancient Peru, Letourneau says: "Every male inherited his father's profession; he
was not allowed to choose another employment. By right of
birth a man was either labourer, miner, artisan, or soldier"
(100. 486). Predestination of state and condition in another
world is a common theological tenet, predestination of state and
condition in this world is a common social theory.

Vast indeed is the lore of birth-days, months and years, seasons and skies — the fictions, myths, and beliefs of the astrolo-
gist, the spiritualist, the fortune-teller, and the almanac-maker —
which we have inherited from those ancestors of ours, who believed in the kinship of all things, who thought that in some way
"beasts and birds, trees and plants, the sea, the mountains, the
wind, the sun, the moon, the clouds, and the stars, day and night,
the heaven and the earth, were alive and possessed of the pas-
sions and the will they felt within themselves" (258. 25). Here
belongs a large amount of folk-lore and folk-speech relating to
the defective, delinquent, and dependent members of human
society, whose misfortunes or misdeeds are assigned to atavistic
causes, to demoniacal influences.

Parenthood.

Among primitive peoples, the advent of a child, besides entail-
ing upon one or both of the parents ceremonies and superstitious
performances whose name and fashion are legion, often makes a
great change in the constitution of society. Motherhood and
fatherhood are, in more than one part of the globe, primitive titles
of nobility and badges of aristocracy. With the birth of a child,

the Chinese woman becomes something more than a mere slave and plaything, and in the councils of uncivilized peoples (as with us to-day) the voice of the father of a family carries more weight than that of the childless. With the civilized races to-day, more marriages mean fewer prison-houses, and more empty jails, than in the earlier days, and with the primitive peoples of the present, this social bond was the salvation of the tribe to the same extent and in the same way.

As Westermarck points out, there are "several instances of husband and wife not living together before the birth of a child." Here belong the temporary marriages of the Creek Indians, the East Greenlanders, the Fuegians, the Essenes, and some other Old World sects and peoples — the birth of a child completes the marriage — "marriage is therefore rooted in family, rather than family in marriage," in such cases. With the Ainos of the island of Yezo, the Khyens of Farther India, and with one of the aboriginal tribes of China, so Westermarck informs us, "the husband goes to live with his wife at her father's house, and never takes her away till after the birth of a child," and with more than one other people the wife remains with her own parents until she becomes a mother (166. 22, 23).

In some parts of the United States we find similar practices among the population of European ancestry. The "boarding-out" of young couples until a child is born to them is by no means uncommon.

Adoption.

Adoption is, among some primitive peoples, remarkably extensive. Among the natives of the Andaman Islands "it is said to be of rare occurrence to find any child above six or seven years of age residing with its parents, and this, because it is considered a compliment and also a mark of friendship for a married man, after paying a visit, to ask his hosts to allow him to adopt one of their children" (498. 57).

Of the Hawaiian Islanders, Letourneau remarks (100. 389, 390): "Adoption was rendered extremely easy; a man would give himself a father or sons almost *ad infinitum.*" In the Marquesas Islands "it was not uncommon to see elderly persons being adopted by children." Moreover, "animals even were adopted.

A chief adopted a dog, to whom he offered ten pigs and some precious ornaments. The dog was carried about by a *kikino*, and at every meal he had his stated place beside his adopted father." Connected with adoption are many curious rites and ceremonies which may be found described in Ploss and other authorities. Dr. Friedrich S. Krauss (280) has recently treated at some length of a special form of adoption symbolized by the cutting of the hair, and particularly known among the southern Slavonians. The cutting off the hair here represents, the author thinks, the unconditional surrendering of one's body or life to another. The origin of the sacrifice of the hair is to be sought in the fact that primitive peoples have believed that the seat of the soul was in the hair and the blood, which were offered to the spirits or demons in lieu of the whole body. The relation between nurse and child has been treated of by Ploss and Wiedmann (167), the latter with special reference to ancient Egypt and the Mohammedan countries. In ancient Egypt the nurse was reckoned as one of the family, and in the death-steles and reliefs of the Middle Kingdom her name and figure are often found following those of the children and parents of the deceased. The wet-nurse was held in especial honour. The milk-relationship sometimes completely takes the place of blood-relationship. The Koran forbids the marriage of a nurse and a man whom, as a child, she has suckled; the laws of the Hanafï forbid a man to marry a woman from whose breast he has imbibed even a single drop of milk. Among the southern Slavonians: "If of two children who have fed at the breast of the same woman, one is a boy and the woman's own child, and the other (adopted) a girl, these two must never marry." If they are both girls, they are like real sisters in love and affection; if both boys, like real brothers. In Dardistan and Armenia also, milk-relationship prevents marriage (167. 263).

In Mingrelia as soon as a child is given to a woman to nurse, she, her husband, children, and grandchildren are bound to it by ties more dear even than those of blood-relationship; she would yield up her life for the child, and the latter, when grown up, is reciprocally dutiful. It is a curious fact that even grown-up people can contract this sort of relationship. "Thus peasant-women are very anxious to have grown-up princesses become then foster-children — the latter simply bite gently the breasts of their foster-mothers, and forthwith a close relationship subsists between them." It is said also that girls obtain protectors in like manner by having youths bite at their breasts, which (lately) they cover with a veil (167. 263). Adoption by the letting or transfusion of blood is also found in various parts of the world and has far-reaching ramifications, as Trumbull, Robertson Smith, and Daniels have pointed out. The last calls attention to the Biblical declaration (Proverbs, xxviii. 24): "There is a friend which sticketh closer than a brother," underlying which seems to be this mystic tie of blood (214. 16).

The mourning for the death of children is discussed in another part of this work. It may be mentioned here, however, that the death of a child often entails other, sometimes more serious, consequences. Among the Dyaks of Borneo, "when a father has lost his child, he kills the first man he meets as he goes out of his house; this is to him an act of duty" (100. 238).

Hereditary Rights.

The hereditary rights of children to share in the property of their parents have been made the subject of an interesting study by Clement Deneus (215), a lawyer of Ghent, who has treated in detail of the limitation of the *patria potestas* in respect to disposition of the patrimony, and the reservation to the children of a portion of the property of their parents — an almost inviolable right, of which they can be deprived only in consequence of the gravest offences. This reservation the author considers "a principle universally recognized among civilized nations," and an institution which marks a progress in the history of law and of civilization" (215. 49), while testamentary freedom is unjust and inexpedient. The author discusses the subject from the points of view of history, statute and natural law, social economy, etc., devoting special attention to pointing out the defects of the system of the school of Le Play, — primogeniture, which still obtains in England, in several parts of Germany, in certain localities of the Pyrenees, and in the Basque provinces.

In the countries of modern Europe, the testamentary power of the father is limited as follows: *Austria* (Code of 1812): One-half of parents' property reserved for children. The law of 1889 makes exception in the case of rural patrimonies of moderate size with dwelling attached, where the father has the right to designate his heir. *Denmark* (Code of 1845): Father can dispose of but one-fourth of the property; nobles, however, are allowed to bestow upon one of their children the half of their fortune. *Germany:* No uniform civil legislation exists as yet for the whole empire. In the majority of the smaller states, in a part of Bavaria, Rügen, eastern Pomerania, Schleswig-Holstein, the *Corpus Juris Civilis* of Justinian is in force, while the Napoleonic code obtains in Rhenish Prussia, Hesse, and Bavaria, in Baden, Berg, Alsace-Lorraine. In Prussia, the reserve is one-third, if there are less than three children; one-half, if there are three or four. In Saxony, if there are five or more children, the reserve is one-half; if there are four or less, one-third. *Greece:* The Justinian novels are followed. *Holland:* The Napoleonic code is in force. *Italy* (Code of 1866): The reserve is one-half. *Norway* (Code of 1637, modified in 1800, 1811, 1825): The father is allowed free disposal of one-half of the patrimony, but for religious charities (*fondations pieuses*) only. *Portugal:* The legitimate is two-thirds. *Roumania* (Code of 1865): The same provision as in the Napoleonic code. *Russia* (Code of 1835): The father can dispose at pleasure of the personal property and property acquired, but the property itself must be divided equally. In Esthonia, this provision also applies to personal property acquired by inheritance. *Spain* (Code of 1889): The father can dispose of one-third of the patrimony to a stranger; to a child he can will two-thirds. He can also, in the case of farming, industry, or commerce, leave his entire property to one of his children, except that the legatee has to pecuniarily indemnify his brothers and sisters. *Sweden* (Code of 1734): In the towns, the father can dispose of but one-sixth of the patrimony; in the country, the patrimonial property must go to the children. The rest is at the will of the father, except that he must provide for the sustenance of his children. *Switzerland:* At Geneva, the Napoleonic code is in force; in the Canton of Uri, the younger son is sometimes specially favoured; in Zürich, the father can dispose of one-sixth in favour of strangers, or one-fifth in favour of a child; in Bâle, he is allowed no disposal; in the cantons of Neuchâtel and Vaud, the reserve is one-half, in Bern and Schaffhausen, two-thirds, and in Friburg and Soleure, three-fourths. *Turkey:* The father can dispose of two-thirds by will, or of the whole by gift (215. 39–41).

In France, article 913 of the civil code forbids the father to dispose, by gift while living, or by will, of more than one-half of the property, if he leaves at his death but one legitimate child; more than one-third, if he leaves two children; more than one-fourth, if he leave three or more children. In the United States great testamentary freedom prevails, and the laws of inheritance belong to the province of the various States.

Among the nations of antiquity, — Egyptians, Persians, Assyrians, Chinese, — according to Deneus (215. 2), the *patria potestas* probably prevented any considerable diffusion of the family estates. By the time of Moses, the Hebrews had come to favour the first-born, and to him was given a double share of the inheritance. With the ancient Hindus but a slight favouring of the eldest son seems to have been in vogue, the principle of co-proprietorship of parent and children being recognized in the laws of Manu. In Sparta, the constitution was inimical to a reserve for all the children; in Athens, the code of Solon forbade a man to benefit a stranger at the expense of his legitimate male children; he had, however, the right to make particular legacies, probably up to one-half of the property. Deneus considers that the *penchant* of the Athenians for equality was not favourable to a cast-iron system of primogeniture, although the father may have been able to favour his oldest child to the extent of one-half of his possessions. In ancient Rome (215. 4–16), at first, a will was an exception, made valid only by the vote of a *lex curiata;* but afterwards the absolute freedom of testamentary disposition, which was approved in 450 B.C. by the Law of the Twelve Tables, — *Uti legassit super pecunia tutelave suæ rei, ita jus esto,* — appears, and the father could even pass by his children in silence and call upon an utter stranger to enjoy his estate and possessions. By 153 B.C., however, the father was called upon to nominally disinherit his children, and not merely pass them over in silence, if he wished to leave his property to a stranger. For some time this provision had little effect, but a breach in the *patria potestas* has really been made, and by the time of Pliny the Younger (61–115 A.D.), who describes the procedure in detail, the disinherited children were given the right of the *querula inofficiosi testamenti*, by which the father was presumed to have died intestate, and his property fell in equal shares to all his children. Thus it was that the right of children in the property of the father was first really recognized at Rome, and the *pars legitima*, the reserve of which made it impossible for the children to attack the will of the father, came into practice. In the last years of the Republic, this share was at least one-fourth of what the legitimate heir would have received in the absence of a will; under Justinian, it was one-third of the part *ab intestate*, if this was at least one-fourth of the estate; otherwise, one-half. The father always retained the right to disinherit, for certain reasons, in law. With this diminution of his rights over property went also a lessening of his powers over the bodies of his children. Diocletian forbade the selling of children, Constantine decreed that the father who exposed his new-born child should lose the *patria potestas*, and Valentinian punished such action with death. Among the ancient Gauls, in spite of the father's power of life and death over his offspring, he could not disinherit them, for the theory of co-proprietorship obtained with these western tribes (215. 16). With the ancient Germans, the father appears to have been rather the protector of his children than their owner or keeper; the child is recognized, somewhat rudely, as a being with some rights of his own. Michelet has aptly observed, as Deneus remarks, that "the Hindus saw in the son the reproduction of the father's soul; the Romans, a servant of the father; the Germans, a child" (215. 17). At first wills were unknown among them, for the system of co-proprietorship, — *hæredes successoresque sui cuique liberi et nullum testamentum*, — and the solidarity of the family and all its members, did not feel the need of any. The inroad of Roman ideas, and especially, Deneus thinks, the fervour of converts to Christianity, introduced testamentary legacies.

The Goths and Burgundians, in their Roman laws, allowed the parent to dispose of three-fourths, the Visigoths one-third or one-fifth, according as the testator disposed of his property in favour of a child or a stranger. The national law of the Burgundians allowed to the father the absolute disposal of his acquisitions, but prescribed the equal sharing of the property among all the children. The ripuarian law of the Franks left the children a reserve of twelve sous, practically admitting absolute freedom of disposition by will (215. 18). The course of law in respect to the inheritance of children during the Middle Ages can be read in the pages of Deneus and the wider comparative aspect of the subject studied in the volumes of Post, Dargun, Engels, etc., where the various effects of mother-right and father-right are discussed and interpreted.

Subdivisions of Land.

In some cases, as in Wurtemburg, Switzerland, Hanover, Thuringia, Hesse, certain parts of Sweden, France, and Russia, the subdivision of property has been carried out to an extent which has produced truly Lilliputian holdings. In Switzerland there is a certain commune where the custom obtains of transmitting by will to each child its proportional share of each parcel; so that a single walnut-tree has no fewer than sixty proprietors. This reminds us of the Maoris of New Zealand, with whom "a portion of the ground is allotted to the use of each family, and this portion is again subdivided into individual parts on the birth of each child." It is of these same people that the story is told that, after selling certain of their lands to the English authorities, they came back in less than a year and demanded payment also for the shares of the children born since the sale, whose rights they declared had not been disposed of. On the islands of the Loire there are holdings "so small that it is impossible to reduce them any less, so their owners have them each in turn a year"; in the commune of Murs, in Anjou, there is "a strip of nine hectares, subdivided into no fewer than thirty-one separate parcels." The limit, however, seems to be reached in Laon, where "it is not rare to find fields scarce a metre (3 ft. 3.37 in.) wide; here an apple-tree or a walnut-tree covers with its branches four or five lots, and the proprietor can only take in his crop in the presence of his neighbours, to whom he has also to leave one-half of the fruit fallen on their lots." No wonder many disputes and lawsuits arise from such a state of affairs. It puts us in mind at once of the story of the sand-pile and the McDonogh farm. The exchange or purchase of contiguous parcels sometimes brings temporary or permanent relief (215. 112, 113).

The following figures show the extent to which this Lilliputian system obtained in France in 1884, according to the returns of the Minister of Finance : —

Nature of Property.	Absolute Number of Holdings.	Per Cent.	Total Hectares.	Per Cent.
Less than 20 ares (100 ares=one hectare) .	4,115,463	29.00	—— ——	——
Less than 50 ares	6,597,843	47.00	1,147,804	2.31
Less than 1 hectare (= 2½ acres)	8,585,523	61.00	2.574,589	5.19
Less than 2 hectares	10,426,368	74.09	5,211,456	10.53
From 2 to 6 hectares	2,174,188	15.47	7,543,347	15.26
From 6 to 50 hectares	1,351,499	9.58	19,217,902	38.94
From 50 to 200 hectares	105,070	0.74	9,398,057	19.04
More than 200 hectares	17,676	0.12	8,017,542	16.23
Totals	14,074,801	100.00	49,388,304	100.00

Deneus gives other interesting figures from Belgium and elsewhere, showing the extent of the system. Other statistics given indicate that this parcelling-out has reached its lowest point, and that the reaction has set in. It is a curious fact, noted by M. Deneus, that of the 1,173,724 tenant-farmers in the United Kingdom of Great Britain and Ireland in the year 1884, no fewer than 852,438 cultivated an acre or less.

Younger Son.

Mr. Sessions, in his interesting little pamphlet (351) calls attention to the important *rôle* assigned in legend and story to the "younger son," "younger brother," as well as the social customs and laws which have come into vogue on his account. Sir Henry Maine argued that "primogeniture cannot be the natural outgrowth of the family, but is a political institution, coming not from clansmen but from a chief." Hence the youngest son, "who continues longest with the father, is naturally the heir of his house, the rest being already provided for." Mr. Sessions observes (351. 2): "Among some primitive tribes, as those of Cape York [Australia] and the adjacent islands, the youngest son inherited a double portion of his deceased father's goods.

Among the Maoris of New Zealand he takes the whole. Among some hill tribes of India, such as the Todas of the Neilgherries, he takes the house and maintains the women of the family, whilst the cattle, which represent the chief personalities, are equally divided. The Mrus and Kolhs and Cotas have similar customs." Somewhat similar to the code of the Todas was that of the Hindu Aryans, as embodied in the laws of Manu, for "the youngest son has, from time immemorial, as well as the eldest, a place in Hindu legislation." The succession of the youngest prevails among the Mongolian Tartars, and "when in Russia the joint family may be broken up, the youngest takes the house." The right of the youngest was known among the Welsh, Irish, and some other Celtic tribes; the old Welsh law gave the youngest son the house and eight acres. the rest of the land being divided equally between all the sons. Mr. Sessions calls attention to the fact that, while in Old Testament Palestine primogeniture was the rule, the line of ancestry of Christ exhibits some remarkable exceptions. And among primitive peoples the hero or demi-god is very often the younger son.

Under the name of "Borough English," the law by which the father's real property descends to the youngest son alone, survives in Gloucester and some few other places in England, — Lambeth, Hackney, part of Islington, Heston, Edmonton, etc.

Another interesting tenure is that of gavelkind, by which the land and property of the father was inherited in equal portions by all his sons, the youngest taking the house, the eldest the horse and arms, and so on. This mode of tenure, before the Conquest, was quite common in parts of England, especially Wales and Northumberland, still surviving especially in the county of Kent. Many things, indeed, testify of the care which was taken even in primitive times to secure that the youngest born, the child of old age, so frequently the best-loved, should not fare ill in the struggle for life.

Child-Nurses.

One important function of the child (still to be seen commonly among the lower classes of the civilized races of to-day) with primitive peoples is that of nurse and baby-carrier. Even of Japan, Mrs. Bramhall gives this picture (189. 33): —

" We shall see hundreds of small children, not more than five or six years of age, carrying, fast asleep on their shoulders, the baby of the household, its tiny smooth brown head swinging hither and thither with every movement of its small nurse, who walks, runs, sits, or jumps, flies kites, plays hop-scotch, and fishes for frogs in the gutter, totally oblivious of that infantile charge, whether sleeping or waking. If no young sister or brother be available, the husband, the uncle. the father, or grandfather hitches on his back the baby, preternaturally good and contented."

The extent to which, in America, as well as in Europe, to-day, young children are entrusted with the care of infants of their family, has attracted not a little attention, and the "beyond their years" look of some of these little nurses and care-takers is often quite noticeable. The advent of the baby-carriage has rather facilitated than hindered this old-time employment of the child in the last century or so. In a recent number (vol. xvii. p. 792) of *Public Opinion* we find the statement that from June 17, 1890, to September 15, 1894, the "Little Mothers' Aid Association," of New York, has been the means of giving a holiday, one day at least of pleasure in the year, to more than eight thousand little girls, who are "little mothers, in the sense of having the care of younger children while the parents are at work." In thrifty New England, children perform not a little of the house-work, even the cooking; and "little mothers" and "little house-keepers" were sometimes left to themselves for days, while their elders in days gone by visited or went to the nearest town or village for supplies.

Child-Marriages.

"Marriages are made in heaven," says the old proverb, and among some primitive peoples we meet with numerous instances of their having been agreed upon and arranged by prospective parents long before the birth of their offspring. Indeed, the betrothal of unborn children by their parents occurs sporadically to-day in civilized lands. Ploss has called attention to child-marriages in their sociological and physiological bearings (125. I. 386–402), and Post has considered the subject in his historical study of family law. In these authorities the details of the subject may be read. In Old Calabar, men who already possess several wives take to their bosom and kiss, as their new wife, babes two or three weeks old. In China, Gujurat, Ceylon, and parts of Brazil, wives of from four to six years of age are occasionally met with. In many parts of the world wives of seven to nine years of age are common, and wives of from ten to twelve very common. In China it is sometimes the case that parents buy for their infant son an infant wife, nursed at the same breast with him (234. xlii.).

Wiedemann, in an article on child-marriages in Egypt (381), mentions the fact that a certain king of the twenty-first dynasty (about 1100 B.C.) seems to have had as one of his wives a child only a few days old. From Dio Cassius we learn that in Rome, at the beginning of the Empire, marriages of children under ten years occasionally took place.

In some parts of the world the child-wife does not belong to her child-husband. "Among the Reddies, of India," Letourneau . informs us, "a girl from sixteen to twenty years of age is married to a boy of five or six. The wife then becomes the real wife of the boy's uncle, or cousin, or of the father of the reputed husband. But the latter is considered to be the legal father of the children of his pretended wife." So it is only when the boy has grown up that he receives his wife, and he, in turn, acts as his relative before him (100. 354). Temple cites the following curious custom in his tales of the Panjâb (542. I. xviii.) : —

"When Râjâ Vasâlî has won a bride from Râjâ Sirkap, he is given a new-born infant and a mango-tree, which is to flower in twelve years, and when it flowers, the girl is to be his wife." The age prescribed by ancient Hindu custom (for the Brahman, Tshetria, and Vysia classes) is six to eight years for the girl, and the belief prevailed that if a girl were to attain her puberty before being married, her parents and brothers go to hell, as it was their duty to have got her married before that period (317. 56). Father Sangermano, writing of Burma a hundred years ago, notices the "habit of the Burmese to engage their daughters while young, in real or fictitious marriages, in order to save them from the hands of the king's ministers, custom having established a rule, which is rarely if ever violated, that no married woman can be seized, even for the king himself" (234. xlii.). The child-marriages of India have been a fruitful theme for discussion, as well as the enforced widowhood consequent upon the death of the husband.

Q

Among the most interesting literature on the subject are the
"Papers relating to Infant Marriage and Enforced Widowhood in
India" (317), Schlagintweit (142), etc. The evils connected with
the child-marriages of India are forcibly brought out by Mrs.
Steel in several of the short stories in her *From the Five Rivers*
(1893), and by Richard Garbe in his beautiful little novel *The
Redemption of the Brahman* (1894).

  But India and other Eastern lands are not the only countries
where "child-marriages" have flourished. Dr. F. J. Furnivall
(234), the distinguished English antiquary and philologist, poring
over at Chester the "Depositions in Trials in the Bishop's Court
from November, 1561 to March, 1565–6," was astonished to find on
the ninth page the record: "that Elizabeth Hulse said she was
married to George Hulse in the Chapel of Knutsford, when she
was but three or four years old, while the boy himself deposed
that he was about seven," and still more surprised when he discovered that the volume contained "no fewer than twenty-seven
cases of the actual marriage in church of the little boys and girls
of middle-class folk." The result of Dr. Furnivall's researches
is contained in the one-hundred-and-eighth volume (original series)
of the Early English Text Society's Publications, dealing with
child-marriages, divorces, ratifications, etc., and containing a
wealth of quaint and curious sociological lore. Perhaps the
youngest couple described are John Somerford, aged about three
years, and Jane Brerton, aged about two years, who were married
in the parish church of Brerton about 1553. Both were carried
in arms to the church, and had the words of the marriage service
said for them by those who carried them. It appears that they
lived together at Brerton for ten years, but without sustaining
any further marital relations, and when the husband was about
fifteen years, we find him suing for a divorce on account of his
wife's "unkindness, and other weighty causes." Neither party
seemed affectionately disposed towards the other (234. 26). Other
very interesting marriages are those of Bridget Dutton (aged under
five years) and George Spurstowe (aged six) (234. 38); Margaret
Stanley (aged five) and Roland Dutton (aged nine), brother of
Bridget Dutton (234. 41); Janet Parker (aged five) and Lawrence
Parker (aged nine to ten). The rest of the twenty-seven couples
were considerably older, the most of the girls ranging between

eight and twelve, the boys between ten and fourteen (234. 28). It would seem that for the most part these young married couples were not allowed to live together, but at times some of the nuptial rites were travestied or attempted to be complied with. In two only of the twenty-seven cases is there mention of "bedding" the newly-married children. John Budge, who at the age of eleven to twelve years, was married to Elizabeth Ramsbotham, aged thirteen to fourteen years, is said to have wept to go home with his father and only by "compulsion of the priest of the Chapel" was he persuaded to lie with his wife, but never had any marital relations with her whatever, and subsequently a petition for divorce was filed by the husband (234. 6). In the case of Ellen Dampart, who at the age of about eight years, was married to John Andrew aged ten, it appears that they slept in the same bed with two of the child-wife's sisters between them. No marital relations were entered upon, and the wife afterwards sues for a divorce (234. 15, 16).

The practice seems to have been for each of the children married to go to live with some relative, and if the marriage were not ratified by them after reaching years of consent, to petition for a divorce. In some nine cases the boy is younger than the girl, and Humfrey Winstanley was under twelve when he was married to Alice Worsley aged over seventeen; in this case no marital relations were entered upon, though the wife was quite willing; and the husband afterwards petitions for a divorce (234. 2–4). Thomas Dampart, who at the age of ten years, was married to Elizabeth Page, appears to have lived with his wife about eight years and to have kept up marital relations with her until she left him of her own motion. Dr. Furnivall (234. 49–52) cites four cases of ratification of child-marriages by the parties after they have attained years of discretion, in one of which the boy and the girl were each but ten years old when married. The most naïve account in the whole book is that of the divorce-petition of James Ballard, who, when about eleven years of age, was married in the parish church of Colne at ten o'clock at night by Sir Roger Blakey, the curate, to a girl named Anne; the morning after the ceremony he is said "to have declared unto his uncle that the said Anne had enticed him with two Apples, to go with her to Colne, and marry her." No marital relations were entered upon, and the curate was punished for his hasty and injudicious action (234. 45).

Dr. Furnivall (234. xxxv.) quotes at some length the legal opinion — the law on infant marriages — of Judge Swinburne (died, 1624), from which we learn that "infants" (*i.e.* children under seven years of age) could not contract spousals or matrimony, and such contracts made by the infants or by their parents were void, unless subsequently ratified by the contracting parties by word or deed, — at twelve the girls ceased to be children, and at fourteen the boys, and were then fully marriageable, as they are to-day in many parts of the world. Of childhood, Judge Swinburne says, "During this age, children cannot contract Matrimony *de præsenti*, but only *de futuro*"; but their spousals could readily be turned into actual marriages after the girls were twelve and the boys fourteen, as Dr. Furnivall points out.

The fifth limitation to his general statement, which the learned judge made, is thus strangely and quaintly expressed : " The fifth Limitation is, when the Infants which do contract Spousals are of that *Wit* and *Discretion*, that albeit they have not as yet accomplished the full Age of Seven Years, yet doth their supraordinary understanding fully supply that small defect of Age which thing is not rare in these days, wherein Children become sooner ripe, and do conceive more quickly than in former Ages " (234. xxxvi.).

First among the causes of these child-marriages Dr. Furnivall is inclined to rank "the desire to evade the feudal law of the Sovereign's guardianship of all infants," for "when a father died, the Crown had the right to hold the person and estate of the propertied orphan until it came of age, and it could be sold in marriage for the benefit of the Crown or its grantee." Moreover, "if the orphan refused such a marriage with a person of its own rank, it had to pay its guardian a heavy fine for refusing his choice, and selecting a spouse of its own" (234. xxxix.). Property-arrangement also figures as a cause of these alliances, especially where the bride is older than the groom : Elizabeth Hulse (aged four) was married to George Hulse (aged seven) "because her friends thought she should have a living by him" (234. 4). When Elizabeth Ramsbotham (aged 13–14) married John Bridge (aged 11–12), "money was paid by the father of the said Elizabeth, to buy a piece of land" (234. 6); according to the father of Joan Leyland (aged 11–12), who married Ralph Whittall (aged 11–12), "they were married because she should have had by him a pretty bargain, if they could have loved, one the other" (234. 12); Thomas Bentham (aged twelve) and Ellen Bolton (aged ten) were married because Richard Bentham, grandfather of Ellen, "was a very wealthy man, and it was supposed that he would have been good unto them, and bestowed some good farm upon them" (234. 32); the marriage of Thomas Fletcher (aged 10–11) and Anne Whitfield (aged about nine) took place because "John Fletcher, father of the said Thomas, was in debt; and, to get some money of William Whitfield, to the discharge of his debts, married and bargained his sonne to the said Whitfield's daughter." The "compulsion of their friends" seems also to have been a cause of the marriages of children; Peter Hope (about thirteen) married Alice Ellis (aged nine), "because it was his mother's mind, he durst not displease her" (234. 20, 23).

So far the evidence has related to unsatisfactory and unfortunate marriages, but, as Dr. Furnivall remarks, "no doubt scores of others ended happily; the child-husband and -wife just lived on together, and — when they had reached their years of discretion (girls twelve, boys fourteen) or attained puberty — ratified their marriage by sleeping in one bed and having children" (234. xix., 203).

Some additional cases of child-marriages in the diocese of Chester are noticed by Mr. J. P. Earwaker (234. xiv.), a pioneer in this branch of antiquarian research, whose studies date back to 1885. The case of John Marden, who, at the age of three years, was married to a girl of five is thus described: "He was carried in the arms of a clergyman, who coaxed him to repeat the words of matrimony. Before he had got through his lesson, the child declared he would learn no more that day. The priest answered: 'You must speak a little more, and then go play you.'" Robert Parr, who, in 1538–9, at the age of three, was married to Elizabeth Rogerson, "was hired for an apple by his uncle to go to church, and was borne thither in the arms of Edward Bunburie his uncle . . . which held him in arms the time that he was married to the said Elizabeth, at which time the said Robert could scarce speak." Mr. Earwaker says that in the *Inquisitiones post mortem*, "it is by no means unfrequent to read that so and so was heir to his father, and then aged, say, ten years, and was already married" (234. xxi.–xxxiii.).

A celebrated child-marriage was that at Eynsham, Oxfordshire, in 1541, the contracting parties being William, Lord Eure, aged 10–11 years, and Mary Darcye, daughter of Lord Darcye, aged four. The parties were divorced November 3, 1544, and in 1548, the boy took to himself another wife. Dr. Furnivall cites from John Smith's *Lives of the Berkeleys*, the statements that Maurice, third Lord Berkeley, was married in 1289, when eight years old, to Eve, daughter of Lord Zouch, and, before he or his wife was fourteen years of age, had a son by her; that Maurice, the fourth Lord Berkeley, when eight years of age, was married in 1338–9, to Elizabeth, daughter of Hugh Lord Spenser, about eight years old; that Thomas, the fourth Lord Berkeley, when about fourteen and one-half years of age, was married, in 1366, to Margaret, daughter of Lord de Lisle, aged about seven. Smith, in quaint fashion, refers to King Josiah (2 Kings, xxiii., xxvi.), King Ahaz (2 Kings, xvi. 2, xviii. 2), and King Solomon (1 Kings, xi. 42, xiv. 21) as having been fathers at a very early age, and remarks: "And the Fathers of the Church do tell us that the blessed Virgin Mary brought forth our Saviour at fifteen years old, or under" (234. xxvii.).

Even during the seventeenth and eighteenth centuries childmarriages are numerously attested. Following are noteworthy cases (234. xxiii.): In 1626 Anne Clopton, aged nearly fourteen, was married to Sir Simonds D'Ewes, aged nearly twenty-four; in 1673, John Power, grandson of Lord Anglesey, was married at Lambeth, by the Archbishop of Canterbury to Mrs. Catherine Fitzgerald, his cousin-german, she being about thirteen, and he eight years old; at Dunton Basset, Leicestershire, in 1669, Mary Hewitt (who is stated to have lived to the good old age of seventyseven) was married when but three years old; in 1672, the only daughter (aged five) of Lord Arlington was married to the Duke of Grafton, and the ceremony was witnessed by John Evelyn, who, in 1679, "was present at the re-marriage of the child couple"; in 1719, Lady Sarah Cadogan, aged thirteen, was married to Charles, Duke of Richmond, aged eighteen; in 1721, Charles Powel, of Carmarthen, aged about eleven, was married to a daughter of

Sir Thomas Powel, of Broadway, aged about fourteen; in 1729, "a girl of nine years and three months was taken from a boarding school by one of her guardians, and married to his son"; Bridget Clarke, in 1883, is reputed to have been twenty-five years old, to have had seven children, and to have been married when only thirteen; at Deeping, Lincolnshire, a young man of twenty-one married a girl of fourteen, and "it was somewhat of a novelty to observe the interesting bride the following day exhibiting her skill on the skipping-rope on the pavement in the street." Mr. Longstaff, who has studied the annual reports of the registrar-general for 1851–81, finds that during these thirty-one years, "out of 11,058,376 persons married, 154 boys married before 17, and 862 girls before 16. Of these, 11 boys of 15 married girls of 15 (four cases), 16, 18 (two cases), 20, and 21. Three girls of 14 married men of 18, 21, and 25. Five girls of 15 married boys of 16; in 29 marriages both girl and boy were sixteen" (234. xxxiii.).

Further comments upon infant marriages may be found in an article in the *Gentleman's Magazine*, for September, 1894, the writer of which remarks: "Within recent years, however, the discovery has been made, that, so far from being confined, as had been supposed, to royal or aristocratic houses, infant marriages were, in the sixteenth century, common in some parts of England among all classes" (367. 322).

It was said "marriages are made in heaven," and that sometimes children are married before they are born; it might also be said "marriages are made for heaven," since some children are married after they are dead. In some parts of China (and Marco Polo reported the same practice as prevalent in his time among the Tartars) "the spirits of all males who die in infancy or in boyhood are, in due time, married to the spirits of females who have been cut off at a like early age" (166. 140).

As Westermarck observes, "Dr. Ploss has justly pointed out that the ruder a people is, and the more exclusively a woman is valued as an object of desire, or as a slave, the earlier in life is she chosen; whereas, if marriage becomes a union of souls as well as of bodies, the man claims a higher degree of mental maturity from the woman he wishes to be his wife."

In so civilized a nation even as the United States, the "age of consent" laws evidence the tenacity of barbarism. The black list of states, compiled by Mr. Powell (180. 201), in a recent article in the *Arena*, reveals the astonishing fact that in three states — Alabama, North Carolina, South Carolina — the "age of consent" is *ten* years; in four states, twelve years; in three states, thirteen years; in no fewer than twenty states, fourteen years; in two states, fifteen years; in twelve states, sixteen years; and in one state (Florida), seventeen years. In Kansas and Wyoming alone is the "age of consent" eighteen years, and it is worthy of note that Wyoming is the only state in the Union in which women have for any considerable length of time enjoyed the right to vote on exactly the same terms as men. In England, the agitation set going by Mr. Stead, in 1885, resulted in the passage of a law raising the "age of consent" from thirteen to six-teen years. It is almost beyond belief, that, in the State of Dela-ware, only a few years ago, the "age of consent" was actually as low as *seven* years (180. 194)! Even in Puritan New England, we find the "age of consent" fixed at thirteen in New Hampshire, and at fourteen in Connecticut, Vermont, and Maine (180. 195). It is a sad comment upon our boasted culture and progress that, as of old, the law protects, and even religion fears to disturb too rudely, this awful sacrifice to lust which we have inherited from our savage ancestors. There is no darker chapter in the history of our country than that which tells of the weak pandering to the modern representatives of the priests of Bacchus, Astarte, and the shameless Venus. The religious aspect of the horrible immolation may have passed away, but wealth and social attrac-tions have taken its place, and the evil works out its destroying way as ever. To save the children from this worse than death, women must fight, and they will win; for once the barbarity, the enormity, the inhumanity of this child-sacrifice is brought home to men they cannot for their own children's sake permit the thing to go on. Here, above all places else, apply the words of Jesus: "Whoso shall cause one of these little ones which believe on me to stumble, it is profitable that a great millstone should be hanged about his neck, and he should be sunk in the depths of the sea."

The marriage-laws of some of the states savour almost as much of prehistoric times and primitive peoples. With the consent of her parents, a girl of twelve years may lawfully contract marriage in no fewer than twenty-two states and territories; and in no fewer than twenty, a boy of fourteen may do likewise. Among the twenty-two states and territories are included: Connecticut, Delaware, Maine, Massachusetts, New Hampshire, New Jersey, Pennsylvania, Rhode Island, Vermont; and among the twenty, Connecticut, Delaware, Maine, Massachusetts, New Hampshire, New Jersey, Pennsylvania, Rhode Island, Vermont. In some of the Southern States the age seems to be somewhat higher than in a number of the Northern. The existence of slavery may have tended to bring about this result; while the same fact in the West is to be accounted for by the vigour and newness of the civilization in that part of the country.

Children's Rights.

Where, as in ancient Rome, for example, the *patria potestas* flourished in primitive vigour, — Mommsen says, "all in the household were destitute of legal rights, — the wife and the child no less than the bullock or the slave" (166. 229), children could in nowise act as members of society. Westermarck (166. 213–239) shows to what extent and to what age the *mundium*, or guardianship of the father over his children, was exercised in Rome, Greece, among the Teutonic tribes, in France. In the latter country even now "a child cannot quit the paternal residence without the permission of the father before the age of twenty-one, except for enrolment in the army. For grave misconduct by his children the father has strong means of correction. A son under twenty-five and a daughter under twenty-one cannot marry without the consent of their parents; and even when a man has attained his twenty-fifth year, and the woman her twenty-first, both are still bound to ask for it, by a formal notification." Westermarck's observations on the general subject are as follows : —

"There is thus a certain resemblance between the family institution of savage tribes and that of the most advanced races. Among both, the grown-up son, and frequently the grown-up daughter, enjoys a liberty unknown among peoples at an intermediate stage of civilization. There are, however, these vital differences: that children in civilized countries are in no respect the property of their parents; that they are born with certain rights guaranteed to them by society ; that the birth of children gives parents no rights over them other than those which conduce to the children's happiness.   These ideas, essential as they are to true civilization, are not many centuries old.   It is a purely modern conception the French Encyclopædist expresses when he says, ' Le pouvoir paternel est plutôt un devoir qu'un pouvoir ' " (166. 239).

The Child at School.

It was in this spirit also that Count Czáky (when Minister of Education in Hungary), replying to the sarcastic suggestion of one of the Deputies, during the debate on the revision of the curriculum of classical studies, that "the lazy children should be asked whether they liked to study Greek or not," said that " when it became necessary, he would willingly listen to the children themselves."   That children have some rights in the matter is a view that is slowly but surely fixing itself in the minds of the people, — that the school should be something more than an intellectual prison-house, a mental and moral tread-mill, a place to put children in out of the way of the family, a dark cave into which happy, freedom-loving, joyous childhood must perforce retire from that communion with nature which makes the health of its body and the salvation of its soul.   This false theory of education is vanishing, however tardily, before the teachings of the new psychology and the new anthropology, which demand a knowledge of what the child is, feels, thinks, before they will be party to any attempt to *make* him be, feel, think, something different.   The school is but a modified form of society, of its fundamental institution, the family.   Dr. Riccardi, in the introduction to his *Antropologia e Pedagogia*, — in which he discusses a mass of psychological, sociological, and anthropological observations and statistics, — well says (336. 12) : —

" The school is a little society, whose citizens are the scholars. The teacher has not merely to instruct the pupil, but ought also to teach him to live in the little school-society and thus fitly prepare him to live in the great society of humanity.   And just as men are classified in human society, so ought to be classified the scholars in the little school-society ; and just as the teacher looks upon the great human world in movement upon the earth, so ought he also to look upon that little world called the school, observing its elements with a positive eye, without preconceptions and without prejudices. The teacher, therefore, in regard to the school-organism, is as a legislator in regard to society. And the true and wise legislator does not give laws to the governed, does not offer security and liberty to the citizens, until after he has made a profound study of his country and of society. Let the teacher try for some time to take these criteria into his school; let him try to apply in the school many of those facts and usages which are commonly employed in human society, and he will see how, little by little, almost unnoticeably, the primitive idea of the school will be modified in his mind, and he will see how the school itself will assume the true character which it ought to have, that is, the character of a microscopic social organism. This legislator for our children, by making the children and youths clearly see of themselves that the school is nothing else but a little society, where they are taught to live, and by making them see the points of resemblance and of contact with the great human society, will engender in the minds of the pupils the conscience of duty and of right; will create in them the primitive feeling of justice and of equity. And the pupils, feeling that there is a real association, feeling that they do form part of a little world, and are not something merely gathered together by chance for a few hours, will form a compact homogeneous scholastic association, in which all will try to be something, and of which all will be proud. In this way will the assemblage of disparate, diverse, heterogeneous elements, with which the school begins the year, be able to become homogeneous and create a true school organism. And if the teacher will persevere, whether in the direction of the school, in the classification of the pupils, or in the different contingencies that arise, in applying those criteria, those ideas, those forms, which are commonly employed in society, he will be favouring the homogeneity of the little organism which he has to instruct and to educate. He will thus have always before his mind all the organic, psychic, and moral characteristics of human society and will see the differences from, and the resemblances to, those of the school-organism. In so far will he have an example, a law, a criterion, a form to follow in the direction of the little human society entrusted to him, with its beautiful and its ugly side, its good and its bad, its vices and its virtues. This idea of the school as an organism, however much it seems destined to overturn ideas of the past, will be the crucible from which will be turned out in the near future all the reforms and many new ideas."

This view of the school as an organism, a social microcosm, a little society within the great human society, having its resemblances to, and its differences from, the family and the nation, is one that the new development of "child-study" seems bound to promote and advance. Rank paternalism has made its exit from the great human society, but it has yet a strong hold upon the school. It is only in comparatively recent times that motherhood, which, as Zmigrodzki says, has been the basis of our civilization, has been allowed to exercise its best influence upon the scholastic microcosm. Paternalism and celibacy must be made to yield up the strong grasp which they have upon the educational institutions of the land, and the early years of the life of man must be confided to the care of the mother-spirit, which the individual man and the race alike have deified in their golden age. The mother who laid so well the foundations of the great human society, the originator of its earliest arts, the warder of its faiths and its beliefs, the mother, who built up the family, must be trusted with some large share in the building of the school.

Child-Sociology.

In *The Story of a Sand-Pile* (255), President G. Stanley Hall has chronicled for us the life-course of a primitive social community — nine summers of work and play by a number of boys with a sand-pile in the yard of one of their parents. Here we are introduced to the originality and imitation of children in agriculture, architecture, industrial arts, trade and commerce, money and exchange, government, law and justice, charity, etc. The results of this spontaneous and varied exercise, which, the parents say, "has been of about as much yearly educational value to the boys as the eight months of school," and in contrast with which "the concentrative methodic unities of Ziller seem artificial, and, as Bacon said of scholastic methods, very inadequate to subtlety of nature," Dr. Hall sums up as follows (255. 696) : —

"Very many problems that puzzle older brains have been met in simpler terms and solved wisely and well. The spirit and habit of active and even prying observation has been greatly quickened. Industrial processes, institutions, and methods of administration and organization have been appropriated and put into practice. The boys have grown more companionable and rational, learning many a lesson of self-control, and developed a spirit of self-help. The parents have been enabled to control indirectly the associations of their boys, and, in a very mixed boy-community, to have them in a measure under observation without in the least restricting their freedom. The habit of loafing, and the evils that attend it, have been avoided, a strong practical and even industrial bent has been given to their development, and much social morality has been taught in the often complicated *modus vivendi* with others that has been evolved. Finally, this may perhaps be called one illustration of the education according to *nature* we so often hear and speak of."

This study of child-sociology is a *rara avis in terra;* it is to be hoped, however, that if any other parents have "refrained from suggestions, and left the hand and fancy of the boys to educate each other under the tuition of the mysterious play-instinct," they may be as fortunate in securing for the deeds of their young offspring, as observant and as sympathetic a historian as he who has told the story of the sand-pile in that little New England town.

Bagehot, in the course of his chapter on "Nation-Making," observes (395. 91) : —

"After such great matters as religion and politics, it may seem trifling to illustrate the subject from little boys. But it is not trifling. The bane of philosophy is pomposity : people will not see that small things are the miniatures of greater, and it seems a loss of abstract dignity to freshen their minds by object lessons from what they know. But every boarding-school changes as a nation changes. Most of us may remember thinking, 'How odd it is that this *half* should be so unlike last *half;* now we never go out of bounds, last half we were always going; now we play rounders, then we played prisoner's base,' and so through all the easy life of that time. In fact, some ruling spirits, some one or two ascendant boys, had left, one or two others had come, and so all was changed. The models were changed, and the copies changed; a different thing was praised, and a different thing bullied."

It was in the spirit of this extract (part of which he quotes), that the editor of the "Johns Hopkins University Studies in Historical and Political Science" happily admitted into that series of monographs, Mr. J. H. Johnson's *Rudimentary Society among Boys* (272), a sociological study of peculiar interest and importance — "a microcosm, not only of the agrarian, but of the political and economic history of society." Mr. Johnson has graphically described the development of society among some fifty boys on the farm belonging to the McDonogh School, not far from the city of Baltimore, Maryland; land-tenure, boy-legislation, judicial procedure, boy-economy, are all treated of in detail and many analogies with the life and habits of primitive peoples brought out, and the author has gone a long way towards realizing the thesis that "To show a decided resemblance between barbarian political institutions and those of communities of civilized children, would be a long step towards founding a science of Social Embryology" (272. 61).

"*Gangs.*"

Mr. Stewart Culin (212) in his interesting account of the "Street Games of Boys in Brooklyn, N.Y." notices *en passant* the existence of "gangs" of boys — boys' societies of the ruder and rougher kind. As evidence of the extent to which these organizations have flourished, the following somewhat complete list of those known to have existed in the city of Philadelphia is given: —

Badgers, Bed Bugs, Bleeders, Blossoms, Bouncers, Buena Vistas, Buffaloes, Bull Dogs, Bullets, Bunker Hills, Canaries, Clippers, Corkies, Cow Towners, Cruisers, Darts, Didos, Dirty Dozen, Dumplingtown Hivers, Dung Hills, Fluters, Forest Rose, Forties, Garroters, Gas House Tarriers, Glassgous, Golden Hours, Gut Gang, Haymakers, Hawk-Towners, Hivers, Killers, Lancers, Lions, Mountaineers, Murderers, Niggers, Pigs, Pluckers, Pots, Prairie Hens, Railroad Roughs, Rats, Ramblers, Ravens, Riverside, Rovers, Schuylkill Rangers, Skinners, Snappers, Spigots, Tigers, Tormentors, War Dogs, Wayne Towners.

Of these Mr. Culin remarks : "They had their laws and customs, their feuds and compacts. The former were more numerous than the latter, and they fought on every possible occasion. A kind of half-secret organization existed among them, and new members passed through a ceremony called 'initiation,' which was not confined to the lower classes, from which most of them were recruited. Almost every Philadelphia boy, as late as twenty years ago, went through some sort of ordeal when he first entered into active boyhood. Being triced up by legs and arms, and swung violently against a gate, was usually part of this ceremony, and it no doubt still exists, although I have no particular information, which indeed is rather difficult to obtain, as boys, while they remain boys, are reticent concerning all such matters" (212. 236).

These street-organizations exist in other cities also, and have their ramifications in the school-life of children, who either belong to, or are in some way subject to, these curious associations. Every ward, nay, every street of any importance, seems to have its "gang," and it is no small experience in a boy's life to pass the ordeal of initiation, battle with alien organizations, and retire, as childhood recedes, unharmed by the primitive *entourage.*

No doubt, from these street-gangs many pass into the junior criminal societies which are known to exist in many great cities, the training-schools for theft, prostitution, murder, the feeding-grounds for the "White Caps," "Molly Maguires," "Ku-Klux," "Mafia," "Camorra," and other secret political or criminal associations, who know but too well how to recruit their numbers from the young. The gentler side of the social instinct is seen in the formation of friendships among children, associations born of the nursery or the school-room which last often through life. The study of these early friendships offers a tempting field for sociological research and investigation.

Secret Societies of the Young.

There are among primitive peoples many secret societies to which children and youth are allowed to belong, or which are wholly composed of such.

Among the secret societies of the Kwakiutl Indians, of British Columbia, Dr. Boas mentions the "Kēki'qalak· (=the crows)," formed from the children (403. 53). The same author speaks of the Tsimshians, another British Columbia tribe, in these terms (403. 57): —

"A man who is not a member of a secret society is a 'common man.' He becomes a middle-class man after the first initiation, and attains higher rank by repeated initiations. The novice disappears in the same way as among the Kwakiutl. It is supposed that he goes to heaven. During the dancing season a feast is given, and while the women are dancing the novice is suddenly said to have disappeared. If he is a child, he stays away four days; youths remain absent six days, and grown-up persons several months. Chiefs are supposed to stay in heaven during the fall and entire winter. When this period has elapsed, they suddenly reappear on the beach, carried by an artificially-made monster belonging to their crest. Then all the members of the secret society to which the novice is to belong gather and walk down in grand procession to the beach to fetch the child. At this time the child's parents bring presents, particularly elk skins, strung on a rope as long as the procession, to be given at a subsequent feast. The people surround the novice and lead him into every house in order to show that he has returned. Then he is taken to the house of his parents and a bunch of cedar-bark is fastened over the door, to show that the place is tabooed, and nobody is allowed to enter." The dance and other ceremonies which follow may be read of in Dr. Boas' report.

Dr. Daniels, in his study of *Regeneration*, has called attention to "seclusion" and "disappearance," followed by reappearance and adoption as members of society, as characteristic practices in vogue among many savage and semi-civilized tribes with respect to children and those approaching the age of puberty — a change of name sometimes accompanies the "entering upon the new life," as it is often called. Of the Australians we read: "The boy at eight or ten years of age must leave the hut of his father and live in common with the other young men of the tribe. He is called by another name than that which he has borne from birth and his diet is regulated to some extent." In New Guinea, in Africa, and among some of the tribes of American aborigines like habits prevail. The custom of certain Indians formerly inhabiting Virginia is thus described: "After a very severe beating the boys are sent into a secluded spot. There they must stay nine months and can associate with no human being. They are fed during this time with a kind of intoxicating preparation of roots to make them forget all about their past life. After their return home everything must seem strange to them. In this way it is thought that they 'begin to live anew.' They are thought of as having been dead for a short time and are 'numbered among the older citizens after forgetting that they once were boys'" (214. 11–13).

In the African district of Quoja existed a secret society called Belly-Paaro, "the members of which had to spend a long time in a holy thicket. Whoever broke the rules of this society was seized upon by the Jannanes, or spirits of the dead, who dwelt in the thicket and brought thither, whence he was unable to return" (127. I. 240). Of this practice Kulischer remarks: "'It is a death and a new birth, since they are wholly changed in the consecrated thicket, dying to the old life and existence, and receiving a new understanding.' When the youths return from the thicket, they act as if they had come into the world for the first time, and had never known where their parents lived or their names, what sort of people they were, how to wash themselves" (214. 12).

Of another part of Africa we read: "In the country of Ambamba each person must die once, and come to life again. Accordingly, when a fetich-priest shakes his calabash at a village, those men and youths whose hour is come fall into a state of death-like torpor, from which they recover usually in the course of three days. But if there is any one that the fetich loves, him he takes into the bush and buries in the fetich-house. Oftentimes he remains buried for a long series of years. When he comes to life again, he begins to eat and drink as before, but his reason is gone, and the fetich-man is obliged to train him and instruct him in the simplest bodily movements, like a little child. At first the stick is only the instrument of education, but gradually his senses come back to him, and he begins to speak. As soon as his education is finished, the priest restores him to his parents. They seldom recognize their son, but accept the express

R

assurance of the feticero, who also reminds them of events in the past. In Ambamba a man who has not passed through the process of dying and coming to life again is held in contempt, nor is he permitted to join in the dance" (529. 56).

Some recollection, perhaps, of similar customs and ideas appears in the game of "Rûripsken," which, according to Schambach, is played by children in Göttingen: One of the children lies on the ground, pretending to be dead, the others running up and singing out "Rûripsken, are you alive yet?" Suddenly he springs up and seizes one of the other players, who has to take his place, and so the game goes on.

Among the Mandingos of the coast of Sierra Leone, the girls approaching puberty are taken by the women of the village to an out-of-the-way spot in the forest, where they remain for a month and a day in strictest seclusion, no one being permitted to see them except the old woman who has charge of their circumcision. Here they are instructed in religion and ceremonial, and at the expiration of the time set, are brought back to town at night, and indulge in a sort of Lady Godiva procession until daybreak. At the beginning of the dry-cool season among the Mundombe "boys of from eight to ten years of age are brought by the 'kilombola-masters' into a lonely uninhabited spot, where they remain for ninety days after their circumcision, during which time not even their own parents may visit them. After the wound heals, they are brought back to the village in triumph" (127. I. 292).

With the Kaffirs the circumcision-rites last five months, "and during this whole time the youths go around with their bodies smeared with white clay. They form a secret society, and dwell apart from the village in a house built specially for them" (127. I. 292). Among the Susu there is a secret organization known as the *Semo*, the members of which use a peculiar secret language, and "the young people have to pass a whole year in the forest, and it is believed right for them to kill any one who comes near the wood, and who is not acquainted with this secret tongue" (127. I. 240). A very similar society exists among the tribes on the Rio Nunez. Here "the young people live for seven or eight years a life of seclusion in the forest." In Angoy there is the secret society of the *Sindungo*, membership in which passes from father to son; in Bomma, the secret orders of the fetich Undémbo; among the Shekiani and the Bakulai, that of the great spirit Mwetyi, the chief object of which is to keep in subjection women and children, and into which boys are initiated when between fourteen and eighteen years old; the Mumbo Jumbo society of the Mandingos, into which no one under sixteen years of age is allowed to enter (127. I. 241-247).

Among the Mpongwe the women have a secret society called *Njembe*, the object of which is to protect them against harsh treatment by the men. The initiation lasts several weeks, and girls from ten to twelve years of age are admissible (127. I. 245).

Of the Indians of the western plains of the United States of America we are told: " At twelve or thirteen these yearnings can no longer be suppressed; and, banded together, the youths of from twelve to sixteen years roam over the country; and some of the most cold-blooded atrocities, daring attacks, and desperate combats have been made by these children in pursuit of fame" (432. 191).

Among the Mandingos of West Africa, during the two months immediately following their circumcision, the youths "form a society called *Solimana*. They make visits to the neighbouring villages, where they sing and dance and are *fêted* by the inhabitants."

In Angola the boys "live for a month under the care of a fetich-priest, passing their time in drum-beating, a wild sort of singing, and rat-hunting." Among the Beit Bidel "all the youths who are to be consecrated as men unite together. They deck themselves out with beads, hire a guitar-player, and retire to the woods, where they steal and kill goats from the herds of their tribe, and for a whole week amuse themselves with sport and song." The Wanika youths of like age betake themselves, wholly naked, to the woods, where they remain until they have slain a man." On the coast of Guinea, after their circumcision, "boys are allowed to exact presents from every one and to commit all sorts of excesses" (127. I. 291-4).

Among the Fulas, boys who have been circumcised are a law unto themselves until the incision has healed. They can steal or take whatever suits them without its being counted an offence.

In Bambuk, for fourteen days after the circumcision-*fête*, the young people are allowed to escape from the supervision of their parents. From sunrise to sunset they can leave the paternal roof and run about the fields near the village. They can demand meat and drink of whomsoever they please, but may not enter a house unless they have been invited to do so." In Darfur, "after their circumcision, the boys roamed around the adjacent villages and stole all the poultry" (127. I. 291).

Modern Aspects.

These secret societies and outbursts of primitive lawlessness recall at once to our attention the condition of affairs at some of our universities, colleges, and larger schools. The secret societies and student-organizations, with their initiations, feasts, and extravagant demonstrations, their harassing of the uninitiated, their despisal of municipal, collegiate, even parental authority, and their oftentime contempt and disregard of all social order, their not infrequent excesses and debauches, carry us back to their analogues in the institutions of barbarism and savagery, the accompaniments of the passage from childhood to manhood. Of late years, the same spirit has crept into our high schools, and is even making itself felt in the grammar grades, so imitative are the school-children of their brothers and sisters in the universities and colleges. Pennalism and fagging, so prevalent of old time in Germany and England, are not without their representatives in this country. The "freshman" in the high schools and colleges is often made to feel much as the savage does who is serving his time of preparation for admission into the mysteries of Mumbo-Jumbo.

In the revels of " May Day," " Midsummer," " Rogation Week," "Whitsuntide," " All Fools' Day," " New Year's Day," " Hallow E'en," " Christmas," " Easter," etc., children throughout England and in many parts of Europe during the Middle Ages took a prominent part and *rôle* in the customs and practices which survive even to-day, as may be seen in Brand, Grimm, and other books dealing with popular customs and festivals, social *fêtes* and merry-makings.

In Tennyson's *May Queen* we read : —

" You must wake and call me early, call me early, mother dear ;
To-morrow'll be the happiest time of all the glad New Year ;
Of all the glad New Year, mother, the maddest, merriest day ;
For I'm to be Queen o' the May, mother, I'm to be Queen o' the May."

And a " mad, merry day " it certainly was in " merry England,"
when the fairest lass in the village was chosen " Queen of the
May," and sang merry songs of Robin Hood and Maid Marian.

Polydore Virgil tells us that in ancient Rome the " youths used
to go into the fields and spend the Calends of May in dancing
and singing in honour of Flora, goddess of fruits and flowers."
Westermarck seems to think some of these popular customs have
something to do with the increase of the sexual function in spring
and early summer (166. 30).

In seizing upon this instinct for society-making among children
and youth lies one of the greatest opportunities for the prevention of crime and immorality the world has ever known. To turn
to good ends this spontaneity of action, to divert into channels
of usefulness these currents of child-activity, will be to add
immensely to the equipment of mankind in the struggle with
vice. A certain bishop of the early Christian Church is credited
with having declared that, if the authorities only took charge of
the children soon enough, there would be no burning of heretics,
no scandalous schisms in the body ecclesiastic; and there is a
good deal of truth in this observation.

The Catholic Church and many of the other Christian churches
have seen the wisdom of appealing to, and availing themselves
of, the child-power in social and socio-religious questions. Not
a little of the great spread of the temperance movement in America and Europe of recent years is due to the formation of children's societies, — Bands of Hope, Blue Ribbon Clubs, Junior
Temperance Societies and Prohibition Clubs, Young Templars'
Associations, Junior Father Matthew Leagues, and the like, —
where a legitimate sphere is open to the ardour and enthusiasm
of the young of both sexes. The great Methodist Church has
been especially quick to recognize the value of this kind of work,
and the junior chapters of the " Epworth League " — whose object
is " to promote intelligence and loyal piety in its young members
and friends and to train them in experimental religion, practical
benevolence, and church work " — now numbers some three thou-

sand, with a membership of about one hundred and twenty thousand. This society was organized at Cleveland, Ohio, May 15, 1889. The " Young People's Society of Christian Endeavour," the first society of which was established at Portland, Maine, February 2, 1881, with the object of " promoting an earnest Christian life among its members, increasing their mutual acquaintance, and making them more useful in the service of God," has now enrolled nearly thirty-four thousand " Companies," with a total membership (active and associate) all over the world of over two million; of these societies 28,696 are in the United States and 2243 in Canada. Another society of great influence, having a membership in America and the Old World of some thirty-five thousand, is the " Ministering Children's League," founded by the Countess of Meath in 1885, and having as objects " to promote kindness, unselfishness, and the habit of usefulness amongst children, and to create in their minds an earnest desire to help the needy and suffering; to give them some definite work to do for others, that this desire may be brought to good effect"; there are also the " Lend-a-Hand Clubs " of the Unitarian Church. The Episcopal Church has its "Girls' Friendly Societies," its "Junior Auxiliaries to the Board of Missions"; its "Brotherhood of St. Andrew," and " Brotherhood of Andrew and Philip," for young men. For those of not too youthful years, the " Young Men's Christian Association," the associations of the " White," " Red," and "Iron Cross " exist in the various churches, besides many other " Guilds," " Alliances," "Leagues," etc. For those outside the churches there are " Boys' Clubs," and " Girls' Societies " in the cities and larger towns. The " Bands of Mercy " and the branches of the "Society for the Prevention of Cruelty to Animals" exert a widespread influence for good; while several of the secret benevolent associations, such as the "Foresters," for example, have instituted junior lodges, from which the youth are later on drafted into the society of their elders. There exist also many social clubs and societies, more or less under the supervision of the older members of the community, in which phases of human life other than the purely religious or benevolent find opportunity to display themselves; and between these and the somewhat sterner church-societies a connecting link is formed by the " Friday Night Clubs " of the Unitarian Church and the " Young People's Associations" of other liberal denominations. In the home itself, this society instinct is recognized, and the list of children's teas, dinners, parties, "receptions," "doll-parties," "doll-shows," etc., would be a long one. Among all peoples, barbarous as well as civilized, since man is by nature a social animal, the instinct for society develops early in the young, and the sociology of childhood offers a most inviting field for research and investigation both in the Old World and in the New.

CHAPTER XV.

THE CHILD AS LINGUIST.

But what am I?
An infant crying in the night :
An infant crying for the light,
And with no language but a cry. — *Tennyson.*

Yet she carried a doll as she toddled alone,
And she talked to that doll in a tongue her own. — *Joaquin Miller.*

Among savages, children are, to a great extent, the originators of idiomatic diversities. — *Charles Rau.*

It was as impossible for the first child endowed with this faculty not to speak in the presence of a companion similarly endowed, as it would be for a nightingale or a thrush not to carol to its mate. The same faculty creates the same necessity in our days, and its exercise by young children, when accidentally isolated from the teachings and influence of grown companions, will readily account for the existence of all the diversities of speech on our globe. — *Horatio Hale.*

SOME scientists have held that mankind began with the *Homo Alalus*, speechless, dumb man, an hypothesis now looked upon by the best authorities as untenable; and the folk have imagined that, were not certain procedures gone through with upon the new-born child, it would remain dumb through life, and, if it were allowed to do certain things, a like result would follow. Ploss informs us that the child, and the mother, while she is still suckling it, must not, in Bohemia, eat fish, else, since fish are mute, the child would be so also; in Servia, the child is not permitted to eat any fowl that has not already crowed, or it would remain dumb for a very long time; in Germany two little children, not yet able to speak, must not kiss each other, or both will be dumb.

The Frenum.

Our English phrase, "an unbridled tongue," has an interesting history and *entourage* of folk-lore. The subject has been quite

248

recently discussed by Dr. Chervin, of the Institute for Stammerers at Paris (205). Citing the lines of Boileau: —

> "Tout charme en un enfant dont la langue sans fard,
> A peine du *filet* encore débarrassée
> Sait d'un air innocent bégayer sa pensée,"

he notes the wide extension of the belief that the cutting of the *filet*, or *frein*, the *frenum*, or "bridle" of the tongue of the new-born infant facilitates, or makes possible, articulate speech. According to M. Sébillot, the cutting of the *sublet*, as it is called, is quite general in parts of Brittany (Haute Bretagne), and M. Moisset states that in the Yonne it is the universal opinion that neglect to do so would cause the new-born child to remain dumb for life; M. Desaivre cites the belief in Poitou that, unless the *lignoux* were cut in the child at birth, it would prevent its sucking, and, later on, its speaking. The operation is usually performed by nurses and midwives, with the nail of the little finger, which is allowed to grow excessively long for the purpose (205. 6). Dr. Chervin discusses the scientific aspects of the subject, and concludes that the statistics of stammering and the custom of cutting the *frenum* of the tongue do not stand in any sort of correlation with each other, and that this ancient custom, noted by Celsus, has no real scientific *raison d'être* (205. 9). We say that a child is "tongue-tied," and that one "makes too free with his tongue"; in French we find: *Il a le filet bien coupé*, "he is a great talker," and in the eighteenth century *Il n'a pas de filet* was in use; a curious German expression for "tongue-tied" is *mundfaul*, "mouth-lazy."

Following up the inquiry of Dr. Chervin in France, M. Höfler of Tölz has begun a similar investigation for Germany (263). He approves of the suggestion of Dr. Chervin, that the practice of cutting the *frenum* of the tongue has been induced by the inept name *frenulum, frein, Bändchen*, given by anatomists to the object in question. According to H. Carstens the *frenulum* is called in Low German *keekel-reem* or *kikkel-reem*, which seems to be derived from *käkeln*, "to cry, shriek," and *reem*, "band, cord," so that the word really signifies "speech-band." If it is cut in children who have difficulty in speaking before the first year of life, or soon after, they will be cured of stuttering and made to speak well. To a man or woman who does a good deal of talking, who has "the gift of the gab," the expression *Em (ehr) is de keekelreem gut snäden* = " His (her) *frenum* has been well cut," is applied. In some parts of Low Germany the operation is performed for quite a different reason, viz., when the child's tongue cannot take hold of the mother's breast, but always slips off. Höfler mentions the old custom of placing beneath the child's tongue a piece of ash-bark (called *Schwindholz*), so that the organ of speech may not vanish (*schwinden*); this is done in the case of children who are hard of speech (263. 191, 281).

Ploss states that in Königsberg (Prussia) tickling the soles of the feet of a little child is thought to occasion stuttering; in Italy the child will learn to stutter, unless, after it has been weaned, it is given to drink for the first time out of a hand-bell (326. II. 286).

Among the numerous practices in vogue to hasten the child's acquisition of speech, or to make him ready and easy of tongue, are the following: some one returned from the communion breathes into the child's mouth (Austrian Silesia); the mother, when, after supper on Good Friday, she suckles the child for the last time, breathes into its mouth (Bohemia); the child is given to drink water out of a cow-bell (Servia); when the child, on the arm of its mother, pays the first visit to neighbours or friends, it is presented with three eggs, which are pressed three times to his mouth, with the words, "as the hens cackle, the child learns to prattle" (Thuringia, the Erzgebirge, Bavaria, Franconia, and the Harz); when a child is brought to be baptized, one of the relatives must make a christening-letter (*Pathenbrief*), and, with the poem or the money contained in it, draw three crosses through the mouth of the child (Königsberg) (326. II. 205).

Speech-Exercises.

Ploss has a few words to say about " Volksgebräuchliche Sprach-Exercitien," or " Zungen-Exercitien," the folk-efforts to teach the child to overcome the difficulties of speech (326. II. 285, 286), and more recently Treichel (373) has treated in detail of the various methods employed in Prussia. In these exercises examples and difficult words are given in several languages, alliteration, sibilation, and all quips and turns of consonantal and vocalic expression, word-position, etc., are in use to test the power of speech alike of child and adult. Treichel observes that in the schools even, use is made of foreign geographical names, names of mountains in Asia, New Zealand, and Aztec names in Mexico; the plain of *Apapurinkasiquinitschiquasaqua*, from Immermann's *Münchhausen*, is also cited as having been put to the like use. The title of doctors' dissertations in chemistry are also recommended (373. 124).

Following are examples of these test sentences and phrases from German: —

(1) Acht und achtzig achteckige Hechtsköpfe; (2) Bierbrauer Brauer braut braun Bier; (3) De dönne Diewel drog den dicke Diewel dorch den dicke Dreck; (4) Esel essen Nesseln gern; (5) In Ulm und um Ulm und um Ulm herum; (6) Wenige wissen, wie viel sie wissen müssen, um zu wissen, wie wenig sie wissen; (7) Es sassen zwei zischende Schlangen zwischen zwei spitzigen Steinen und zischten dazwischen; (8) Näge mal de Boll Boll Boll Boll Boll Boll Boll Boll Boll; (9) Fritz, Fritz, friss frische Fische, Fritz; (10) Kein klein Kind kann keinen kleinen Kessel Kohl kochen.

There are alliterative sentences for all the letters of the alphabet, and many others more or less alliterative, while the humorous papers contain many exaggerated examples of this sort of thing. Of the last, the following on "Hottentottentaten" will serve as an instance: —

> "In dem wilden Land der Kaffern,
> Wo die Hottentotten trachten
> Hohe Hottentottentitel
> Zu erwerben in den Schlachten,
> Wo die Hottentottentaktik
> Lässt ertönen fern und nah
> Auf dem Hottentottentamtam
> Hottentottentattratah;
> Wo die Hottentottentrotteln,
> Eh' sie stampfen stark und kühn,
> Hottentottentätowirung
> An sich selber erst vollzieh'n,
> Wo die Hottentotten tuten
> Auf dem Horn voll Eleganz

Und nachher mit Grazie tanzen
Hottentottentotentanz, —
Dorten bin ich mal gewesen
Und ich habe schwer gelitten,
Weil ich Hottentotten trotzte,
Unter Hottentottentritten ;
So 'ne Hottentottentachtel,
Die ist nämlich fürchterlich
Und ich leid' noch heute
An dem Hottentottentatterich " (373. 222).

In our older English and American readers and spelling-books we meet with much of a like nature, and the use of these test-phrases and sentences has not yet entirely departed from the schools. Familiar are: "Up the high hill he heaved a huge round stone; around the rugged riven rock the ragged rascal rapid ran; Peter Piper picked a peck of prickly pears from the prickly-pear trees on the pleasant prairies," and many others still in use traditionally among the school-children of to-day, together with linguistic exercises of nonsense-syllables and the like, pronouncing words backwards, etc.

In French we have: (1) L'origine ne se désoriginalisera jamais de son originalité; (2) A la santé de celle, qui tient la sentinelle devant la citadelle de votre cœur! (3) Car Didon dîna, dit-on, Du dos d'un dodu dindon.

In Polish: (1) Bydło by*ł*o, byd*ł*o będzie (It was cattle, it remains cattle); (2) Podawa*ł*a baba babie przez piec malowane grabie (A woman handed the woman over the stove a painted rake); (3) Chrząszcz brzmi w trzinie (The beetle buzzes in the pipe).

Latin and Greek are also made use of for similar purpose. Treichel cites, among other passages, the following: (1) Quamuis sint sub aqua, sub aqua maledicere tentant (Ovid, *Metam.* VI. 376); (2) At tuba terribili sonitu taratantara dixit (Virgil, *Aen.* IX. 503); (3) Quadrupedante putrem sonitu quatit ungula campum (Virgil, *Aen.* VIII. 596); (4) Αὖτις ἔπειτα πέδονδε κυλίνδετο λᾶας ἀναιδής (Homer, *Odyss.* II. 598); (5) Τριχθὰ τε καὶ τέτραχθὰ · διέσχεσεν ἲς ἀνέμοιο (Homer, *Odyss.* IX. 71, *Il.* III. 363); (6) Ὦ μάκαρ Ἀτρείδη μοιρηγενὲς ὀλβιοδαίμον (Homer, *Il.* III. 182).

These customs are not confined, however, to the civilized nations of Europe. Dr. Pechuel-Loesche tells us that, among the negroes of the Loango coast of Africa, the mother teaches the child little verses, just as illogical as the test-sentences often are which are employed in other parts of the world, and containing intentionally difficult arrangements of words. The child whose skilful tongue can repeat these without stumbling, is shown to visitors and is the cause of much admiration and merriment. And this exhibition of the child's linguistic and mnemonic powers finds vogue among other races than those of the dark continent (373. 125).

Alphabet-Rhymes.

A very curious development of child-linguistics is seen in the so-called *ABC Rhymes.* H. A. Carstensen reports from Risummoor in Low Germany the following arrangement and interpretation of the letters of the alphabet (199. 55): —

A	B	C(K)		A	B	C(K)
Aewel	baeget	Kaege		Abel	bakes	cakes.
D	**E**	**F**		**D**	**E**	**F**
Detlef	ēt	fåle.		Detlef	eats	much.
G	**H**	**J K**		**G**	**H**	**J K**
Grutte Hans jaeget Kraege.				Great Jack hunts crows.		
L	**M**	**N**		**L**	**M**	**N**
Lötte	maeget	noerne.		Lütje	makes	names.
O	**P**	**Q**		**O**	**P**	**Q**
Okke	plökket	Kuerde.		Okke	makes	wool-cards.
R	**S**	**T**		**R**	**S**	**T**
Rikkert	sâit	tuffle.		Richard	sews	slippers
U	**V**	**W**		**U**	**V**	**W**
Uethet	Völkert	waeder?		Fetches	Volkert	water?

From the North Frisian islands of Silt and Föhr the following ABC rhymes have been recorded, consisting mostly of personal names (199. 192): —

1. From Silt: *A*nna *B*oyken, *C*hristian *D*ojken, *E*rkel *F*redden, *G*ondel *H*ansen, *J*ens *K*uk, *L*orenz *M*ommen, *N*iels *O*tten, *P*eter *Q*uotten, *R*ink *S*wennen, *T*heide *U*wen, *V*olkert, *W*ilhelm, exerzére.

2. From Föhr: *A*rest *B*uhn, *C*ike *D*uhn, *E*hlen *F*rödden, *G*irrǝ *H*ayen, *I*ngke *K*ayen, *L*urenz *M*unje, *N*ahmen *O*tt, *P*eter *Q*uott, *R*ekkert *s*kär, *T*rintje *u*n, qui *w*eg, *x*, *y*, *z*.

3. From Föhr: *A*ntje *b*rawt; *C*isele *d*rug; *E*hlen *f*ald; *G*öntje *h*olp; *I*ngke *k*näd; *L*ena *m*äd; *N*ahmen *O*kken; *P*eter *Q*uast;

*R*örd *R*ütjer; *S*ab *S*ütjer; *S*onk *S*tein; *T*hur *O*rdert; *W*ögen *w*uhlet; *Y*ng *Z*uhlet.

From Ditmarschen we have the following (199. 290): —

1. From Süderstapel in Stapelholm: *A*-*B*eeter, *C*-*D*eeter, *E*-*E*fter, *G*-*H*ater, *I*-*K*ater, *L*-*E*mder, *N*-*O*ter, *P*eter Rüster sien Swester harr Büxsen von Manchester, harr'n Kleed vun Kattun, weer Köfft bi Jud'n (Peter Rüster his sister has breeches from Manchester, has a dress of cotton, who buys of Jews).

2. From Tönningstedt and Feddringen: *A*-*B*eeter, *C*-*D*eeter, *E*-*E*fter, *G*-*H*ater, *J*-*K*ater, *L*-*E*mder, *N*-*O*ter, *P*-*K*uter, *L*-*E*ster, *T*-*U*ter, *V*-*W*eeter, *X*-*Z*eeter.

In Polish we have a rather curious rhyme (199. 260): *A*dam *B*abkie *C*ukier *Da*ſ, *E*wa *F*igi *G*ryzſa; *H*anko, *J*eko, *K*arol *L*erch *N*osi *O*rla *P*apa *R*uskigo (Adam to the old woman sugar gave, Eve figs nibbled; Hanko, Jeko, Karol, and Lerch carry the eagle of the Ruthenian priest). Another variant runs: *A*dam *B*abi *C*ucker *d*aje *E*wa *f*igi *g*rizi *H*ala *i*dzie *K*upić *l*ala *m*ama *n*ie *p*ozwala (199. 150).

At Elberfeld, according to O. Schell, the following rhyme was in use about the middle of this century (199. 42): *A*braham *B*öckmann; *C*epter *D*ickmann; *E*ngel *F*uawenkel; *G*retchen *H*ahn; *I*saak *K*reier; *L*ottchen *M*eyer; *N*ikolas *O*lk; *P*itter *Q*uack; *R*udolf *S*imon; *T*ante *U*hler; *V*ater *W*ettschreck; *X*erxes *Y*ork.

From Leipzig, L. Fränkel reports the following as given off in a singing tone with falling rhythm: —

B a ba, b e be, b i bi — babebi; b o bo, b u bu — bobu; ba, be, bi, bo, bu — babebibobu. C a ca (pron. *za*, not *ka*), c e ce, c i ci — caceci; c o co, c u cu — cocu; ca, ce, ci, co, cu — cacecicocu, etc.

From various parts of Ditmarschen come these rhymes: —

A–B ab,	A–B ab,
Mus sitt in't Schapp,	Mouse sits in the cupboard,
Kater darfår,	Cat in front,
Mak apen de Dår.	Open the door.

These child-rhymes and formulæ from North Germany find their cognates in our own nursery-rhymes and explanatory letter-lists, which take us back to the very beginnings of alphabetic writing. An example is the familiar: —

"*A* was an Archer that shot at a frog,
B was a Butcher that had a big dog," etc., etc.

Letter-Formulæ.

Here belong also the curious formulæ known all over the United States and English-speaking Canada, to which attention has recently been called by Professor Frederick Starr. When the word *Preface* is seen, children repeat the words, "*P*eter *R*ice *E*ats *F*ish and *C*atches *E*els," or backwards, "*E*els *C*atch *A*lligators; *F*ather *E*ats *R*aw *P*otatoes." Professor Starr says that the second formula is not quite so common as the first; the writer's experience in Canada leads him to express just the opposite opinion. Professor Starr gives also formulæ for *Contents* and *Finis* as follows: "*F*ive *I*rish *N*iggers *I*n *S*pain," backwards "*S*ix *I*rish *N*iggers *I*n *F*rance"; "*C*hildren *O*ught *N*ot *T*o *E*at *N*uts *T*ill *S*unday" (355. 55). Formulæ like these appear to be widespread among school-children, who extract a good deal of satisfaction from the magic meaning of these quaint expressions.

Another series of formulæ, not referred to by Professor Starr, is that concerned with the interpretation of the numerous abbreviations and initials found in the spelling-book and dictionary. In the manufacture of these much childish wit and ingenuity are often expended. In the writer's schoolboy days there was quite a series of such expansions of the letters which stood for the various secret and benevolent societies of the country. *I. O. G. T.* (Independent Order of Good Templars), for example, was made into "I Often Get Tight (*i.e.* drunk)," which was considered quite a triumph of juvenile interpretative skill. Another effort was in the way of explaining the college degrees: *B.A.* = "Big Ape," *M.A.* = "Matured Ape," *B.D.* = "Bull-Dog," *LL.D.* = "Long Legged Devil," etc. Still another class is represented by the interpretations of the German *u. A. w. g.* (our R. S. V. P.), *i.e.* "um Antwort wird gebeten" (an answer is requested), for which A. Treichel records the following renderings: um Ausdauer wird gebeten (perseverance requested); und Abends wird getanzt (and in the evening there is dancing); und Abends wird gegeigt (and in the evening there is fiddling); und Abends wird gegessen (and in the evening there is eating); und Andere werden gelästert (and others are abused) (392. V. 114). This side of the linguistic inventiveness of childhood, with its *double-entendre*, its puns, its folk-etymologies, its keen discernment of hidden resemblances and analogies, deserves more study than it has apparently received.

The formulæ and expressions belonging to such games as marbles are worthy of consideration, for here the child is given an opportunity to invent new words and phrases or to modify and disfigure old ones.

Formulæ of Defiance, etc.

The formulæ of defiance, insult, teasing, etc., rhymed and in prose, offer much of interest. Peculiarities of physical constitution, mental traits, social relationships, and the like, give play to childish fancy and invention. It would be a long list which should include all the material corresponding to such as the following, well known among English-speaking school-children : —

1. Georgie Porgie, Puddin' Pie,
   Kissed a girl and made her cry !
2. Blue-eyed beauty,
   Do your mother's duty !
3. Black eye, pick a pie,
   Turn around and tell a lie !
4. Nigger, nigger, never-die,
   Black face and shiny eye !

Interesting is the following scale of challenging, which Professor J. P. Fruit reports from Kentucky (430. 229) : —

"I dare you ; I dog dare you ; I double dog dare you.
I dare you ; I black dog dare you ; I double black dog dare you."

The language of the school-yard and street, in respect to challenges, fights, and contests of all sorts, has an atmosphere of its own, through which sometimes the most clear-sighted older heads find it difficult to penetrate.

The American Dialect Society is doing good work in hunting out and interpreting many of these contributions of childhood to the great mosaic of human speech, and it is to be hoped that in this effort they will have the co-operation of all the teachers of the country, for this branch of childish activity will bear careful and thorough investigation.

Plant-Names.

In the names of some of the plants with which they early come into contact we meet with examples of the ingenuity of children. In Mrs. Bergen's (400) list of popular American plant-names are included some which come from this source, for example: "frog-plant (*Sedum Telephium*)," from the children's custom of "blowing up a leaf so as to make the epidermis puff up like a frog"; "drunkards (*Gaulteria procumbens*)," because "believed by children to intoxicate"; "bread-and-butter (*Smilax rotundifolia*)," because "the young leaves are eaten by children"; "velvets (*Viola pedata*)," a corruption of the "velvet violets" of their elders; "splinter-weed (*Antennaria plantaginifolia*)," from "the appearance of the heads"; "ducks (*Cypripedium*)," because "when the flower is partly filled with sand and set afloat on water, it looks like a duck"; "pearl-grass (*Glyceria Canadensis*)," a name given at Waverley, Massachusetts, "by a few children, some years ago." This list might easily be extended, but sufficient examples have been given to indicate the extent to which the child's mind has been at work in this field. Moreover, many of the names now used by the older members of the community, may have been coined originally by children and then adopted by the others, and the same origin must probably be sought out for not a few of the folk-etymologies and word-distortions which have so puzzled the philologists.

"Physonyms."

In an interesting paper on "physonyms,"—*i.e.* "words to which their signification is imparted by certain physiological processes, common to the race everywhere, and leading to the creation of the same signs with the same meaning in totally sundered linguistic stocks"—occurs the following passage (193. cxxxiii.):—

"One of the best known and simplest examples is that of the widespread designation of 'mother' by such words as *mama, nana, ana;* and of 'father' by such as *papa, baba, tata.* Its true explanation has been found to be that, in the infant's first attempt to utter articulate sounds, the consonants *m, p,* and *t* decidedly preponderate; and the natural vowel *a,* associated with these,

B

yields the child's first syllables. It repeats such sounds as *ma-ma-ma* or *pa-pa-pa*, without attaching any meaning to them; the parents apply these sounds to themselves, and thus impart to them their signification."

Other physonyms are words of direction and indication of which the radical is *k* or *g*; the personal pronouns radical in *n, m* (first person), *k, t, d* (second person); and demonstratives and locatives whose radical is *s*. The frequency of these sounds in the language of children is pointed out also by Tracy in his monograph on the psychology of childhood. In the formation and fixation of the onomatopes with which many languages abound some share must be allotted to the child. A recent praiseworthy study of onomatopes in the Japanese language has been made by Mr. Aston, who defines an onomatope as "the artistic representation of an inarticulate sound or noise by means of an articulate sound" (394. 333). The author is of opinion that from the analogy of the lower animals the inference is to be drawn that "mankind occupied themselves for a long time with their own natural cries before taking the trouble to imitate for purposes of expression sounds not of their own making" (394. 334). The latter process was gradual and extended over centuries. For the child or the "child-man" to imitate the cry of the cock so successfully was an inspiration; Mr. Aston tells us that "the formation of a word like *cock-a-doodle-do*, is as much a work of individual genius as Hamlet or the Laocoön" (394. 335). Of certain modern aspects of onomatopœia the author observes: "There is a kindred art, viz. that of the *exact* imitation of animal cries and other sounds, successfully practised by some of our undergraduates and other young people, as well as by tame ravens and parrots. It probably played some part in the development of language, but I can only mention it here" (394. 333).

College Yells.

The "college yells" of the United States and Canada offer an inviting field for study in linguistic atavism and barbaric vocal expression. The *New York World Almanac* for 1895 contains a list of the "yells" of some three hundred colleges and universities in the United States. Out of this great number, in which there is a plenitude of "Rah! rah! rah!" the following are especially noteworthy: —

> *Benzonia:* Kala, kala, kala! Sst, Boom, Gah! Benzo, Benzon-iah! Whooo!
> *Buchtel:* Ye-ho! Ye-hesa! Hisa! Wow wow! Buchtel!
> *Dartmouth:* Wah, who, wah! wah who wah! da-da-da, Dartmouth! wah who wah! T-i-g-e-r!
> *Heidelberg:* Killi-killick! Rah, rah, Zik, zik! Ha! Ha! Yi! Hoo! Baru! Zoo! Heidelberg!

The "yell" of *Ohio Wesleyan University,* "O-wee-wi-wow! Ala-ka-zu-ki-zow! Ra-zi-zi-zow! Viva! Viva! O. W. U.!" is enough to make the good man for whom the institution is named turn uneasily in his grave. The palm must, however, be awarded to the *University of North Dakota,* whose remarkable "yell" is this: "Odz-dzo-dzi! Ri-ri-ri! Hy-ah! Hy-ah! North Dakota! and Sioux War-Cry." Hardly have the ancestors of Sitting Bull and his people suspected the immortality that awaited their ancient slogan. It is curious that the only "yell" set to proper music is that of the girls of *Wellesley College,* who sing their cheer, "Tra la la la, Tra la la la, Tra la la la la la la, W-E-L-L-E-S-L-E-Y, Welles-ley."

As is the case with other practices in collegiate life, these "yells" seem to be making their way down into the high and grammar schools, as well as into the private secondary schools, the popularity and excitement of field-sports and games, baseball, foot-ball, etc., giving occasion enough for their frequent employment.

Here fall also the spontaneous shouts and cries of children at work and at play, the *Ki-yah!* and others of a like nature whose number is almost infinite.

Mr. Charles Ledyard Norton, in his *Political Americanisms* (New York, 1890), informs us that "the peculiar staccato cheer, 'rah, rah, rah!'" was probably invented at Harvard in 1864. In the Blaine campaign of 1884 it was introduced into political meetings and processions together with "the custom, also borrowed from the colleges, of spelling some temporarily significant catch-word in unison, as, for instance, 'S-o-a-p!' the separate letters being pronounced in perfect time by several hundred voices at once." The same authority thinks that the idea of calling out "Blaine —

Blaine — James G. Blaine!" in cadenced measure after the manner of the drill-sergeants, "Left — left — left — right — left!" an idea which had many imitations and elaborations among the members of both the great political parties, can be traced back to the Columbia College students (p. 120).

The Child as an Innovator in Language.

But the *rôle* of the child in the development of language is concerned with other things than physonyms and onomatopes. In his work on Brazilian ethnography and philology, Dr. von Martius writes (522. 43): "A language is often confined to a few individuals connected by relationship, forming thus, as it were, a *family institute*, which isolates those who use it from all neighbouring or distant tribes so completely that an understanding becomes impossible." This intimate connection of language with the family, this preservation and growth of language, as a family institution, has, as Dr. von Martius points out, an interesting result (522. 44): —

"The Brazilians frequently live in small detachments, being kept apart by the chase; sometimes only a few families wander together; often it is one family alone. Within the family the language suffers a constant remodelling. One of the children will fail to catch precisely the radical sound of a word; and the weak parents, instead of accustoming it to pronounce the word correctly, will yield, perhaps, themselves, and adopt the language of the child. We often were accompanied by persons of the same band; yet we noticed in each of them slight differences in accentuation and change of sound. His comrades, however, understood him, and they were understood by him. As a consequence, their language never can become stationary, but will constantly break off into new dialects." Upon these words of von Martius (reported by Dr. Oscar Peschel), Dr. Charles Rau comments as follows (522. 44): "Thus it would seem that, among savages, *children* are to a great extent the originators of idiomatic diversities. Dr. Peschel places particular stress on this circumstance, and alludes to the habit of over-indulgent parents among refined nations of conforming to the humours of their children by conversing with them in a kind of infantine language, until they are several years old. Afterward, of course, the rules of civilized life compel these children to adopt the proper language; but no such necessity exists among a hunter family in the primeval forests of South America; here the deviating form of speech remains, and the foundation of a new dialect is laid."

Children's Languages.

But little attention has been paid to the study of the language of children among primitive people. In connection with a brief investigation of child-words in the aboriginal tongues of America, Mr. Horatio Hale communicated to the present writer the following observation of M. l'Abbé Cuoq, of Montreal, the distinguished missionary and linguist: "As far as the Iroquois in particular are concerned, it is certain that this language [langage enfantin] is current in every family, and that the child's relatives, especially the mothers, teach it to their children, and that the latter consequently merely repeat the words of which it is composed" (201. 322). That these "child-words" were invented by children, the Abbé does not seem to hint.

The prominence of the mother-influence in the child's linguistic development is also accentuated by Professor Mason, who devotes a chapter of his recent work on woman's part in the origin and growth of civilization to woman as a linguist. The author points out how "women have helped to the selection and preservation of language through onomatopœia," their vocal apparatus being "singularly adapted to the imitation of many natural sounds," and their ears "quick to catch the sounds within the compass of the voice" (113. 188–204). To the female child, then, we owe a good deal of that which is now embodied in our modern speech, and the debt of primitive races is still greater. Many a traveller has found, indeed, a child the best available source of linguistic information, when the idling warriors in their pride, and the hard-working women in their shyness, or taboo-caused fear, failed to respond at all to his requests for talk or song.

Canon Farrar, in his *Chapters on Language*, makes the statement: "It is a well-known fact that the neglected children, in some of the Canadian and Indian villages, who are left alone for days, can and do invent for themselves a sort of *lingua franca,* partially or wholly unintelligible to all except themselves" (200. 237). Mr. W. W. Newell speaks of the linguistic inventiveness of children in these terms (313. 24) : —

"As infancy begins to speak by the free though unconscious combination of linguistic elements, so childhood retains in language a measure of freedom. A little attention to the jargons invented by children might have been serviceable to certain philologists. Their love of originality finds the tongue of their elders too commonplace; besides, their fondness for mystery requires secret ways of communication. They, therefore, often create (so to speak) new languages, which are formed by changes in the mother-speech, but sometimes have quite complicated laws of structure and a considerable arbitrary element." The author cites examples of the "Hog Latin" of New England school-children, in the elaboration of which much youthful ingenuity is expended. Most interesting is the brief account of the "cat" language : —

"A group of children near Boston invented the *cat language,* so called because its object was to admit of free intercourse with cats, to whom it was mostly talked, and by whom it was presumed to be comprehended. In this tongue the cat was naturally the chief subject of nomenclature; all feline positions were observed and named, and the language was rich in such epithets, as Arabic contains a vast number of expressions for *lion.* Euphonic changes were very arbitrary and various, differing for the same termination; but the adverbial ending *-ly* was always *-osh; terribly, terriblosh.* A certain percentage of words were absolutely independent, or at least of obscure origin. The grammar tended to Chinese or infantine simplicity; *ta* represented any case of any personal pronoun. A proper name might vary in sound according to the euphonic requirements of the different Christian names by which it was preceded. There were two dialects, one, however, stigmatized as *provincial.* This invention of language must be very common, since other cases have fallen under our notice in which children have composed dictionaries of such" (313. 25).

This characterization of child-speech offers not a few points of contact with primitive languages, and might indeed almost have been written of one of them.

More recently Colonel Higginson (262) has given some details of "a language formed for their own amusement by two girls of thirteen or thereabouts, both the children of eminent scientific men, and both unusually active-minded and observant." This dialect "is in the most vivid sense a living language," and the inventors, who keep pruning and improving it, possess a manu-script dictionary of some two hundred words, which, it is to be hoped, will some day be published. An example or two from those given by Colonel Higginson will serve to indicate the gen-eral character of the vocabulary : —

bojiwassis, "the feeling you have just before you jump, don't you know — when you mean to jump and want to do it, and are just a little bit afraid to do it."

spygri, "the way you feel when you have just jumped and are awfully proud of it."

pippadolify, "stiff and starched like the young officers at Washington."

Other information respecting this "home-made dialect," with its revising academy of children and its standard dictionary, must be sought in the entertaining pages of Colonel Higginson, who justly says of this triumph of child-invention : "It coins thought into syllables, and one can see that, if a group of children like these were taken and isolated until they grew up, they would forget in time which words were their own and which were in Worcester's Dictionary ; and *stowish* and *krono* and *bojiwassis* would gradually become permanent forms of speech" (262. 108).

In his valuable essay on *The Origin of Languages* (249), Mr. Horatio Hale discusses a number of cases of invention of languages by children, giving interesting, though (owing to the neglect of the observers) not very extensive, details of each.

One of the most curious instances of the linguistic inventive-ness of children is the case of the Boston twins (of German descent on the mother's side) born in 1860, regarding whose lan-guage a few details were given by Miss E. H. Watson, who says : "At the usual age these twins began to talk, but, strange to say, *not* their 'mother-tongue.' They had a language of their own, and no pains could induce them to speak anything else. It was in vain that a little sister, five years older than they, tried to make them speak their *native language*, — as it would have been.

They persistently refused to utter a syllable of English. Not even the usual first words, 'papa,' 'mamma,' 'father,' 'mother,' it is said, did they ever speak; and, said the lady who gave this information to the writer, — who was an aunt of the children, and whose home was with them, — they were never known during this interval to call their mother by that name. They had their own name for her, but never the English. In fact, though they had the usual affections, were rejoiced to see their father at his returning home each night, playing with him, etc., they would seem to have been otherwise completely taken up, absorbed, with each other. . . . The children had not yet been to school; for, not being able to speak their 'own English,' it seemed impossible to send them from home. They thus passed the days, playing and talking together in their own speech, with all the liveliness and volubility of common children. Their accent was *German,* — as it seemed to the family. They had regular words, a few of which the family learned sometimes to distinguish; as that, for example, for carriage [*ni-si-boo-a*], which, on hearing one pass in the street, they would exclaim out, and run to the window " (249. 11). We are further informed that, when the children were six or seven years old, they were sent to school, but for a week remained "perfectly mute"; indeed, "not a sound could be heard from them, but they sat with their eyes intently fixed upon the children, seeming to be watching their every motion, — and no doubt, listening to every sound. At the end of that time they were induced to utter some words, and gradually and naturally they began, for the first time, to learn their 'native English.' With this accomplishment, the other began also naturally to fade away, until the memory with the use of it passed from their mind" (249. 12).

Mr. Horatio Hale, who resumes the case just noticed in his address before the Anthropological Section of the American Association for the Advancement of Science (Buffalo, 1886), gives also valuable details of the language of a little four-year-old girl and her younger brother in Albany, as reported by Dr. E. R. Hun (249. 13). The chief facts are as follows: "The mother observed when she was two years old that she was backward in speaking, and only used the words 'papa' and 'mamma.' After that she began to use words of her own invention, and

though she readily understood what was said, never employed the
words used by others. Gradually she extended her vocabulary
until it reached the extent described below [at least twenty-one
distinct words, many of which were used in a great variety of
meanings]. She has a brother eighteen months younger than
herself, who has learned her language, so that they talk freely
together. He, however, seems to have adopted it only because
he has more intercourse with her than with others; and in some
instances he will use a proper word with his mother, and his sister's word with her. She, however, persists in using only her
own words, though her parents, who are uneasy about her peculiarity of speech, make great efforts to induce her to use proper
words."

More may be read concerning this language in the account of
Dr. Hun (published in 1868).

Mr. Hale mentions three other cases, information regarding
which came to him. The inventors in the first instance were a
boy between four and five years old, said to have been "unusually
backward in his speech," and a girl a little younger, the children of a widower and a widow respectively, who married; and,
according to the report of an intimate friend: "He and the little
girl soon became inseparable playmates, and formed a language
of their own, which was unintelligible to their parents and
friends. They had names of their own invention for all the
objects about them, and must have had a corresponding supply of
verbs and other parts of speech, as their talk was fluent and
incessant." This was in Kingston, Ontario, Canada (249. 16).

The second case is that of two young children, twins, a boy
and a girl: "When they were three or four years old they were
accustomed, as their elder sister informs me, to talk together in a
language which no one else understood. . . . The twins were
wont to climb into their father's carriage in the stable, and 'chat-
ter away,' as my informant says, for hours in this strange language. Their sister remembers that it sounded as though the
words were quite short. But the single word which survives in
the family recollection is a dissyllable, the word for milk, which
was *cully*. The little girl accompanied her speech with gestures,
but the boy did not. As they grew older, they gradually gave up
their peculiar speech" (249. 17).

The third case cited by Mr. Hale is that of two little boys of Toronto, Canada, — five or six years of age, one being about a year older than the other, who attended a school in that city: "These children were left much to themselves, and had a language of their own, in which they always conversed. The other children in the school used to listen to them as they chattered together, and laugh heartily at the strange speech of which they could not understand a word. The boys spoke English with difficulty, and very imperfectly, like persons struggling to express their ideas in a foreign tongue. In speaking it, they had to eke out their words with many gestures and signs to make themselves understood; but in talking together in their own language, they used no gestures and spoke very fluently. She remembers that the words which they used seemed quite short" (249. 18).

Mr. Hale's studies of these comparatively uninvestigated forms of human speech led him into the wider field of comparative philology and linguistic origins. From the consideration of these data, the distinguished ethnologist came to regard the child as a factor of the utmost importance in the development of dialects and families of speech, and to put forward in definite terms a theory of the origin and growth of linguistic diversity and dialectic profusion, to the idea of which he was led by his studies of the multitude of languages within the comparatively restricted area of Oregon and California (249. 9). Starting with the language-faculty instinct in the child, says Mr. Hale: "It was as impossible for the first child endowed with this faculty not to speak in the presence of a companion similarly endowed, as it would be for a nightingale or a thrush not to carol to its mate. The same faculty creates the same necessity in our days, and its exercise by young children, when accidentally isolated from the teachings and influence of grown companions, will readily account for the existence of all the diversities of speech on our globe" (249. 47). Approaching, in another essay, one of the most difficult problems in comparative philology, he observes: "There is, therefore, nothing improbable in the supposition that the first Aryan family — the orphan children, perhaps, of some Semitic or Accadian fugitives from Arabia or Mesopotamia — grew up and framed their new language on the southeastern seaboard of Persia." Thus, he thinks, is the Aryo-Semitic problem most satisfactorily solved (467. 675). In a second paper (250) on *The Development of Language,* Mr. Hale restates and elaborates his theory with a wealth of illustration and argument, and it has since won considerable support from the scientists of both hemispheres.

Professor Romanes devotes not a few pages of his volume on *Mental Evolution in Man,* to the presentation of Mr. Hale's theory and of the facts upon which it is based (338. 138–144).

Secret Languages.

That the use of secret languages and the invention of them by children is widespread and prevalent at home, at school, in the playground, in the street, is evident from the exhaustive series of articles in which Dr. F. S. Krauss (281) of Vienna has treated of "Secret Languages." Out of some two hundred forms and fashions there cited a very large proportion indeed belong to the period of childhood and youth and the scenes of boyish and girlish activity. We have languages for games, for secret societies, for best friends, for school-fellows, for country and town, for boys and girls, etc. Dr. Oscar Chrisman (206) has quite recently undertaken to investigate the nature and extent of use of these secret languages in America, with gratifying results. A study of the child at the period in which the language-making instinct is most active cannot be without interest to pedagogy, and it would not be without value to inquire what has been the result of the universal neglect of language-teaching in the primary and lower grade grammar schools — whether the profusion of secret languages runs parallel with this diversion of the child-mind from one of its most healthful and requisite employments, or whether it has not to some extent atrophied the linguistic sense.

The far-reaching ramifications of "secret languages" are evidenced by the fact that a language called "Tut" by school-children of Gonzales, Texas, is almost identical in its alphabet with the "Guitar Language," of Bonyhad, in Hungary, the "Bob Language," of Czernowitz, in Austria, and another language of the same sort from Berg. The travels of the Texas secret language are stated by Dr. Chrisman to be as follows: "This young lady . . . learned it from her mother's servant, a negro girl; this girl learned it from a negro girl who got it at a female negro school at Austin, Texas, where it was brought by a negro girl from Galveston, Texas, who learned it from a negro girl who had come from Jamaica" (206. 305).

Evidence is accumulating to show that these secret languages of children exist in all parts of the world, and it would be a useful and instructive labour were some one to collect all available material and compose an exhaustive scientific monograph on the subject.

Interesting, for comparative purposes, are the secret languages and jargons of adults. As Paul Sartori (528) has recently shown, the use of special or secret languages by various individuals and classes in the communities is widespread both in myth and reality. We find peculiar dialects spoken by, or used in addressing, deities and evil spirits; giants, monsters; dwarfs, elves, fairies; ghosts, spirits; witches, wizards, "medicine men"; animals, birds, trees, inanimate objects. We meet also with special dialects of secret societies (both of men and of women); sacerdotal and priestly tongues; special dialects of princes, nobles, courts; women's languages, etc.; besides a multitude of jargons, dialects, languages of trades and professions, of peasants, shepherds, soldiers, merchants, hunters, and the divers slangs and jargons of the vagabonds, tramps, thieves, and other outcast or criminal classes.

Far-reaching indeed is the field opened by the consideration of but a single aspect of child-speech, that doll-language which Joaquin Miller so aptly notes : —

> " Yet she carried a doll, as she toddled alone,
> And she talked to that doll in a tongue her own."

Diminutives.

Both the golden age of childhood and the golden age of love exercise a remarkable influence upon language. Mantegazza, discussing "the desire to merge oneself into another, to abase oneself, to aggrandize the beloved," etc., observes: "We see it in the use of diminutives which lovers and sometimes friends use towards each other, and which mothers use to their children; we lessen ourselves thus in a delicate and generous manner in order that we may be embraced and absorbed in the circle of the creature we love. Nothing is more easily possessed than a small object, and before the one we love we would change ourselves into a bird, a canary — into any minute thing that we might be held utterly in the hands, that we might feel ourselves pressed on all sides by the warm and loving fingers. There is also another secret reason for the use of diminutives. Little creatures are loved tenderly, and tenderness is the supreme sign of every great force which is dissolved and consumes itself. After the wild, passionate, impetuous embrace there is always the tender note, and then diminutives, whether they belong to expression or to language, always play a great part" (499. 137). The fondness of boys for calling each other by the diminutives of their surnames belongs here.

In some languages, such as the Nipissing dialect of Algonkian in North America, the Modern Greek or Romaic, Lowland Scotch, and Plattdeutsch, the very frequent employment of diminutives has come to be a marked characteristic of the common speech of the people. The love for diminutives has, in some cases, led to a charm of expression in language which is most attractive; this is seen perhaps at its best in Castilian, and some of the Italian dialects (202 and 219). A careful study of the influence of the child upon the forms of language has yet to be made.

CHAPTER XVI.

The Child as Actor and Inventor.

The child is a born actor.

The world's a theatre, the earth a stage,
Which God and Nature do with actors fill. — *Heywood.*

Man is an imitative creature, and the foremost leads the flock. — *Schiller.*

Imitative Games.

In her article on *Imitation in Children*, Miss Haskell notes the predilection of children for impersonation and dramatic expression, giving many interesting examples. S. D. Warren, in a paper read before the American Association for the Advancement of Science, at the Brooklyn Meeting, 1894 (*Proc.*, Vol. xliii., p. 335), also notes these activities of children, mentioning, among other instances, "an annual celebration of the surrender of Cornwallis at Yorktown," "playing railroad," playing at pulling hand fire-engines, as the representatives of two rival villages.

The mention of the celebration of Cornwallis' surrender by children brings up the question of the child as recorder. As historian and chronicler, the child appears in the countless games in which he preserves more or less of the acts, beliefs, and superstitions of our ancestors. Concerning some of these, Miss Alice Gomme says: "It is impossible that they have been invented by children by the mere effort of imagination, and there is ample evidence that they have but carried on interchangeably a record of events, some of which belong to the earliest days of the nation" (242. 11).

As Miss Gomme points out, many of the games of English children are simply primitive dramas, — of the life of a woman ("When I was a Young Girl"), of courtship and marriage ("Here comes Three Dukes a-Riding," "Poor Mary sits a-Weeping"), of funerals ("Jenny Jones," "Green Gravel"), of border warfare ("We are the Rovers"), etc. Mr. W. W. Newell had previously remarked the importance of the dramatic element in children's games, citing as historical plays "Miss Jennia Jones" (funeral), "Down she comes as White as Milk," "Green Gravel," "Uncle John," "Barbara Allen," and others more or less partaking of this character, based upon historical ballads, of some of which traces only are now preserved.

By means of carved or graven images in wood or stone, given to children as playthings or as targets to practise skill in shooting or striking with miniature bow-and-arrow or spear, an early acquaintance is formed with many animals. The imitation of animals, their habits and peculiarities, often forms no small part of the dances and games of children of the lower races.

The Child as Actor.

Wallaschek, in his study of the primitive drama and pantomime (546. 214–229), notes the presence of children as dancers and performers among the Andaman Islanders, the Tagals of the Philippines, the Tahitians, Fijis, Polynesians and other more or less primitive races. Of Tibet and some portions of China Mr. Rockhill, in his *Diary of a Journey through Mongolia and Tibet, in* 1891 *and* 1892 (Washington, D. C., 1894), informs us that the lads in every village give theatrical performances, the companies of young actors being known as *Hsiao sheng huei,* "young men's amateur theatrical company" (p. 68).

Among the aborigines of the New World we find also children as actors and participants in the ceremonies and ritual performances of various tribes. In certain ceremonials of the Sia, as Mrs. Stevenson informs us, young children take part. A boy of eight was allowed to hear the sacred songs on one occasion, and to witness the making of the "medicine-water," but a boy of four was not permitted to be present; the boy also took part in the dance (538. 79). In the rain ceremonial of the "Giant Society," a little girl, eight years old, painted the fetiches quite as dexterously as her elders, and took apparently quite as much interest in the proceedings. In the rain ceremonial of the "Knife

Society," boys assist, and in the rain ceremonial of the Querränna, a child (boy) with wand and rattle joins in the celebration of the rites, "requiring no rousing to sing and bend his tiny body to the time of the rattle, and joining in the calls upon the cloud-people to gather to water the earth, with as much enthusiasm as his elders." When children, boys or girls, are about ten or twelve years of age, and have, as the Indians say, "a good head," they are initiated, if they so desire, into some of the mysteries of the dances of the Ka'tsuna, in charge of the Querränna Society (538. 106–117).

Dr. J. W. Fewkes, in his detailed article on the *Flute Observ-ance* of the Tusayan Indians of Walpi, an interesting study of primitive dramatization, notes the part played by children in these ceremonies. The principal characters are the "Snake Boy," the "Snake Girl," and some girl carriers of the sacred corn, besides lads as acolytes.

The story of the child as an actor has yet to be written. When the ancient Greeks crowded the theatres to hear and see the masterpieces of dramatic and histrionic genius, their "women, slaves, and children" were for the most part left at home, though we do find that later on in history, front seats were provided for the chief Athenian priestesses. No voices of children were heard in chorus, and childhood found no true interpreter upon the stage. In France, in the middle of the seventeenth century, women appear as actors; in England it was not until long after the death of her greatest dramatist that (in 1660) women could fill a *rôle* upon the stage without serious hindrance or molestation; in Japan, even now, play-acting is not looked upon as a respectable profession for women. For a long time in England and else-where, female parts were taken by children and youths. Here also we meet with companies of child-actors, such as the "Boys of the Grammar School at Westminster," "The Children of Paul's," etc. The influence which produced these survives and flourishes to-day in the fondness of high-school pupils and university students for dramatic performances and recitations, and the number of schools of gesture, elocution, and the like, testifies to the abiding interest of the young in the mimic art. This is also evidenced by the number of child actors and actresses in the theatrical world, and the remarkable precocity of the members of the profession in all lands. In England, the pantomime offers a special outlet for this current of expression, and there the child is a most important factor in stage-life. The precocity of girls in these respects is noteworthy.

The Child as Inventor.

Borrowing his figure of speech from the environment of childhood, C. J. Weber has said: "*Die Gesellschaft ist die Grossmutter der Menschheit durch ihre Töchter, die Erfindungen,* — Society is the grandmother of humanity through her daughters, the inventions," and the familiar proverb — Necessity is the mother of invention — springs from the same source. Isaac Disraeli aptly says: "The golden hour of invention must terminate like other hours; and when the man of genius returns to the cares, the duties, the vexations, and the amusements of life, his companions behold him as one of themselves, — the creature of habits and infirmities," and not a few of the "golden hours of invention" seem to belong to the golden age of childhood. Even in these "degenerate" days the child appears as an inventor. A contributor to the periodical literature of the day remarks: "Children have taken out a number of patents. The youngest inventor on record is Donald Murray Murphy, of St. John, Canada, who, at the age of six years, obtained from the United States exclusive rights in a sounding toy. Mabel Howard, of Washington, at eleven years, invented an ingenious game for her invalid brother and got a patent for it. Albert G. Smith, of Richwood, Illinois, at twelve years invented and patented a rowing apparatus" (*Current Lit.,* N. Y., xiv. 1893, p. 138).

The works of Newell (313), Bolton (187), Gomme (243), amply reveal the riot of childish variation and invention in games and plays. Mr. Newell observes: "It would be strange if children who exhibit so much inventive talent [in language] did not contrive new games; and we find accordingly that in many families a great part of the amusements of the children are of their own devising. The earliest age of which the writer has authentic record of such ingenuity is two and a half years" (313. 25). And among the primitive peoples the child is not without like invention; some, indeed, of the games our children play, were invented

T

by the savage young ones, whose fathers have been long forgotten in the mist of prehistoric ages — the sports of their children alone surviving as memorials of their existence.

Theal tells us that the Kaffir children, when not engaged in active exercise, "amuse themselves by moulding clay into little images of cattle, or by making puzzles with strings. Some of them are skilful in forming knots with thongs and pieces of wood, which it taxes the ingenuity of the others to undo. The cleverest of them sometimes practise tricks of deception with grains of maize" (543. 221). The distinguished naturalist, Mr. A. R. Wallace, while on his visit to the Malay Archipelago, thought to show the Dyak boys of Borneo something new in the way of the "cat's cradle," but found that he was the one who needed to learn, for the little brown aborigines were able to show him several new tricks (377. 25).

Miklucho-Maclay notes that among the Papuans of north-eastern New Guinea, while the women showed no tendency to ornament pottery, young boys "found pleasure in imprinting with their nails and a pointed stick a sort of ornamental border on some of the pots" (42. 317).

Paola Lombroso, daughter of Professor Cesare Lombroso, the celebrated criminologist, in her recent study of child psychology, observes: "Games (and plays) are the most original creation of the child, who has been able to create them, adapt them to his needs, making of them a sort of gymnastics which enables him to develop himself without becoming fatigued, and we, with the aid of memory, can hardly now lay hold of that feeling of infinite, intense pleasure." Moreover, these popular traditional plays and games, handed down from one generation to another of children, "show how instinctive are these forms of muscular activity and imitative expression, which have their roots in a true physiological and psychic necessity, being a species of tirocinium for the experience of childhood" (301. 136).

The *magnum opus*, perhaps, of the child as inventor, is the lyre, the discovery of which, classical mythology attributes to the infant Mercury or Hermes. Four hours after his birth the baby god is said to have found the shell of a tortoise, through the opposite edges of which he bored holes, and, inserting into these cords of linen, made the first stringed instrument. The English poet,

Aubrey de Vere, singing of an Athenian girl, thus refers to the quaint myth:—

> " She loves to pace the wild sea-shore —
> Or drop her wandering fingers o'er
> The bosom of some chorded shell :
> Her touch will make it speak as well
> As infant Hermes made
> That tortoise in its own despite
> Thenceforth in Heaven a shape star-bright."

CHAPTER XVII.

The Child as Poet, Musician, etc.

Poeta nascitur, non fit. — *Latin Proverb.*

As yet a child, nor yet a fool to fame,
I lisp'd in numbers, for the numbers came. — *Pope.*

The Child and Music.

" Music," said quaint old Thomas Fuller, "is nothing else but wild sounds civilized into time and tune," and Wallaschek, in his recent volume on *Primitive Music,* has shown how every nation under heaven, even the most savage and barbarous of peoples, have had a share in the work of civilization. Music has been called "the language of the gods," "the universal speech of mankind," and, early in the golden age of childhood, the heaven of infancy, is man made captive by "music's golden tongue." As Wallaschek has said of the race, Tracy says of the individual, "no healthy, normal child is entirely lacking in musical 'ear.'" The children of primitive races enjoy music, as well as their fellows in civilized communities. The lullaby, that *quod semper ubique et ab omnibus* of vocal art, early engages and entrances the infantile ear, and from the musical demonstrations of his elders, the child is not always or everywhere excluded. Indeed, the infant is often ushered into the world amid the din and clamour of music and song which serve to drown the mother's cries of pain, or to express the joy of the family or the community at the successful arrival of the little stranger.

Education in music and the dance begins very early with many peoples. At the school of midwifery at Abu-Zabel in Egypt, according to Clot-Bey, in cases of difficult childbirth, a child is made to hop and dance about between the legs of the mother in order to induce the fœtus to imitate it (125. II. 159).

As understudies and assistants to shamans, "medicine-men," and "doctors," children among many primitive peoples soon become acquainted with dance and song.

In Ashanti, boy musicians, singers, and dancers figure in the processions of welcome of the chiefs and kings, and young girls are engaged in the service of the fetiches (438. 258). At a funeral dance of the Latuka, an African tribe, "the women remained outside the row of dancers dancing a slow, stupid step, and screaming a wild and most inharmonious chant, whilst boys and girls in another row beat time with their feet." Burchell, while *en route* for the Kaffir country, found among certain tribes that "in the evening a whole army of boys would come to his hut and listen with manifest pleasure to the tones of his violin, and would repeat the melodies he played with surprising accuracy" (546. 3, 199).

The *meke-meke*, a dance of the Fiji Islanders, "is performed by boys and girls for whom an old musician plays"; at Tahiti the children "are early taught the 'ubus,' songs referring to the legends or achievements of the gods," and "Europeans have at times found pleasure in the pretty, plaintive songs of the children as they sit in groups on the sea-shore" (546. 35, 180, 208). In some of the Polynesian Islands, young girls are "brought up to dance the timorodea, a most lascivious dance, and to accompany it with obscene songs" (100. 62). At Tongatabu, according to Labillardière, a young girl "sang a song, the simple theme of which she repeated for half-an-hour" (546. 31). Wallaschek calls attention to the importance of the child in song in the following words (546. 75) : —

"In some places the children, separated from the adults, sing choruses among themselves, and under certain circumstances they are the chief support of the practice of singing. On Hawaii, Ellis found boys and girls singing in chorus, with an accompaniment of seven drums, a song in honour of a quondam celebrated chief. Even during supper with the Governor, table-music was performed by a juvenile bard of some twelve or fourteen summers, who sang a monotonous song to the accompaniment of a small drum. . . . In Fiji a man of position deems it beneath him to sing, and he leaves it to his wife and children, so that women sing with women only, and children with children."

Speaking of the natives of Australia, with whom he came into contact, Beckler says "the octaves of the women and children at the performance he attended were perfectly in tune, as one rarely hears in a modern opera chorus, they were in exact accord." In the Kuri dance, witnessed by Angas, a number of boys take part (546. 37, 223).

In New Guinea "the Tongala-up, a stick with a string whirled in the air, is played by women and children." Among the Tagals of the Philippines, Volliner found (with perhaps a little Spanish influence) "a chorus was performed in a truly charming manner by twelve young girls formed in a circle, one girl standing in the middle to direct." In the Andaman Islands, where the men only, as a rule, sing, "the boys were far the best performers" (546. 24, 27, 75).

Among the Apache Indians of Arizona and Mexico, "old matrons and small children dance until no longer able to stand, and stop for very exhaustion" (546. 46).

The Child as Poet.

Victor Hugo, in one of his rhapsodies, exclaims: "The most sublime psalm that can be heard on this earth is the lisping of a human soul from the lips of childhood," and the rhythm within whose circle of influence the infant early finds himself, often leads him precociously into the realm of song. Emerson has said, "Every word was once a poem," and Andrew Lang, in his facetious *Ballade of Primitive Man,* credits our Aryan ancestors with speaking not in prose, but "in a strain that would scan." In the statement of the philosopher there is a good nugget of truth, and just a few grains of it in the words of the wit.

The analogy between the place and effect of rhythm, music, and poetry in the life of the child and in the life of the savage has been frequently noted. In his recent study of *Rhythm* (405 a), Dr. Bolton has touched up some aspects of the subject. With children "the habit of rhyming is almost instinctive" and universal. Almost every one can remember some little sing-song or nonsense-verse of his own invention, some rhyming pun, or rhythmic adaptation. The enormous range of variation in the wording of counting-out rhymes, game-songs, and play-verses, is evidence enough of the fertility of invention of child-poets and child-poetesses. Of the familiar counting-out formula *Eeny, meeny, miny, mo,* the variants are simply legion.

The well-known lines of Pope: —

> " As yet a child, nor yet a fool to fame,
>   I lisp'd in numbers, for the numbers came,"

receive abundant illustration from the lives of the great geniuses of song.

Among primitive peoples, if anywhere, *poeta nascitur, non fit.* In her article on *Indian Songs*, Miss Alice C. Fletcher says: " Children make songs for themselves, which are occasionally handed down to other generations. These juvenile efforts sometimes haunt the memory in maturer years. An exemplary old man once sang to me a composition of his childhood, wherein he had exalted the pleasures of disobedience; but he took particular care that his children should not hear this performance. Young men sing in guessing-games, as they gambol with their companions, tossing from hand to hand a minute ball of buffalo hair or a small pebble, moving their arms to the rhythm of the music." This, and the following statement made of the Omaha Indians, will hold for not a few other savage and barbarous tribes: " Children compose ditties for their games, and young men add music to give zest to their sports " (445).

Dr. F. Boas says of the Eskimo of Baffin Land (402. 572): " Children tell one another fables and sing short songs, especially comic and satirical ones." The heroes of the Basque legend of Aquelarre are thus described by Miss Monteiro (505. 22): —

" Izar and Lañoa were two orphan children; the first was seven years of age, and the latter nine. These poor children, true wandering bards, frequented the mountains, earning a livelihood by singing ballads and national airs in sweet, infantile voices, in return for a bed of straw and a cupful of meal. Throughout the district these children were known and loved on account of their sad state, as well as for their graceful forms and winning ways."

Mr. Chatelain, in his recent work on African folk-tales, says of the natives of Angola: " No Angola child finds difficulty at any time in producing extemporaneous song."

Dr. Gatschet, in his study of the Klamath Indians, gives examples of many songs composed and sung by young people, especially girls; and many other Indian tribes, Algonkian, Iroquois, etc., possess such as well. When Darwin reached Tahiti, his arrival was "sung by a young girl in four improvised strophes, which her fellow-maidens accompanied in a pretty chorus"; and among the song-loving people of the islands of the South Sea, the poetic talent develops quite early in both sexes. Among the aborigines of Peake River, in Australia, when a youth — at puberty — has undergone the ceremony of tattooing, and, his wounds having healed, is about to return to his fellows, "a young girl selected for the purpose, sings in her own way a song which she has composed, and, amid dancing, merriment, and feasting, the youth is welcomed back to his family and his kin" (326. II. 241). Throughout the Orient woman is a dancer and a singer. India has her bayadères and nautch-girls, whose dancing and singing talents are world-known.

The Gypsies, too, that wander-folk of the world, are famed for their love-songs and fortune-telling rhymes, which the youth and girlhood among them so often know how to make and use. Crawford, who has translated the Kalevala, the great epic of the Finns, tells us, "The natural speech of this people is poetry. The young men and maidens, the old men and matrons, in their interchange of ideas unwittingly fall into verse" (423. I. xxvi.). Among the young herdsmen and shepherdesses of the pastoral peoples of Europe and Asia, the same precocity of song prevails. With songs of youth and maiden, the hills and valleys of Greece and Italy resound as of old. In his essay on the *Popular Songs of Tuscany*, Mr. J. A. Symonds observes (540. 600, 602): "Signor Tigri records by name a little girl called Cherubina, who made *Rispetti* by the dozen, as she watched her sheep upon the hills." When Signor Tigri asked her to dictate to him some of her songs, she replied: "Oh Signore! ne dico tanti quando li canto!... ma ora... bisognerebbe averli tutti in visione; se no, proprio non vengono, — Oh Sir! I say so many, when I sing... but now... one must have them all before one's mind... if not, they do not come properly." World-applicable as the boy grows out of child-hood — with some little change of season with the varying clime — are the words of Tennyson: —

"In the spring a young man's fancy lightly turns to thoughts of love,"

and everywhere, if poetry and song be not indeed the very off-spring of love, they are at least twin-born with it.

Lombroso, in his discussion of the man of genius, gives many examples of precocious poetical and musical talent: Dante (who at nine years of age wrote sonnets), Tasso (wrote at ten years of age), Wieland (who wrote an epic at 16), Lope de Vega (who wrote verses at 12), Calderon (at 13), Metastasio (who composed at 10), Handel (who wrote a mass at 13, and was director of opera at 19), Eichhorn, Mozart, and Eibler (all three of whom gave concerts at 6), Beethoven (who wrote sonatas at 13), Weber (who wrote his first opera at 14), Cherubini (who wrote a mass at 15), etc. (300. 15).

Among English poets whose precocity was marked, we find the most noteworthy to be Robert Browning, whose first poetic effusion is ascribed to his fourth year. It is now known, however, that poetry is much more common among children than was at first supposed, and early compositions are not to be expected from geniuses alone, but often from the scions of the ruder commonalty.

In her interesting study of individual psychology, Dr. Caroline Miles informs us that out of ninety-seven answers to the question, "Did you express yourself in any art-form before eighteen years of age?" fourteen stated that the person replying used verses alone, fourteen used stories and poetry, three used poetry and drawing or painting, two used poetry and painting. Dr. Miles notes that "those who replied 'no,' seemed to take pride in the fact that they had been guilty of no such youthful folly." This is in line with the belief parents sometimes express that the son or daughter who poetizes early is "loony." Some who were not ashamed of these child-expressions volunteered information concerning them, and we learn: "Most interesting was one who wrote a tragedy at ten, which was acted on a little stage for the benefit of her friends; from ten to thirteen, an epic; at thirteen, sentimental and religious poems" (310. 552, 553).

Dr. H. H. Donaldson, in his essay on the *Education of the Nervous System*, cites the fact that of the musicians whose biographies were examined by Sully, 95% gave promise before twenty years of age, and 100% produced some work before reaching thirty; of the poets, 75% showed promise before twenty, and 92% produced before they were thirty years of age (216. 118). Precocity and genius seem to go together.

CHAPTER XVIII.

The Child as Teacher and Wiseacre.

The child is father of the man.— *Wordsworth.*

And wiser than the gray recluse
This child of thine.— *Whittier.*

And still to Childhood's sweet appeal
The heart of genius turns,
And more than all the sages teach
From lisping voices learns. — *Whittier.*

Wisdom of Childhood.

In his beautiful verses — forming part of one of the best child-poems in our language —

> " And still to childhood's sweet appeal
> The heart of genius turns,
> And more than all the sages teach
> From lisping voices learns," —

Whittier has expressed that instinctive faith in the wisdom of childhood that seems perennial and pan-ethnic. Browning, in *Pippa's Song,* has sounded even a deeper note : —

> " Overhead the tree-tops meet,
> Flowers and grass spring 'neath one's feet ;
> There was nought above me, nought below,
> My childhood had not learned to know :
> For, what are the voices of birds
> — Aye, and of beasts, — but words, our words,
> Only so much more sweet ?
> The knowledge of that with my life begun.
> But I had so near made out the sun,
> And counted your stars, the seven and one,

> Like the fingers of my hand:
> Nay, I could all but understand
> Wherefore through heaven the white moon ranges;
> And just when out of her soft fifty changes
> No unfamiliar face might overlook me —
> Suddenly God took me."

The power and wisdom of the child are quaintly and naïvely brought out in the legends and folk-lore of the various races of men, not alone of the present day, but of all eras of the world's history. As an illustration of the truth contained in the words of a great child-lover, "A little child shall lead them," and their echo in those of the Quaker poet, —

> " God hath his small interpreters;
> The child must teach the man,"

nothing could be more artless and natural than the following legend of the Penobscot Indians of Maine, recorded by Mr. Leland, which tells of the origin of the "crowing of babies" (488. 121) : —

When Glooskap, the culture-hero of these Indians, had conquered all his enemies, giants, sorcerers, magicians, evil spirits and ghosts, witches, devils, goblins, cannibals, *et id genus omne*, pride rose within him, and he said to a certain woman, that now his work was done, for he had conquered all. But she told him that he was mistaken; there yet remained "one whom no one has ever yet conquered or got the better of in any way, and who will remain unconquered to the end of time." This was *Wasis*, "the baby," who was sitting contentedly on the floor of the wigwam chewing a piece of maple-sugar. The great Glooskap, so the story runs, "had never married or had a child; he knew nought of the way of managing children" — yet he thought he knew all about it. So he smiled graciously at baby, and, " in a voice like that of a summer bird," bade him come to him. But baby sat still and went on sucking his sugar. Then Glooskap got angry, and in a terrible voice, ordered baby to crawl to him at once. But baby merely cried out and yelled, stirring not. Then Glooskap tried his last resort, magic, "using his most awful spells, and singing the songs which raise the dead and scare the devils." Still baby only smiled, and never budged an inch. At last the great Glooskap could do no more; he gave up the attempt in despair, whereupon " baby, sitting on the floor in the sunshine, went '*goo! goo!*' and crowed lustily." And to this day, the Indians, when they hear "a babe well-contented going '*goo! goo!*' and crowing, and no one can tell why," know that it is because he "remembers the time when he overcame the great Master, who had conquered all things. For of all beings that have been since the beginning, baby is alone the invincible one."

Manabozho, the culture-hero of the Chippeways and other Algonkian tribes of the Great Lakes, and probably identical with his eastern analogue, Glūskap, was, like the latter, discomfited by a child. This is the legend : —

" One day Manabozho appeared upon the earth in an ill-humour. Walking along, he espied a little child sitting in the sun, curled up with his toe in his mouth. Somewhat surprised at this, and being of a dauntless and boastful nature, he set himself down beside the child; and, picking up his own toe, he essayed to place it in his mouth after the manner of the child. He could not do it. In spite of all twisting and turning, his toe could not be brought to reach his mouth. As he was getting up in great discomfiture to get away, he heard a laugh behind him, and did no more boasting that day, for he had been outwitted by a little child."

This characteristic attitude of the child has also been noted by the folk-historians of India; for when, after the death of Brahma, the waters have covered all the worlds, " Vishnu [the 'Preserver,' in the Hindoo Trinity] sits, in the shape of a tiny infant, on a leaf of the pipala (fig-tree), and floats on the sea of milk, sucking the toe of his right foot " (440. 366), and, as Mrs. Emerson points out, " the feat that Manabozho sought in vain to perform is accomplished by the more flexible and lithe Hindoo god, Narayana " (440. 367).

In another Micmac legend, given by Leland, Glūskap appears somewhat more to advantage. Of the Turtle [Mikchich], the " Uncle" of Glūskap, for whom the latter had obtained a wife, we read (488. 57) : —

" And Turtle lived happily with his wife, and she had a babe. Now it happened in after-days that Glooskap came to see his uncle, and the child cried. ' Dost thou know what he says?'

exclaimed the Master. 'Truly, not I,' answered Mikchich, 'unless it be the language of the Mu-se-gisk (spirits of the air), which no man knoweth.' 'Well,' replied Glooskap, 'he is talking of eggs, for he says, '*Hoowah! hoowah!*' which, methinks, is much the same as '*waw-wun, waw-wun.*' And this in Passamaquoddy means 'egg.' 'But where are there any?' asked Mikchich. Then Glooskap bade him seek in the sand, and he found many, and admired and marvelled over them greatly; and in memory of this, and to glorify the jest of Glooskap, the turtle layeth eggs even to this day."

In Mr. Leland's collection, as in the later volume of Dr. Rand, there are many other delicate touches of childhood that show that these aborigines have a large measure of that love for children which is present with all races of mankind.

In the legends of the saints and heroes of the Christian Church we meet with numberless instances of the wisdom and instruction that came to them from the mouths of little children.

Among the stories in the life of St. Augustine is the following: "While St. Augustine was composing his book *On the Trinity*, and was at Cività Vecchia, he saw a little child making a hole in the seashore, and asked him what he was doing. The child replied: 'I am making a hole to contain the water of the sea.' The doctor smiled, telling the child it would not be possible to do so; but the child made answer: 'Not so, Augustine. It would be far easier to drain off the waters of the great deep than for the finite to grasp the Infinite'; and so he vanished. Augustine then knew that the child was an angel of God, sent to warn him, and he diligently set to work to revise what he had written" (191. 355).

The best of mankind can still sit at the feet of childhood and learn of its wisdom. But of many a one must it be said: —

"He hath grown so foolish-wise
He cannot see with childhood's eyes ;
He hath forgot that purity
And lowliness which are the key
Of Nature's mysteries."

CHAPTER XIX.

The Child as Judge.

So, Holy Writ in Babes hath judgment shown,
Where Judges have been babes. — *Shakespeare.*

O wise young judge ! — *Shakespeare.*

The Child as Judge.

Shakespeare in *All's Well that Ends Well*, makes Helen say to the King : —

> " He that of greatest works is finisher,
> Oft does them by the weakest minister :
> So, Holy Writ in babes hath judgment shown,
> When judges have been babes."

And in the history of the human race, appeal has often been made to the innocence and imputed discernment of the child.

As one of the glories of God, David sang in Israel of old : "Out of the mouths of babes and sucklings hast thou ordained strength, because of thine enemies, that thou mightest still the enemy and the avenger." And the disciple Matthew reiterates the thought : "Thou hast hid these things from the wise and prudent, and hast revealed them unto babes"; and, again : "Out of the mouths of babes and sucklings hast thou perfected praise."

Solomon.

The stories told of Solomon — the judgments of the wise Hebrew monarch, when a child, were as remarkable as those which he made after attaining man's estate — have their counterparts in other lands. One of the most celebrated decisions was rendered by Solomon when he was but thirteen years of age. Weil gives the story as follows (547. 192): —

"The accuser had sold some property to the other, who, in clearing out a cellar, had found a treasure. He now demanded that the accused should give up the treasure, since he had bought the property without it; while the other maintained that the accuser possessed no right to the treasure, since he had known nothing of it, and had sold the property with all that it contained. After long meditation, David adjudged that the treasure should be divided between them. But Solomon inquired of the accuser whether he had a son, and, when he replied that he had a son, he inquired of the other if he had a daughter; and he also answering in the affirmative, Solomon said: 'If you will adjust your strife so as not to do injustice one to the other, unite your children in marriage, and give them this treasure as their dowry.'"

In many other difficult cases, David, after the loss of the tube which, according to legend, the angel Gabriel brought him, was aided in judgment by the wisdom and far-sightedness of his young son. A decision similar to that of Solomon is attributed to Buddha, when a child, and to Christ.

Child-Judgments.

Müllenhoff records two cases of child-judgments in his collection of the folk-lore of Schleswig-Holstein. The first is as follows: "A branch of the river Widau, near Tondern, is named Renzau, from the little village Renz in the parish of Burkall. Where the banks are pretty high and steep, a man fell into the water once upon a time, and would have been drowned had not a certain person, hearing his cries, hastened to the river, and, holding out a pole, enabled the drowning man to help himself out. In doing so, however, he put out an eye. The rescued man appeared at the next thing (court), entered a complaint against the other, and demanded compensation for his lost eye. The judges, not knowing what to make of the case, put it off till the next thing, in order to meditate upon it in the meantime. But the third thing came, and the district-judge had not made up his mind about it. Out of humour, he mounted his horse and rode slowly and thoughtfully in the direction of Tondern, where the thing was then held.   He reached Rohrkarrberg, and, opposite the house which is still standing there, lay a stone heap, upon which sat three herd-boys, apparently busy with something of importance. 'What are you doing there, children?' asked the judge. 'We are playing thing' (court), was the answer. 'What is the matter before the court?' continued the judge. 'We are trying the case of the man who fell into the Renzau,' they answered, and the judge held his horse to await the verdict. The boys did not know him, for he was well hidden in his cloak, and his presence did not disturb them.   The judgment rendered was, that the man who had been rescued should be thrown into the stream again at the same spot; if he was able to save himself, then he should receive compensation for the eye he had lost; if he could not, the decision was to be in favour of the other. Before the district-judge went away, he put his hand into his pocket and gave the boys some money; then, merrily riding to Tondern, he rendered the same judgment as the boys had given. The fellow was unable to save himself without assistance, and was like to have been drowned; consequently, his rescuer won the case " (508. 87, 88).   The other case, said to have occurred at Rapstede, was this: —

" A tailor and a peasant, both possessing nothing more than a wretched hut, made a bargain for so and so many bushels of corn at such and such a price, although the tailor knew that the peasant had no money, and the peasant knew that the tailor had a needle, but no corn.   Soon the price of corn rose, and the peasant appeared before the court to demand that the tailor should fulfil his part of the bargain.   The judges were at a loss to decide such a matter.   In this case, also, boys rendered judgment.   The decision was, that the agreement was invalid, for both, being neighbours, had known each other's circumstances, and yet both were culpable for having entered into such a deceitful bargain " (508. 88).

These decisions belong to the same category as that rendered by Solomon in the case of the two women, who both claimed the same child, — a judgment which has gone upon record in the Bible (1 Kings, iii. 16–28), — and a multitude of similar interpretations of justice found all over the world (191. 290).

Mr. Newell, speaking of children's games in which judicial

procedures are imitated, but from whose decisions no serious results ever come, observes (313. 123): —

" In the ancient world, however, where the courts were a place of resort, and law was not a specialized profession, the case was different. Maximus of Tyre tells us that the children had their laws and tribunals; condemnation extended to the forfeiture of toys. Cato the younger, according to Plutarch, had his detestation of tyranny first awakened by the punishment inflicted on a playmate by such a tribunal. One of the younger boys had been sentenced to imprisonment; the doom was duly carried into effect; but Cato, moved by his cries, rescued him."

Children's Ideas of Right.

Mr. Brown, of the Normal School at Worcester, Massachusetts, has given us an excellent collection of *Thoughts and Reasonings of Children* (194), and Signora Paola Lombroso, in her interesting and valuable *Essays on Child-Psychology*, has also contributed to the same subject (301. 45–72). A very recent study is that of *Children's Rights*, by Margaret E. Schallenberger (341), of Leland Stanford, Jr. University, California. The last author has charted the opinions of a large number — some three thousand papers were collected — of boys and girls from six to sixteen years of age, upon the following case, the story being employed as specially appealing to children (341. 89): —

" Jennie had a beautiful new box of paints; and, in the afternoon, while her mother was gone, she painted all the chairs in the parlour, so as to make them look nice for her mother. When her mother came home, Jennie ran to meet her, and said, 'Oh mamma! come and see how pretty I have made the new parlour'; but her mamma took her paints away and sent her to bed. If you had been her mother, what would you have done or said to Jennie?"

From this extensive and most ingenious investigation, the following results are thought to have been obtained: " Young children are less merciful than older ones. When they appear cruel and resentful, we know that they are exercising what they honestly consider the right of revenge. Boys are less merciful than girls. Young children judge of actions by their results, older ones

υ

look at the motives which prompt them. If a young child dis-
obeys a command and no bad result follows, he doesn't see that
he has done wrong. Punishments which have in them the idea
of restitution are common to all ages. Girls consider the why
more than boys; they explain to Jennie oftener than boys do.
Threats and forced promises do not impress children" (341. 96).

Jurisprudence of Child's Play.

Pitré, the great Italian folklorist, has made a special study,
though a very brief one, of the judgments rendered by children in
games and plays, — the jurisprudence of child's play (323). His
essay, which is devoted to the island of Sicily, touches upon a field
which is likely to yield a rich harvest all over the world. The
rules of the game; who shall play and who shall not; what is
"out," "taw," "in"; when is one "it," "caught," "out"; what
can one "bar," and what "choose," — all these are matters which
require the decisions of the youthful judiciary, and call for the
frequent exercise of judgment, and the sense of justice and equity.
Of the "Boy Code of Honour" some notice is taken by Gregor
(246. 21-24). Mr. Newell thus describes the game of "Judge and
Jury," as played at Cambridge, Massachusetts (312. 123): "A child
is chosen to be judge, two others for jurors (or, to speak with our
little informant, *juries*), who sit at his right and left hand. Each
child must ask the permission of the judge before taking any
step. A platter is brought in, and a child, rising, asks the judge,
'May I go into the middle of the room?' 'May I turn the platter?' 'On which side shall it fall?' If the platter falls on the
wrong side, forfeit must be paid." In Germany and Switzerland
there is a game of the trial of a thief. In the former country:
"There is a king, a judge, an executioner, an accuser, and a thief.
The parts are assigned by drawing lots, but the accuser does not
know the name of the thief, and, if he makes an error, has to
undergo the penalty in his stead. The judge finally addresses the
king, inquiring if his majesty approves of his decision; and the
king replies, 'Yes, your sentence entitles you to my favour'; or,
'No, your sentence entitles you to so many blows.' Thus we see
how modern child's play respects the dignity of the king as the
fountain of law." In the Swiss version, as Mr. Newell remarks,

"the memory of the severity of ancient criminal law is preserved," for "the thief flies, and is chased over stock and stone until caught, when he is made to kneel down, his cap pushed over his brows, and his head immediately struck off with the edge of a board" (313. 124).

Boy-Moots.

The most interesting section, perhaps, of Mr. Johnson's *Rudimentary Society among Boys*, is that devoted to "Judicial Procedure" (272. 35–48). Fighting, arbitration, the ordeal and the wager have all been in use as modes of settling quarrels at the McDonogh School — such matters of dispute as arose having been left for the boys to settle among themselves without the control of the faculty. Indeed, the advice which Polonius gives to Laertes seems to have been ever present in the earlier days: —

> " Beware
> Of entrance to a quarrel ; but being in,
> Bear't that th' opposed may beware of thee."

Following the appeal to fists came the appeal to chance and luck — the "odd or even" marbles, the "longest straw," and like devices came into vogue. The arbitration of a bystander, particularly of "a big boy who could whip the others," and the "expedient of laying a wager to secure the postponement of a quarrel," are very common. But the most remarkable institution at McDonogh is undoubtedly the boy-moot, one of whose decisions is reported in detail by Mr. Johnson, — an institution in action "almost daily," and part and parcel of the life of the school. None but the author's own words can justly portray it (272. 47, 48): —

"The crowd of boys assembled about the contestants, whose verdict decides the controversy, is, in many respects, the counterpart of a primitive assembly of the people in the folk-moot. Every boy has the right to express an opinion, and every boy present exercises his privilege, though personal prowess and great experience in matters of law have their full influence on the minds of the judges. The primitive idea that dispensing justice is a public trust, which the community itself must fulfil towards its members, is embodied in this usage of the 'McDonogh boys.'

The judges are not arbitrators chosen by the disputants, nor are they public functionaries whose sole business is to preside over the courts; but the whole body of the population declares by word of mouth the right and wrong of the matter. This tumultuous body of school-fellows, giving decisions in quarrels, and determining questions of custom, reproduces with remarkable fidelity the essential character of the primitive assembly."

Mr. Johnson was struck with "the peace and good order generally prevalent in the community," which speaks well for the judicial system there in vogue.

The editor, in his introductory remarks, observes: —

"Every schoolboy and every college student in his upward way to real manhood represents the evolution of a primitive savage into a civilized being. Every school and college reproduces the developmental process of a human society in some of its most interesting aspects, such as government and law. There are all stages of social development in the student class, from actual savagery, which frequently crops out in the very best schools and colleges, to effeminate forms of modern civilization. There are all degrees of institutional government, from total anarchy and patriarchal despotism to Roman imperialism and constitutional government; although it must be admitted that self-government among the student class — said to obtain in some American schools and colleges — is not yet a chartered right. The regulation of student society by itself, or by all the powers that be, presents all phases of judicature, from the most savage ordeals to the most humane. Student customs are full of ancient survivals, and some editions of 'College Laws' are almost as archaic as the Code of Manu. One of these days we shall perhaps find men investigating college jurisprudence, college government, and college politics from the comparative point of view, and writing the natural history of the student class" (272. 3).

In the community of the sand-pile studied by Dr. Hall, "a general habit of settling disputes, often brought to issue with fists, by means of meetings and specifications, arose." There is room for a volume on the jurisprudence of childhood and youth, and every page would be of intensest interest and of value in the history of the evolution of the ideas of justice in the human race.

CHAPTER XX.

The Child as Oracle-Keeper and Oracle-Interpreter.

Enfants et fous sont devins [Children and fools are soothsayers].—*French Proverb.*

Children pick up words as chickens peas,
And utter them again as God shall please.—*English Proverb.*

The fresh face of a child is richer in significance than the forecasting of the most indubitable seer.—*Novalis.*

Child-Oracles.

"Children and fools speak the truth," says an old and widespread proverb, and another version includes him who is drunken, making a trinity of truth-tellers. In like manner have the frenzy of wine and the madness of the gods been associated in every age with oracle and sign, and into this oracular trinity enters also the child. Said De Quincey: "God speaks to children also, in dreams and by the oracles that lurk in darkness," and the poet Stoddard has clothed in exquisite language a similar thought:—

"Nearer the gate of Paradise than we,
Our children breathe its air, its angels see;
And when they pray, God hears their simple prayer,
Yea, even sheathes his sword in judgment bare."

The passage in Joel ii. 28, "Your old men shall dream dreams, your young men shall see visions," might stand for not a few primitive peoples, with whom, once in childhood (or youth) and once again in old age, man communes with the spirits and the gods, and interprets the events of life to his fellows.

The Darien Indians, we are told, "used the seeds of the *Datura sanguinea* to bring on in children prophetic delirium in which they revealed hidden treasures" (545. II. 417).

293

One of the most curious of the many strange practices which the conservatism of the Established Church of England has continued down to the present is one in vogue at the parish church of St. Ives, in Huntingdonshire. A certain Dr. Robert Wilde, who died in 1678, "bequeathed £50, the yearly interest of which was to be expended in the purchase of six Bibles, not exceeding the price of 7s. 6d. each, which should be 'cast for by dice' on the communion table every year by six boys and six girls of the town." The vicar was also to be paid 10s. a year for preaching an appropriate sermon on the Holy Scriptures. Public opinion has within recent years caused the erection of a table on the chancel steps, where the dice-throwing now takes place, instead of on the communion table as of old. Every May 26th the ceremony is performed, and in 1888 we are told: "The highest throw this year (three times with three dice) was 37, by a little girl. The vicar (the Rev. E. Tottenham) preached a sermon from the words, 'From a child thou hast known the Holy Scriptures'" (390 (1888). 113).

The Child as Vision-Seer.

In the history of the Catholic Church one cannot fail to be struck by the part played by children in the seeing of visions, especially of the Virgin. To St. Agnes of Monte Pulciano (A.D. 1274–1317), when fourteen years of age, the Virgin appeared and told her she should build a monastery before she died (191. 24); Jeanne de Maillé (1332–1414) was but eleven when the Virgin Mary with the infant Jesus came before her in a vision; Catherine of Racconigi (1486–1547) was visited by the Virgin when only five years of age (191. 108); in 1075, Hermann of Cologne, while still a boy, saw in a vision the Virgin, who kissed him, and made a secret deposit of food on a certain stone for his benefit. In 1858 a vision of the Immaculate Conception appeared to Bernadetta Soubirous, a sickly child of fourteen, at Lourdes, in the Hautes Pyrenees. No one else saw this vision, said to have occurred on Shrove Tuesday (Feb. 11), four years after Pius IX. had proclaimed the dogma of the Immaculate Conception. The vision lasted for fourteen successive days (191. 484). On Jan. 17, 1871, the Virgin is alleged to have appeared at Pontmain to several children, and a detailed account of the vision has been given by Mgr. Guérin, chamberlain of Pius IX., in his *Vie des Saints*, and this is digested in Brewer. The children who saw the apparition are described as follows: "Eugène Barbedette was the second son of a small farmer living in the village of Pontmain, in the diocese of Laval. He was twelve years old, and his brother Joseph was ten. The other two [Françoise Richer, Jeanne Marie Lebossé] were children from neighbouring cottages, called in to witness the sight. The parents of the children, the pastor of the village, Sister Vitaline, the abbot Guérin, all present, could see nothing, nor could any of the neighbours of outlying villages, who flocked to the place. Only the children mentioned, a sick child, and a babe in the arms of its grandmother, saw the apparition." The description of the Virgin, as seen by Eugène Barbedette that starlight winter night, is quaint and naïve in the extreme: "She was very tall, robed in blue, and her robe studded with stars. Her shoes were also blue, but had red rosettes. Her face was covered with a black veil, which floated to her shoulders. A crown of gold was on her head, but a red line was observed to run round the crown, symbolic of the blood shed by Christ for the sins of the world. Beneath her feet was a scroll, on which were written these words: 'Mais priez, mes enfants, Dieu vous exaucera, en peu de temps mon fils se laisse toucher' (Pray, my children, God will hear you, before long my son will be moved)." Mgr. Guérin thus comments upon the miracle: "In order to make herself manifest to men, the Holy Virgin has chosen rather the simple eyes of childhood; for, like troubled waters, sinful souls would have but ill reflected her celestial image" (191. 26).

Flower- and Animal-Oracles.

Mr. Newell has a chapter on "Flower-Oracles" (313. 105–114), in which he gives many illustrations of the practice noted in the lines of that nature-loving mediæval German singer, with which he prefaces his remarks: —

> "A spire of grass hath made me gay;
> It saith I shall find mercy mild.
> I measured in the self-same way
> I have seen practised by a child.

> " Come look and listen if she really does:
> She does, does not, she does, does not, she does.
> Each time I try, the end so augureth.
> That comforts me, — 'tis right that we have faith."

The ox-eye daisy, the common daisy, the marguerite, the corn-flower, the dandelion, the rose, the pansy, the clover, and a score of other flowers and plants (to say nothing of bushes and trees) have their leaves and petals pulled off, their seeds counted, their fruit examined, their seed-tufts blown away, their markings and other peculiarities deciphered and interpreted to determine the fortune of little questioners, the character of the home they are to live in, the clothes they are to be married in, what they are to ride in, the profession they are to adopt, whether they are to marry, remain single, become monk or nun, whether they are to be drowned or hanged, rich or poor, honest or criminal, whether they are to go to hell, purgatory, or paradise.

The use of drawing straws or blades of grass from the hand to determine who is " it," or who shall begin the game, the blowing of the dandelion in seed, the counting of apple-pips, or the leaves on a twig, and a hundred other expedients belong to the same category. All these are oracles, whose priest and interpreter is the child; first, in "those sweet, childish days that were as long as twenty days are now," and then again when love rules the heart and the appeal to the arbitrament of nature — for not alone all mankind but all nature loves a lover — is made in deepest faith and confidence. In the golden age of childhood and in the spring-time of love all nature is akin to man. The dandelion is espe-cially favoured as an oracle of children, and of those who are but "children of a larger growth." To quote from Folkard (448. 309) : —

"The dandelion is called the rustic oracle ; its flowers always open about 5 A.M. and shut at 8 P.M., serving the shepherd for a clock.

> ' Leontodons unfold
> On the swart turf their ray-encircled gold,
> With Sol's expanding beam the flowers unclose,
> And rising Hesper lights them to repose.' — *Darwin.*

As the flower is the shepherd's clock, so are the feathery seed-tufts his barometer, predicting calm or storm. These downy seed-

balls, which children blow off to find out the hour of day, serve
for other oracular purposes. Are you separated from the object
of your love ? Carefully pluck one of the feathery heads; charge
each of the little feathers composing it with a tender thought;
turn towards the spot where the loved one dwells; blow, and the
seed-ball will convey your message faithfully. Do you wish to
know if that dear one is thinking of you ? blow again; and if
there be left upon the stalk a single aigrette, it is a proof you are
not forgotten. Similarly, the dandelion is consulted as to whether
the lover lives east, west, north, or south, and whether he is coming or not.

> ' Will he come ? I pluck the flower leaves off,
> And, at each, cry yes, no, yes ;
> I blow the down from the dry hawkweed,
> Once, twice—hah ! it flies amiss! ' — *Scott.*"

Many interesting details about flower-oracles may be read in the
pages of Friend (453) and Folkard (448) and in Mr. Dyer's chapters on *Plants and the Ceremonial Use* (435. 145–162), *Children's
Rhymes and Games* (435. 232–242), etc.

Beasts, birds, and insects are also the child's oracles. Mr.
Callaway tells us that among the Amazulu, when cattle are lost,
and the boys see the bird called *Isi pungumangati* sitting on a
tree, "they ask it where the cattle are, and go in the direction in
which it points with its head." The insect known as the *mantis*,
or "praying insect," is used for a similar purpose (417. 339). In
the Sollinger forest (Germany), on St. Matthew's day, February
24, the following practice is in vogue: A girl takes a girl friend
upon her back and carries her to the nearest sheep-pen, at the
door of which both knock. If a lamb is the first to bleat, the
future husbands of both girls will be young; if an old sheep bleats
first, they will both marry old men (391. II. 10).

The Child as Oracle in the Primitive Community.

In primitive social economy the services of the child, as an
unprejudiced or oracular decider of fates and fortunes, were often
in demand. In the community of Pudu-vayal, in the Carnatic
(southeastern India), "when the season for cultivation arrives,
the arable land in the village is allotted to the several shareholders

in the following manner: The names of each lot and each share-holder are written on pieces of the leaf of the palm-tree, such as is used for village records, and the names of each division of land to be allotted are placed in a row. A child, selected for the purpose, draws by lot a leaf with the name of the principal share-holder, and places under it a number, thus, —

1	2	3	4
Tannappa.	Nina.	Narrappa.	Malliyan.

It is thus settled by lottery that Tannappa and his under-share-holders are to cultivate the land of the principal share lotted under No. 1. Tannappa next proceeds to settle in the same way each under-shareholder's portion included in his principal share, and so on, until the sixty-four shareholders receive each his allot-ment (461. 32)."

At Haddenham, in the county of Buckingham, England, a some-what similar practice survived: "The method of deciding the ownership, after the meadow was plotted out, was by drawing lots. This was done by cutting up a common dock-weed into the required number of pieces to represent the lots, a well understood sign being carved on each piece, representing crows' feet, hog-troughs, and so on. These were placed in a hat and shaken up. Before this could be done, however, notice must be given by one of the men, calling out, at the top of his voice, 'Harko,' and using some sort of rigmarole, calling people to witness that the lots were drawn fairly and without favour. . . . The hat being shaken up, and one of the boys standing by, looking on with the greatest interest, is pitched upon as a disinterested person to draw the lots, and each owner had to 'sup up' with the lot that fell to him" (461. 270).

In the manor of Aston, in the parish of Bampton, Oxfordshire, a like custom prevailed: "When the grass was fit to cut, the grass stewards and Sixteens [stewards] summoned the freeholders and tenants to a general meeting, and the following ceremony took place: Four of the tenants came forward, each bearing his mark cut on a piece of wood, which, being thrown into a hat, were shaken up and drawn by a boy. The first drawing entitled its owner to have his portion of the common meadow in set one, the second drawn in set two, etc., and thus four of the tenants have obtained their allotments. Four others then came forward, and the same process is repeated until all the tenants have received their allotments" (461. 166).

In Kilkenny, "when the division is made out, lots are prepared. Each man takes a bit of stick or particular stone, well marked; these are enveloped in a ball of clay, and a child or stranger is called to place each ball upon some one of the lots, by which each man's share is determined" (461. 141).

The Kaffir boy who is to tend the calves in the kraal, while his fellows sport and romp about, is selected by lot: "As many blades of grass as there are boys are taken, and a knot is made on the end of one of them. The biggest boy holds the blades between the fingers and thumb of his closed hand, and whoever draws the blade with the knot has to act as herdsman" (543. 221).

Nowadays, children are employed to turn roulette-wheels, sort cards, pick out lottery-tickets, select lucky numbers, set machinery going for the first time, and perform other like actions; for, though men are all "children of fortune," there is something about real children that brings luck and prospers all enterprises of chance and hazard.

Unconscious action and selection by children have no doubt profoundly influenced individual men and society at times. De Quincey tells us that "the celebrated Dr. Doddridge is said to have been guided in a primary act of choice, influencing his whole after life, by a few chance words from a child reading aloud to his mother." The story of the conversion of drunken John Stirling by the naïve remark of his four-year-old boy, as the mother was reading Matthew xxv. 31–33, "Will father be a goat, then, mother?" finds parallels in other lives and other lands (191. 356).

Here may be considered as belonging some of the "guessing-games," certain of which, in forms remarkably like those in use to-day, were known to the ancients, as Mr. Newell has pointed out, from references in Xenophon and Petronius Arbiter (313. 147–152).

Oracular Games.

As we of to-day see in the sports and games of children some resemblance to the realities of life of our ancestors of long ago, and of those primitive peoples who have lingered behind in the march of culture, so have the folk seen in them some echo, some oracular reverberation, of the deeds of absent elders, some forecast of the things to come.

Among the Shushwap Indians of British Columbia, the following belief is current regarding twins : " While they are children their mother can see by their plays whether her husband, when he is out hunting, will be successful or not. When the twins play about and feign to bite each other, he will be successful ; if they keep quiet, he will return empty-handed " (404. 92).

In Saxon Transylvania, " when children play games in which dolls and the like are buried, play church, or sing hymns in the street, it is thought to foretell the approaching death of some one in the place " (392 (1893). 18).

Similar superstitions attach to others of the games and sports of childhood, in which is reproduced the solemn earnest of an earlier manhood; for, with some peoples, the conviction that what is acted in pantomime must occur at a later date in all its reality, finds ready acceptance, and hence children are sometimes even now debarred from carrying out some of their games, from a vague fear that ill will come of them in the manner indicated.

CHAPTER XXI.

The Child as Weather-Maker.

Rain, rain, go away,
Come again, another day. — *Children's Rhyme.*

PERHAPS the most naïve tale in which the child figures as a weather-maker occurs in the life-story of St. Vincent Ferrier (1357–1419 A.D.), who is credited with performing, in twenty years, no fewer than 58,400 miracles. While the saint was not yet a year old, a great dearth prevailed in Valencia, and one day, while his mother was lamenting over it, "the infant in swaddling-clothes said to her distinctly, 'Mother, if you wish for rain, carry me in procession.' The babe was carried in procession, and the rain fell abundantly" (191. 356). Brewer informs us that in 1716 "Mrs. Hicks and her daughter (a child nine years of age) were hung at Huntingdon [England], for 'selling their souls to the devil; and raising a storm by pulling off their stockings and making a lather of soap'" (191. 344). Saints and witches had power to stop rains and lay storms as well as to bring them on.

H. F. Feilberg has given us an interesting account of "weather-making," a folk-custom still in vogue in several parts of Denmark. It would appear that this strange custom exists in Djursland, Samsø, Sejerø, Nexelø, in the region of Kallundborg. Here "the women 'make weather' in February, the men in March, all in a fixed order, usually according to the numbers of the tax-register. The pastor and his wife, each in his and her month, 'make weather' on the first of the month, after them the other inhabitants of the village. If the married men are not sufficient to fill out the days of the months, the unmarried ones and the servants are called upon, — the house-servant perhaps 'making weather' in the morning, the hired boy in the afternoon, and in like manner the kitchen-maid and the girl-servant" (392 (1891). 56, 58). In this case we have a whole family, household, community of "weather-makers," old and young, and are really taken back to a culture-stage similar to that of the Caribs and Chibchas of America, with whom the chief was weather-maker as well as ruler of his people (101. 57).

The " Bull-Roarer."

In Mr. Andrew Lang's *Custom and Myth* there is an entertaining chapter on "The Bull Roarer," which the author identifies with the ῥόμβος mentioned by Clemens of Alexandria as one of the toys of the infant Dionysus. The "bull-roarer," known to the modern English boy, the ancient Greek, the South African, the American Indian, etc., is in actual use to-day by children, — Mr. Lang does not seem to be aware of the fact, — as a " wind-raiser," or " weather-maker." Mr. Gregor, speaking of northeastern Scotland, says : " During thunder it was not unusual for boys to take a piece of thin wood a few inches wide and about half a foot long, bore a hole in one end of it, and tie a few yards of twine into the hole. The piece of wood was rapidly whirled around the head under the belief that the thunder would cease, or that the thunder-bolt would not strike. It went by the name of the "thunner-spell'" (246. 153).

Among the Kaffirs, according to Mr. Theal : —

" There is a kind of superstition connected with the *nowidu* [the South African 'bull-roarer'], that playing with it invites a gale of wind. Men will, on this account, often prevent boys from using it when they desire calm weather for any purpose" (543. 223).

Dr. Boas tells us that the Shushwap Indians of British Columbia attribute supernatural powers to twins, and believe : "They can make good and bad weather. In order to produce rain they take a small basket filled with water, which they spill into the air. For making clear weather, they use a small stick to the end of which a string is tied. A small flat piece of wood is attached to the end of the string, and this implement is shaken. Storm is produced by strewing down on the ends of spruce branches" (404. 92).

The Nootka Indians have a like belief regarding twins: "They have the power to make good and bad weather. They produce rain by painting their faces with black colour and then washing them, or by merely shaking their heads" (404. 40).

Among some of the Kwakiutl Indians, upon the birth of twins "the father dances for four days after the children have been born, with a large square rattle. The children, by swinging this rattle, can cure disease and procure favourable winds and weather" (404. 62).

In Prussia, when it snows, the folk-belief is "the angels are shaking their little beds," and Grimm's story of "Old Mother Frost" has another rendering of the same myth: "What are you afraid of, my child! Stop with me: if you will put all things in order in my house, then all shall go well with you; only you must take care that you make my bed well, and shake tremendously, so that the feathers fly; then it snows upon earth. I am Old Mother Frost."

An Eskimo legend states that thunder and lightning are caused by an adult person and a child, who went up in the sky long, long ago; they carry a dried seal-skin, which, when rattled, makes the thunder, and torches of tar, which, when waved, cause the lightning.

The Mississaga Indians explain a fierce storm of thunder and lightning by saying that "the young thunder-birds up in the sky are making merry and having a good time." In like manner, the Dakotas account for the rumbling of thunder, "because the old thunder-bird begins the peal and the young ones take it up and continue."

In the poetry of the ancient Aryans of Asia the wind is called "the heavenly child," some idea of which survives in the old pictures in books representing the seasons, and in maps, where infants or cherubs are figured as blowing at the various points of the compass. But to return to rain-making. Grimm has called attention to several instances in Modern Europe where the child figures as " rain-maker."

Girl Rain-Makers.

One of the charms in use in the Rhine country of Germany in the eleventh century, as recorded by Burchard of Worms, was this: "A little girl, completely undressed and led outside the town, had to dig up henbane with the little finger of her right hand, and tie it to the little toe of her right foot; she was then solemnly conducted by the other maidens to the nearest river, and splashed with water" (462. II. 593).

In Servia the rain-maker is well known, and the procedure is as follows: "A girl, called the *dodola*, is stript naked, but so wrapt up in grass, herbs, and flowers, that nothing of her person is to be seen, not even the face. Escorted by other maidens, *dodola* passes from house to house; before each house they form a ring, she standing in the middle and dancing alone. The good-wife comes out and empties a bucket of water over the girl, who keeps dancing and whirling all the while; her companions sing songs, repeating after every line the burden *oy dodo, oy dodo le.*" Following is one of the rain-songs: —

> "To God doth our doda call, oy dodo oy dodo le !
> That dewy rain may fall, oy dodo oy dodo le !
> And drench the diggers all, oy dodo oy dodo le !
> The workers great and small, oy dodo oy dodo le !
> Even those in house and stall, oy dodo oy dodo le ! "

Corresponding to the Servian *dodola*, and thought to be equally efficacious, is the πυρπηροῦνα of the Modern Greeks. With them the custom is: "When it has not rained for a fortnight or three weeks, the inhabitants of villages and small towns do as follows. The children choose one of themselves, who is from eight to ten years old, usually a poor orphan, whom they strip naked and deck from head to foot with field herbs and flowers : this child is called πυρπηροῦνα. The others lead her round the village, singing a hymn, and every housewife has to throw a pailful of water over the pyrperuna's head and hand the children a para ($\frac{1}{4}$ of a farthing) " (462. I. 594).

In a Wallachian song, sung by children when the grain is troubled by drought, occurs the following appeal: "Papaluga (Father Luga), climb into heaven, open its doors, and send down rain from above, that well the rye may grow ! " (462. II. 593). This brings us naturally to the consideration of the rain-rhymes in English and cognate tongues.

Rain-Rhymes.

Mr. Henderson, treating of the northern counties of England, tells us that when the rain threatens to spoil a boy's holiday, he will sing out: —

> " ' Rain, rain, go away,
> Come again another summer's day ;
> Rain, rain, pour down,
> And come no more to our town.'

or : —

> ' Rain, rain, go away,
> And come again on washing day,'

or, more quaintly, yet : —

> ' Rain, rain, go to Spain ;
> Fair weather, come again,'

and, *sooner* or *later*, the rain will depart. If there be a rainbow, the juvenile devotee must look at it all the time. The Sunderland version runs thus : —

> ' Rain, rain, pour down
> Not a drop in our town,
> But a pint and a gill
> All a-back of Building Hill.' "

Mr. Henderson remarks that "such rhymes are in use, I believe, in every nursery in England," and they are certainly well known, in varying forms in America. A common English charm for driving away the rainbow brings the child at once into the domain of the primitive medicine-man. Schoolboys were wont, "on the appearance of a rainbow, to place a couple of straws or twigs across on the ground, and, as they said, ' cross out the rainbow.' The West Riding [Yorkshire] receipt for driving away a rainbow is: ' Make a cross of two sticks and lay four pebbles on it, one at each end ' " (469. 24, 25).

Mr. Gregor, for northeastern Scotland, reports the following as being sung or shouted at the top of the voice by children, when a rainbow appears (246. 153, 154) : —

(1)
> " Rainbow, rainbow,
> Brack an gang hame,
> The coo's wi' a calf,
> The yow's wi' a lam,
> An' the coo 'ill be calvt,
> Or ye win hame."

(2)
>   "Rainbow, rainbow,
>   Brack an gang hame;
>   Yir father an yir mither's aneth the layer-stehn;
>   Yir coo's calvt, yir mare's foalt,
>   Yir wife'll be dead
>   Or ye win hame."

(3)
>   "Rainbow, rainbow,
>   Brack an gang hame,
>   Yir father and mither's aneth the grave stehn."

Even more touching is the appeal made by the children in Berwickshire, according to Mr. Henderson (469. 24, 25) : —

>   "Rainbow, rainbow, haud awa' hame,
>   A' yer bairns are dead but ane,
>   And it lies sick at yon gray stane,
>   And will be dead ere you win hame.
>   Gang owre the Drumaw [a hill] and yont the lea
>   And down by the side o' yonder sea ;
>   Your bairn lies greeting [crying] like to dee,
>   And the big tear-drop is in his e'e."

Sometimes the child-priest or weather-maker has to employ an intermediary. On the island of Rügen and in some other parts of Germany the formula is (466 a. 132) : —

>   "Leeve Katriene
>   Lat de sünnen schienen,
>   Lat'n rägen övergahn,
>   Lat de sünnen wedder kam'n."
>   ["Dear (St.) Catharine,
>   Let the sun shine,
>   Let the rain pass off,
>   Let the sun come again."]

In Rügen the glow-worm is associated with "weather-making." The children take the little creature up, put it on their hand and thus address it (466 a. 133) : —

>   "Sünnskürnken fleeg weech,
>   Bring mi morgen good wäder,
>   Lat 'en rägen övergahn,
>   Lat de sünnen wedder kam'n,
>   Bring mi morgen good wäder."

If the insect flies away, the good weather will come; if not, there will be rain.

The Altmark formula, as given by Danneil (*Worterb.*, p. 81) is: —

" Herrgottswörmk'n, flêg nao'n Himmel, segg dîn Vaoder un Mutter, dat't morgen un äöwermorg'n gôd Wäd'r wart." [" Little God's-worm, fly to heaven, tell your father and mother to make it fine weather to-morrow and the day after to-morrow."]

Another rain-rhyme from Altmark, sung by children in the streets when it rains, is harsh in tone, and somewhat derisive as well (p. 153): —

> " Räg'n blatt, maok mi nich natt,
> Maok den olln Paop'n natt
> De'n Büd'l vull Geld hat."
> [" Rain, don't make me wet,
> Make the old priest wet,
> Who has a purse full of money."]

Concerning the Kansa Indians, Rev. J. Owen Dorsey informs us that the members of the Tcihaci^n or Ka^{n}ze gens are looked upon as "wind people," and when there is a blizzard the other Kansa appeal to them: "O, Grandfather, I wish good weather! Please cause one of your children to be decorated!" The method of stopping the blizzard is as follows: "Then the youngest son of one of the Ka^{n}ze men, say one over four feet high, is chosen for the purpose, and painted with red paint. The youth rolls over and over in the snow and reddens it for some distances all around him. This is supposed to stop the storm" (433. 410).

With the Kwakiutl Indians of Vancouver Island, as with the Shushwaps and Nootka, twins are looked upon in the light of wonderful beings, having power over the weather. Of them it is said "while children they are able to summon any wind by motions of their hands, and can make fair or bad weather. They have the power of curing diseases, and use for this purpose a rattle called K·'oā'qaten, which has the shape of a flat box about three feet long by two feet wide." Here the "weather-maker" and the "doctor" are combined in the same person. Among the Tsimshian Indians, of British Columbia, twins are believed to control the weather, and these aborigines "pray to wind and rain: 'Calm down, breath of the twins'" (403. 51).

In the creation-legend of the Indians of Mt. Shasta (California), we are told that once a terrific storm came up from the sea and shook to its base the wigwam,—Mt. Shasta itself,— in which lived the "Great Spirit" and his family. Then "The 'Great Spirit' commanded his daughter, little more than an infant, to go up and bid the wind be still, cautioning her at the same time, in his fatherly way, not to put her head out into the blast, but only to thrust out her little red arm and make a sign before she delivered her message." But the temptation to look out on the world was too strong for her, and, as a result, she was caught up by the storm and blown down the mountain-side into the land of the grizzly-bear people. From the union of the daughter and the grizzly-bear people sprang a new race of men. When the "Great Spirit" was told his daughter still lived, he ran down the mountain for joy, but finding that his daughter had become a mother, he was so angry that he cursed the grizzly-people and turned them into the present race of bears of that species; them and the new race of men he drove out of their wigwam,—Little Mt. Shasta,—then "shut to the door, and passed away to his mountains, carrying his daughter; and her or him no eye has since seen." Hence it is that "no Indian tracing his descent from the spirit mother and the grizzly, will kill a grizzly-bear; and if by an evil chance a grizzly kill a man in any place, that spot becomes memorable, and every one that passes casts a stone there till a great pile is thrown up" (396. III. 91).

Here the weather-maker touches upon deity and humanity at once.

CHAPTER XXII.

The Child as Healer and Physician.

Fingunt se medicos quivis idiota, sacerdos, Iudæus, monachus, histrio, rasor, anus. [Any unskilled person, priest, Jew, monk, actor, barber, old woman, turns himself into a physician.]—*Medical Proverb*.

The Child as Healer and Physician.

Though Dr. Max Bartels' (397) recent treatise — the best book that has yet appeared on the subject of primitive medicine — has no chapter consecrated to the child as healer and physician, and Mr. Black's *Folk-Medicine* (401) contains but a few items under the rubric of personal cures, it is evident from data in these two works, and in many other scattered sources, that the child has played a not unimportant *rôle* in the history of folk-medicine. Among certain primitive peoples the healing art descends by inheritance, and in various parts of the world unbaptized children, illegitimate children, and children born out of due time and season, or deformed in some way, have been credited with special curative powers, or looked upon as "doctors born."

In Spain, to kiss an unbaptized child before any one else has done so, is a panacea against toothache (258. 100). In northeastern Scotland, "a seventh son, without a daughter, if worms were put into his hand before baptism, had the power of healing the disease (ring-worm) simply by rubbing the affected part with his hand. The common belief about such a son was that he was a doctor by nature" (246. 47). In Ireland, the healing powers are acquired "if his hand has, before it has touched anything for himself, been touched with his future medium of cure. Thus, if silver is to be the charm, a sixpence, or a three-penny piece, is put into his hand, or meal, salt, or his father's hair, 'whatever

309

substance a seventh son rubs with must be worn by his parents as long as he lives.'" In some portions of Europe, the seventh son, if born on Easter Eve, was able to cure tertian or quartan fevers. In Germany, "if a woman has had seven sons in succession, the seventh can heal all manner of hurt," — his touch is also said to cure wens at the throat (462. III. 1152). In France, the *marcou*, or seventh son, has had a great reputation; his body is said to be marked with a *fleur-de-lis*, and the cure is effected by his simply breathing upon the diseased part, or by allowing the patient to touch a mark on his body. Bourke calls attention to the fact that among the Cherokee Indians of the southeastern United States is this same belief that the seventh son is "a natural-born prophet with the gift of healing by touch" (406. 457). In France similar powers have also been attributed to the fifth son. The seventh son of a seventh son is still more famous, while to the twenty-first son, born without the intervention of a daughter, prodigious cures are ascribed.

Nor is the other sex entirely neglected. In France a "seventh daughter" was believed to be able to cure chilblains on the heels (462. III. 1152), and in England, as recently as 1876, the seventh daughter of a seventh daughter claimed great skill as an herb-doctor.

In northeastern Scotland, "a posthumous child was believed to possess the gift of curing almost any disease by looking on the patient" (246. 37), and in Donegal. Ireland, the peasants "wear a lock of hair from a posthumous child, to guard against whooping-cough," while in France, such a child was believed to possess the power of curing wens, and a child that has never known its father was credited with ability to cure swellings and to drive away tumours (462. III. 1152).

Twins, in many countries, have been regarded as prodigies, or as endowed with unusual powers. In Essex, England, "a 'left twin' (*i.e.* a child who has survived its fellow-twin) is thought to have the power of curing the thrush by blowing three times into the patient's mouth, if the patient is of the opposite sex" (469. 307). Among the Kwakiutl Indians of British Columbia, twins are said to be able to cure disease by swinging a rattle, and in Liberia (Africa) they are thought to possess great healing powers, for which reason most of them become doctors (397. 75).

In Sweden, "a first-born child that has come into the world with teeth can cure a bad bite." In Scotland, "those who were born with their feet first possessed great power to heal all kinds of sprains, lumbago, and rheumatism, either by rubbing the afflicted part, or by trampling on it. The chief virtue lay in the feet" (246. 45). In Cornwall, England, the mother of such a child also possessed the power to cure rheumatism by trampling on the patients. The natives of the island of Nias, off the western coast of Sumatra, consider children born with their feet first specially gifted for the treatment of dislocations (397. 75). Among the superstitions prevalent among the Mexicans of the Rio Grande region in Texas, Captain Bourke mentions the belief: "To cure rheumatism, stroke the head of a little girl three times — a golden-haired child preferred" (407. 139). The Jews of Galicia seek to cure small-pox by rubbing the pustules with the tresses of a girl, and think that the scrofula will disappear "if a *Bechôr*, or first-born son, touches it with his thumb and little finger" (392 (1893). 142).

The power of curing scrofula — touching for the "King's Evil" — possessed by monarchs of other days, was thought to be hereditary, and seems to have been practised by them at a tender age. In England this "cure" was in vogue from the time of Edward the Confessor until 1719, when, according to Brewer, the "office" disappeared from the Prayer-book. The French custom dated back to Anne of Clovis (A.D. 481). In the year of his coronation (1654 A.D.), when Louis XV. was but eleven years old, he is said to have touched over two thousand sufferers (191. 308).

Blood of Children.

In the dark ages the blood of little children had a wide-spread reputation for its medicinal virtue. The idea that diseased and withered humanity, having failed to discover the fountain of eternal youth, might find a new well-spring of life in bathing in, or being sprinkled with, the pure blood of a child or a virgin, had long a firm hold upon the minds of the people. Hartmann von Aue's story, *Der arme Heinrich*, and a score of similar tales testify of the folk-faith in the regeneration born of this horrible baptism — a survival or recrudescence of the crassest form of the doctrine that the life dwells in the blood. Strack, in his valuable treatise on "Human Blood, in Superstition and Ceremonial," devotes a brief section to the belief in the cure of leprosy by means of human blood (361. 20–24). The Targumic gloss on Exodus ii. 23 — the paraphrase known as the Pseudo-Jonathan — explains "that the king of Egypt, suffering from leprosy, ordered the firstborn of the children of Israel to be slain that he might bathe in their blood," and the Midrasch Schĕmôth Rabba accounts for the lamentation of the people of Israel at this time, from the fact that the Egyptian magicians had told the king that there was no cure for this loathsome disease, unless every evening and every morning one hundred and fifty Jewish children were slain and the monarch bathed twice daily in their blood. Pliny tells us that the Egyptians warmed with human blood the seats in their baths as a remedy against the dreaded leprosy.

According to the early chroniclers, Constantine the Great, on account of his persecution of the Christians, was afflicted with leprosy, which would yield neither to the skill of native nor to that of foreign physicians. Finally, the priests of Jupiter Capitolinus recommended a bath in the blood of children. The children were gathered together, but "the lamentations of their mothers so affected the Emperor, that he declared his intention of suffering the foul disease, rather than be the cause of so much woe and misery." Afterwards he was directed in a dream to Pope Sylvester, was converted, baptized into the Church, and restored to health (361. 22).

Other instances of this fearful custom are mentioned in the stories of Percival (in the history of the Holy Grail), of Giglan de Galles et Geoffroy de Mayence, and the wide-spread tale of Amicus and Amelius and its variants, Louis and Alexander, Engelhard and Engeltrut, Oliver and Arthur, etc., in all of which one of the friends is afflicted with leprosy, but is cured through the devotion of the other, who sacrifices his own children in order to obtain the blood by which alone his friend can be restored to health. Usually, we are told, God rewards his fidelity and the children are restored to life.

The physicians of King Richard I. of England are said, in one of the fictions which grew up about his distinguished personality, to have utterly failed to give relief to the monarch, who was suffering from leprosy. At last a celebrated Jew, after exhausting his skill without curing the monarch, told him that his one chance of recovery lay in bathing in the fresh blood of a new-born child, and eating its heart just as it was taken out of the body. That the king adopted this horrible remedy we are left to doubt, but of Louis XI. of France, several chroniclers affirm that he went even farther than the others, and, in order to become rejuvenated, drank large quantities of the blood of young children. In all these cases the character of the child as fetich seems to be present, and the virtues ascribed to the blood drawn from children (not always killed) belong not alone to medicine, but also to primitive religion (361. 23).

Even the dead body of a child or some one of its members plays a *rôle* in folk-medicine in many parts of the globe. Grimm cites from a document of 1408 A.D., a passage recording the cure of a leper, who had been stroked with the hand of a still-born (and, therefore, sinless) child, which had been rubbed with salve (361. 34). In Steiermark, so Dr. Strack informs us, " a favourite cure for birth-marks is to touch them with the hand of a dead person, especially of a child " (361. 35). Among the charges made by the Chinese against the foreigners, who are so anxious to enter their dominions, is one of " kidnapping and buying children in order to make charms and medicines out of their eyes, hearts, and other portions of their bodies." This belief induced the riot of June, 1870, an account of which has been given by Baron Hübner, and similar incidents occurred in 1891 and 1892. Somewhat the same charges have been made (in 1891, for example) by the natives of Madagascar against the French and other foreigners (361. 37).

Medicine-Men.

Among many primitive peoples, as is the case with the Zulus, Bechuana, Japanese (formerly), Nez Percés, Cayuse, Walla-Wallas, Wascos, etc., the office of " doctor " is hereditary, and is often exercised at a comparatively early age (397. 275). Dr. Pitré has recently discussed some interesting cases in this connection in modern Italy (322).

Among certain Indian tribes of the Rocky Mountain region of the northwestern United States, although he cannot properly practise his art until he reaches manhood, the "medicine-man" (here, doctor) begins his candidacy in his eighth or tenth year. Of the "wizards," or "doctors" of the Patagonians, Falkner says, that they "are selected in youth for supposed qualifications, especially if epileptic" (406. 456). While among the Dieyerie of South Australia, the "doctor" is not allowed to practise before having been circumcised, or to enter upon the duties of his office before completing his tenth year, those young people become "doctors," who, as children, "have seen the devil," *i.e.* have seen in a troubled dream the demon *Kutchie*, or have had the nightmare. The belief is, that in this way, the power to heal has been imparted to the child (397. 75). Among the Yuki Indians of California, "the 'poison-doctor' is the most important member of the profession. The office is hereditary; a little child is prepared for holding it by being poisoned and then cured, which, in their opinion, renders him invulnerable ever afterward" (519. 131). Among the Tunguses, of Siberian Russia, a child afflicted with cramps or with bleeding at the nose and mouth, is declared by an old shaman ("medicine-man," or "medicine-woman") to be called to the profession, and is then termed *hudildon*. After the child has completed its second year, it is taken care of by an old shaman, who consecrates it with various ceremonies; from this time forth it is called *jukejeren*, and is instructed by the old man in the mysteries of his art (482. III. 105). With these people also the female shamans have the assistance of boys and girls to carry their implements and perform other like services (397. 66). An excellent account of shamanism in Siberia and European Russia has been given by Professor Mikhailovskii (504), of Moscow, who gives among other details a notice of the *kamlanie*, or spirit-ceremonial of a young shaman belonging to one of the Turkish tribes of the Altai Mountains (504. 71). Among the Samoyeds and Ostiaks of Siberia, "the shamans succeed to the post by inheritance from father to son" (504. 86). On the death of a shaman, "his son, who desires to have power over the spirits, makes of wood an image of the dead man's hand, and by means of this symbol succeeds to his father's power. Those destined to be shamans spend their youth in practices which irritate the nervous system and excite the imagination."

Among the Buryats of southern Siberia, it is thought that "the

dead ancestors who were shamans choose from their living kins-
folk a boy who is to inherit their power. This child is marked by
signs; he is often thoughtful, fond of solitude, a seer of prophetic
visions, subject, occasionally, to fits, during which he is unconscious. The Buryats believe that at such a time the boy's soul
is with the spirits, who are teaching him; if he is to be a white
shaman, with the western spirits; if he is to be a black shaman,
among the eastern spirits." Usually, the youth does not enter
upon his duties until he has reached his twentieth year (504. 87).

The tribes of the Altai believe that "the ability to shamanize
is inborn; instruction only gives a knowledge of the chants,
prayers, and external rites." There is in early life an innate
tendency to sickness and frenzy, against which, we are told, the
elect struggle in vain (504. 90): "Those who have the shamanist
sickness endure physical torments; they have cramps in the arms
and legs, until they are sent to a *kam* [shaman] to be educated.
The tendency is hereditary; a *kam* often has children predis-
posed to attacks of illness. If, in a family where there is no
shaman, a boy or a girl is subject to fits, the Altaians are persuaded that one of its ancestors was a shaman. A *kam* told
Potanin that the shamanist passion was hereditary, like noble
birth. If the *kam's* own son does not feel any inclination, some
one of the nephews is sure to have the vocation. There are cases
of men becoming shamans at their own wish, but these *kams* are
much less powerful than those born to the profession." Thus the
whole training of the *kam* from childhood up to exercise of his
official duties is such as "to augment his innate tendencies, and
make him an abnormal man, unlike his fellows." When fully
qualified, he functions as "priest, physician, wizard, diviner."

Moses.

Of the childhood of Moses Oriental legend has much to say.
One story tells how the daughter of Pharaoh, a leper, was healed
as she stretched out her hand to the infant whom she rescued from
the waters of Nile. Weil thus resumes the tale (547. 122): —

"The eldest of the seven princesses first discovered the little
ark and carried it to the bank to open it. On her removing the
lid, there beamed a light upon her, which her eyes were not able

to endure. She cast a veil over Moses, but at that instant her own face, which hitherto had been covered with scars and sores of all the most hideous colours imaginable, shone like the moon in its brightness and purity, and her sisters exclaimed in amazement, 'By what means hast thou been so suddenly freed from leprosy?' 'By the miraculous power of this child,' replied the eldest. The glance which beamed upon me when I beheld it unveiled, has chased away the impurity of my body, as the rising sun scatters the gloom of night.' The six sisters, one after the other, now lifted the veil from Moses' face, and they, too, became fair as if they had been formed of the finest silver. The eldest then took the ark upon her head, and carried it to her mother, Asia, relating to her in how miraculous a manner both she and her sisters had been healed."

We also learn that when Moses was six years old, being teased by Pharaoh until he was angry, he kicked the throne over so that the king fell and injured himself so that he bled at the mouth and nose. The intercession of Asia and the seven princesses seemed vain, and the king was about to thrust Moses through with his sword, when "there flew a white cock toward the king, and cried: 'Pharaoh, if thou spill the blood of this child, thy daughters shall be more leprous than before.' Pharaoh cast a glance upon the princesses; and, as if from dread and fright, their faces were already suffused with a ghastly yellow, he desisted again from his bloody design" (547. 127).

Child-Saints.

To other heroes, kings, saints, the power to heal which characterized their years of discretion is often ascribed to them in childhood, especially where and when it happens that the same individual is prophet, priest, and king. In the unnumbered miracles of the Church children have often figured. Lupellus, in his life of St. Frodibert (seventh century A.D.), says: "When Frodibert was a mere child he cured his mother's blindness, as, in the fulness of love and pity, he kissed her darkened eyes, and signed them with the sign of the cross. Not only was her sight restored, but it was keener than ever" (191. 45). Of St. Patrick (373–464 A.D.) it is told: "On the day of his baptism he gave sight to a man born blind; the blind man took hold of the babe's hand, and with it made on the ground a sign of the cross." Another account makes the miracle a triple one: "A blind man, taking hold of St. Patrick's right hand, guided it into making on the ground a cross, when instantly three miracles ensued: (1) A spring of water bubbled from the dry ground; (2) the blind man, bathing his eyes with this water, received his sight; and (3) the man, who before could neither write nor read, was instantly inspired with both these gifts" (191. 237).

Brewer relates other instances of the miraculous power of the child-saint from the lives of St. Géneviève (423–512, A.D.), St. Vitus, who at the age of twelve caused the arms and legs of the Emperor Aurelian to wither, but on the Emperor owning the greatness of God, the "child-magician," as the monarch had termed him, made Aurelian whole again; St. Sampson (565 A.D.), who cured a fellow schoolboy of a deadly serpent's bite; Mari- anne de Quito (1618–1645 A.D.), who cured herself of a gangrened finger (191. 442).

In his interesting chapters on *Fairy Births and Human Mid- wives*, Mr. Hartland informs us that young girls have some- times been called upon to go to fairy-land and usher into the world of elves some little sprite about to be born. Instances of this folk- belief are cited from Pomerania, Swabia, Silesia. Rewards and presents are given the maiden on her return, and often her whole family is blest, if she has acted well (258. 37–92).

Close, indeed, are often the ties between the saint and the physician; the healer of the soul and the healer of the body are frequently the same. Other links bind the doctor to the hero and to the god. Of Æsculapius, the great son of Apollo, exposed in childhood by his mother, but nurtured by the goat of the shep- herd Aresthanas, and guarded by his dog, when he grew up to manhood, became so skilled in the uses of herbs and other medi- cines that he received divine honours after his death and came to be looked upon as the inventor of medicine as well as god of the healing art.

Origin of the Healing Art.

With some primitive peoples even the child is their Æscula- pius, at once human and divine, hero and god. An Iroquois legend recorded by Mrs. Smith attributes to a boy the discovery of witch-charms: "A certain boy while out hunting came across a beautiful snake. Taking a great fancy to it, he caught it and cared for it, feeding it on birds, etc., and made a bark bowl in which he kept it. He put fibres, down, and small feathers into the water with the snake, and soon found that these things had become living beings. From this fact he naturally conjectured that the snake was endowed with supernatural powers." So he went on experimenting, and discovered many of the virtues of the snake water: rubbing it on his eyes would make him see in the dark and see hidden things; pointing his finger, after having dipped it in the bowl, at any one would bewitch that person; by using it in certain other ways he could become like a snake, travel very fast, even become invisible; deadly indeed were arrows dipped in this liquid, and pointing a feather so dipped at any game-animal would cause it to start for the creature and kill it. In this fashion the boy learned the secret art of witch-craft. Afterwards, by experimenting, he discovered, among the various roots and herbs, the proper antidotes and counteracting agents (534. 69, 70).

In his detailed account of the medicine-society of the Ojibwa, Dr. Hoffman tells how the mysteries of the "Grand Medicine" were taught to the Indians by the Sun-spirit, who at the request of the great Manido, came down to earth and dwelt among men in the form of a little boy, raising to life again his dead play-mate, the child of the people who adopted him. After his mission was fulfilled, he "returned to his kindred spirits, for the Indians would have no need to fear sickness, as they now possessed the Grand Medicine which would enable them to live. He also said that his spirit could bring a body to life but once, and he would now return to the sun, from which they would feel his influence." So the institution of "medicine" among the Ojibwa is called *Kwi-wi-sĕns' wĕ-di'-shi-tshi gĕ-wi-nip*, "Little-boy-his-work" (473. 172, 173).

CHAPTER XXIII.

The Child as Shaman and Priest.

Nearer the gates of Paradise than we
Our children breathe its air, its angels see;
And when they pray, God hears their simple prayer,
Yea, even sheathes his sword, in judgment bare. — *R. H. Stoddard.*

The youth, who daily farther from the east
Must travel, still is nature's priest. — *Wordsworth.*

Priestly Training.

Instruction in the priestly art in Africa begins sometimes almost at birth. Bastian informs us (529. 58) : —

"Women who have been long barren, or who have lost their children, are wont to dedicate to the service of the fetich the unborn fruit of the womb, and to present to the village priest the new-born babe. He exercises it, at an early age, in those wild dances with deafening drum-accompaniment, by means of which he is accustomed to gain the requisite degree of spiritual exaltation; and in later years he instructs his pupil in the art of understanding, while his frame is wracked with convulsions, the inspirations of the demon and of giving fitting responses to questions proposed."

Of the one sex we read (529. 56) : —

"Every year the priests assemble the boys who are entering the state of puberty, and take them into the forest. There they settle and form an independent commonwealth, under very strict regulations, however; and every offence against the rules is sternly punished. The wound given in circumcision commonly heals in one week, yet they remain in the woods for a period of six months, cut off from all intercourse with the outside world, and in the meanwhile each receives separate instruction how to prepare his medicine-bag. Forever after, each one is mystically united with the fetich who presides over his life. Even their nearest relatives are not allowed to visit the boys in this retreat; and women are threatened with the severest punishment if they be only found in the neighbourhood of a forest containing such a boy-colony. When the priest declares the season of probation at an end, the boys return home and are welcomed back with great rejoicings."

Concerning the other, Bosman, as reported by Schultze, says that among the negroes of Whida, where snake-worship prevails (529. 80) —

"Every year the priestesses, armed with clubs, go about the country, picking out and carrying away girls of from eight to twelve years of age, for the service of the god. These children are kindly treated and instructed in songs and dances *in majorem gloriam* of his snakeship. In due time they are consecrated by tattooing on their bodies certain figures, especially those of serpents. The negroes suppose it is the snake himself that marks his elect thus. Having received their training and consecration, which are paid for by the parents according to their means, the children return home; and when they attain their majority are espoused to the Serpent."

In Ashanti, according to Ellis, the children of a priest or of a priestess "are not ordinarily educated for the priestly profession, one generation being usually passed over [a curious primitive recognition of the idea in our common saying, "genius skips a generation"], and the grand-children selected" (438. 121). At the village of Suru several children (male and female) and youths are handed over to the priests and priestesses to be instructed in the service of the gods, when the goddess was thought to be offended, and in the ceremonials when the new members are tested, youths and children take part, smeared all over with white (438. 130).

Among the natives of the Andaman Islands, as Mr. Man informs us, sometimes even "a young boy is looked upon as a coming ôko-pai·ad-." The word signifies literally "dreamer," and such individuals are "credited with the possession of supernatural powers, such as second sight" (498. 28).

Captain Bourke, in his detailed account of the "medicine-men" of the Apaches, speaking of the Pueblos Indians, says: "While I was at Tusayan, in 1881, I heard of a young boy, quite a child, who was looked up to by the other Indians, and on special occasions made his appearance decked out in much native finery of beads and gewgaws, but the exact nature of his duties and supposed responsibilities could not be ascertained." He seems to have been a young "medicine-man" (406. 456).

Into the "medicine-society" of the Delaware Indians "the boys were usually initiated at the age of twelve or fourteen years, with very trying ceremonies, fasting, want of sleep, and other tests of their physical and mental stamina." Of these same aborigines the missionary Brainerd states: "Some of their diviners (or priests) are endowed with the spirit in infancy; others in adult age. It seems not to depend upon their own will, nor to be acquired by any endeavours of the person who is the subject of it, although it is supposed to be given to children sometimes in consequence of some means which the parents use with them for that purpose" (516. 81).

Among the Chippeway (Ojibwa), also, children are permitted to belong to the "Midéwewin or 'Grand Medicine Society,'" of which Dr. W. J. Hoffman has given so detailed a description — Sikassige, a Chippeway of Mille Lacs, having taken his "first degree" at ten years of age (473. 172).

The Angakok.

Among the Eskimo the *angakok*, or shaman, trains his child from infancy in the art of sorcery, taking him upon his knee during his incantations and conjurations. In one of the tales in the collection of Rink we read (525. 276): "A great *angakok* at his conjurations always used to talk of his having been to Akilinek [a fabulous land beyond the ocean], and his auditors fully believed him. Once he forced his little son to attend his conjurations, sitting upon his knee. The boy, who was horribly frightened, said: 'Lo! what is it I see? The stars are dropping down in the old grave on yonder hill.' The father said: 'When the old grave is shining to thee, it will enlighten thy understanding.' When the boy had been lying in his lap for a while, he again burst out: 'What is it I now see? The bones in the old grave

Y

are beginning to join together.' The father only repeating his last words, the son grew obstinate and wanted to run away, but the father still kept hold of him. Lastly, the ghost from the grave came out, and being called upon by the *angakok*, he entered the house to fetch the boy, who only perceived a strong smell of maggots, and then fainted away. On recovering his senses, he found himself in the grave quite naked, and when he arose and looked about, his nature was totally altered — he found himself able at a sight to survey the whole country to the farthest north, and nothing was concealed from him. All the dwelling-places of man appeared to be close together, side by side; and on looking at the sea, he saw his father's tracks stretching across to Akilinek. When going down to the house, he observed his clothes flying through the air, and had only to put forth his hands and feet to make them cover his body again. But on entering the house he looked exceedingly pale, because of the great *angakok* wisdom he had acquired down in the old grave. After he had become an *angakok* himself, he once went on a flight to Akilinek."

Besides this interesting account of an *angakok* séance, the same authority, in the story of the *angakok* Tugtutsiak, records the following (525. 324): "Tugtutsiak and his sister were a couple of orphans, and lived in a great house. It once happened that all the grown-up people went away berry-gathering, leaving all children at home. Tugtutsiak, who happened to be the eldest of them, said: 'Let us try to conjure up spirits'; and some of them proceeded to make up the necessary preparations, while he himself undressed, and covered the door with his jacket, and closed the opening at the sleeves with a string. He now commenced the invocation, while the other children got mortally frightened, and were about to take flight. But the slabs of the floor were lifted high in the air, and rushed after them. Tugtutsiak would have followed them, but felt himself sticking fast to the floor, and could not get loose until he had made the children come back, and ordered them to uncover the door, and open the window, on which it again became light in the room, and he was enabled to get up."

Girls, too, among the Eskimo, could become *angakoks* or shamans. Rink tells of one who visited the under-world, where she received presents, but these, while she was carrying them home, "were wafted out of her hands, and flew back to their first owners."

Of the Pawnee Indians, Mr. Grinnell informs us that the legend of their wanderings tells of a boy in whose possession was the sacred " medicine-bundle " of the tribe, and who was regarded as the oracle-interpreter (480 (1893). 125).

Witches.

As Dr. Mackay has remarked, in all the woeful annals of the witch-persecutions, there is nothing so astounding and revolting as the burning and putting to death of mere children for practising the arts of the devil. Against innocents of both sexes counting no more than ten or twelve years, there appear on the records the simple but significant words *convicta et combusta* — convicted and burned. Here the degradation of intellect and morals reaches its lowest level; it was Satan and not Jesus who bade the children come unto him; their portion was the kingdom of hell, not that of heaven. In Würzburg, between 1627 and 1629, no fewer than 157 persons suffered death for witchcraft (guilty and innocent), and among these were included "the prettiest girl in the town "; two mere boys; a wandering boy of twelve; a maiden of nine and her sister, younger in years; two boys of twelve; a girl of fifteen; a boy of ten and a boy of twelve; three boys of from ten to fifteen years of age. At Lille, in 1639, a whole school of girls — fifty in number — barely escaped burning as witches (496 a. II. 266–287). Everywhere the maddened, deluded people made sacrifice of their dearest and holiest, tainted, they thought, with the touch of the evil one (496 a. II. 285). It is a sad comment upon civilization that the last execution for witchcraft in England, which took place in 1716, was that of "Mrs. Hicks and her daughter, *a child nine years of age*, who were hung at Huntingdon, for 'selling their souls to the devil; and raising a storm, by pulling off their stockings and making a lather of soap'" (191. 344).

In the *London Times* for Dec. 8, 1845, appeared the following extract from the *Courier*, of Inverness, Scotland: "Our Wick contemporary gives the following recent instance of gross ignorance and credulity: 'Not far from Louisburg there lives a girl who, until a few days ago, was suspected of being a witch. In order to cure her of the witchcraft, a neighbour actually put her into a creed half-filled with wood and shavings, and hung her above a fire, setting the shavings in a blaze. Fortunately for the child and himself, she was not injured, and it is said that the gift of sorcery has been taken away from her. At all events, the intelligent neighbours aver that she is not half so witch-like in appearance since she was singed " (408. III. 14).

Concerning the sect of the Nagualists or "Magicians" of Mexico and Central America Dr. Brinton tells us much in his interesting little book (413). These sorcerers recruited their ranks from both sexes, and "those who are selected to become the masters of these arts are taught from early childhood how to draw and paint these characters and are obliged to learn by heart the formulas, and the names of the ancient Nagualists, and whatever else is included in these written documents " (413. 17).

We learn that "in the sacraments of Nagualism, woman was the primate and hierophant," the admission of the female sex to the most exalted positions and the most esoteric degrees being a remarkable feature of this great secret society (413. 33). Indeed, Aztec tradition, like that of Honduras, speaks of an ancient sorceress, mother of the occult sciences, and some of the legends of the Nagualists trace much of their art to a mighty enchantress of old (413. 34).

In 1713, the Tzendals of Chiapas rose in insurrection under the American Joan of Arc, an Indian girl about twenty years of age, whose Spanish name was Maria Candelaria. She was evidently a leader of the Nagualists, and after the failure of the attempt at revolution disappeared in the forest and was no more heard of (413. 35). Dr. Brinton calls attention to the fact that Mr. E. G. Squier reports having heard, during his travels in Central America, of a "*sukia*" woman, as she was called by the coast Indians, one who lived alone amid the ruins of an old Maya temple, a sorceress of twenty years, loved and feared, holding death and life in her hands " (413. 36). There are many other instances of a like nature showing the important position assigned to girls and young women in the esoteric rites, secret societies, magic, sorcery, and witchcraft of primitive peoples.

" Boy-Bishop."

A curious custom attached itself to the day of St. Nicholas, of Patara in Lycia (died 343 A.D.), the patron saint of boys, after whom the American boys' magazine *St. Nicholas* is aptly named. Brewer, in his *Dictionary of Phrase and Fable*, has the following paragraph concerning the "Boy-Bishop," as he is termed : "The custom of choosing a boy from the cathedral choir, etc., on St. Nicholas day (6th December), as a mock bishop is very ancient. The boy possessed episcopal honour for three weeks, and the rest of the choir were his prebends. If he died during the time of his prelacy, he was buried *in pontificalibus*. Probably the reference is to Jesus Christ sitting in the Temple among the doctors while he was a boy. The custom was abolished in the reign of Henry Eighth" (p. 110). Brand gives many details of the election and conduct of the "Boy-Bishops," and the custom seems to have been in vogue in almost every parish and collegiate church (408. I. 415–431). Bishop Hall thus expresses himself on the subject: "What merry work it was here in the days of our holy fathers (and I know not whether, in some places it may not be so still), that upon St. Nicholas, St. Katherine, St. Clement, and Holy Innocents' Day, children were wont to be arrayed in chimers, rochets, surplices, to counterfeit bishops and priests, and to be led with songs and dances from house to house, blessing the people, who stood grinning in the way to expect that ridiculous benediction. Yea, that boys in that holy sport were wont to sing masses, and to climb into the pulpit to preach (no doubt learnedly and edifyingly) to the simple auditory. And this was so really done, that in the cathedral church of Salisbury (unless it be lately defaced) there is a perfect monument of one of these Boy-Bishops (who died in the time of his young pontificality), accoutred in his episcopal robes, still to be seen. A fashion that lasted until the later times of King Henry the Eighth, who, in 1541, by his solemn Proclamation, printed by Thomas Bertlet, the king's printer, *cum privilegio*, straitly forbad the practice."

When King Edward First was on his way to Scotland, in 1299, we are told, "he permitted one of these Boy-Bishops to say vespers before him in his Chapel at Heton, near Newcastle-upon-Tyne, and made a considerable present to the said bishop, and certain other boys that came and sang with him on the occasion, on the 7th of December, the day after St. Nicholas's Day" (408. I. 422).

The records of the churches contain many particulars of the election, duties, and regalia of these boy-bishops, whence it would appear that expense and ceremony were not spared on these occasions.

Another boy-bishop was paid "thirteen shillings and sixpence for singing before King Edward the Third, in his chamber, on the day of the Holy Innocents" (408. I. 428).

The Boy-Bishop of Salisbury, whose service set to music is printed in the *Processionale et usum insignis et preclare Ecclesie Sarum*, 1566, is actually said "to have had the power of disposing of such prebends there as happened to fall vacant during the days of his episcopacy" (408. I. 424). With the return of Catholicism under Mary, as Brand remarks, the Boy-Bishop was revived, for we find an edict of the Bishop of London, issued Nov. 13, 1554, to all the clergy of his diocese, to the effect that "they should have a Boy-Bishop in procession," and Warton notes that "one of the child-bishop's songs, as it was sung before the Queen's Majesty, in her privy chamber; at her manor of St. James in the Field's on St. Nicholas's Day, and Innocents' Day, 1555, by the child-bishop of St. Paul's, with his company, was printed that year in London, containing a fulsome panegyric on the queen's devotions, comparing her to Judith, Esther, the Queen of Sheba, and the Virgin Mary" (408. I. 429–430). The places at which the ceremonies of the Boy-Bishop have been particularly noted are: Canterbury, Eton, St. Paul's, London, Colchester, Winchester, Salisbury, Westminster, Lambeth, York, Beverly, Rotherham, Newcastle-upon-Tyne, etc. The Boy-Bishop was known also in Spain and in France; in the latter country he was called Pape-Colas. In Germany, at the Council of Salzburg, in 1274, on account of the scandals they gave rise to, the *ludi noxii quos vulgaris eloquentia* Episcopatus Puerorum *appellat*, were placed under the ban (408. I. 426).

It would appear from the mention of "children strangely decked and apparelled to counterfeit priests, bishops, and women," that on these occasions "divine service was not only performed by boys, but by little girls," and "there is an injunction given to the Benedictine Nunnery of Godstowe in Oxfordshire, by Archbishop Peckham, in the year 1278, that on Innocents' Day the public prayers should not any more be said in the church of that monastery *per parvulas, i.e.* little girls" (408. I. 428).

Though with the Protestantism of Elizabeth the Boy-Bishop and his revels were put down by the authorities, they continued to survive, in some places at least, the end of her reign. Puttenham, in his *Art of Poesie* (1589), observes: "On St. Nicholas's night, commonly, the scholars of the country make them a bishop, who, like a foolish boy, goeth about blessing and preaching with such childish terms as make the people laugh at his foolish counterfeit speeches" (408. 427). Brand recognizes in the *iter ad montem* of the scholars at Eton the remnants of the ceremonies of the Boy-Bishop and his associates (408. 432); and indeed a passage which he cites from the *Status Scholæ Etonensis* (1560) shows that "in the Papal times the Eton scholars (to avoid interfering, as it should seem, with the boy-bishop of the college there on St. Nicholas's Day) elected *their* boy-bishop on St. Hugh's Day, in the month of November." In the statutes (1518) of St. Paul's School, we meet with the following: "All these children shall every Childermas Day come to Pauli's Church, and hear the Child-bishop sermon; and after he be at the high mass, and each of them offer a 1*d.* to the Child-bishop, and with them the masters and surveyors of the school." Brand quotes Strype, the author of the *Ecclesiastical Memorials*, as observing: "I shall only remark, that there might be this at least said in favour of this old custom, that it gave a spirit to the children; and the hopes that they might one time or other attain to the real mitre made them mind their books."

In his poem, *The Boy and the Angel*, Robert Browning tells how Theocrite, the boy-craftsman, sweetly praised God amid his weary toil. On Easter Day he wished he might praise God as Pope, and the angel Gabriel took the boy's place in the workshop, while the latter became Pope in Rome. But the new Pope sickened of the change, and God himself missed the welcome praise of the happy boy. So back went the Pope to the workshop and boyhood, and praise rose up to God as of old. Somewhat different from the poet's story is the tale of the lama of Tibet, a real boy-pope. The Grand Lama, or Pope, is looked upon as an incarnation of Buddha and as immortal, never suffering death, but merely transmigration (100. 499).

Among various peoples, the child has occupied all sacerdotal positions from acolyte to pope — priest he has been, not in barbarism alone, but in the midst of culture and civilization, where often the jest begun has ended in sober earnest. In the ecclesiastical, as well as in the secular, kingdom, the child has often come to his throne when "young in years, but in sage counsel old."

CHAPTER XXIV.

The Child as Hero, Adventurer, Etc.

O wonderful son, that can so astonish a mother ! — *Shakespeare.*

Who can foretell for what high cause
This Darling of the Gods was born ? — *Marvell.*

The haughty eye shall seek in vain
What innocence beholds ;
No cunning finds the keys of heaven,
No strength its gate unfolds.

Alone to guilelessness and love
That gate shall open fall ;
The mind of pride is nothingness,
The childlike heart is all. — *Whittier.*

CARLYLE has said: " The History of the World is the Biography of Great Men." He might have added, that in primitive times much of the History of the World is the Biography of Great Children. Andrew Lang, in his edition of *Perrault's Tales,* speaking of *Le Petit Poucet* (Hop o' My Thumb), says: " While these main incidents of Hop o' My Thumb are so widely current, the general idea of a small and tricksy being is found frequently, from the Hermes of the Homeric Hymn to the Namaqua Heitsi Eibib, the other *Poucet,* or Tom Thumb, and the Zulu Uhlakanyana. Extraordinary precocity, even from the day of birth, distinguishes these beings (as Indra and Hermes) in *myth.* In *Märchen,* it is rather their smallness and astuteness than their youth that commands admiration, though they are often very precocious. The general sense of the humour of ' infant prodigies' is perhaps the origin of these romances " (p. cx.).

This world-homage to childhood finds apt expression in the verses of Mrs. Darmesteter: —

> " Laying at the children's feet
> Each his kingly crown,
> Each, the conquering power to greet,
> Laying humbly down
> Sword and sceptre as is meet."

All over the globe we find wonder-tales of childhood, stories of the great deeds of children, whose venturesomeness has saved whole communities from destruction, whose heroism has rid the world of giants and monsters of every sort, whose daring travels and excursions into lands or skies unknown have resulted in the great increase of human knowledge and the advancement of culture and civilization. In almost all departments of life the child-hero has left his mark, and there is much to tell of his wonderful achievements.

Finnish Child-Heroes.

In Finnish story we meet with *Pikku mies*, the dwarf-god, and in Altaic legend the child *Kan Püdai*, who was fed upon two hundred hares, who tames wild animals, makes himself a bow and bow-string, and becomes a mighty hero. In Esthonian folk-lore we have the tale of the seven-year-old wise girl, the persecution to which she was subjected at the hands of her stepmother, and the great deeds she accomplished (422. II. 144, 147, 154). But, outside of the wonderful infancy of Wäinämöinen, the culture-hero of the Finns, whom the *Kalevala* has immortalized, we find some striking tributes to the child-spirit. In the closing canto of this great epic, which, according to Andrew Lang, tells. in savage fashion, the story of the introduction of Christianity, we learn how the maiden Marjatta, " as pure as the dew is, as holy as stars are that live without stain," was feeding her flocks and listening to the singing of the golden cuckoo, when a berry fell into her bosom, and she conceived and bore a son, whereupon the people despised and rejected her. Moreover, no one would baptize the infant: " The god of the wilderness refused, and Wäinämöinen would have had the young child slain. Then the infant rebuked the ancient demi-god, who fled in anger to the sea." As

Wäinämöinen was borne away in his magic barque by the tide, he lifted up his voice and sang how when men should have need of him they would look for his return, "bringing back sunlight and moonshine, and the joy that is vanished from the world." Thus did the rebuke of the babe close the reign of the demi-gods of old (484. 171–177).

Italian.

On the other hand, it is owing to a child, says a sweet Italian legend, that "the gates of heaven are forever ajar." A little girl-angel, up in heaven, sat grief-stricken beside the gate, and begged the celestial warder to set the gates ajar: —

> "I can hear my mother weeping;
> She is lonely ; she cannot see
> A glimmer of light in the darkness,
> Where the gates shut after me.
> Oh ! turn the key, sweet angel,
> The splendour will shine so far !"

But the angel at the gate dared not, and the childish appeal seemed vain until the mother of Jesus touched his hand, when, lo! "in the little child-angel's fingers stood the beautiful gates ajar." And they have been so ever since, for Mary gave to Christ the keys, which he has kept safe hidden in his bosom, that every sorrowing mother may catch a glimpse of the glory afar (379. 28–30).

Persian Deed-Maiden.

I fatti sono maschi, le parole femmine, — deeds are masculine, words feminine, — says the Italian proverb. The same thought is found in several of our own writers. George Herbert said bluntly: "Words are women, deeds are men"; Dr. Madden: "Words are men's daughters, but God's sons are things"; Dr. Johnson, in the preface to his great dictionary, embodies the saying of the Hindus: "Words are the daughters of earth, things are the sons of heaven."

In compensation for so ungracious a distinction, perhaps, the religion of Zoroaster, the ancient faith of Persia, teaches that, on the other side of death, the soul is received by its good deeds in the form of a beautiful maiden who conducts it through the three heavens to Ahura (the deity of good), and it is refreshed with celestial food (470. II. 421). That children should be brought into close relationship with the stars and other celestial bodies is to be expected from the *milieu* of folk-life, and the feeling of kinship with all the phenomena of nature.

Moon-Children.

In his exhaustive essay on *Moon Lore*, Rev. Mr. Harley tells us that in the Scandinavian mythology, Mâni, the moon, "once took up two children from the earth, Bill and Hiuki, as they were going from the well of Byrgir, bearing on their shoulders the bucket Sœg, and the pole Simul," and placed them in the moon, "where they could be seen from the earth." The modern Swedish folk-lore represents the spots on the moon as two children carrying water in a bucket, and it is this version of the old legend which Miss Humphrey has translated (468. 24–26). Mr. Harley cites, with approval, Rev. S. Baring-Gould's identification of Hiuki and Bill, the two moon-children, with the Jack and Jill of the familiar nursery rhyme:—

> "Jack and Jill went up the hill,
>   To fetch a pail of water ;
> Jack fell down and broke his crown,
>   And Jill came tumbling after."

According to Mr. Duncan, the well-known missionary to certain of the native tribes of British Columbia, these Indians of the far west have a version of this legend: "One night a child of the chief class awoke and cried for water. Its cries were very affecting — 'Mother, give me to drink!' but the mother heeded not. The moon was affected and came down, entered the house, and approached the child, saying, 'Here is water from heaven: drink.' The child anxiously laid hold of the pot and drank the draught, and was enticed to go away with the moon, its benefactor. They took an underground passage till they got quite clear of the village, and then ascended to heaven" (468. 35, 36). The story goes on to say that "the figure we now see in the moon is that very child; and also the little round basket which it had in its hand when it went to sleep appears there."

The Rev. George Turner reports a Polynesian myth from the Samoan Islands, in which the moon is represented as coming down one evening and picking up a woman and her child, who was beating out bark in order to make some of the native cloth. There was a famine in the land; and "the moon was just rising, and it reminded her of a great bread-fruit. Looking up to it, she said, 'Why cannot you come down and let my child have a bit of you?' The moon was indignant at the idea of being eaten, came down forthwith, and took her up, child, board, mallet, and all." To this day the Samoans, looking at the moon, exclaim: "Yonder is Sina and her child, and her mallet and board." Related myths are found in the Tonga Islands and the Hervey Archipelago (468. 59).

The Eskimo of Greenland believed that the sun and the moon were originally human beings, brother and sister. The story is that "they were playing with others at children's games in the dark, when *Malina*, being teased in a shameful manner by her brother *Anninga*, smeared her hands with the soot of the lamp, and rubbed them over the face and hands of her persecutor, that she might recognize him by daylight. Hence arise the spots in the moon. *Malina* rushed to save herself by flight, but her brother followed at her heels. At length she flew upwards, and became the sun. *Anninga* followed her, and became the moon; but being unable to mount so high he runs continually round the sun in hopes of some time surprising her" (468. 34). There are many variants of this legend in North and in Central America.

In her little poem *The Children in the Moon*, Miss Humphrey has versified an old folk-belief that the "tiny cloudlets flying across the moon's shield of silver" are a little lad and lass with a pole across their shoulders, at the end of which is swinging a water-bucket. These children, it is said, used to wander by moonlight to a well in the northward on summer nights to get a pail of water, until the moon snatched them up and "set them forever in the middle of his light," so that—

> " Children, ay, and children's children,
> Should behold my babes on high;
> And my babes should smile forever,
> Calling others to the sky ! "

Thus it is that —

> " Never is the bucket empty,
>   Never are the children old,
>   Ever when the moon is shining
>   We the children may behold " (224. 23–25).

In Whittier's *Child Life*, this poem is given as "from the Scandinavian," with the following additional stanzas : —

> " Ever young and ever little,
>   Ever sweet and ever fair !
>   When thou art a man, my darling,
>   Still the children will be there.

> " Ever young and ever little,
>   They will smile when thou art old ;
>   When thy locks are thin and silver,
>   Theirs will still be shining gold.

> " They will haunt thee from their heaven,
>   Softly beckoning down the gloom ;
>   Smiling in eternal sweetness
>   On thy cradle, on thy tomb " (379. 115–117).

The Andaman Islanders say that the sun is the wife of the moon, and the stars are their children — boys and girls — who go to sleep during the day, and are therefore not seen of men (498. 92). The sun is termed *chä·n·a bo·do*, "Mother Sun"; the moon, *mai·a ·o-gar*, " Mr. Moon " (498. 59). In many other mythologies the stars, either as a whole, or in part, figure as children. In the figurative language of ancient records the patriarchs are promised descendants as numerous as the stars of heaven, and in the Tshi language of Western Africa, the stars are termed *woh-rabbah*, from *woh*, "to breed, multiply, be fruitful," and *abbah*, " children." The South Australian natives thought the stars were groups of children, and even in the classic legends of Greece and Rome more than one child left earth to shine in heaven as a star.

In the belief of the natives of the Hervey Islands, in the South Pacific, the double star μ^1 and μ^2 *Scorpii* is a brother and sister, twins, who, fleeing from a scolding mother, leapt up into the sky. The bright stars υ and λ *Scorpii* are their angry parents who follow in pursuit, but never succeed in overtaking their runaway children, who, clinging close together, — for they were very fond of each other, — flee on and on through the blue sky. The girl, who is the elder, is called *Inseparable*, and Mr. Gill tells us that a native preacher, alluding to this favourite story, declared, with a happy turn of speech, that "Christ and the Christian should be like these twin stars, ever linked together, come life, come death." He could scarcely have chosen a more appropriate figure. The older faith that was dying lent the moral of its story to point the eloquence of the new (458. 40–43).

Hindu Child-Heroes.

In the Rig-Veda we have the story of the three brothers, the youngest of whom, Tritas, is quite a child, but accomplishes wonderful things and evinces more than human knowledge; also the tale of Vikramâdityas, the wise child (422. II. 136).

In the interesting collection of Bengalese folk-tales by Rev. Lal Behari Day we find much that touches upon childhood: The story of the "Boy whom Seven Mothers Suckled," and his wonderful deeds in the country of the Rakshasis (cannibals) — how he obtained the bird with whose life was bound up that of the wicked queen, and so brought about her death; the tale of the "Boy with the Moon on his Forehead" — how he rescued the beautiful Lady Pushpavati from the power of the Rakshasis over-sea! We have also the wonder-tales of Buddha.

In a tale of the Panjâb, noted by Temple (542. II. xvi.), "a couple of gods, as children, eat up at a sitting a meal meant for 250,000 people"; and in a Little Russian story "a mother had a baby of extraordinary habits. When alone, he jumped out of the cradle, no longer a baby, but a bearded old man, gobbled up the food out of the store, and then lay down again a screeching babe." He was finally exorcised (258. 119). A huge appetite is a frequent characteristic of changelings in fairy-stories (258. 108).

Japanese Child-Heroes.

The hero of Japanese boys is Kintarō, the "Wild Baby," the "Golden Darling." Companionless he played with the animals, put his arm around their necks, and rode upon their backs. Of him we are told : "He was prince of the forest; the rabbits, wild boars, squirrels and pheasants and hawks, were his servants and messengers." He is the apotheosis of the child in Japan, "the land of the holy gods," as its natives proudly termed it (245. 121).

Another boy-hero is Urashima, who visited Elysium in a fishing-boat. A third phenomenal child of Japanese story is "Peach Darling," who, while yet a baby, lifted the wash-tub and balanced the kettle on his head (245. 62). We must remember, however, that the Japanese call their beautiful country "the land of the holy gods," and the whole nation makes claim to a divine ancestry. Visits to the other world, the elfin-land, etc., are found all over the world.

German.

In Germany and Austria we have the stories of (258. 140–160): The girl who stole the serpent-king's crown; the Pomeranian farmer's boy who, after quenching his thirst with the brown beer of the fairies, tried to run off with the can of pure silver in which it was contained (in a Cornish legend, however, the farmer's boy pockets one of the rich silver goblets which stood on the tables in the palace of the king of the piskies, or fairies, and proves the truth of the story he has afterwards to tell by producing the goblet, "which remained in the boy's family for generations, though unfortunately it is no longer forthcoming for the satisfaction of those who may still be sceptical." A like origin has been suggested for the celebrated "Luck of Edenhall," and the "Horn of Oldenburg," and other like relics); the Carinthian girl, who, climbing a mountain during the noon-hour, entered through a door in the rock, and remained away a whole year, though it seemed but a little while; the baker's boy who visited the lost Emperor in the mountain — the Barbarossa-Otto legend; the baker's daughter of Ruffach, who made her father rich by selling bread to the soldiers in a great subterranean camp; the girl of Silesia, who is admitted into a cavern, where abides a buried army; and many more of a similar nature, to be read in Grimm and the other chroniclers of fairy-land (258. 216, 217).

Among the Danish legends of kindred type we find the tales of : The boy who ran off with the horn out of which an elf-maiden offered him a drink, and would not return it until she had promised to bestow upon him the strength of twelve men, with which, unluckily, went also the appetite of twelve men (258. 144).

Celtic.

Among the Welsh tales of the child as hero and adventurer are: The visit of Elidorus (afterwards a priest), when twelve years old, to the underground country, where he stole a golden ball, which, however, the pigmies soon recovered; the youths who were drawn into the fairies' ring and kept dancing for a year and a day until reduced to a mere skeleton; the little farmer's son, who was away among the fairies for two years, though he thought he had been absent but a day; corresponding is the Breton tale of the girl who acts as godmother to a fairy child, and remains away for ten long years, though for only two days in her own mind (258. 135, 136, 168, 170).

Very interesting is the Breton legend of the youth who undertook to take a letter to God, — *Monsieur le Bon Dieu,* — in Paradise. When he reaches Paradise, he gives the letter to St. Peter, who proceeds to deliver it. While he is away, the youth, noticing the spectacles on the table, tries them on, and is astonished at the wonders he sees, and still more at the information given him by St. Peter on his return, that he has been gazing through them five hundred years. Another hundred years he passes in looking at the seat kept for him in Paradise, and then receives the answer to the letter, which he is to take to the parish priest. After distributing in alms the hundred crowns he is paid for his services, he dies and goes to Paradise to occupy the seat he has seen. As Mr. Hartland remarks, "the variants of this traditional Pilgrim's Progress are known from Brittany to Transylvania, and from Iceland to Sicily" (258. 192).

Basque.

A remarkable child-hero tale is the Basque legend of the orphans, Izar (seven years old) and Lañoa (nine years old), and their adventures with Satan and the witches, — how Izar cured the Princess and killed the great toad which was the cause of her complaint, and how Lañoa defied Satan to his face, meeting death by his action, but gaining heaven (505. 19–41).

z

American Indian Child-Heroes.

In a legend of the Tlingit Indians concerning the visit of Ky'itlāc', a man who had killed himself, to the upper country ruled by Tahīt, whither go such as die a violent death, we read that —

" When he looked down upon the earth, he saw the tops of the trees looking like so many pins. But he wished to return to the earth. He pulled his blanket over his head and flung himself down. He arrived at the earth unhurt, and found himself at the foot of some trees. Soon he discovered a small house, the door of which was covered with mats. He peeped into it, and heard a child crying that had just been born. He himself was that child, and when he came to be grown up he told the people of Tahīt. They had heard about him before, but only then they learnt everything about the upper world " (403. 48, 49).

In a legend of the Kwakiutl Indians of Vancouver Island, a chief killed by a rival goes to the other world, but returns to earth in his grandson: "It was Ank·oaˀlagyilis who was thus born again. The boy, when a few years old, cried and wanted to have a small boat made, and, when he had got it, asked for a bow and arrows. His father scolded him for having so many wishes. Then the boy said, 'I was at one time your father, and have returned from heaven.' His father did not believe him, but then the boy said, 'You know that Ank·oaˀlagyilis had gone to bury his property, and nobody knows where it is. I will show it to you.' He took his father right to the place where it lay hidden, and bade him distribute it. There were two canoe-loads of blankets. Now the people knew that Ank·oaˀlagyilis had returned. He said, 'I was with *āta* [the deity], but he sent me back.' They asked him to tell about heaven, but he refused to do so." The boy afterwards became a chief, and it is said he refused to take revenge upon his murderer (404. 59).

In the mythology of the Siouan tribes we meet with the " Young Rabbit," born of a piece of the clotted blood of the Buffalo killed by Grizzly Bear, which the Rabbit had stolen. According to legend the Rabbit "addressed the blood, calling it his son, and ordering it to become a little child, and when he had ordered it to advance from infancy, through boyhood to youth, and from youth to manhood, his commands were obeyed." The "Young Rabbit" kills the Grizzly and delivers his own father (480 (1892). 293–304).

The legend of the "Blood-clot Boy" is also recorded from the narration of the Blackfeet Indians by Rev. John MacLean and Mr. Grinnell. The tale of his origin is as follows: "There lived, a long time ago, an old man and his wife, who had three daughters and one son-in-law. One day, as the mother was cooking some meat, she threw a clot of blood into the pot containing the meat. The pot began to boil, and then there issued from it a peculiar hissing noise. The old woman looked into the pot, and was surprised to see that the blood-clot had become transformed into a little boy. Quickly he grew, and, in a few moments, he sprang from the pot, a full-grown young man." Kûtoyĭs, as the youth was named, became an expert hunter, and kept the family in food. He also killed his lazy and quarrelsome brother-in-law, and brought peace to the family. Of Kûtoyĭs it is said he "sought to drive out all the evil in the world, and to unite the people and make them happy" (480 (1893). 167).

Concerning the Micmac Indians of Nova Scotia, Mr. Rand informs us (521. xlii.): —

"Children exposed or lost by their parents are miraculously preserved. They grow up suddenly to manhood, and are endowed with superhuman powers; they become the avengers of the guilty and the protectors of the good. They drive up the moose and the caribou to their camps, and slaughter them at their leisure. The elements are under their control; they can raise the wind, conjure up storms or disperse them, make it hot or cold, wet or dry, as they please. They can multiply the smallest amount of food indefinitely, evade the subtlety and rage of their enemies, kill them miraculously, and raise their slaughtered friends to life."

A characteristic legend of this nature is the story of Noojekĕsĭgŭnodăsĭt and the "magic dancing-doll." Noojekĕsĭgŭnodăsĭt, — "the sock wringer and dryer," so-called because, being the youngest of the seven sons of an Indian couple, he had to wring and dry the moccasin-rags of his elders, — was so persecuted by the eldest of his brothers, that he determined to run away, and "requests his mother to make him a small bow and arrow and thirty pairs of moccasins." He starts out and "shoots the arrow ahead, and runs after it. In a short time he is able to outrun the arrow and reach the spot where it is to fall before it strikes the ground. He then takes it up and shoots again, and flies on swifter than the arrow. Thus he travels straight ahead, and by night he has gone a long distance from home." His brother starts in pursuit, but, after a hundred days, returns home discouraged. Meanwhile, the boy travels on and meets a very old man, who tells him that the place from whence he came is a long way off, for "I was a small boy when I started, and since that day I have never halted, and you see that now I am very old." The boy says, however, that he will try to reach the place, and, after receiving from the old man a little box in return for a pair of moccasins, — for those of the traveller were quite worn out, — he goes his way. By and by the boy's curiosity leads him to open the box, and

" As soon as he has removed the cover, he starts with an exclamation of surprise, for he sees a small image, in the form of a man, dancing away with all his might, and reeking with perspiration from the long-continued exertion. As soon as the light is let in upon him, he stops dancing, looks up suddenly, and exclaims, ' Well, what is it? What is wanted?' The truth now flashes over the boy. This is a supernatural agent, a *mănitoo*, a god, from the spirit world, which can do anything that he is requested to do." The boy wished " to be transported to the place from whence the old man came," and, closing the box, " suddenly his head swims, the darkness comes over him, and he faints. When he recovers he finds himself near a large Indian village." By the aid of his doll — *weedăpcheejŭl,* " little comrade," he calls it — he works wonders, and obtains one of the daughters of the chief as his wife, and ultimately slays his father-in-law, who is a great " medicine-man." This story, Mr. Rand says he " wrote down from the mouth of a Micmac Indian in his own language"; it will bear comparison with some European folk-tales (521. 7–13).

Another story of boy wonder-working, with some European trappings, however, is that of " The Boy who was transformed into a Horse." Of this wonderful infant it is related that " at the age of eighteen months the child was able to talk, and immediately made inquiries about his elder brother [whom his father had 'sold to the devil']." The child then declares his intention of finding his lost brother, and, aided by an "angel," — this tale is strangely hybrid, — discovers him in the form of a horse, restores him to his natural shape, and brings him safely home; but changes the wicked father into a horse, upon whose back an evil spirit leaps and runs off with him (521. 31).

Other tales of boy adventure in Dr. Rand's collection are: "The History of Kĭtpooseägŭnow" [*i.e.* "taken from the side of his mother," as a calf of a moose or a caribou is after the mother has fallen] (521. 62–80); "The Infant Magician"; "The Invisible Boy," who could change himself into a moose, and also become invisible (521. 101–109); "The Badger and his Little Brother" (521. 263–269), in which the latter helps the former decoy the water-fowl to destruction, but, repenting at the wanton slaughter, gives the alarm, and many birds escape; "The Little Boy who caught a Whale" (521. 280–281). The story of "The Small Baby and the Big Bird" contains many naïve touches of Indian life. The hero of the tale is a foundling, discovered in the forest by an old woman, "so small that she easily hides it in her mitten." Having no milk for the babe, which she undertakes to care for, the woman "makes a sort of gruel from the scrapings of the inside of raw-hide, and thus supports and nourishes it, so that it thrives and does well." By and by he becomes a mighty hunter, and finally kills the old culloo (giant bird) chief, tames the young culloo, and discovers his parents (521. 81–93).

In the mythologic tales of the Iroquois, the child appears frequently as a hero and an adventurer. Mrs. Erminnie A. Smith, in treating of *The Myths of the Iroquois* (534), relates the stories of the infant nursed by bears; the boy whom his grandmother told never to go west, but who at last started off in that direction, and finally killed the great frog (into which form the man who had been tormenting them turned himself); the boy who, after interfering with his uncle's magic wand and kettle, and thereby depriving. the people of corn, set out and managed to return home with plenty of corn, which he had pilfered from the witches who guarded it, — all interesting child exploits.

Among the myths of the Cherokees, — a people related in speech to the Iroquois, — as reported by Mr. James Mooney, we find a story somewhat similar to the last mentioned, — "Kǎnǎ́tĭ

and Sélu: the Origin of Corn and Game" (506. 98–105), the
heroes of which are *Ināgĕ Utāsŭhĭ*, "He who grew up Wild," a
wonderful child, born of the blood of the game washed in the
river; and the little son of Kănátĭ ("the lucky hunter") and
Sélu ("Corn," his wife), his playmate, who captures him. The
"Wild Boy" is endowed with magic powers, and leads his
"brother" into all sorts of mischief. They set out to discover
where the father gets all the game he brings home, and, finding
that he lifted a rock on the side of a mountain, allowing the
animal he wished to come forth, they imitated him some days
afterwards, and the result was that the deer escaped from the
cave, and "then followed droves of raccoons, rabbits, and all the
other four-footed animals. Last came great flocks of turkeys,
pigeons, and partridges." From their childish glee and tricksi-
ness the animals appear to have suffered somewhat, for we are
told (506. 100): "In those days all the deer had their tails hanging down like other animals, but, as a buck was running past, the
'wild boy' struck its tail with his arrow, so that it stood straight
out behind. This pleased the boys, and when the next one ran
by, the other brother struck his tail so that it pointed upward.
The boys thought this was good sport, and when the next one
ran past, the 'wild boy' struck his tail so that it stood straight
up, and his brother struck the next one so hard with his arrow
that the deer's tail was curled over his back. The boys thought
this was very pretty, and ever since the deer has carried his tail
over his back." When Kănátĭ discovered what had occurred
(506. 100), "he was furious, but, without saying a word, he went
down into the cave and kicked the covers off four jars in one
corner, when out swarmed bedbugs, fleas, lice, and gnats, and got
all over the boys." After they had been tortured enough, Kănátĭ
sent them home, telling them that, through their folly, "whenever they wanted a deer to eat they would have to hunt all over
the woods for it, and then may be not find one." When the boys
got home, discovering that Sélu was a witch, they killed her and
dragged her body about a large piece of ground in front of the
house, and wherever the blood fell Indian corn sprang up. Kănátĭ
then tried to get the wolves to kill the two boys, but they trapped
them in a huge pound, and burned almost all of them to death.
Their father not returning from his visit to the wolves, the boys

set out in search of him, and, after some days, found him. After killing a fierce panther in a swamp, and exterminating a tribe of cannibals, who sought to boil the "wild boy" in a pot, they kept on and soon lost sight of their father. At "the end of the world, where the sun comes out," they waited "until the sky went up again" [in Cherokee cosmogony "the earth is a flat surface, and the sky is an arch of solid rock suspended above it. This arch rises and falls continually, so that the space at the point of juncture is constantly opening and closing, like a pair of scissors"], and then "they went through and climbed up on the other side." Here they met Kănătĭ and Sélu, but, after staying with them seven days, had to "go toward the sunset land, where they are still living."

Dr. G. M. Dawson records, from the Shushwap Indians of British Columbia, the story of an old woman, — husbandless, childless, companionless, — who, "for the sake of companionship, procured some pitch and shaped from it the figure of a girl, which became her daughter," whom many adventures befell (425. 33).

There is a very interesting Tahitian myth telling of the descent of little Tavai to the invisible world. Tavai was his mother's pet, and one day, for some slight fault, was beaten by the relatives of his father. This made Ouri, his mother, so angry, that Oemā, her husband, out of shame, went down to Hawaii, the under-world, whither Tavai, accompanied by his elder brother, journeyed, and, after many adventures, succeeded in bringing their mother the bones of Oemā, who had long been dead when they found him (458. 250).

Legion in number and world-wide in their affiliations are the stories of the visits of children and youths, boys and girls, to heaven, to the nether-world, to the country of the fairies, and to other strange and far-off lands, inhabited by elves, dwarfs, pigmies, giants, "black spirits and white." Countless are the variants of the familiar tale of "Jack and the Bean Stalk," "Jack, the Giant-Killer," and many another favourite of the nursery and the schoolroom. Tylor, Lang, Clouston, and Hartland have collated and interpreted many of these, and the books of fairy-tales and kindred lore are now numbered by the hundred, as may be seen from the list given by Mr. Hartland in the appendix to his work on fairy-tales. Grimm, Andersen, and the *Arabian Nights* have become household names.

For children to speak before they are born is a phenomenon of frequent occurrence in the lives of saints and the myths of savage peoples, especially when the child about to come into the world is an incarnation of some deity. Of Glūskap, the Micmac culture-hero, and Malumsis, the Wolf, his bad brother, we read (488. 15, 16) : —

"Before they were born, the babes consulted to consider how they had best enter the world. And Glooskap said: 'I will be born as others are.' But the evil Malumsis thought himself too great to be brought forth in such a manner, and declared that he would burst through his mother's side. And, as they planned it, so it came to pass. Glooskap as first came quietly to light, while Malumsis kept his word, killing his mother." Another version of the same story runs: "In the old time, far before men knew themselves in the light before the sun, Glooskap and his brother were as yet unborn. They waited for the day to appear. Then they talked together, and the youngest said: 'Why should I wait? I will go into the world and begin my life at once;' when the elder said: 'Not so, for this were a great evil.' But the younger gave no heed to any wisdom; in his wickedness he broke through his mother's side, he rent the wall; his beginning of life was his mother's death" (488. 106). Very similar is the Iroquois myth of the "Good Mind" and the "Bad Mind," and variants of this American hero-myth may be read in the exhaustive treatise of Dr. Brinton.

Very interesting is the Maya story of the twins Hun-Ahpu and Xbalanque, sons of the virgin Xquiq, who, fleeing from her father, escaped to the upper world, where the birth took place. Of these children we are told "they grew in strength, and performed various deeds of prowess, which are related at length in the *Popul Vuh* [the folk-chronicle of the Quichés of Guatemala], and were at last invited by the lords of the underworld to visit them." The chiefs of the underworld intended to slay the youths, as they had previously slain their father and uncle, but through their oracular and magic power the two brothers pretended to be burned, and, when their ashes were thrown into the river, they rose from its waters and slew the lords of the nether world. At this the inhabitants of Hades fled in terror and the twins "released the prisoners and restored to life those who had been slain. The latter rose to the sky to become the countless stars, while Hunhun-Ahpu and Vukub-Hun-Ahpu [father and uncle of the twins] ascended to dwell, the one in the sun, the other in the moon" (411. 124).

Born of a virgin mother were also Quetzalcoatl, the culture-hero of Mexico, and other similar characters whose lives and deeds may be read in Dr. Brinton's *American Hero-Myths.*

From the Indians of the Pueblo of Isleta, New Mexico, Dr. A. S. Gatschet has obtained the story of the "Antelope-Boy," who, as the champion of the White Pueblo, defeated the Hawk, the champion of the Yellow Pueblo, in a race around the horizon. The "Antelope-Boy" was a babe who had been left on the prairie by its uncle, and brought up by a female antelope who discovered it. After some trouble, the people succeeded in catching him and restoring him to his mother. Another version of the same tale has it that "the boy-child, left by his uncle and mother upon the prairie, was carried to the antelopes by a coyote, after which a mother-antelope, who had lost her fawn, adopted the tiny stranger as her own. By an ingenious act of the mother-antelope the boy was surrendered again to his real human mother; for when the circle of the hunters grew smaller around the herd, the antelope took the boy to the northeast, where his mother stood in a white robe. At last these two were the only ones left within the circle, and when the antelope broke through the line on the northeast, the boy followed her and fell at the feet of his own human mother, who sprang forward and clasped him in her arms." The Yellow Pueblo people were wizards, and so confident were they of success that they proposed that the losing party, their villages, property, etc., should be burnt. The White Pueblo people agreed, and, having won the victory, proceeded to exterminate the conquered. One of the wizards, however, managed to hide away and escape being burned, and this is why there are wizards living at this very day (239. 213, 217).

In the beginning, says the Zuñi account of the coming of men upon earth, they dwelt in the lowermost of four subterranean caverns, called the "Four Wombs of the World," and as they began to increase in numbers they became very unhappy, and the children of the wise men among them besought them to deliver them from such a life of misery. Then, it is said, "The 'Holder of the Paths of Life,' the Sun-Father, created from his own being two children, who fell to earth for the good of all beings. The Sun-Father endowed these children with immortal youth, with power even as his own power, and created for them a bow (the Rainbow) and an arrow (the Lightning). For them he made also a shield like unto his own, of magic power, and a knife of flint. . . . These children cut the face of the world with their magic knife, and were borne down upon their shield into the caverns in which all men dwelt. There, as the leaders of men, they lived with their children, mankind." They afterwards led men into the second cavern, then into the third, and finally into the fourth, whence they made their way, guided by the two children, to the world of earth, which, having been covered with water, was damp and unstable and filled with huge monsters and beasts of prey. The two children continued to lead men "Eastward, toward the Home of the Sun-Father," and by their magic power, acting under the directions of their creator, the Sun-Father, they caused the surface of the earth to harden and petrified the fierce animals who sought to destroy the children of men (which accounts for the fossils of to-day and the animal-like forms of rocks and boulders) (424. 13). Of this people it could have been said most appropriately, "a little child shall lead them."

Mr. Lummis' volume of folk-tales of the Pueblos Indians of New Mexico contains many stories of the boy as hero and adventurer. The "Antelope-Boy" who defeats the champion of the witches in a foot-race (302. 12–21); Nah-chu-rú-chu (the "Bluish Light of the Dawn"), the parentless hero, "wise in medicine," who married the moon, lost her, but found her again after great trouble (302. 53–70); the boy who cursed the lake (302. 108–121); the boy and the eagle, etc. (302. 122–126). But the great figures in story at the Pueblo of Quēres are the "hero-twins," Máw-Sahv and Oó-yah-wee, sons of the Sun, wonderful and astonishing children, of whom it is said that "as soon as they were a minute old, they were big and strong and began playing" (302. 207). Their mother died when they were born, but was restored to life by the Crow-Mother, and returned home with her two children, whose hero-deeds, "at an age when other boys were toddling about the house," were the cause of infinite wonder. They killed the Giant-Woman and the Giant-Baby, and performed unnumbered other acts of heroism while yet in childhood and youth. To the same cycle seems to belong also the story of "The Magic Hide-and-Seek" (302. 87–98).

From the Pueblo of Sia, Mrs. Stevenson has recorded the story of the twins Ma'asewe and U'yuuyewĕ, sons of the Sun-Father by the virgin Ko'chinako; how they visited their father, and the adventures that befell them on their long journey; how they killed the wolf of the lake, the cougar, the bear, the bad eagles, burned the cruel witch, and other great enemies of the people, organized the cult societies, and then "made their home in the Sandia Mountain, where they have since remained." At the entrance to the crater, we are told, "the diminutive footprints of these boys are yet to be seen by the good of heart" (538. 43–57). Among the American Indians it is difficult, if not impossible, to distinguish the child-hero from the divinity whom he so often closely resembles.

CHAPTER XXV.

THE CHILD AS FETICH, DEITY, GOD.

Childhood shall be all divine. — *Proctor.*

A baby's feet, like sea-shells pink,
Might tempt, should Heaven see meet,
An angel's lips to kiss. — *Swinburne.*

Their glance might cast out pain and sin,
Their speech make dumb the wise,
By mute glad godhead felt within
A baby's eyes. — *Swinburne.*

The Child as Fetich.

It is easy to understand how, among barbarous or semi-civilized peoples, children born deformed or with any strange marking or defect should be looked upon as objects of fear or reverence, fetiches in fact. Post informs us regarding certain African tribes (127. I. 285, 286): —

"The Wanika, Wakikuyu, and Wazegua kill deformed children; throttle them in the woods and bury them. The belief is, that the evil spirit of a dead person has got into them, and such a child would be a great criminal. The Somali let misformed children live, but regard them with superstitious fear. In Angola all children born deformed are considered 'fetich.' In Loango dwarfs and albinos are regarded as the property of the king, and are looked upon as sacred and inviolable."

Here we see at least some of the reasons which have led up to the eulogy and laudation, as well as to the dread suspicion, of the dwarf and the hunchback, appearing in so many folk-tales. We might find also, perhaps, some dim conception of the occasional simultaneity of genius with physical defects or deformities, a fact of which a certain modern school of criminal sociologists has made so much.

Concerning albinos Schultze says (529. 82) : —

"In Bornoo albinos are objects of fear, as beings gifted with supernatural power; in Senegambia, if they are slaves, they are given their freedom, are exempted from all labour, and are cheerfully supported at others' expense. In Congo the king keeps them in his palace as 'fetiches which give him influence over the Europeans.' They are held in such respect that they may take whatever they will; and he who is deprived of his property by them, esteems himself honoured. In Loango they are esteemed above the Gangas (priests), and their hair is sold at a high price as a holy relic. Thus may a man become a fetich." At Moree, in West Africa, Ellis informs us, "Albinos are sacred to Aynfwa, and, on arriving at puberty, become her priests and priestesses. They are regarded by the people as the mouth-pieces of the goddess." At Coomassie a boy-prisoner was painted white and consecrated as a slave to the tutelary deity of the market (438. 49, 88). Coeval with their revival of primitive language-moulds in their slang, many of our college societies and sporting clubs and associations have revived the beliefs just mentioned in their mascots and luck-bringers — the other side of the shield showing the "Jonahs" and those fetiches of evil import. Even great actors, stock-brokers, and politicians have their mascots. We hear also of mascots of regiments and of ships. A little hunchback, a dwarf, a negro boy, an Italian singing-girl, a child dressed in a certain style or colour, all serve as mascots. Criminals and gamblers, those members of the community most nearly allied in thought and action with barbarous and primitive man, have their mascots, and it is from this source that we derive the word, which Andran, in his opera *La Mascotte*, has lifted to a somewhat higher plane, and now each family may have a mascot, a fetich, to cause them to prosper and succeed in life (390 (1888). 111, 112).

One of the derivations suggested for this word, viz. from *masqué* = *coiffé*, in the expression *né coiffé*, "born with a caul," would make the *mascot* to have been originally a child born with the caul on its head, a circumstance which, as the French phrase *être né coiffé*, "to be born lucky," indicates, betokened happiness and good-fortune for the being thus coming into the world. In German the caul is termed "Glückshaube," "lucky hood," and Ploss gives many illustrations of the widespread belief in the luck that falls to the share of the child born with one. A very curious custom exists in Oldenburg, where a boy, in order to be fortunate in love, carries his caul about with him (326. I. 12–14).

Other accidents or incidents of birth have sufficed to make fetiches of children. Twins and triplets are regarded in many parts of the world as smacking of the supernatural and uncanny. The various views of the races of mankind upon this subject are given at length in Ploss (326. II. 267–275), and Post has much to say of the treatment of twins in Africa. In Unyoro twins are looked upon as "luck-bringers, not only for the family, but for the whole village as well. Great feasts are held in their honour, and if they die, the house in which they were born is burned down." Among the Ishogo, from fear that one of the pair may die, twins are practically isolated and *taboo* until grown up (127. I. 282, 284).

To the Ovaherero, according to Ploss, "the birth of twins is the greatest piece of good-fortune that can fall to the lot of mortals," and such an event makes the parents "holy." Among this Kaffir people, moreover: "Every father of twins has the right to act as substitute for the village-chief in the exercise of his priestly functions. If the chief is not present, he can, for example, exorcise a sick person. Even the twin-child himself has all priestly privileges. For a twin boy there is no forbidden flesh, no forbidden milk, and no one would ever venture to curse him. If any one should kill a twin-child, the murderer's whole village would be destroyed. As a twin-boy, he inherits the priestly dignity at the death of the chief, and even when an older brother succeeds the father as possessor of the village, it is, however, named after the younger twin-brother, who is clothed with the priestly dignity" (326. II. 271–274).

Among the Songish Indians of Vancouver Island, it is believed that "twins, immediately after their birth, possess supernatural powers. They are at once taken to the woods and washed in a pond in order to become ordinary men." The Shushwap Indians believe that twins retain this supernatural power throughout their lives (404. 22, 92).

Of children whose upper teeth break out before the lower, some primitive tribes are in fear and dread, hastening to kill them, as do the Basutos, Wakikuyu, Wanika, Wazegua, and Wasawahili. Among the Wazaramo, another African people, such children "are either put to death, given away, or sold to a slave-holder, for the belief is that through them sickness, misfortune, and death would enter the house." The Arabs of Zanzibar, "after reading from the Koran, administer to such a child an oath that it will do no harm, making it nod assent with its head" (127. I. 287).

From what has preceded, we can see how hard it is sometimes to draw the line between the man as fetich and the priest, between the divinity and the medicine-man.

Fetiches of Criminals.

It is a curious fact that St. Nicholas is at once the patron saint of children and of thieves, — the latter even Shakespeare calls "St. Nicholas's clerks." And with robbers and the generality of evil-doers the child, dead or alive, is much of a fetich. Anstey's *Burglar Bill* is humorously exaggerated, but there is a good deal of superstition about childhood lingering in the mind of the law-breaker. Strack (361) has discussed at considerable length the child (dead) as fetich among the criminal classes, especially the use made of the blood, the hand, the heart, etc. Among the thieving fraternity in Middle Franconia it is believed that "blood taken up from the genitals of an innocent boy on three pieces of wood, and carried about the person, renders one invisible when stealing" (361. 41). The same power was ascribed to the eating of the hearts (raw) of unborn children cut out of the womb of the mother. Male children only would serve, and from the confession of the band of the robber-chief "King Daniel," who so terrified all Ermeland in the middle of the seventeenth century, it would appear that they had already killed for this purpose no fewer than fourteen women with child (361. 59). As late as 1815, at Heide in Northditmarsch, one Claus Dau was executed for "having killed three children and eaten their hearts with the belief of making himself invisible" (361. 61).

This eating of little children's hearts was thought not alone to confer the gift of invisibility, but "when portions of nine hearts had been eaten by any one, he could not be seized, no matter what theft or crime he committed, and, if by chance he should fall into the power of his enemies, he could make himself invisible and thus escape." The eating of three hearts is credited with the same power in an account of a robber of the Lower Rhine, in 1645. In the middle of the last century, there was executed at Bayreuth a man "who had killed eight women with child, cut them open, and eaten the warm, palpitating hearts of the children, in the belief that he would be able to fly, if he ate the hearts of nine such children" (361. 58).

Only a few years ago (April, 1888), at Oldenburg, a workman named Bliefernicht was tried for having killed two girls, aged six and seven years. The examination of the remains showed that "one of the bodies not only had the neck completely cut through, but the belly cut open, so that the entrails, lungs, and liver were exposed. A large piece of flesh had been cut out of the buttocks and was nowhere to be found, the man having eaten it. His belief was, that whoever ate of the flesh of innocent girls, could do anything in the world without any one being able to make him answer for it" (361. 62).

Strack has much to say of the *main-de-gloire* and the *chandelle magique*. Widespread among thieves is the belief in the "magic taper." At Meesow, in the Regenwald district of Pomerania, these tapers are made of the entrails of unborn children, can only be extinguished with milk, and, as long as they burn, no one in the house to be robbed is able to wake. It is of the hands, however, of unbaptized or unborn children that these tapers were most frequently made. At Nürnberg, in 1577 and 1701, there were executed two monsters who killed many women in their pursuit for this fetich; at Vechta, in Oldenburg, the finger of an unborn child "serves with thieves to keep asleep the people of the house they have entered, if it is simply laid on the table"; at Konow, the fat of a woman with child is used to make a similar taper. In the Ukrain district of Poland, it is believed that the hand of the corpse of a five-year-old child opens all locks (361. 42). This belief in the *hand-of-glory* and the *magic candle* may be due to the fact that such children, being unbaptized and unborn, were presumed to be under the influence of the Evil One himself. Of the wider belief in the *chandelle magique* and *main-de-gloire* (as obtained from criminal adults) in Germany, France, Spain, etc., nothing need be said here.

At Konow, in the Kammin district of Pomerania, "if a thief takes an unborn child, dries it, puts it in a little wooden box, and carries it on his person, he is rendered invisible to everybody, and can steal at will" (361. 41).

The history of the robbers of the Rhine and the Main, of Westphalia, the Mark, and Silesia, with whom the child appears so often as a fetich, evince a bestiality and inhumanity almost beyond the power of belief.

Magic.

But it is not to the criminal classes alone that superstitions of this nature belong. Of the alchemy, magic, black art, sorcery, and "philosophy" of the Dark Ages of Europe, the practice of which lingered in some places well on into the seventeenth century, horrible stories are told, in which children, their bodies, their souls even, appear as fetishes. The baptism of blood is said still to be practised in parts of Russia by parents "to preserve their child from the temptations of the prince of darkness," and in 1874, "a country-school teacher of the Strassburg district, and his wife, upon the advice of a somnambulist, struck their own aunt with the fire-tongs until the blood flowed, with which they sprinkled their child supposed to have been bewitched by her" (361. 73). Here it is the blood of adults that is used, but the practice demands the child's also. According to C. F. A. Hoffmann (1817), there lived in Naples "an old doctor who had children by several women, which he inhumanly killed, with peculiar ceremonies and rites, cutting the breast open, tearing out the heart, and from its blood preparing precious drops which were preservative against all sickness." Well known is the story of Elizabeth Bathori, a Hungarian woman of the early part of the seventeenth century, who, it is said, receiving on her face a drop of blood which spurted from a waiting-girl whose ears she had severely boxed, and noticing afterward, when she wiped it away, that her skin at that spot appeared to be more beautiful, whiter, and finer than before, resolved to bathe her face and her whole body in human blood, in order to increase her charms and her

2 A

beauty. Before her monstrous actions were discovered, she is thought to have caused the death of some 650 girls with the aid of accomplioes (361. 46).

Fetiches of Religion.

The use of human blood in ritual has been treated of in detail by Strack, and in his pages many references to children will be found. He also discusses in detail the charge of the Anti-Semitics that the Jews kill little children of their Christian neighbours for the purpose of using their blood and certain parts of their bodies in religious rites and ceremonies, showing alike the antiquity of this libel as well as its baselessness. Against the early Christians like charges appear to have been made by the heathen, and later on by the Saracens; and indeed, this charge is one which is generally levelled at new-comers or innovators in the early history of Christian religion and civilization. Strack points out also that, during the contest of the Dominicans and Franciscans in Bern, in 1507 A.D., it was charged that the former used the blood of Jewish children, the eyebrows and hair of children, etc., in their secret rites (361. 68, 69).

Brewer, who gives little credit to the stories, cites the account of numerous crucifixions of children alleged to have been carried out by Jews in various parts of Europe, for the purpose of using their flesh and blood in their rituals, or merely out of hatred to the Christian religion. The principal cases are: Andrew of Innspruck; Albert of Swirnazen in Podolia, aged four (1598); St. Hugh of Lincoln, aged eleven (1255); St. Janot of Cologne (1475); St. Michael of Sappendelf in Bavaria, aged four and one-half (1340); St. Richard of Pontoise, aged twelve (1182); St. Simon of Trent, aged twenty-nine months and three days (1475); St. William of Norwich, aged twelve (1137); St. Wernier (Garnier), aged thirteen (1227). The *Acta Sanctorum* of the Bollandists give a long list of nameless children, who are claimed to have suffered a like fate in Spain, France, Hungary, Austria, Germany, Italy, etc. The later charges, such as those made in the celebrated case of the girl Esther Solymasi, whose death was alleged to have been brought about by the Jews of Tisza-Eszlar in Hungary, in 1882, are investigated by Strack, and shown to be utterly without foundation of fact, merely the product of frenzied Anti-Semitism (191. 171–175).

The use of blood and the sacrifice of little children, as well as other fetichistic practices, have been charged against some of the secret religious sects of modern Russia.

Dead Children.

In Annam the natives "surround the beds of their children suffering from small-pox with nets, and never leave them alone, fearing lest a demon, in the form of a strange child, should sneak in and take possession of them" (397. 169, 242). This belief is akin with the widespread superstitions with respect to changelings and other metamorphoses of childhood, to the discussion of which Ploss and Hartland have devoted much space and attention, the latter, indeed, setting apart some forty pages of his book on fairy-tales to the subject.

In Devonshire, England, it was formerly believed lucky to put a stillborn child into an open grave, "as it was considered a sure passport to heaven for the next person buried there." In the Border country, on the other hand, it is unlucky to tread on the graves of unbaptized children, and "he who steps on the grave of a stillborn or unbaptized child, or of one who has been overlaid by its nurse, subjects himself to the fatal disease of the grave-merels, or grave-scab." In connection with this belief, Henderson cites the following popular verses, of considerable antiquity : —

> " Woe to the babie that ne'er saw the sun,
>   All alane and alane, oh !
> His bodie shall lie in the kirk 'neath the rain,
>   All alane and alane, oh !

> " His grave must be dug at the foot o' the wall,
>   All alane and alane, oh !
> And the foot that treadeth his body upon
>   Shall have scab that will eat to the bane, oh !

> " And it ne'er will be cured by doctor on earth,
>   Tho' every one should tent him, oh !
> He shall tremble and die like the elf-shot eye,
>   And return from whence he came, oh ! " (409. 13).

Among the natives of the Andaman Islands, after a dead child
has been buried and the parents have mourned for about three
months, the remains are exhumed, cleansed at the seashore by
the father, and brought back to the hut, where the bones are
broken up to make necklaces, which are distributed to friends
and relatives as mementos. Moreover, "the mother, after painting the skull with *kòi-ob-* [a mixture of yellow ochre, oil, etc.]
and decorating it with small shells attached to pieces of string,
hangs it round her neck with a netted chain, called *rab-*. After
the first few days her husband often relieves her by wearing it
himself" (498. 74, 75).

According to Lumholtz, "a kind of mummy, dried by the aid
of fire and smoke, is also found in Australia. Male children are
most frequently prepared in this manner. The corpse is then
packed into a bundle, which is carried for some time by the
mother. She has it with her constantly, and at night sleeps with
it at her side. After about six months, when nothing but the
bones remain, she buries it in the earth. Full-grown men are
sometimes treated in this manner, particularly the bodies of
great heroes" (495. 278).

Among the western Eskimo, "the mother who loses her nurs-
ling places the poor 'papoose' in a beautifully ornamented box,
which she fastens on her back and carries about her for a long
while. Often she takes the miserable mummy in her arms and
makes it a kind of toilette, disinfecting it, and removing the
mouldiness" (523. 102).

According to the traveller Lander, a woman of Yoruba, in
Africa, "carries for some time a wooden figure of her lost child,
and, when she eats, puts part of her food to its lips"; and Catlin
writes of the Mandan Indians: "They place the skulls of their
dead in a circle. Each wife knows the skull of her former husband or child, and there seldom passes a day that she does not
visit it with a dish of the best cooked food. . . . There is
scarcely an hour in a pleasant day, but more or less of these
women may be seen sitting or lying by the skull of their dead
child or husband, talking to it in the most pleasant and endearing language they can use (as they were wont to do in former
days), and seemingly getting an answer back" (Spencer, *Princ.
of Soc.*, 1882, I. 332, 326).

Of the Nishinam Indians of California, Mr. Powers tells us: "When a Nishinam wife is childless, her sympathizing female friends sometimes make out of grass a rude image of a baby, and tie it in a miniature baby-basket, according to the Indian custom. Some day, when the woman and her husband are not at home, they carry this grass baby and lay it in their wigwam. When she returns and finds it, she takes it up, holds it to her breast, pretends to nurse it, and sings it lullaby songs. All this is done as a kind of conjuration, which they hope will have the effect of causing the barren woman to become fertile" (519. 318).

Of certain Indians of the northern United States we read, in the early years of the present century: "The traders on the river St. Peter's, Mississippi, report that some of them have seen in the possession of the Indians a petrified child, which they have often wished to purchase; but the savages regard it as a deity, and no inducement could bribe them to part with it" (*Philos. Mag.* XXIX., p. 5).

Child-Worship.

As Count D'Alviella has pointed out, we have in the apocryphal book of the *Wisdom of Solomon* the following interesting passage: "For a father afflicted with untimely mourning, when he hath made an image of his child soon taken away, now honoured him as a god, which was then a dead man; and delivered to those that were under him ceremonies and sacrifices."

Mrs. Stevenson, in a Zuñi tale of motherly affection, relates how, in crossing a river in the olden time, the children clinging to their mothers were transformed into such ugly and mischievous shapes that the latter let many of them fall into the river. Some held their children close, and on the other side these were restored to their natural forms. Those who had lost their children grieved and would not be comforted; so two twin-brothers — sons of the sun, they are called — went beneath the waters of a lake to the dwelling of the children, who asked them to tell how it fared with their mothers. Their visitors told them of the grief and sorrow of the parents, whereupon the children said: "Tell our mothers we are not dead, but live and sing in this beautiful place, which is the home for them when they sleep. They will wake here and be always happy. And we are here to intercede with the sun, our father, that he may give to our people rain and the fruits of the earth, and all that is good for them." Since that time these children have been "worshipped as ancestral gods, bearing the name of *kōk-ko*" (358. 541). This reminds us strikingly of the great Redeemer, of whom it was said that he is "an Advocate for us with the Father," and who himself declared: "In my Father's house are many mansions; if it were not so I would have told you; for I go to prepare a place for you."

In not a few mythologies we meet with the infant god in the arms of its mother or of some other woman. Of the goddess of pity in the Celestial Empire we read: "The Chinese Lady of Mercy in her statues is invariably depicted as young, symmetrical, and beautiful. Sometimes she stands or sits alone. Sometimes she holds an infant god in her lap. Sometimes she holds one, while a second plays about her knee. Another favourite picture and statue represents her standing on the head of a great serpent, with a halo about her face and brows, and spirits encircling her. In the sixth, she stands upon a crescent, awaiting a bird approaching her from the skies. In a seventh, she stands smiling at a beautiful child on the back of a water-buffalo. In an eighth, she is weeping for the sins of either humanity or the female portion of it. She is the patron saint of all her sex, and intercedes for them at the great throne of Heaven. She is a very old divinity. The Chinese themselves claim that she was worshipped six thousand years ago, and that she was the first deity made known to mankind. The brave Jesuit missionaries found her there, and it matters not her age; she is a credit to herself and her sex, and aids in cheering the sorrowful and sombre lives of millions in the far East." We also find "the saintly infant Zen-zaï, so often met with in the arms of female representations of the androgynous Kwanon."

Mr. C. N. Scott, in his essay on the "Child-God in Art" (344), is hesitant to give to many mythologies any real child-worship or artistic concept of the child as god. Not even Rama and Krishna, or the Greek Eros, who had a sanctuary at Thespiæ in Bœotia, are beautiful, sweet, naïve child-pictures; much less even is Hercules, the infant, strangling the serpents, or Mercury running off with the oxen of Admetus, or bacchic Dionysus. In

Egypt, in the eleventh or twelfth dynasty, we do find a family of gods, the triad, father (Amun), mother (Maut), child (Khuns). Mr. Scott follows Ruskin in declaring that classic Greek art gives no real child-concept; nor does Gothic art up to the thirteenth century, when the influence of Christianity made itself felt, that influence which made art lavish its genius upon the Madonna and the Santo Bambino — the Virgin and the Christ-Child.

CHAPTER XXVI.

The Christ-Child.

The holy thing that is to be born shall be called the Son of God. — *Luke* i. 35.

There is born to you this day in the city of David a Saviour, which is anointed Lord. — *Luke* ii. 11.

> Great little One! whose all-embracing birth
> Lifts Earth to Heaven, stoops Heaven to Earth. — *Richard Crashaw.*

> Our Babe, to show his Godhead true,
> Can in his swaddling bands control the damnèd crew. — *Milton.*

> The heart of Nature feels the touch of Love;
>   And Angels sing:
>   "The Child is King!
> See in his heart the life we live above." — *E. P. Gould.*

During the nineteen centuries that have elapsed since Jesus of Nazareth was born, art and music, eloquence and song, have expended their best talents in preserving forever to us some memories of the life and deeds of Him whose religion of love is winning the world. The treasures of intellectual genius have been lavished in the interpretation and promulgation of the faith that bears his name. At his shrine have worshipped the great and good of every land, and his name has penetrated to the uttermost ends of the earth.

But in the brief record of his history that has come down to us, we read: "The common people heard him gladly"; and to these, his simple life, with its noble consecration and unselfish aims, appealed immeasurably more even than to the greatest and wisest of men. This is evident from a glance into the lore that has grown up among the folk regarding the birth, life, and death of the Christ. Those legends and beliefs alone concern us here which cluster round his childhood, — the tribute of the lowly

and the unlearned to the great world-child, who was to usher in
the Age of Gold, to him whom they deemed Son of God and Son
of Man, divinely human, humanly divine.

Nature and the Christ-Birth.

The old heathen mythologies and the lore of the ruder races of
our own day abound in tales of the strange and wonderful events
that happened during the birth, passion, and death of their heroes
and divinities. Europe, Africa, Asia, America, and the Isles of
the Sea, bring us a vast store of folk-thought telling of the sympathy of Mother Nature with her children; how she mourned
when they were sad or afflicted, rejoiced when they were fortunate and happy. And so has it been, in later ages and among
more civilized peoples, with the great good who have made their
influence felt in the world, — the poets, musicians, artists, seers,
geniuses of every kind, who learned to read some of the secrets
of the universe and declared them unto men. They were a part
of Nature herself, and she heralded their coming graciously and
wept over them when they died. This deep feeling of kinship
with all Nature pervades the writings of many of our greatest
poets, who "live not in themselves," but are become "a portion
of that around them." In the beautiful words of Scott: —

> "Call it not vain; they do not err
> Who say, that, when the poet dies,
> Mute Nature mourns her worshipper,
> And celebrates his obsequies;
> Who say, tall cliff, and cavern lone,
> For the departed bard make moan;
> That mountains weep in crystal rill;
> That flowers in tears of balm distil;
> Through his loved groves the breezes sigh,
> And oaks, in deeper groan, reply;
> And rivers teach their rushing wave
> To murmur dirges round his grave."

And with a holier fervour, even, are all things animate and
inanimate said to feel the birth of a great poet, a hero, a genius,
a prophet; all Nature thrills with joy at his advent and makes
known her satisfaction with the good that has fallen to the lot

of earth. With such men, as Goethe said, Nature is in eternal league, watching, waiting for their coming.

How Nature must have rejoiced on that auspicious day, nineteen centuries ago, when the Messiah, long looked for, long expected, came! The sacred historians tell us that the carol of angels heralded his birth and the bright star in the East led the wise men to the modest manger where he lay. Never had there been such gladness abroad in the world since

> "The morning stars sang together,
> And all the sons of God shouted for joy."

Shakespeare, in *Hamlet,* — a play in which so many items of folk-lore are to be found, — makes Marcellus say : —

> " It faded on the crowing of the cock.
> Some say that ever 'gainst that season comes
> Wherein our Saviour's birth is celebrated,
> The bird of dawning singeth all night long :
> And then, they say, no spirit dares stir abroad ;
> The nights are wholesome ; then no planets strike,
> No fairy takes, nor witch hath power to charm,
> So hallow'd and so gracious is the time,"

to which Horatio replies : —

> " So have I heard, and do in part believe it."

This belief in the holy and gracious season of the birth of Christ, — a return to the old ideas of the Golden Age and the kinship of all Nature, — finds briefest expression in the Montenegrin saying of Christmas Eve: "To-night, Earth is blended with Paradise." According to Bosnian legend, at the birth of Christ: "The sun in the East bowed down, the stars stood still, the mountains and the forests shook and touched the earth with their summits, and the green pine tree bent; heaven and earth were bowed." And when Simeon took the Holy Child from the mother's arms : —

" The sun leaped in the heavens and the stars around it danced. A peace came over mountain and forest. Even the rotten stump stood straight and healthy on the green mountain-side. The grass was beflowered with opening blossoms, and incense sweet as myrrh pervaded upland and forest, and birds sang on the mountain-top, and all gave thanks to the great God" (*Macmillan's Mag.*, Vol. XLIII., p. 362).

Relics of the same thoughts crop out from a thousand Christmas songs and carols in every country of Europe, and in myriads of folk-songs and sayings in every language of the Continent.

And in those southern lands, where, even more than with us, religion and love are inseparable, the environment of the Christ-birth is transferred to the beloved of the human heart, and, as the Tuscans sing in their *stornelli* (415. 104) : —

> " Quando nascesti tu, nacque un bel fiore ;
> La luna si fermò di camminare,
> Le stelle si cambiaron di colore,"

in Mrs. Busk's translation : —

> " Thy birth, Love, was the birth of a fair flower ;
> The moon her course arrested at that hour,
> The stars were then arrayed in a new colour,"

so, in other lands, has the similitude of the Golden Age of Love and the Golden Time of Christmas been elaborated and adorned by all the genius of the nameless folk-poets of centuries past.

Folk-Lore of Christmas Tide.

Scottish folk-lore has it that Christ was born "at the hour of midnight on Christmas Eve," and that the miracle of turning water into wine was performed by Him at the same hour (246. 160). There is a belief current in some parts of Germany that "between eleven and twelve the night before Christmas water turns to wine"; in other districts, as at Bielefeld, it is on Christmas night that this change is thought to take place (462. IV. 1779).

This hour is also auspicious for many actions, and in some sections of Germany it was thought that if one would go to the cross-roads between eleven and twelve on Christmas Day, and listen, he "would hear what most concerns him in the coming year." Another belief is that "if one walks into the winter-corn on Holy Christmas Eve, he will hear all that will happen in the village that year."

Christmas Eve or Christmas is the time when the oracles of the folk are in the best working-order, especially the many processes by which maidens are wont to discover the colour of their lover's hair, the beauty of his face and form, his trade and occupation, whether they shall marry or not, and the like.

The same season is most auspicious for certain ceremonies and practices (transferred to it from the heathen antiquity) of the peasantry of Europe in relation to agriculture and allied industries. Among those noted by Grimm are the following: —

On Christmas Eve thrash the garden with a flail, with only your shirt on, and the grass will grow well next year.

Tie wet strawbands around the orchard trees on Christmas Eve and it will make them fruitful.

On Christmas Eve put a stone on every tree, and they will bear the more (462. IV. 1790–1825).

Beat the trees on Christmas night, and they will bear more fruit (448. 337).

In Herefordshire, Devonshire, and Cornwall, in England, the farmers and peasantry " salute the apple-trees on Christmas Eve," and in Sussex they used to " worsle," *i.e.* " wassail," the apple-trees and chant verses to them in somewhat of the primitive fashion (448. 219).

Some other curious items of Christmas folk-lore are the following, current chiefly in Germany (462. IV. 1779–1824): —

If after a Christmas dinner you shake out the table-cloth over the bare ground under the open sky, crumb-wort will grow on the spot.

If on Christmas Day, or Christmas Eve, you hang a wash-clout on a hedge, and then groom the horses with it, they will grow fat.

As often as the cock crows on Christmas Eve, the quarter of corn will be as dear.

If a dog howls the night before Christmas, it will go mad within the year.

If the light is let go out on Christmas Eve, some one in the house will die.

When lights are brought in on Christmas Eve, if any one's shadow has no head, he will die within a year; if half a head, in the second half-year.

If a hoop comes off a cask on Christmas Eve, some one in the house will die that year.

If on Christmas Eve you make a little heap of salt on the

table, and it melts over night, you will die the next year; if, in the morning, it remain undiminished, you will live.

If you wear something sewed with thread spun on Christmas Eve, no vermin will stick to you.

If a shirt be spun, woven, and sewed by a pure, chaste maiden on Christmas Day, it will be proof against lead or steel.

If you are born at sermon-time on Christmas morning, you can see spirits.

If you burn elder on Christmas Eve, you will have revealed to you all the witches and sorcerers of the neighbourhood (448. 319).

If you steal hay the night before Christmas, and give the cattle some, they thrive, and you are not caught in any future thefts.

If you steal anything at Christmas without being caught, you can steal safely for a year.

If you eat no beans on Christmas Eve, you will become an ass.

If you eat a raw egg, fasting, on Christmas morning, you can carry heavy weights.

The crumbs saved up on three Christmas Eves are good to give as physic to one who is disappointed (462. IV. 1788–1801).

It is unlucky to carry anything forth from the house on Christmas morning until something has been brought in.

It is unlucky to give a neighbour a live coal to kindle a fire with on Christmas morning.

If the fire burns brightly on Christmas morning, it betokens prosperity during the year; if it smoulders, adversity (246. 160).

These, and many other practices, ceremonies, beliefs, and superstitions, which may be read in Grimm (462), Gregor (246), Henderson (469), De Gubernatis (427, 428), Ortwein (315), Tilte (370), and others who have written of Christmas, show the importance attached in the folk-mind to the time of the birth of Christ, and how around it as a centre have fixed themselves hundreds of the rites and solemnities of passing heathendom, with its recognition of the kinship of all nature, out of which grew astrology, magic, and other pseudo-sciences.

Flowers of the Christ-Child.

Many flowers are believed to have first sprung into being or to have first burst into blossom at the moment when Christ was born, or very near that auspicious hour.

The Sicilian children, so Folkard tells us, put pennyroyal in their cots on Christmas Eve, "under the belief that at the exact hour and minute when the infant Jesus was born this plant puts forth its blossom." Another belief is that the blossoming occurs again on Midsummer Night (448. 492).

In the East the Rose of Jericho is looked upon with favour by women with child, for "there is a cherished legend that it first blossomed at our Saviour's birth, closed at the Crucifixion, and opened again at Easter, whence its name of Resurrection Flower" (448. 528).

Gerarde, the old herbalist, tells us that the black hellebore is called "Christ's Herb," or "Christmas Herb," because it "floweth about the birth of our Lord Jesus Christ" (448. 281).

Certain varieties of the hawthorn also were thought to blossom on Christmas Day. The celebrated Abbey of Glastonbury in England possessed such a thorn-tree, said to have sprung from the staff of Joseph of Arimathea, when he stuck it into the ground, in that part of England, which he is represented as having converted. The "Glastonbury Thorn" was long believed to be a convincing witness to the truth of the Gospel by blossoming without fail every Christmas Day (448. 352, 353).

Many plants, trees, and flowers owe their peculiarities to their connection with the birth or the childhood of Christ. The *Ornithogalum umbellatum* is called the "Star of Bethlehem," according to Folkard, because "its white stellate flowers resemble the pictures of the star that indicated the birth of the Saviour of mankind" (448. 553). The *Galium verum*, "Our Lady's Bedstraw," receives its name from the belief that the manger in which the infant Jesus lay was filled with this plant (448. 249).

The flight of the Holy Family into Egypt has attracted to it as a centre a large group of legends belonging to this category, many of which are to be found in Folkard and Busk.

Of a certain tree, with leaves like the sensitive plant, in Arabia, we read that this peculiarity arose from the fact that when near the city of Heliopolis "Joseph led the dromedary that bore the blessed Mother and her Divine Son, under a neighbouring tree, and as he did so, the green branches bent over the group, as if paying homage to their Master."

Near Mataria there was said to be a sycamore-tree, called "the

Tree of Jesus and Mary," which gave shelter at nightfall to the
Holy Family, and to this fact the Mohammedans are reported
to attribute the great longevity and verdure of the sycamore
(448. 558).

A widespread tradition makes the "Rose of Jericho," called
also "St. Mary's Rose," spring up on every spot where the Holy
Family rested on their way to Egypt. The juniper owes the
extraordinary powers with which it is credited in the popular
mind to the fact that it once saved the life of the Virgin and the
infant Christ. The same kind offices have been attributed to the
hazel-tree, the fig, the rosemary, the date-palm, etc. Among
the many legends accounting for the peculiarity of the aspen there
is one, preserved in Germany, which attributes it to the action of
this tree when the Holy Family entered the dense forest in which
it stood (448. 230) : —

"As they entered this wilderness, all the trees bowed themselves down in reverence to the infant God; only the Aspen, in
her exceeding pride and arrogance, refused to acknowledge Him,
and stood upright." In consequence of this "the Holy Child
pronounced a curse against her . . .; and, at the sound of His
words, the Aspen began to tremble through all her leaves, and
has not ceased to tremble to this day." According to a Sicilian
legend, "the form of a hand is to be seen in the interior of the
fruit of the pine," representing "the hand of Jesus blessing the
tree which had saved Him during the flight into Egypt by screen-
ing Him and His mother from Herod's soldiers" (448. 490).

We have from Rome the following tradition (415. 173) : —

"One day the Madonna was carrying the Bambino through a
lupine-field, and the stalks of the lupines rustled so, that she
thought it was a robber coming to kill the Santo Bambino. She
turned, and sent a malediction over the lupine-field, and immediately the lupines all withered away, and fell flat and dry on the
ground, so that she could see there was no one hidden there.
When she saw there was no one hidden there, she sent a blessing
over the lupine-field, and the lupines all stood straight up again,
fair and flourishing, and with ten-fold greater produce than they
had at first." In a Bolognese legend the lupines are cursed by
the Virgin, because, "by the clatter and noise they made, certain
plants of this species drew the attentions of Herod's minions to

the spot where the tired and exhausted travellers had made a brief halt" (448. 473). Another tradition, found over almost all Italy, says that when the Holy Family were fleeing from the soldiers of King Herod: —

"The brooms and the chick-peas began to rustle and crackle, and by this noise betrayed the fugitives. The flax bristled up. Happily for her, Mary was near a juniper; the hospitable tree opened its branches as arms and enclosed the Virgin and Child within their folds, affording them a secure hiding-place. Then the Virgin uttered a malediction against the brooms and the chick-peas, and ever since that day they have always rustled and crackled." The story goes on to tell us that the Virgin "pardoned the flax its weakness, and gave the juniper her blessing," which accounts for the use of the latter for Christmas decorations, — like the holly in England and France (448. 395).

Birds of the Christ-Child.

Several birds are associated with the infant Christ in the folklore of Europe and the East. In Normandy, the wren is called *Poulette de Dieu, Oiseau de Dieu,* "God's Chicken," "God's Bird," — corresponding to the old Scotch "Our Lady's Hen," — because, according to legend, "she was present at the birth of the Infant Saviour, made her nest in his cradle, and brought moss and feathers to form a coverlet for the Holy Child" (539. 35).

A Tyrolian folk-tale informs us that in days of yore the ravens were "beautiful birds with plumage white as snow, which they kept clean by constant washing in a certain stream." It happened, once upon a time, that "the Holy Child, desiring to drink, came to this stream, but the ravens prevented him by splashing about and befouling the water. Whereupon he said: 'Ungrateful birds! Proud you may be of your beauty, but your feathers, now so snowy white, shall become black and remain so till the judgment day!'" In consequence of their uncharitable action have the ravens continued black ever since (539. 92).

In his childhood Christ is often represented as playing with the other little Jewish children. One Sabbath day He and His playmates amused themselves by making birds out of clay, and after the children had been playing a while, a Sadducee chanced to pass that way. The story goes on to tell that "He was very old and very zealous, and he rebuked the children for spending their Sabbath in so profane an employment. And he let it not rest at chiding alone, but went to the clay birds and broke them all, to the great grief of the children. Now, when Christ saw this, He waved His hands over all the birds He had fashioned, and they became forthwith alive, and soared up into the heavens" (539. 181). From Swainson we learn that in the Icelandic version of the legend the birds are thought to have been the golden plover "whose note 'deerin' sounds like to the Iceland word 'dyrdhin,' namely 'glory,' for these birds sing praise to their Lord, for in that He mercifully saved them from the merciless hand of the Sadducee."

A Danish legend, cited by Swainson, accounts for the peculiar cry of the lapwing, which sounds like "Klyf ved! klyf ved!" *i.e.* "Cleave wood! cleave wood!" as follows (539. 185):—

"When our Lord was a wee bairn, He took a walk out one day, and came to an old crone who was busy baking. She desired Him to go and split her a little wood for the oven, and she would give Him a new cake for His trouble. He did as He was bid, and the old woman went on with her occupation, sundering a very small portion of the dough for the promised recompense. But when the batch was drawn, this cake was equally large with the rest. So she took a new morsel of the dough still less than before, and made and baked another cake, but with the like result. Hereupon she broke out with 'That's a vast overmuckle cake for the likes o' you; thee's get thy cake anither time.' When our Lord saw her evil disposition, His wrath was stirred, and He said to the woman: 'I split your wood as you asked me, and you would not so much as give me the little cake you promised me. Now you shall go and cleave wood, and that, too, as long as the world endures!' With that he changed her into a weep (*vipa*) [lapwing]."

Among the many legends of Isa, as Jesus is called by the Moslems, current among the Mohammedan peoples is a variant of the story of the clay-birds, as follows: "When Isa was seven years old, he and his companions made images in clay of birds and beasts, and Isa, to show his superiority, caused his images to fly and walk at his command." Clouston informs us that this

2 B

story is also found in the Gospel of the Pseudo-Matthew, and in
that of the Infancy (422. II. 408).

In Champagne, France, legend makes the cuckoo to have issued
from a Christmas log (462. I. 113), and in a Latin poem of the
Middle Ages we are told that "the crossbill hatches its eggs at
Christmas and the young birds fly in full plumage at Easter"
(539. 67).

Animals.

At Christmas certain animals become more human, or express
their joy at the birth of Christ in unmistakable fashion.

There was an old Scottish belief that "at the exact hour of the
Saviour's birth bees in their hive emitted a buzzing sound" (246.
147). According to a Breton folk-tale the ox and the ass can
converse for a single hour, "between eleven and twelve on Christmas night." At the same hour, in German folk-lore, all cattle
stand up; another version, however, makes them devoutly kneel
(462. IV. 1481).

Among the animals which folk-thought has brought into connection with the Christ-Child is the horse. A Russian legend
tells us that the flesh of the horse is deemed unclean because
"when the infant Saviour was hidden in the manger, the horse
kept eating the hay under which the babe was concealed, whereas
the ox not only would not touch it, but brought back hay on its
horns to replace what the horse had eaten" (520. 334). From a
Spanish-American miracle-play, we learn that the oxen and asses
around the manger kept the little babe warm with their breath.

In Ireland the following folk-beliefs obtain regarding the ass
and the cow : —

"Joseph and Mary fled into Egypt with the infant Jesus, on
an ass. Since that date the ass has had a cross on its back.
This same ass returned to Nazareth seven years later with them
on its back, travelling in the night, since which time it has been
the wisest of all animals ; it was made sure-footed for Christ to
ride on his triumphal entry into Jerusalem, and it remains the
most sure-footed of all beasts. The ass and cow are looked upon
as sacred, because these animals breathed upon the infant Jesus in
the manger and kept the child warm. Old women sprinkle holy
water on these animals to drive away disease" (480 (1893) 264).

In *I Henry IV.* (Act II. Sc. 4) Falstaff says: "The lion will not touch the true Prince," and the divinity which hedged about the princes of human blood was ever present with the son of Joseph and Mary, whose divinity sprang from a purer, nobler fount than that of weak humanity.

The Holy Family.

We have several word-pictures of the Holy Family from the mouth of the folk. Among the hymns sung by the Confraternities of the Virgin in Seville, is one in which occurs the following figure (*Catholic World*, XXIV. 19):—

> " Es María la nave de gracia,
> San José la vela, el Niño el timon ;
> Y los remos son las buenas almas
> Que van al Rosario con gran devocion."

i.e.

> ["Mary is the ship of grace,
> St. Joseph is the sail,
> The Child (Jesus) is the helm,
> And the oars are the pious souls who devoutly pray."]

One of the little Italian songs called *razzi neddu*, recorded by Mrs. Busk, is even briefer:—

> " Maruzza lavava,
> Giuseppe stinnia,
> Gesù si stricava
> Ca minna vulia."

> ["Sweet Mary was washing,
> Joseph was hanging out the clothes to dry,
> Jesus was stretching Himself on the ground,
> For so His mother willed."]

A popular Spanish lullaby recorded by De Gubernatis in his great study of birth customs and usages, runs as follows in translation (500. 310):—

> "The Baby Child of Mary,
> Now cradle He has none ;
> His father is a carpenter,
> And he shall make Him one.

"The Lady, good St. Anna,
The Lord St. Joachim,
They rock the Baby's cradle,
That sleep may come to Him.

"Then sleep, thou too, my baby,
My little heart so dear ;
The Virgin is beside thee,
The Son of God is near."

Among the many versions and variants of the familiar child's prayer, "Now I lay me down to sleep," cited by the Countess Martinengo-Cesaresco (500. 202–213), is to be included the following, found among the Greeks of the Terra d'Otranto, in Italy : —

"I lay me down to sleep in my little bed; I lay me down to sleep with my Mamma Mary ; the Mamma Mary goes hence and leaves me Christ to keep me company."

Some of the most naïve legends are those which deal with the Child and His mother in the early years of life. "Our Lady's Thistle" (*Carduus Marianus*) receives its name "because its green leaves have been spotted white ever since the milk of the Virgin fell upon it, when she was nursing Jesus, and endowed it with miraculous virtues." A German tradition tells the same story of the *Polypodium vulgare* (Marienmilch), based upon an older legend of the goddess Freia, many of whose attributes, with the lapse of heathendom, passed over to the central female figure of Christianity (448. 499). A similar origin of the white lily from the milk of Juno is given in Greek mythology (462. 1V. 1671).

In Devonshire, the custom of burning a faggot of ash at Christmas, is traced back to the fact that "the Divine Infant at Bethlehem was first washed and dressed by a fire of ash-wood" (448. 235).

In Spain the rosemary is believed to blossom on the day of Christ's passion, and the legend accounting for this tells us that "the Virgin Mary spread on a shrub of rosemary the underlinen and little frocks of the infant Jesus." The peasantry believe that rosemary "brings happiness on those families who employ it in perfuming the house on Christmas night" (448. 526).

Joseph and Mary.

The suspicions entertained by Joseph (as indicated in the narrative of St. Matthew i. 19), when the birth of the child of Mary was first announced, have found deep expression in folk-thought. According to one Oriental legend, the infant Christ himself spoke, declaring that "God had created Him by His word, and chosen Him to be His servant and prophet" (547. 254).

Another tradition, cited by Folkard, states that (448. 279): " Before the birth of our Saviour, the Virgin Mary longed extremely to taste of some tempting cherries which hung upon a tree high above her head ; so she requested Joseph to pluck them. Joseph, however, not caring to take the trouble, refused to gather the cherries, saying sullenly, ' Let the father of thy child present thee with the cherries if he will ! ' No sooner had these words escaped his lips, than, as if in reproof, the branch of the cherry-tree bowed spontaneously to the Virgin's hand, and she gathered its fruit and ate it. Hence the cherry is dedicated to the Virgin Mary."

In Finland the white side of the flounder " is said to have been caused by the Virgin Mary's laying her hand upon it," and an Eastern legend states that " the Angel Gabriel restored a sole to life, to assure the Virgin Mary of the truth of the miraculous conception." Ralston cites from the Kherson Government in Russia the following : —

" At the time of the Angelic Salutation, the Blessed Virgin told the Archangel Gabriel that she would give credit to his words, if a fish, one side of which had already been eaten, were to come to life again. That moment the fish came to life, and was put back into the water." This legend, accounting for the shape of the sole, finds perhaps its origin in " the old Lithuanian tradition that the Queen of the Baltic Sea once ate half of it and threw the other half into the sea again " — another example of the transference of older stories to the cycle of the Virgin Mary (520. 334).

De Gubernatis records from Andalusia, in Spain, a legend which tells how the Holy Family, journeying one day, came to an orange-tree guarded by an eagle. The Virgin " begged of it one of the oranges for the Holy Child. The eagle miraculously fell asleep, and the Virgin thereupon plucked not one but three oranges, one of which she gave to the infant Jesus, another to

Joseph, and the third she kept for herself. Then, and not till then, the eagle that guarded the orange-tree awoke" (448. 478).

A beautiful pendant to this Spanish tale is found in the Roumanian story cited by Folkard: —

"'The infant Jesus, in the arms of the Blessed Virgin, becomes restless, will not go to sleep, and begins to cry. The Virgin, to calm the Holy Child, gives Him two apples. The infant throws one upwards and it becomes the Moon; He then throws the second, and it becomes the Sun. After this exploit, the Virgin Mary addresses Him and foretells that He will become the Lord of Heaven" (448. 222).

In his recent book on *Childhood in Literature and Art*, Mr. Scudder treats of the Christ-Child and the Holy Family in mediæval and early Christian art and literature (350. 57–65, 83–99), calling special attention to a series of twelve prints executed in the Netherlands, known as *The Infancy of our Lord God and Saviour, Jesus Christ*, in which we have "a reproduction of the childhood of the Saviour in the terms of a homely Netherland family life, the naturalistic treatment diversified by the use of angelic machinery" (350. 91).

Moslem Lore of the Christ.

In the *Toldoth Jesú*, which Clouston terms "a scurrilous Jewish 'Life of Christ,'" — the Hebrew text with a Latin translation and explanatory notes, appeared at Leyden in 1705, under the title *Historiæ Jeschuæ Nazareni*, — the many wonders admitted to have been performed by Christ are ascribed to his "having abstracted from the Temple the Ineffable Name and concealed it in his thigh," — an idea thought to be of Indian origin. Clouston goes so far as to say: "Legends of the miracles of 'Isa, son of Maryam, found in the works of Muslim writers, seem to have been derived from the Kurán, and also from early Christian, or rather *quasi*-Christian traditions, such as those in the apocryphal gospels, which are now for the most part traceable to Buddhist sources." One belief of the Mohammedans was that "the breath of the Messiah had the virtue of restoring the dead to life" (422. II. 395, 408, 409).

In the first volume of the *Orientalist*, Muhammed Casim Siddi Lebbe gives an account of the views of Arabian writers regarding the Virgin Mary and Jesus. Weil has also devoted a section of his work on Mussulman legends to "John, Mary, and Christ." When the child Jesus was born, we are told, the withered trunk of a date tree against which the Virgin leaned, "blossomed, and its withered branches were covered with fresh dates," while "a fountain of fresh water gushed forth from the earth at her feet" (547. 249–264).

The Christ-Child To-day.

Folk-stories and churchly legends tell us that the Christ-Child still walks the earth, and appears unto the saints and sinners of this world.

Folkard reports a tradition from the Havel country in North Germany : —

"One Christmas Eve a peasant felt a great desire to eat cabbage and, having none himself, he slipped into a neighbour's garden to cut some. Just as he had filled his basket, the Christ-Child rode past on his white horse, and said: ' Because thou hast stolen on the holy night, thou shalt immediately sit in the moon with thy basket of cabbage.' " And so, we are told, " the culprit was immediately wafted up to the moon," and there he can still be seen as " the man in the moon " (448. 265).

Brewer gives many of the churchly legends in which the Christ-Child appears to men and women upon earth, either in the arms of the Virgin, as he came to St. Agnes of Monte Pulciano and to Jeanne Marie de Maillé, or as a glorious child, in which form he appeared alone to St. Alexander and Quirinus the tribune, in the reign of Hadrian; to St. Andrew Corsini, to call him to the bishopric of Fiesole; to St. Anthony of Padua, many times; to St. Cuthbert, to rebuke him (a child of eight years) for wasting his time in play; to St. Emiliana of Florence, with the same purpose; to St. Oxanna, and to St. Veronica of Milan (191. 59, 60).

Among the rude peasantry of Catholic Europe belief in the visitations of the Christ-Child lingers, especially at the season of His birth. With them, as Milton thought, —

" Millions of spiritual creatures walk the earth."

Yet not unseen, but seen often of the good and wise, the simple and innocent, and greatest of these visitants of earth is the Child Jesus, ever occupied about His Father's business.

CHAPTER XXVII.

PROVERBS, SAYINGS, ETC., ABOUT PARENTS, FATHER AND MOTHER.

1. BE a father to virtue, but a father-in-law to vice.

2. Bread is our father, but *kasha* [porridge] is our mother.
— *Russian.*

3. Call not that man wretched, who, whatever ills he suffers, has a child he loves. — *Southey.*

4. Children suck the mother when they are young, and the father when they are old.

5. Children see in their parents the past, they again in their children the future; and if we find more love in parents for their children than in children for their parents, this is sad and natural. Who does not fondle his hopes more than his recollections?
— *Eötvös.*

6. Choose a good mother's daughter, though her father were the devil. — *Gaelic.*

7. Die Menschheit geben uns Vater und Mutter, die Menschlichkeit aber gibt uns nur die Erziehung. [Human nature we owe to father and mother, but humanity to education alone.]
— *Weber.*

8. Die Mütter geben uns von Geiste Wärme, und die Väter Licht. [Our mothers give us warmth of spirit; our fathers, light.]
— *Jean Paul.*

9. Die Mutter sagt es, der Vater glaubt es, ein Narr zweifelt daran. [The mother says it, the father believes it, the fool doubts it.] — *Pistorius.*

10. Dos est magna parentum Virtus. [The virtue of parents is a great dowry.] — *Horace.*

11. En olle kan beter söfen kinner erneren, as söfen kinner ên

olle. [A parent can more easily maintain seven children than seven children one parent.] — *Low German.*

12. Fader og Moder ere gode, end er Gud bedre. [Father and mother are kind, but God is better.] — *Danish.*

13. He knows not what love is that hath no children.

14. He that loveth father and mother more than me is not worthy of me. — *Jesus.*

15. If poverty is the mother of crimes, want of sense is the father of them. — *La Bruyère.*

16. Keep thy father's commandment, and forsake not the law of thy mother. — *Bible.*

17. La buena vida padre y madre olvida. [Prosperity forgets father and mother.] — *Spanish.*

18. Laus magna natis obsequi parentibus. [Great praise comes to children for having complied with the wishes of their parents.]
— *Phædrus.*

19. Look at home, father priest, mother priest; your church is a hundred-fold heavier responsibility than mine can be. Your priesthood is from God's own hands. — *Henry Ward Beecher.*

20. One mother is more venerable than a thousand fathers.
— *Laws of Manu.*

21. Parents are the enemies of their children, if they refuse them education. — *Eastern Proverb.*

22. Parents' blessings can neither be drowned in water, nor consumed in fire.

23. Parents we can have but once. — *Dr. Johnson.*

24. Parents say: "Our boy is growing up." They forget his life is shortening. — *Afghan.*

25. Respect for one's parents is the highest duty of civil life.
— *Chinese.*

26. The bazaar knows neither father nor mother. — *Turkish.*

27. The crow says: "O my son, whiter than muslin." — *Afghan.*

28. The eye that mocketh at his father, and despiseth to obey his mother, the ravens of the valley shall pick it out, and the young eagles shall eat it. — *Bible.*

29. The house of the childless is empty; and so is the heart of him that hath no wife. — *Hitopadesa.*

30. The joys of parents are secret, and so are their griefs and fears. — *Bacon.*

31. These are my jewels. — *Cornelia (mother of the Gracchi).*

32. They who have lost an infant are never, as it were, without an infant child. — *Leigh Hunt.*

33. To a father, when his child dies, the future dies; to a child, when his parents die, the past dies. — *Auerbach.*

34. To make a boy despise his mother's care is the straightest way to make him also despise his Redeemer's voice; and to make him scorn his father and his father's house, the straightest way to make him deny his God and his God's heaven. — *Ruskin.*

35. Unworthy offspring brag most of their worthy descent.

— Danish.

36.   Vom Vater hab' ich die Statur,
            Des Lebens ernstes Führen;
            Von Mütterchen die Frohnatur
            Und Lust zu fabulieren.
         [My father's stature I possess
            And life's more solemn glory;
         My mother's fund of cheerfulness,
            Her love for song and story.] — *Goethe.*

37. Was der Mutter an's Herz geht, das geht dem Vater nur an die Kniee. [What goes to the mother's heart goes only to the father's knees.] — *German.*

38. Wer nicht Kinder hat, der weiss nicht, warum er lebt. [Who has not children knows not why he lives.] — *German.*

39. Whoso curseth his father or his mother, his lamp shall be put out in obscure darkness. — *Bible.*

40. Whoso robbeth his father or his mother, and saith, It is no transgression, the same is the companion of a destroyer.

— Bible.

CHAPTER XXVIII.

Proverbs, Sayings, etc., about the Child, Mankind, Genius, etc.

1. Argument is like an arrow from a cross-bow, which has great force, though shot by a child. — *Bacon.*

2. Childhood often holds a truth in its feeble fingers, which the grasp of manhood cannot retain, and which it is the pride of utmost age to recover. — *Ruskin.*

3. Children always turn toward the light. — *Hare.*

4. Der grösste Mensch bleibt stets ein Menschenkind. [The greatest man always remains a son of man.] — *Goethe.*

5. Dieu aide à trois sortes de personnes, — aux fous, aux enfants, et aux ivrognes. [God protects three sorts of people, — fools, children, and drunkards.] — *French.*

6. Enfants et fous sont devins. [Children and fools are sooth-sayers.] — *French.*

7. Every child is, to a certain extent, a genius, and every genius is, to a certain extent, a child. — *Schopenhauer.*

8. Except ye be converted, and become as little children, ye cannot enter into the kingdom of heaven. — *Jesus.*

9.   Fede ed innocenzia son reperte
        Solo ne' pargoletti.
        [Faith and innocence we find
        Only in the children's mind.] — *Dante.*

10. Genius is the power of carrying the feelings of childhood into the powers of manhood. — *Coleridge.*

11. Genius must be born, and never can be taught. — *Dryden.*

12. Genius should be the child of genius, and every child should be inspired. — *Emerson.*

379

13. God is kind to fou [*i.e.* drunken] folk and bairns. — *Scotch.*
14. God watches over little children and drunkards.
— *Russian.*
15. Heaven lies about us in our infancy. — *Wordsworth.*
16. I love God and little children. — *Jean Paul.*
17. If children grew up according to early indications, we should have nothing but geniuses. — *Goethe.*
18. Infancy presents body and spirit in unity; the body is all animated. — *Coleridge.*
19. Ingenio non ætate adipiscitur sapientia. [Wisdom comes by nature, not by age.] — *Latin.*
20. Kinder und Narren sprechen die Wahrheit. [Children and fools tell the truth.] — *German.*
21. Kloke kinner ward nît old. [Wise children don't live long.]
— *Frisian.*
22. L'homme est toujours l'enfant, et l'enfant toujours l'homme. [The man is always the child, and the child is always the man.]
— *French.*
23. Mankind at large always resembles frivolous children; they are impatient of thought, and wish to be amused. — *Emerson.*
24.   Men are but children of a larger growth;
Our appetites are apt to change as theirs,
And full as craving, too, and full as vain. — *Dryden.*
25. Men are unwiser than children; they do not know the hand that feeds them. — *Carlyle.*
26. Men deal with life as children with their play,
Who first misuse, then cast their toys away. — *Cowper.*
27. Men fear death as children to go into the dark. — *Bacon.*
28. Nature is full of freaks, and now puts an old head on young shoulders, and then a young heart beating under fourscore winters. — *Emerson.*
29. Nothing is so intelligible to the child, nothing seems so natural to him as the marvellous or the supernatural. — *Zachariä.*
30. Odi puerulos præcoci ingenio. [I hate boys of precocious genius.] — *Cicero.*
31. ὃν οἱ θεοὶ φιλοῦσιν ἀποθνῄσκει νέος. [He whom the gods love dies young.] — *Menander.*
32. Poeta nascitur, non fit. [A poet is born, not made.]
— *Latin.*

33.　　Prophete rechts, Prophete links,
　　　Das Weltkind in der Mitten.
　　[Prophets to right of him, prophets to left of him,
　　　The world-child in the middle.] — *Goethe.*

34. So wise, so young, they say, do ne'er live long.
　　　　　　　— *Shakespeare* (Rich. III. iii. 1).

35. Suffer little children to come unto me, and forbid them not, for of such is the kingdom of heaven. — *Jesus.*

36. The best architecture is the expression of the mind of manhood by the hands of childhood. — *Ruskin.*

37. The birth of a child is the imprisonment of a soul.
　　　　　　　　　— *Simons.*

38. The boy's story is the best that is ever told. — *Dickens.*

39. The child is father of the man. — *Wordsworth.*

40.　　The childhood shows the man
　　　As morning shows the day. — *Milton.*

41. The wisest doctor is gravelled by the inquisitiveness of a child. — *Emerson.*

42.　　These moving things, ca'ed wife and weans,
　　　Wad move the very heart o' stanes. — *Burns.*

43. They who have lost an infant are never, as it were, without an infant child. — *Leigh Hunt.*

44. To be young is to be as one of the immortals. — *Hazlitt.*

45.　　Wage du zu irren und zu träumen:
　　　Hoher Sinn liegt oft im kind'schen Spiel.
　　　[Dare thou to err and dream;
　　　Oft deep sense a child's play holds.] — *Schiller.*

46. Wer darf das Kind beim rechten Namen nennen? [Who dare give the child its right name?] — *Goethe.*

47. Whilst we converse with what is above us, we do not grow old but grow young. — *Emerson.*

48. Whosoever shall not receive the kingdom of God as a little child, he shall not enter therein. — *Jesus.*

49. Ye are but children. — *Egyptian Priest (to Solon).*

CHAPTER XXIX.

Proverbs, Sayings, etc., about the Mother and Child.

1. A child may have too much of its mother's blessing.
2. A kiss from my mother made me a painter. — *Benj. West.*
3. Ama sinhesten, ezduenac, ain zuna. [Who does not follow his mother will follow his stepmother, *i.e.* who will not hear must feel.] — *Basque.*
4. A mother curses not her son. — *Sanskrit.*
5. An ounce o' mother-wit is worth a pound o' clergy.

— *Scotch.*

6. As if he had fallen out of his mother's mouth (*i.e.* so like his mother). — *Low German.*
7. Barmherzige Mütter ziehen grindige Töchter. [Compassionate mothers bring up scabby daughters.] — *German.*
8. Choose cloth by its edge, a wife by her mother. — *Persian.*
9. Das Kind, das seine Mutter verachtet, hat einen stinkenden Atem. [The child that despises its mother has a fetid breath.]

— *German.*

10. Das Kind fällt wieder in der Mutter Schooss. [The child falls back into its mother's bosom.] — *German.*
11. Das Kind folgt dem Busen. [The child follows the bosom.] — *German.*
12. Die Mutter eine Hexe, die Tochter auch eine Hexe. [Mother a witch, daughter also a witch.] — *German.*
13. Die Tochter ist wie die Mutter. [Like mother, like daughter.] — *German.*
14. Es meinet jede Frau, ihr Kind sei ein Pfau. [Every woman thinks her child a peacock.] — *German.*
15. Es ist kein' so böse Mutter, sie zöhe gern ein frommes

Kind. [There is no mother so bad but that she will bring up a good child.] — *German.*

16. Fleissige Mutter hat faule Tochter. [A diligent mother has a lazy daughter.] — *German.*

17. God pardons like a mother who kisses the offence into everlasting forgetfulness. — *Henry Ward Beecher.*

18. Happy is the boy whose mother is tired of talking non-sense to him before he is old enough to know the sense of it.

— *Hare.*

19. He deceives thee, who tells thee that he loves thee more than thy mother does. — *Russian.*

20. He has faut [*i.e.* need] o' a wife that marries.mam's pet.

— *Scotch.*

21. He that is born of a hen must scrape for a living.

22. I have always found that the road to a woman's heart lies through her child. — *Haliburton.*

23. I would desire for a friend the son who never resisted the tears of his mother. — *Lacretelle.*

24. If the world were put into one scale and my mother into the other, the world would kick the beam. — *Lord Langdale.*

25. In a matter of life and death don't trust even your mother; she might mistake a black bean [nay] for a white one [yea]. — *Alcibiades.*

26. Ist eine Mutter noch so arm, so giebt sie ihrem Kinde warm. [However poor a mother is, she keeps her child warm.]

— *German.*

27. It is not as thy mother says, but as thy neighbours say.

— *Hebrew.*

28. Jedes Mutterkind ist schön. [Every mother's child is beautiful.] — *German.*

29. Keine Mutter trägt einen Bastart. [No mother bears a bastard.] — *German.*

30. La madre pitiosa fa la figluola tignosa. [A merciful mother makes a scabby daughter.] — *Italian.*

31. Like mother, like daughter.

32. Mãi aguçosa, filha preguiçosa. [Diligent mother, idle daughter.] — *Portuguese.*

33. Mère piteuse fait sa fille rogneuse. [A merciful mother makes her daughter scabby.] — *French.*

34. Milk with water is still milk [*i.e.* though your mother is bad, she is nevertheless your mother]. — *Badaga.*

35. Mothers' darlings are but milksop heroes.

36. Mothers' love is the cream of love.

37. Muttertreu wird täglich neu. [Mother's truth keeps constant youth.] — *German.*

38.   Mysterious to all thought,
           A mother's prime of bliss,
           When to her eager lips is brought
           Her infant's thrilling kiss. — *Keble.*

39. Nature sent women into the world that they might be mothers and love children, to whom sacrifices must ever be offered, and from whom none can be obtained. — *Jean Paul.*

40. No bones are broken by a mother's fist. — *Russian.*

41. No hay tal madre come la que pare. [There is no mother like her who bears.] — *Spanish.*

42. O l'amour d'une mère! amour que nul n'oublie!
    Pain merveilleux, que Dieu partage et multiplie!
    Table toujours servie au paternel foyer!
    Chacun en a sa part, et tous l'ont tout entier.
    [O mother-love! love that none ever forgets!
    Wonderful bread, that God divides and multiplies!
    Table always spread beside the paternal hearth!
    Each one has his part of it, and each has it all!]
                                    — *Victor Hugo.*

43. One good mother is worth a hundred schoolmasters.

44. One scream of fear from a mother may resound through the whole life of her daughter. — *Jean Paul.*

45.   Seem I not as tender to him
           As any mother?
           Ay, but such a one
           As all day long hath rated at her child,
           And vext his day, but blesses him asleep.
                                    — *Tennyson.*

46. Sind die Kinder klein, so treten sie der Mutter auf den Schooss; sind die Kinder gross, so treten sie der Mutter auf das Herz. [When the children are small they tread upon the mother's breast; when they are large they tread upon the mother's heart.]
                                    — *German.*

47. So moder, so dogter. [Like mother, like daughter.]

— *Frisian.*

48.   Stabat Mater dolorosa

      Juxta crucem lacrymosa

      Quo pendebat Filius.

      [Sorrow-stricken stood the Mother

      Weeping by the cross

      On which hung her Son.]

— *Mediæval Latin Hymn.*

49. Tendresse maternelle toujours se renouvelle. [A mother's affection is forever new.] — *French.*

50. The child is often kissed for the mother's (nurse's) sake.

51. The elephant does not find his trunk heavy, nor the mother her babe. — *Angolese* (Africa).

52. The future destiny of the child is always the work of the mother. — *Napoleon.*

53. The good mother says not " Will you? " but gives.

— *Italian.*

54. The mother's heart is always with her children.

55. The mother's breath is aye sweet. — *Scotch.*

56. The mother knows best if the child be like the father.

57. The mother makes the house or mars it.

58. The nurse's bread is better than the mother's cake.

— *Frisian.*

59. The prayer of the mother fetches her child out of the bottom of the sea. — *Russian.*

60.   The watchful mother tarries nigh,

    Though sleep has closed her infant's eye. — *Keble.*

61. There is nothing more charming to see than a mother with her child in her arms, and there is nothing more venerable than a mother among a number of her children. — *Goethe.*

62. Though a mother be a wolf, she does not eat her cub's flesh. — *Afghan.*

63. Timidi mater non flet. [The coward's mother need not weep.] — *Latin.*

64. To a child in confinement its mother's knee is a binding-post. — *Hitopadesa.*

65. Unhappy is the man for whom his own mother has not made all mothers venerable. — *Jean Paul.*

2 c

66. Unless the child cries even the mother will not give it suck. — *Telugu.*

67. Wer ein säugendes Kind hat, der hat eine singende Frau. [Whoever has a suckling child, has a singing wife.] — *German.*

68. Wer dem Kinde die Nase wischt, küsst der Mutter den Backen. [Whoever wipes a child's nose kisses the mother's cheek.] — *German.*

69. What a mother sees coils itself up, but does not come out [*i.e.* the faults of her child]. — *Angolese* (Africa).

70. You desire, O woman, to be loved ardently and forever until death; be the mothers of your children. — *Jean Paul.*

71. Zu solchen Kindern gehört eine solche Mutter. [To such children belongs such a mother.] — *German.*

CHAPTER XXX.

PROVERBS, SAYINGS, ETC., ABOUT FATHER AND CHILD.

1. AN dem Kind kennt man den Vater wohl. [The father is known from the child.] — *German.*

2. Bone does not let go flesh, nor father son. — *Angolese.*

3. Böse Kinder machen den Vater fromm. [Bad children make the father good.] — *German.*

4. Chi non ha figliuoli non sa qualche cosa sia amore. [Who has not children knows not what love is.] — *Italian.*

5. Child's pig, but father's bacon.

6. Ein Vater ernährt eher zehn Kinder, denn zehn Kinder einen Vater. [One father can better nourish ten children, than ten children one father.] — *German.*

7. Fathers alone a father's heart can know. — *Young.*

8. Fathers first enter bonds to Nature's ends,
    And are her sureties ere they are a friend's.
    — *George Herbert.*

9. Fathers that wear rags
    Do make their children blind;
    But fathers that wear bags
    Do make their children kind.
    — *Shakespeare* (King Lear, ii. 4).

10. Fathers their children and themselves abuse,
    That wealth a husband for their daughters choose.
    — *Shirley.*

11. Happy is he that is happy in his children.

12. Happy is the child whose father went to the devil.

13. Haur nizar-galeac aitari bizzarra thira. [The child that will cry, pulls at its father's beard.] — *Basque.*

14. He has of [*i.e.* is like] his father. — *Russian.*

15. He is a chip of the old block.

16. He is cut out of his father's eyes [*i.e.* very like his father]. — *Frisian.*

17. He is the son of his father.

18. He is a wise child that knows his own father.

19. He that can discriminate is the father of his father. — *Veda.*

20. He that hath wife and children wants not business.

21. He that marries a widow and three children marries four thieves. — *Spanish.*

22. He that hath a wife and children hath given hostages to fortune; for they are impediments to great enterprises, either of virtue or mischief. — *Bacon.*

23. He was scant o' news that told that his father was hanged.
— *Scotch.*

24. He who hath but one hog makes him fat; he who hath but one son makes him a fool. — *Italian.*

25. It is a wise father that knows his own child.
— *Shakespeare* (Merch. of Venice, ii. 2).

26. Like father, like son. — *Arabic.*

27. Man sieht dem Kind an, was er für einen Vater hat. [By the child one sees what sort of man his father is.] — *German.*

28. Many a father might say. . . "I put in gold into the furnace, and there came out this calf." — *Spurgeon.*

29. Many a good father has a bad son.

30. On est toujours le fils de quelqu'un. Cela console. [One is always the son of somebody. That is a consolation.]
— *French.*

31. Patris est filius. [He is the son of his father.] — *Latin.*

32. Such a father, such a son. — *Spanish.*

33. Tel père, tel fils. [Like father, like son.] — *French.*

34. The child is the father of the man. — *Wordsworth.*

35. The child has a red tongue like its father.

36. The Devil's child, the Devil's luck.

37. The father can no more destroy his son than the cloud can extinguish by water the lightning which precedes from itself.
— *Raghuvansa.*

38. The fathers have eaten sour grapes, and the children's teeth are set on edge. — *Bible.*

39. The glory of children are their fathers. — *Bible.*

40. The gods do not avenge on the son the misdeeds of the

father. Each, good or bad, reaps the just reward of his own actions. The blessing of the parents, not their curse, is inherited.

— *Goethe.*

41. The ungrateful son is a wart on his father's face; to leave it is a blemish, to cut it a pain. — *Afghan.*

42. The words that a father speaks to his children in the privacy of home are not heard by the world, but, as in whispering-galleries, they are clearly heard at the end and by posterity.

— *Jean Paul.*

43. To a father, who is growing old, there is nothing dearer than a daughter. — *Euripides.*

44. To a father, when his child dies, the future dies; to a child, when his parents die, the past dies. — *Auerbach.*

45. Vinegar the son of wine [*i.e.* an unpopular son of a popular father]. — *Talmud.*

46. Whoso wishes to live without trouble, let him keep from step-children and winter-hogs. — *Low German.*

CHAPTER XXXI.

Proverbs, Sayings, etc., about Childhood, Youth, and Age.

1. A' are guid lasses, but where do a' the ill wives come frae?
— *Scotch.*

2. Age does not make us childish, as people say; it only finds us still true children. — *Goethe.*

3. Aliud legunt pueri, aliud viri, aliud senes. [Children read one way, men another, old men another.] — *Terence.*

4. A man at five may be a fool at fifteen.

5. A man at sixteen will prove a child at sixty.

6. An old knave is no babe.

7. A smiling boy seldom proves a good servant.

8. Auld folk are twice bairns. — *Scotch.*

9. Aus gescheidenen Kindern werden Gecken. [From clever children come fools.] — *German.*

10. Aus Kindern werden Leute, aus Jungfern werden Bräute. [From children come grown-up people, from maidens come brides.]
— *German.*

11. Better bairns greet [*i.e.* weep] than bearded men. — *Scotch.*

12. Childhood and youth see all the world in persons.
— *Emerson.*

13. Childhood often holds a truth in its feeble fingers, which the grasp of manhood cannot retain, and which it is the pride of utmost age to recover. — *Ruskin.*

14. Childhood shows the man, as morning shows the day.
— *Milton.*

15. Der Jüngling kämpft, damit der Greis geniesse. [The youth fights, in order that the old man may enjoy.] — *Goethe.*

16. Een diamant van een dochter wordt een glas van eene vrouw. [A diamond of a daughter becomes a glass of a wife.]
— *Dutch.*

17. Eident [*i.e.* diligent] youth makes easy age. — *Scotch.*

18.
Ewig jung zu bleiben
Ist, wie Dichter schreiben,
Höchstes Lebensgut;
Willst du es erwerben,
Musst du frühe sterben.
[To remain ever-young
Is, as poets write,
The highest good of life;
If thou wouldst acquire it,
Thou must die young.] — *Rückert.*

19. Fanciulli piccioli, dolor di testa; fanciulli grandi dolor di cuore. [Little children bring head-ache, big children, heart-ache.]
— *Italian.*

20. Giovine santo, diavolo vecchio. [Young saint, old devil.]
— *Italian.*

21. Hang a thief when he's young, and he'll no steal when he's auld. — *Scotch.*

22. Happy child! the cradle is still to thee an infinite space; once grown into a man, and the boundless world will be too small to thee. — *Schiller.*

23. He cometh to you with a tale which holdeth children from play, and old men from the chimney-corner.
— *Sir Philip Sidney.*

24.
He who mocks the infant's faith
Shall be mocked in age and death. — *Blake.*

25. How little is the promise of the child fulfilled in the man!
— *Ovid.*

26. If you lie upon roses when young, you will lie upon thorns when old.

27. Ihr Kinder, lernet jetzt genug,
Ihr lernt nichts mehr in alten Zeiten.
[Ye children, learn enough now;
When time has passed, you will learn nothing more.]
— *Pfeffel.*

28. In childhood a linen rag buys friendship. — *Angolese.*

29. In childhood be modest, in youth temperate, in manhood just, and in old age prudent. — *Socrates.*

30. In the opening bud you see the youthful thorns. — *Talmud.*

31. In youth one has tears without grief; in age, grief without tears. — *Jean Paul.*

32. Invention is the talent of youth, and judgment of age.
— *Swift.*

33. It's no child's play, when an old woman dances.
— *Low German.*

34. Jong rijs is te buigen, maar geen oude boomen. [A young twig can be bent, but not old trees.] — *Dutch.*

35. Jonge lui, domme lui; oude lui, koude lui. [Young folk, silly folk; old folk, cold folk.] — *Dutch.*

36. Junge Faullenzer, alte Bettler. [Young idlers, old beggars.]
— *German.*

37. Just at the age 'twixt boy and youth
When thought is speech, and speech is truth. — *Scott.*

38. La jeunesse devrait être une caisse d'épargne. [Youth ought to be a savings-bank.] — *Mme. Svetchin.*

39.   Learn young, learn fair;
    Learn auld, learn mair. — *Scotch.*

40.   Let the young people mind what the old people say,
    And where there is danger, keep out of the way.

41. Levity is artlessness in a child, a shameful fault in men, and a terrible folly in old age. — *La Rochefoucauld.*

42. Maids are May when they are maids, but the sky changes when they are wives. — *Shakespeare* (As You Like It, iv. 1).

43. Man schont die Alten, wie man die Kinder schont. [We spare old people, as we spare children.] — *Goethe.*

44. Man mut de kinner bugen, so lange se junk sünt. [Children must be bent while they are young.] — *Frisian.*

45. Man's second childhood begins when a woman gets hold of him. — *Barrie.*

46.   My son's my son till he hath got him a wife,
    But my daughter's my daughter all the days of her life.

47. Nicht die Kinder bloss speist man mit Märchen ab. [Not children alone are put off with tales.] — *Lessing.*

48. Old head and young hand.

49. Old heads will not suit young shoulders.

50. Old men are twice children. — *Greek.*

51. Once a man and twice a child.

52. Se il giovane sapesse, se il vecchio potesse, e' non c' è cosa che non si facesse. [If the youth but knew, if the old man but could, there is nothing which would not be done.] — *Italian.*

53. Study is the bane of boyhood, the element of youth, the indulgence of manhood, and the restorative of age. — *Landor.*

54. The household is the home of the man as well as of the child. — *Emerson.*

55. The man whom grown-up people love, children love still more. — *Jean Paul.*

56. There are in man, in the beginning, and at the end, two blank book-binder's leaves, — childhood and age. — *Jean Paul.*

57. We are children for the second time at twenty-one, and again when we are gray and put all our burden on the Lord.

— Barrie.

58. We bend the tree when it is young. — *Bulgarian.*

59. When bairns are young they gar their parents' heads ache; when they are auld they make their hearts break. — *Scotch.*

60. When children, we are sensualists, when in love, idealists.
— Goethe.

61. Wie die Alten sungen, so zwitschern auch die Jungen. [As the old birds sing, the young ones twitter.] — *German.*

62. Wir sind auch Kinder gewesen. [We too were once children.] — *German.*

63. Young men think that old men are fools; but old men know young men are fools. — *Chapman.*

64. Youth is a blunder; manhood, a struggle; old age, a regret.
— Disraeli.

65.　　Youth is full of sport, age's breath is short;
　　　Youth is nimble, age is lame;
　　Youth is hot and bold, age is weak and cold;
　　　Youth is wild, and age is tame. — *Shakespeare.*

CHAPTER XXXII.

PROVERBS, SAYINGS, ETC., ABOUT THE CHILD AND CHILDHOOD.

1. A beltless bairn cannot lie. — *Scotch.*
2. A burnt child dreads the fire.
3. A child is a Cupid become visible. — *Novalis.*
4. A daft nurse makes a wise wean. — *Scotch.*
5. A growing youth has a wolf in his belly.
6. A hungry belly has no ears.
7. A lisping lass is good to kiss.
8. All work and no play makes Jack a dull boy.
9.   An infant crying in the night,
       An infant crying for the light;
       And with no language but a cry. — *Tennyson.*
10. A pet lamb makes a cross ram.
11. A reasonable word should be received even from a child or a parrot. — *Sanskrit.*
12.   A simple child
       That lightly draws its breath,
       And feels its life in every limb,
       What should it know of death ? — *Wordsworth.*
13. As sair greets [as much weeps] the bairn that's paid at e'en as he that gets his whawks in the morning. — *Scotch.*
14. A tarrowing bairn was never fat. — *Scotch.*
15. Auld men are twice bairns. — *Scotch.*
16. Auld wives and bairns make fools of physicians. — *Scotch.*
17. Bairns are certain care, but nae sure joy. — *Scotch.*
18. Be born neither wise nor fair, but lucky. — *Russian.*
19. Behold the child, by Nature's kindly law,
Pleased with a rattle, tickled with a straw. — *Pope.*

20. Better be unborn than untaught. — *Gaelic.*

21. Birth's good, but breeding's better. — *Scotch.*

22. Bon sang ne peut mentir. Qui naquit chat court après les souris. [Good blood cannot lie. The kitten will chase the mouse.] — *French.*

23. Broken bread makes hale bairns. — *Scotch.*

24. By sports like these are all their cares beguil'd,
The sports of children satisfy the child. — *Goldsmith.*

25. Ce que l'enfant entend au foyer, est bientôt connu jusqu'au Moistre. [What children hear at the fireside is soon known as far as Moistre (a town in Savoy).] — *French.*

26. Che nasce bella nasce maritata. [A beautiful girl is born married.] — *Italian.*

27. Childhood and youth see the world in persons. — *Emerson.*

28. Childhood is the sleep of Reason. — *Rousseau.*

29. Children and chickens are always a-picking.

30. Children and drunken people tell the truth.

31. Children and fools speak the truth. — *Greek.*

32. Children and fools have many lives.

33. Children are certain sorrows, but uncertain joys. — *Danish.*

34. Children are the poor man's wealth. — *Danish.*

35. Children are very nice observers, and they will often perceive your slightest defects. — *Fénelon.*

36. Children cry for nuts and apples, and old men for gold and silver.

37. Children have more need of models than of critics.

— *Joubert.*

38. Children have wide ears and long tongues.

38a. Children increase the cares of life, but they mitigate the remembrance of death.

39. Children, like dogs, have so sharp and fine a scent, that they detect and hunt out everything — the bad before all the rest. — *Goethe.*

40. Children of wealth, or want, to each is given
One spot of green, and all the blue of heaven. — *Holmes.*

41.   Children pick up words as chickens peas,
And utter them again as God shall please.

42. Children should have their times of being off duty, like soldiers. — *Ruskin.*

43. Children to bed, and the goose to the fire.

44. Children should laugh, but not mock; and when they laugh, it should not be at the weaknesses and faults of others.
— *Ruskin.*

45. Children sweeten labours, but they make misfortunes more bitter. — *Bacon.*

46. Children tell in the streets what they hear round the hearth. — *Portuguese.*

47. Das kann ein Kind machen. [A child can do that — that is very easy.] — *German.*

48. Das Kind mit dem Bade verschütten. [To throw away the child with the bath — to reject the good along with the bad.]
— *German.*

49. Dat is en kinnerspil. [That's child's play — very easy.]
— *Frisian.*

50. Dat lütjeste un lefste. [The youngest and dearest.]
— *Frisian.*

51. Dawted [*i.e.* petted] bairns dow bear little. — *Scotch.*

52. Dawted dochters mak' dawly [slovenly] wives. — *Scotch.*

53.   Delightful task ! to rear the tender thought,
    To teach the young idea how to shoot. — *Thomson.*

54. De wesen wil bemint, de nem sin naver kind. [Who would be loved, let him take his neighbour's child.] — *Frisian.*

55. Die Kinder sind mein liebster Zeitvertreib. [Children are my dearest pastime.] — *Chamisso.*

56. Dochders zijn broze waaren. [Daughters are brittle ware.] — *Dutch.*

57. Do not meddle wi' the de'il and the laird's bairns. — *Scotch.*

58. Do not talk of a rape [rope] to a chiel whose father was hangit. — *Scotch.*

59. Do not train boys to learning by force or harshness; but direct them to it by what amuses their minds, so that you may be the better able to discover with accuracy the peculiar bent of the genius of each. — *Plato.*

60. Education begins its work with the first breath of life.
— *Jean Paul.*

61. Education commences at the mother's knee, and every word spoken within the hearing of little children tends towards the formation of character. — *Ballou.*

62. Eet maar Brod, dann wardst du grôt. [Eat bread and you'll grow.]—*Frisian.*

63. Ein Kind, kein Kind, zwei Kind, Spielkind, drei Kind, viel Kind, vier Kind, ein ganzes Hausvoll Kinder. [One child, no child; two children, playing children; three children, many children; four children, a whole house full of children.]
—*German* (with numerous variants).

64. Ein Laster kostet mehr als zwei Kinder. [One crime costs more than two children.]—*German.*

65. Es ist besser zehn Kinder gemacht, als ein einziges umgebracht. [It is better to have made ten children than to have destroyed one.]—*German.*

66. Fools and bairns shouldna see things half done.—*Scotch.*

67. Fools with bookish learning are children with edged tools; they hurt themselves, and put others in pain.—*Zimmermann.*

68. Fremde Kinder, wir lieben sie nie so sehr als die eignen. [We never love the children of others so well as our own.]
—*Goethe.*

69. Fremde Kinder werden wohl erzogen. [Other people's children are well brought up.]—*German.*

70.　　　Gie a bairn his will,
　　　And a whelp his fill,
　　　Nane o' them will e'er do well.—*Scotch.*

71. Give a child till he craves, and a dog while his tail doth wag, and you'll have a fair dog, but a foul knave.

72. Gie a dog an ill name and he'll soon be hanged.—*Scotch.*

73. God is kind to fou [*i.e.* drunken] folk and bairns.
—*Scotch.*

74. God ne'er sent the mouth but He sent the meat wi' t.
—*Scotch.*

75. God watches over little children and drunkards.—*Russian.*

76. Gude bairns are eith [easy] to lear [teach].—*Scotch.*

77. Happy is he that is happy in his children.

78. He who sends mouths will send meat.

79. Heimerzogen Kind ist bei den Leuten wie ein Rind. [A home-bred child acts like a cow.]—*German.*

80. He that's born to be hanged will never be drowned.

81. He that is born under a tippeny [two-penny] planet will ne'er be worth a groat.—*Scotch.*

82. I cuori fanciulli non veston a bruno. [A child's heart puts on no mourning.] — *Zendrini.*

83. If our child squints, our neighbour's has a cast in both eyes.

84. Ill bairns are best heard at hame. — *Scotch.*

85. It is the squalling child that gets the milk. — *Turkish.*

86. Je lieberes Kind, je schärfere Rute. [The dearer the child, the sharper the rod.] — *German.*

87. Kinder hat man, Kinder kriegt man. [Children bring children.] — *German.*

88. Kinder kommen von Herzen und gehen zu Herzen. [Children come from the heart, and go to the heart.] — *German.*

89. Kinder und Bienstöcke nehmen bald ab bald zu. [Children and bee-hives now decrease, now increase.] — *German.*

90.　　　　Kind's hand is ball füllt,
　　　　Kind's zurn is ball stillt.
　　　[A child's hand is soon filled,
　　　　A child's anger is soon stilled.] — *Low German.*

91. Late children are early orphans. — *Spanish.*

92. Les enfants sont ce qu'on les fait. [Children are what we make them.] — *French.*

93. Let thy child's first lesson be obedience, and the second will be what thou wilt. — *Franklin.*

94. Liebe Kinder haben viele Namen. [Dear children have many names.] — *German.*

95. Lieber ungezogene, als verzogene Kinder. [Better unbred children than ill-bred ones.] — *German.*

96. Like the wife wi' the mony daughters, the best comes hindmost. — *Scotch.*

97. Little pitchers have big ears.

98. Little ones are taught to be proud of their clothes before they can put them on. — *Locke.*

99. Lütze potten hebben ok oren [*i.e.* little children have ears]. — *Low German.*

100. Man is wholly man only when he plays. — *Schiller.*

101. Maxima debetur pueris reverentia. [The greatest respect is due to boys (youth).] — *Juvenal.*

102. Men are generally more careful of the breed of their horses and dogs than of their children. — *William Penn.*

103. Mony a ane kisses the bairn for love of the nurice. — *Scotch.*

104. More children, more luck. — *German.*

105. Nessuno nasce maestro. [No one is born master.]
— *Italian.*

106. 'N gôd Kind, wen't slöpt. [A good child, when it sleeps.]
— *Frisian.*

107. O banish the tears of children! Continual rains upon the blossoms are hurtful. — *Jean Paul.*

108. O formose puer, nimium ne crede colori. [Oh, beauteous boy, trust not too much to thy rosy cheeks.] — *Virgil.*

109. Of bairns' gifts ne'er be fain,
Nae sooner they give but they seek them again.
— *Scotch.*

110. One chick keeps a hen busy.

111. Our young men are terribly alike. — *Alex. Smith.*

112. Pars minima est ipsa puella sui. [The girl herself is the smallest part of herself.] — *Ovid.*

113. Parvum parva decent. [Small things become the small.]
— *Horace.*

114. Play is the first poetry of the human being. — *Jean Paul.*

115. Qui aime bien, châtie bien. [Who loves well chastises well.] — *French.*

116. Qui parcit virgæ odit filium. [Who spareth the rod hateth his child.] — *Latin.*

117. Reckless youth maks ruefu' eild [age]. — *Scotch.*

118. Royet [wild] lads may make sober men. — *Scotch.*

119. Rule youth well, for eild will rule itself. — *Scotch.*

120. Salt and bread make the cheeks red. — *German.*

121. Seven nurses cost the child an eye. — *Russian.*

122. Small birds [*i.e.* children] must have meat.

123. Sores are not to be shown to flies, and children are not to be taught to lie. — *Malay.*

124. Spare the rod and spoil the child.

125. Teach your children poetry; it opens the mind, lends grace to wisdom, and makes the heroic virtues hereditary. — *Mahomet.*

126. Tenez la bride haute à votre fils. [Keep a tight rein over your son.] — *French.*

127. That's the piece a step-bairn never gat. — *Scotch.*

128. The bairn speaks in the field what he hears at the fireside.
— *Scotch.*

129. The bearing and the training of a child is woman's wisdom. — *Tennyson.*

130. The best horse needs breeding and the aptest child needs teaching. — *Arabic.*

131. The boy's will is the wind's will. — *Lapp.*

132. The chief art is to make all that children have to do sport and play. — *Locke.*

133. The child says nothing but what he heard at the fireside. — *Spanish.*

134. The de'il's bairns hae the de'il's luck. — *Scotch.*

135. The heart is a child; it desires what it sees. — *Turkish.*

136. The heart of childhood is all mirth. — *Keble.*

137. The king is the strength of the weak; crying is the strength of children. — *Sanskrit.*

138. The right law of education is that you take the best pains with the best material. — *Ruskin.*

139. The spring is the youth of trees, wealth is the youth of men, beauty is the youth of women, intelligence is the youth of the young. — *Sanskrit.*

140. The plays of children are the germinal leaves of all later life. — *Froebel.*

141. The time of breeding is the time of doing children good. — *George Herbert.*

142. They were scant o' bairns that brought you up. — *Scotch.*

143. The youth gets together his materials to build a bridge to the moon, or perchance a palace on the earth; at length middle-aged, he concludes to build a woodshed with them. — *Thoreau.*

144. They who educate children well are more to be honoured than they who produce them; these gave them life only, those the art of well-living. — *Aristotle.*

145. To a child all weather is cold.

146. To endure is the first and most necessary lesson a child has to learn. — *Rousseau.*

147. To write down to children's understandings is a mistake; set them on the scent, and let them puzzle it out. — *Scott.*

148. Un enfant brûlé craint le feu. [A burnt child dreads the fire.] — *French.*

149. Ungezogene Kinder gehen zu Werk wie Rinder. [Unbred children go to work like cattle.] — *German.*

150. Viel Kinder viel Vaterunser, viel Vaterunser viel Segen. [Many children, many Paternosters; many Paternosters, many blessings.] — *German.*

151. We ought not to teach the children the sciences, but give them a taste for them. — *Rousseau.*

152. Wen de gôsen wâter sên, dan willen se drinken. [When the geese (*i.e.* children) see water, they want to drink.] — *Frisian.*

153. Wenn das Kind ertrunken ist, deckt man den Brunnen. [When the child is drowned, the well is covered.] — *German.*

154. Wenn Kinder und Narren zu Markte gehen, lösen die Krämer Geld. [When children and fools go to market, the dealers make money.] — *German.*

155. Wenn Kinder wohl schreien, so leben sie lange. [When children cry well, they live long.] — *German.*

156. Wer wil diu kint vraget, der wil si liegen leren. [Who asks children many questions teaches them to lie.]
— *Old High German.*

157. What children hear at home soon flies abroad.

158. When children remain quiet, they have done something wrong.

159. Women and bairns lein [hide] what they ken not.
— *Scotch.*

160. Women and children should retire when the sun does.
— *Portuguese.*

161. You should lecture neither child nor woman. — *Russian.*

Index to Proverbs, etc.

Following is an index of peoples and authors for the foregoing proverbs and sayings (the references are to pages): —

A, PEOPLES.

2 D

B, AUTHORS, ETC.

For the collection of proverbs and sayings here given, the writer acknowledges his indebtedness to the numerous dictionaries of quotations and proverbs, of which he has been able to avail himself.

CHAPTER XXXIII.

Conclusion.

In these pages the "Child in Primitive Culture" has been considered in many lands and among many peoples, and the great extent of the activities of childhood among even the lowest races of men fully demonstrated. That the child is as important to the savage, to the barbarous peoples, as to the civilized, is evident from the vast amount of lore and deed of which he is the centre both in fact and in fiction. The broader view which anthropologists and psychologists are coming to take of the primitive races of man must bring with it a larger view of the primitive child. Still less than the earliest men, were their children, mere animals; indeed, possibly, nay even probably, the children of primitive man, while their childhood lasts, are the equals, if not the superiors, of those of our own race in general intellectual capacity. With the savage as with the European of to-day, the "child is father of the man."

The primitive child, as language and folk-lore demonstrate, has been weighed, measured, and tested physically and mentally by his elders, much as we ourselves are doing now, but in ruder fashion—there are primitive anthropometric and psychological laboratories as proverb and folk-speech abundantly testify, and examinations as harassing and as searching as any we know of to-day. Schools, nay primitive colleges, even, of the prophets, the shamans, and the *magi*, the race has had in earlier days, and everywhere through the world the activities of childhood have been appealed to, and the race has wonderfully profited by its wisdom, its *naïveté*, its ingenuity, and its touch of divinity.

Upon language, religion, society, and the arts the child has had a lasting influence, both passive and active, unconscious, suggest-

403

ive, creative. History, the stage, music, and song have been its debtors in all ages and among all peoples.

To the child language owes many of its peculiarities, and the multiplicity of languages perhaps their very existence. Religion has had the child long as its servant, and from the faith and confidence of youth and the undying mother-love have sprung the thought of immortality and the Messiah-hope that greets us all over the globe. Even among the most primitive races, it is the children who are " of the Kingdom of Heaven," and the " Fall of Man" is not from a fabled Garden of Eden, but from the glory of childhood into the stern realities of manhood. As a social factor the child has been of vast importance; children have sat upon thrones, have dictated the policies of Church and of State, and from them the wisest in the land have sought counsel and advice. As oracles, priests, shamans, and *thaumaturgi*, children have had the respect and veneration of whole peoples, and they have often been the very mouth-piece of deity, standing within the very gates of heaven. As hero and adventurer, passing over into divinity, the child has explored earth, sea, and sky, descending into nethermost hell to rescue the bones of his father, and setting ajar the gates of Paradise, that the radiant glory may be seen of his mother on earth. Finally, as Christ sums up all that is divine in men, so does the Christ-Child sum up all that is God-like in the child. The Man-Jesus stands at the head of mankind, the Child-Jesus is the first of the children of men. All the activities and callings of the child, the wisdom, the beauty, the innocence of childhood find in folk-belief and folk-faith their highest, perfect expression in the Babe of Bethlehem.

True is it as ten thousand years ago : —

> " Before life's sweetest mystery still
> The heart in reverence kneels ;
> The wonder of the primal birth
> The latest mother feels."

Motherhood and childhood have been the world's great teachers, and the prayer of all the race should be : —

> " Let not (the) cultured years make less
> The childhood charm of tenderness."

BIBLIOGRAPHY.

THE Bibliography here given is intended to serve the double purpose of enabling readers of this book to verify the statements made and the citations from the numerous authorities referred to in the compilation of the work, with as little difficulty as possible, and of furnishing to such as may desire to carry on extended reading in any of the subjects touched upon in the book a reasonable number of titles of the more recent and valuable treatises dealing with such topics.

All references in the body of the book to works listed in the Bibliography are by number and page. Thus: 6. 26 means that the quotation is from, or the opinion is derived from, *Bachofen, J. J.*, Das Mutterrecht, S. 26; 127. II. 180 means *Post, A. H.*, Afrikanische Jurisprudenz, II. Th., S. 180; 300. 15 means *Lombroso, C.*, The Man of Genius, p. 15; 480 (1893). 140 means *Journal of American Folk-Lore*, 1893, p. 140.

A. MOTHER, FATHER, FAMILY, SOCIETY.

1. ACHELIS, T. : Die Entwickelung der Ehe. Berlin, 1893. 125 S. 8vo.
2. Actes du congrès international des œuvres et institutions féminines. Paris, 1890. 530 pp. 8vo.
3. ADAM, L. : Du genre dans les diverses langues. Paris, 1883. 36 pp. 8vo.
4. ANDERSEN, HANS C. : La Mère. Conte de Hans Christian Andersen en 22 Langues. St. Pétersbourg, 1894.
5. AVERY, J. : Polyandry in India and Thibet. *Amer. Antiq. and Or. Journ.* Vol. IV., pp. 48–53.
6. BACHOFEN, J. J. : Das Mutterrecht. Eine Untersuchung über die Gynokratie der alten Welt nach ihrer religiösen und rechtlichen Natur. Stuttgart, 1861. xl, 435 S. 4to.
7. BACON, ALICE M. : Japanese Girls and Women. London, 1891. 330 pp. 8vo.
8. BANDELIER, A. F. : On the Social Organization and Mode of Government of the Ancient Mexicans. *Rep. Peab. Mus.* II., pp. 557–699.
9. BASTIAN, A. : Matriarchat und Patriarchat. *Ztschr. f. Ethnol. (Berlin), Verhndl.*, 1886, S. 331–341.

10. Bawa, —: Marriage Customs of the Moors of Ceylon. *Journ. Ceylon Branch Roy. Asiatic Soc.* Vol. X. (1888), pp. 219–262.

11. Belilovski, K. A.: [Woman in Siberia (Medico-ethnographical Sketch)]. *Sborn. rabot akush i zhensk. bolez.* . . . *Slavjanski* [etc.]. St. Petersburg, 1894. Vol. I., pp. 527–629.

12. Bergel, Jos.: Die Eheverhältnisse der alten Juden. Leipzig, 1881.

13. Bernhöft, F.: Verwandschaftsnamen und Eheformen der nordamerikanischen Volksstämme. Rostock, 1888.

14. Bertholon, M.: Les formes de la famille chez les premiers habitants de l'Afrique du nord d'après les écrivains de l'antiquité et des coutumes modernes. *Arch. de l'Anthr. Crim.* Vol. VIII. (1893), pp. 581–614.

15. Bertillon, J.: Études démographiques du divorce et de la séparation de corps dans les différents pays de l'Europe. Paris, 1883. 2 vols. 116, 257 pp. 8vo.

16. Bloomfield, M.: Women as Mourners in the Atharva-Veda. *Proc. Amer. Orient. Soc.* Vol. XV. (1890), pp. xlix. ff.

16 a. Blyth, D.: Notes on the Traditions and Customs of the Natives of Fiji in relation to Conception, Pregnancy, and Parturition. *Glasgow Med. Journ.* Vol. XXVIII. (1887), pp. 176–186.

17. Boshaftes von der Gattin und Schwiegermutter. Sammlung von Sprüchen, Reimen und Anekdoten. Leipzig, 1882.

18. Budge, E. A. W.: The Mummy: Chapters on Egyptian Funeral Archæology. Cambridge, 1893. xvi, 404 pp. 8vo.

19. Buschmann, J. C. E.: Ueber den Naturlaut. *Königl. Akad. d. Wissensch. (Berlin), Abh. a. d. J.* 1852. III. Th., S. 391–423. Reprinted (separate) as: Buschmann, J. C. E., Ueber den Naturlaut. Berlin, 1853. 34 S. 4to. Translation: On Natural Sounds, by Prof. J. C. E. Buschmann. Transl. by Campbell Clarke. . . . *Philol. Soc. (London) Proc.* Vol. VI. (1855), pp. 188–206.

20. Camboulives, M.: L'Homme et la Femme à tous les Âges de la Vie. Étude hygiénique, médicale, physiologique, sociale et morale. Paris, 1890. 388 pp. 8vo.

21. Carr, L.: Social and Political Status of Woman among the Iroquois Indians. *Rep. Peab. Mus.* (Cambridge, Mass.). III., pp. 207–232.

22. Chamberlain, A. F. · Primitive Woman as Poet. *Proc. Am. Ass. Adv. Sci.* XLII. (1893), Salem, 1894, p. 317.

23. Chauvin, Jeanne: Étude historique sur les professions accessibles aux Femmes. Paris, 1892. 296 pp. 8vo.

24. Child, L. M.: History of the Condition of Women in Various Ages and Nations. 2 vols. 1832.

25. Codrington, R. H.: Social Regulations in Melanesia. *Journ. Anthr. Inst.* (London). Vol. XVIII. (1889), pp. 300–313.

25 a. Convers, D.: Marriage and Divorce in the United States. Philadelphia, 1894.

26. Coriveaud, A.: Hygiène des Familles. Paris, 1890. 328 pp. 8vo.

27. Corre, A.: La Mère et l'Enfant dans les Races humaines. Paris, 1882.

28. Crawley, A. E.: Sexual Taboo: A Study in the Relations of the Sexes. *Journ. Anthr. Inst.* (London). Vol. XXIV. (1894-5), pp. 126-158, 219-235.

29. Dahn, F.: Das Weib im altgermanischen Recht und Leben. Samml. gemeinnütz. Vorträge. Prag. No. 71.

30. Danks, B.: Marriage Customs of the New Britain Group. *Journ. Anthr. Inst.* (London). Vol. XVIII. (1889), pp. 281-284.

31. Dargun, L.: Mutterrecht und Raubehe und ihre Reste im germanischen Recht und Leben. Breslau, 1883.

32. Dargun, L.: Studien zum ältesten Familienrecht: Erster Theil. Mutter- und Vaterrecht. Leipzig, 1892. 155 S. 8vo.

33. De Gubernatis, A.: Storia comparata degli usi natalizi in Italia e presso gli altri popoli Indo-Europei. Milano, 1878.

34. Devine, E. T.: The Economic Function of Woman. *Ann. Amer. Acad. Polit. and Soc. Sci.* (Philadelphia). Vol. V. (1894-5), pp. 45-60.

35. Dorsey, J. O.: Omaha Sociology. *Third Ann. Rep. Bur. Ethn.* (1881-2), Washington, 1884, pp. 205-370.

36. Drummond, II.: The Evolution of Man. Being the Lowell Lectures delivered at Boston, Mass., April, 1893, by Professor Henry Drummond. Edited by William Templeton. Philadelphia, 1893. 244 pp. 12mo.

37. Drummond, II.: The Ascent of Man (Lowell Lectures). New York, 1894. 346 pp. 8vo.

38. Ebers, G.: Woman in Ancient Egypt. *Catholic World*, 1880-1881, pp. 563-572.

39. Eckart, R.: Mutterliebe und -Leben in den schönsten Liedern verherrlicht. Herausg. v. Rudolf Eckart. Stuttgart, 1890.

40. Ellis, A. B.: On Polyandry. *Pop. Sci. Mo.* (New York). Vol. XXXIX. (1891), pp. 801-809.

41. Ellis, A. B.: Marriage and Kinship among the Ancient Israelites. *Ibid.* Vol. XLII. (1892-3), pp. 325-337.

42. Ellis, Havelock: Man and Woman: A Study of Human Secondary Sexual Characters. London and New York, 1894. xiv, 409 pp. 8vo.

43. Engelmann, G.: Labor [Parturition] amongst Primitive Peoples. St. Louis, 1883. 227 pp. 8vo. Also German Transl., Wien, 1884.

44. Engels, F.: Der Ursprung der Familie, des Privateigenthums und des Staats. Hottingen-Zürich, 1884.

45. Faust, J. H.: "Das, was Wir lieben," im Rahmen des Sprichwortes. Humor, Witz und Satire über die Töchter Eva's. 2te Aufl. Hamburg. 102 S.

46. Fawcett, F.: On basivis: Women, who, through dedication to a deity, assume masculine privileges. *Journ. Anthr. Soc.* (Bombay). Vol. II. (1891), pp. 322-354.

47. Felice, L. V. de: Il divorzio e la donna. Napoli, 1893. 63 pp. 16mo.

48. FELKIN, R. W. : Ueber Lage und Stellung der Frau bei der Geburt, auf Grund eigener Beobachtung bei den Negervölkern der oberen Nil-Gegenden. Marburg, 1885. 72 S. 8vo.

49. FÉRÉ, CH. : La famille névropathique. Théorie tératologique de l'hérédité et de la dégénérescence. Paris, 1894. 334 pp. 12mo.

50. FERRERO, G. : The Problem of Woman from a Bio-Sociological Point of View. *Monist* (Chicago). Vol. IV. (1894), pp. 261-274.

51. FEWKES, J. W. : The Kinship of a Tañoan-speaking Community. *Amer. Anthrop.* (Washington). Vol. VII. (1894), pp. 162-167.

52. FEWKES, J. W. : Kinship of the Tusayan Villagers. *Ibid.* 394-417.

53. FINCK, H. T. : Romantic Love and Personal Beauty. Their Development, Causal Relations, Historic and National Peculiarities. 2 vols. London, 1887. 8vo.

54. FISCHER, F. C. J. : Ueber die Probenächte der deutschen Bauernmädchen. Zürich. o. J.

55. FISON, L., and HOWITT, A. W. : Kamilaroi and Kurnai. Group-Marriage and Relationship, and Marriage by Elopement, etc. Melbourne, 1880.

56. FISON, L. : Australian Marriage Laws. *Journ. Anthr. Inst.* (London). Vol. IX., pp. 354-358.

57. FISON, L. : Group-Marriage and Relationship. *Rep. Austral. Ass. Adv. Sci.* (Vol. IV., 1892.) Hobart, 1893. pp. 688-697.

58. FLOESSEL, E. : Die Schwiegermutter. Kulturgeschichtliche Beiträge. Dresden, 1890.

59. FOL, H. : La ressemblance entre époux. *Rev. Scientif.* (Paris). XLVII. (1891), pp. 47-49.

60. GAMBLE, ELIZA B. : The Evolution of Woman. An Inquiry into the Dogma of her Inferiority to Man. New York, 1894. 356 pp. 8vo.

61. GARNETT, Miss L. M. J. : The Women of Turkey and their Folk-Lore. With Chapters on the Ethnography of Turkey, Folk-Conceptions of Nature, and the Origin of Matriarchy by J. S. Stuart Glennie. Christian, Jewish, and Moslem Women. London, 1890-1. 2 vols. 461, 632 pp. 8vo.

62. GARNIER, A. : Anomalies Sexuelles. Paris, 1889. 544 pp. 8vo.

63. GATSCHET, A. S. : Sex-Denoting Nouns in American Languages. *Trans. Amer. Philol. Assoc.* Vol. XX. (1891), pp. 159-171.

64. GEDDES, P., and J. H. THOMPSON : The Evolution of Sex. London and New York, 1890. xvi, 332 pp. 8vo.

65. GESSMANN, G. W. : Die Männerhand und ihre Bedeutung für die Erforschung des männlichen Charakters. Eine physiognomische Studie. Berlin, 1894. 92 S. 8vo. 29 Abbild.

66. GESSMANN, G. W. : Die Frauenhand und ihre Bedeutung für die Erkenntniss des weiblichen Charakters. Eine physiognomische Studie. Berlin, 1894. 92 S. 8vo. 21 Abbild.

67. GIRARD-TEULON, A. : La Mère chez certains peuples de l'Antiquité. Paris, 1867. 60 pp. 8vo.

68. GIRARD-TEULON, A.: Les Origines du Mariage et de la Famille. Paris, 1884. xxiii, 525 pp. 8vo.

69. GONCOURT, EDMOND ET JULES DE: La Femme aux dix-huitième Siècle. Nouv. éd. Paris, 1877.

70. GRINNELL, G. B.: Marriage among the Pawnees. *Amer. Anthrop.* Vol. IV. (1891), pp. 275–281.

71. HABERLANDT, C.: Altjungfernschicksal nach dem Tode. *Globus.* XXXIV. Bd. (1878).

72. HALBERT, H. C.: Courtship and Marriage among the Choctaws of Mississippi. *American Naturalist.* March, 1882.

73. HARRISON, C.: Religion and Family among the Haidas (Queen Charlotte Islands). *Journ. Anthr. Inst.* (London). Vol. XXI. (1891), pp. 14–29.

74. HAUPT, P.: The Babylonian Woman's Language. *Amer. Journ. Philol.* (Baltimore). Vol. V., pp. 68–84.

75. HELD, Jos. v.: Königtum und Göttlichkeit. *Am Ur-Quell* (Lunden). III. Bd. (1892), S. 119–124, 152–157, 195–197, 220–225, 241–243.

76. HELLWALD, F. VON: Die menschliche Familie. Leipzig, 1889.

77. HENNE AM RHYN, O.: Die Frau in der Kulturgeschichte. 2. Aufl. Berlin, 1892.

78. HERING, O.: Die Frauen Japans im Spiegel der für sie bestimmten Literatur. *Mitth. d. deutsch. Gesellsch. f. Natur- und Völkerkunde Ostasiens* (Tokio). V. Bd., Yokohama, 1889, Heft 41, S. 10–27.

79. HIGGINSON, T. W.: Common Sense about Women. Boston, 1892. 403 pp. 8vo.

80. HOWITT, A. W., and LORIMER FISON. From Mother-Right to Father-Right. *Journ. Anthr. Inst.* (London). Vol. XII. (1882).

80 a. JESSUP, H. H.: The Women of the Arabs. London, 1874.

81. KATSCHER, L.: Bilder aus dem chinesischen Leben. Mit besonderer Rücksicht auf Sitten und Gebräuche. Leipzig u. Heidelberg, 1881.

82. KIDD, BENJ.: Social Evolution. New ed. New York, 1894. x, 348 pp. 8vo.

83. KIRKITAR, K. R.: On the ceremonies observed among Hindus during Pregnancy and Parturition. *Journ. Anthr. Soc.* (Bombay). Vol. I. (1889), pp. 394–404.

84. KOVALEVSKY, M.: Modern Customs and Ancient Laws of Russia (Ilchester Lectures for 1889–90). London, 1891. x, 260 pp. 8vo.

85. KRABBES, TH.: Die Frau im altfranzösischen Carlsepos. Marburg, 1884.

86. KRAFFT-EBING, FREIH. R. v.: Psychopathia Sexualis. Eine klinisch-forensische Studie. Stuttgart, 1886.

87. KRAUSS, F. S.: Sitte und Brauch bei den Südslaven. Wien, 1885.

88. KRAUSS, F. S.: Das Mundschaftsrecht des Mannes über die Ehefrau bei den Südslaven. *Mitth. d. anthr. Gesellsch.* (Wien). XV. Bd. (1885).

89. KUBARY, J. S.: Aus dem samoanischen Familienleben. *Globus.* XLVII. Bd. (1885).

90. KULISCHER, M. : Die geschlechtliche Zuchtwahl bei dem Menschen in der Urzeit. *Ztschr f. Ethnol.* (Berlin). VIII. Bd. (1876), S. 140–157.

91. KULISCHER, M. : Intercommunale Ehe durch Raub und Kauf. *Ibid.* X. Bd. (1878), S. 193–225.

92. KULISCHER, M. : Die communale "Zeitehe" und ihre Ueberreste. *Arch. f. Anthrop.* (Braunschweig). XI. Bd. (1879), S. 215–229.

93. LACOMBE, P.: La Famille dans la société Romaine, étude de Moralité comparée. Paris, 1889.

94. LEA, H. C. : An Historical Sketch of Sacerdotal Celibacy in the Christian Church. Boston, 1884.

95. LE BON, G. : L'Homme et les Sociétés. Paris, 1881. 2 vols. 8vo.

96. LECKY, W. E. H. : History of European Morals from Augustus to Charlemagne. London, 1877. 2 vols.

97. LEGOUVÉ, E. : Histoire morale des Femmes. Paris, 1882. vii, 432 pp. 8vo.

98. LEHMANN, K. : Verlobung und Hochzeit in den nordgermanischen Rechten des frühesten Mittelalters. München, 1882.

99. LETOURNEAU, CH. : The Evolution of Marriage and the Family. London, 1891.

100. LETOURNEAU, CH.: Sociology based upon Ethnography. Transl. H. M. Trollope. New ed. London, 1893. xv, 608 pp. 8vo.

101. LETOURNEAU, CH. : L'Évolution Politique dans les diverses Races humaines. Paris, 1890. xxiii, 561 pp. 8vo.

102. LICHTSCHEIN, L. : Die Ehe nach mosaisch-talmudischer Auffassung. Leipzig, 1889.

103. LIPPERT, G. : Die Geschichte der Familie. Stuttgart, 1884. 260 S. 8vo.

104. LOMBROSO, C., and G. FERRERO: The Female Offender. New York, 1895. xxvi, 313 pp. 8vo.

105. LOTI, P. : Woman in Japan. *Harper's Monthly* (New York). Vol. LXXXII. (1890), pp. 119–131.

105 a. LÜBBEN, A. : "Modersprak." *Correspbl. f. niederd. Sprachfrschg.* VI. *Jahrg.* (1881), S. 64–66; VII., S. 7, 63; VIII., S. 75; XII., S. 55–56; XIII., S. 16.

106. LUCKOCK, H. M.: The History of Marriage, Jewish and Christian, in Relation to Divorce and Certain Forbidden Degrees. London, 1894.

107. LUMHOLTZ, C. : Tarahumari Life and Customs. *Scribner's Mag.* (New York). Vol. XVI. (1894), pp. 296–311.

108. MACFARLANE, A. : Analysis of Relationships of Consanguinity and Affinity. *Journ. Anthr. Inst.* (London). Vol. XII. (1882).

109. MAINOV, W. N. : Wedding Customs and Legal Observances among the Mordwins [in Finnish]. 2 pts. Helsingfors, 1883–1888.

110. MANTEGAZZA, P. : Anthropologisch-culturhistorische Studien über die Geschlechtsverhältnisse des Menschen. Jena, 1886.

111. Mason, O. T.: The Human Beast of Burden. *Smithson. Rep.*, 1886–1887. Pt. II., pp. 237–295.

112. Mason, O. T.: Woman's Share in Primitive Culture. *Amer. Antiq. and Orient. Journ.* Vol. XI., pp. 1–13.

113. Mason, O. T.: Woman's Share in Primitive Culture. New York, 1894. xiii, 295 pp. 8vo.

114. McLennan, J. F.: The Patriarchal Theory. London, 1885.

115. McLennan, J. F.: Studies in Ancient History, comprising a reprint of Primitive Marriage. A new ed. London, 1886. xxxi, 387 pp. 8vo.

116. Miklucho-Maclay, v.: Geschlechtlicher Umgang mit Mädchen vor der Geschlechtsreife derselben. *Ztschr. f. Ethnol.* (Berlin), 1880. S. 88.

117. Morgan, L. H.: Ancient Society. New York, 1878. xvi, 500 pp. 8vo.

118. Morgan, L. H.: Systems of Consanguinity and Affinity of the Human Family. (*Smithson. Contrib. to Knowl.*, Vol. XVII.) Washington, 1871. xii, 590 pp. 4to.

119. Morgan, L. H.: Houses and House-Life of the American Aborigines. (*Contrib. to North Amer. Ethnol.*, Vol. V.) Washington, 1881. xiv, 281 pp. 4to.

120. Morley, Margaret W.: A Song of Life. Chicago, 1891. 156 pp. 8vo.

121. Mortillet, G. de: Origines de la chasse, de la pêche et de l'agriculture. I. Chasse, pêche, domestication. Paris, 1890. xiii, 570 pp. 8vo.

122. Morton, F. W.: Woman in Epigram. Flashes of Wit, Wisdom and Satire from the World's Literature. Compiled by Frederick W. Morton. Chicago, 1894.

123. Parker, E. H.: Comparative Chinese Family Law. *China Review* (Hong-Kong). Vol. VIII. (1879–1880).

124. Pischon, C. N.: Der Einfluss des Islâm auf das häusliche, sociale und politische Leben seiner Bekenner. Leipzig, 1881.

125. Ploss, H.: Das Weib in der Natur- und Völkerkunde. Anthropologische Studien von Dr. H. Ploss. Dritte umgearb. u. stark verm. Aufl. Nach d. Tode des Verf. bearb. u. herausgeg. v. Dr. Max Bartels. Leipzig, 1891. 2 Bde., xxiii, 575; vii, 684 S. 8vo.

126. Porter, Rose: About Women: What Men have Said. Chosen and arranged by Rose Porter. New York and London, 1894. 207 pp.

127. Post, A. H.: Afrikanische Jurisprudenz. Ethnologisch-juristische Beiträge zur Kenntniss der einheimischen Rechte Afrikas. 2 Thle. in einem Bd. Oldenburg u. Leipzig, 1887. xx, 480; xxx, 192 S. 8vo.

128. Post, A. H.: Die Geschlechtsverhältnisse der Urzeit und die Entstehung der Ehe. Oldenburg, 1875.

129. Post, A. H.: Studien zur Entwickelungsgeschichte des Familienrechtes. Ein Beitrag zu einer allgemeinen vergleichenden Rechtswissenschaft auf ethnologischer Basis. Oldenburg u. Leipzig, 1890.

130. Post, A. H.: Grundriss der ethnologischen Jurisprudenz. Oldenburg, 1894–1895. 2 Bde. Gr. 8vo. I. Bd., 1894, xii, 473 S.; II. Bd., 1895, xv, 744 S.

130 a. Rademacher, C.: Ueber die Bedeutung des Herdes. *Am Ur-Quell*, 1893. S. 57–60.

131. Raphael, A.: Die Sprache der Proverbia qui dicuntur super naturam feminarum. Berlin, 1887. 8vo.

132. Reinsberg-Düringsfeld, O. Freih. v.: Die Frau im Sprichwort. Leipzig, 1862.

133. Rocco, G.: La filosofia del matrimonio ed i mali individuali e sociali del divorzio. Napoli, 1892. 121 pp. 8vo.

134. Roger, C.: Social Life in Scotland from Early to Recent Times. 3 Vols. Edinburgh, 1884–1886.

135. Rosenbaum, J.: Geschichte der Lustseuche im Alterthume. 3 Abdr. Halle, 1882.

136. Sabelljin, J.: History of Russian Life from the Oldest Times. [In Russian.] Moscow, 1876–1879. 1167 pp.

137. Savage, M. J.: Man, Woman, and Child. Boston, 1884. 211 pp. 8vo.

138. Sayce, A. H.: Social Life among the Assyrians and Babylonians. London, 1893. 126 pp.

139. Schellong, O.: Ueber Familien-Leben und Gebräuche der Papuas der Umgebung von Finschhafen. *Ztschr. f. Ethnol.* (Berlin). XXI., Bd. (1889), S. 10–25.

140. Scherer, O.: Bilder aus dem serbischen Volks- und Familienleben. Neusatz, 1882.

141. Scheurl, O. v.: Das gemeine deutsche Eherecht. Erlangen, 1882.

142. Schlagintweit, E.: Die Hindu-Wittwe in Indien. *Globus.* XLIII. Bd. (1883).

143. Schmidt, K.: Jus primæ noctis. Freiburg im B., 1881.

144. Schmidt, K.: Der Streit über das jus primæ noctis. *Ztschr. f. Ethnol.* (Berlin). XVI. Bd. (1884), S. 18–59.

145. Schroeder, L. v.: Die Hochzeitsgebräuche der Esten und einiger anderer finnisch-ugrischen Völkerschaften in Vergleichung mit denen der indogermanischen Völker. Berlin, 1888.

146. Schwieriger-Lerchenfeld, A. Freih. v.: Das Frauenleben der Erde. Wien-Pest-Leipzig, 1881.

147. Sibree, J.: Relationships and the Names used for them among the Peoples of Madagascar, etc. *Journ. Anthr. Inst.* (London). Vol. IX. (1879).

148. Sighele, L.: La foule criminelle. Paris, 1892. 185 pp. 8vo.

149. Smith, E. M.: Woman in Sacred Song. A Library of Hymns, Religious Poems, and Sacred Music by Women. Compiled and edited by E. M. Smith (Mrs. G. C. S.). Boston, 1885. xl, 883 pp. 4to.

150. Smith, Mrs. Burton: The Mother in Woman's Advancement. *Pop Sci. Mo.* (New York). Vol. XLVI. (1895), pp. 622–626.

151. Smith, W. R.: Marriage and Kinship in Early Arabia. Cambridge, (Engl.), 1885.

152. Starcke, C. N.: The Primitive Family in its Origin and Development. New York, 1889. 315 pp. 8vo.

153. Stein, L. v.: Die Frau auf dem Gebiete der Nationalökonomie. 4. Aufl. Stuttgart, 1876.

154. Stricker, W.: Ethnographische Untersuchungen über die kriegerischen Weiber (Amazonen) der alten und neuen Welt. *Arch. f. Anthr.* (Braunschweig). V. Bd. (1872), S. 220 ff., S. 451.

155. Thulié, H.: La Femme. Essai de sociologie, physiologie. Ce qu'elle a été, ce qu'elle est. Les théories : ce qu'elle doit être. Paris, 1885. 8vo.

156. Trask, K.: Motherhood and Citizenship. *Forum* (New York). Vol. XVIII. (1895), pp. 607–618.

157. Treichel, A.: Lactation beim männlichen Geschlechte. *Am Ur-Quell.* IV. Bd. (1893), S. 70–71.

158. Trumbull, J. H.: On Algonkin Names for Man. *Amer. Philol. Assoc. Trans.* (1871), Hartford (Conn.), 1872, pp. 138–159.

159. Trumbull, H. C.: Studies in Oriental Social Life. Philadelphia, 1894.

160. Uzanne, O.: La femme à Paris. Nos Contemporaines. Paris, 1894. Gr. 8vo.

161. Villemont, M.: Dictionnaire historique et scientifique de l'amour et du mariage. Paris, 1886. 480 pp. 12mo.

162. Volkov, T.: Rites et usages nuptiaux en Ukraine. *Anthropologie* (Paris). Vol. II. (1891), pp. 537–587 ; Vol. III. (1892), pp. 541–588.

163. Wake, C. S.: The Development of Marriage and Kinship. London, 1889.

164. Wasserzieher, Dr.: Das Weib in der Sprache. *Am Ur-Quell*, III. Bd., S. 214–215.

165. Weinhold, K.: Die deutschen Frauen in dem Mittelalter. 2 Bde. 2. Aufl. Wien, 1882.

166. Westermarck, C.: The History of Human Marriage. 2d ed. London and New York, 1894. xx, 644 pp. 8vo.

167. Wiedemann, A.: Die Milchverwandschaft im alten Aegypten. *Am. Ur-Quell.* III. Bd. (1892), S. 260–267.

168. Wilken, G. A.: Das Matriarchat bei den alten Arabern. (Germ. Trans.) Leipzig, 1884.

169. Winternitz, M.: On a Comparative Study of Indo-European Customs with Special Reference to the Marriage Customs. *Trans. Intern. Folk-Lore Congr.* London, 1891.

170. Wlislocki, H. v.: Aus dem Volksleben der Magyaren. Ethnologische Mittheilungen. München, 1893.

171. Wlislocki, H. v.: Volksglaube und Volksbrauch der Siebenbürger Sachsen. Berlin, 1893.

172. Wlislocki, H. v.: Die Stamm- und Familienverhältnisse der transsilvanischen Zeltzigeuner. *Globus.* L. Bd. (1888), S. 183 ff.

173. ZANETTI, Z. : La medicina delle nostre donne. Studio folklorico. Castello, 1892. xviii, 271 pp. 8vo.

174. ZMIGRODZKI, M. v. : Die Mutter bei den Völkern des arischen Stammes. Eine anthropologisch-historische Skizze als Beitrag zur Lösung der Frauenfrage. München, 1886. 444 S. 8vo.

175. ZUCCARELLI, A. : Divorzio e scienza antropologica. Napoli, 1893. 46 pp.

Following is a subject-index to the titles of Section A : —

B. CHILDREN, CHILDHOOD, CHILD-LIFE, ETC.

176. "A.," and MENELLA SMEDLEY: Poems Written for a Child.

177. "A.," and MENELLA SMEDLEY: The Child's World.

178. ADAMS, J. D.: Child-Life and Girlhood of Remarkable Women. New York, 1894.

179. AMÉLINEAU, E.: La Morale Égyptienne quinze siècles avant notre ère. Paris, 1892. lxxxviii, 261 pp. 8vo.

180. America's Shame: Symposium on the Age of Consent Laws in the United States. *Arena* (Boston). Vol. XI. (1895), pp. 192–215.

180 a. AYRTON, M. C.: Child-Life in Japan. London, 1879. xx, 125 pp.

181. BABCOCK, W. H.: Games of Washington Children. *Amer. Anthrop.* (Washington). Vol. I. (1888), pp. 243–284.

182. BALDWIN, J. M.: Mental Development in the Child and the Race. Vol. I. Methods and Processes. New York, 1895. xvi, 496 pp. 8vo.

183. BALL, V.: Wolf-Reared Children in India. *Journ. Anthr. Inst.* (London). Vol. IX. (1879), pp. 465–474.

184. BAMFORD, MARY E.: Child-Life among the California Foot-Hills. *Overl. Mo.* (San Francisco). 2d ser. Vol. II. (1883), pp. 56–59.

184 a. BARNES, EARLE: Theological Life of a California Child. *Pedag. Sem.* (Worcester, Mass.). Vol. II., 442–448.

185. BÄRNSTEIN, A. P. v.: Beiträge zur Geschichte und Literatur des deutschen Studententhumes. Würzburg, 1882. xiii, 156 S. 8vo.

186. BOAS, F.: The Game of Cat's Cradle. *Intern. Arch. f. Ethnogr.* I. Bd. (1888), S. 229.

187. BOLTON, H. C.: The Counting-Out Rhymes of Children, their Antiquity, Origin, and Wide Distribution. A Study in Folk-Lore. New York, 1888. ix, 123 pp. Gr. 8vo.

188. BONFIGLI, C.: Dei fattori sociali della pazzia in rapporto con l' educazione infantile. Roma, 1894.

189. BRAMHALL, MAE ST. JOHN: The Wee Ones of Japan. New York, 1894. 137 pp. 12mo.

190. BRAMLEY, H. R., and JOHN STAINER: Christmas Carols New and Old. London, n.d. 94 pp.

191. BREWER, E. C.: A Dictionary of Miracles. London, 1884. xliv, 582 pp. 8vo.

192. BREWER, W. H.: The Instinctive Interest of Children in Bear and Wolf Stories. *Proc. Amer. Ass. Adv. Sci.* Vol. XLII. (1893), Salem, 1894, pp. 309–311.

193. BRINTON, D. G.: On the Physiological Correlations of Certain Linguistic Radicals. *Amer. Orient. Soc. Proc.*, March, 1894, pp. cxxxiii–iv.

194. BROWN, H. W.: Some Records of the Thoughts and Reasonings of Children. From the Collection of Observations at the State Normal School at Worcester, Mass. *Pedag. Sem.* Vol. II. (1893), pp. 358–396.

195. Bulwer-Lytton, E. R.: Fables in Song. London, 1874.

196. Burnham, W. H.: The Study of Adolescence. *Pedag. Sem.* Vol. I. (1891), pp. 174–198.

197. Campbell Helen: Child-Life in the Slums of New York. *Demorest's Fam. Mag.* (New York), 1892.

198. Carstens, H.: Die Schwalbe im Volksmunde und im Kinderlied. *Am. Urdhs-Brunnen.* II. Bd., S. 240–242.

198 a. Carstens, H.: Der Storch als heiliger Vogel im Volksmund und im Kinderlied. *Am Urdhs-Brunnen.* Heft 1, 1881, S. 12–14.

199. Carstensen, H. H.: A B C Spiel. *Am Ur-Quell.* IV. Bd. (1893), S. 55, 150, 200; V. Bd. (1894), S. 114, 192, 290; VI. Bd. (1895), 42–3.

200. Chamberlain, A. F.: Notes on Indian Child-Language. *Amer. Anthr.* Vol. III. (1890), pp. 237–241.

201. Chamberlain, A. F.: Further Notes on Indian Child-Language. *Ibid.* Vol. VI. (1893), pp. 321–322.

202. Chamberlain, A. F.: The Use of Diminutives in *-ing* by Some Writers in Low German Dialects. *Public. Mod. Lang. Asso. Amer.* Vol. VII. (1892), pp. 212–247.

203. Chamberlain, A. F.: The Coyote and the Owl (Tales of the Kootenay Indians). *Mem. Intern. Congr. Anthr.* (1893), Chicago, 1894, pp. 282–284.

204. Chamberlain, A. F.: Human Physiognomy and Physical Characteristics in Folk-Lore and Folk-Speech. *Journ. Amer. Folk-Lore.* Vol. VI. (1893), pp. 13–24.

205. Chervin, A.: Faut-il couper le frein de la Langue (Extr. de *La Voix Parlée et Chantée*, février, 1894). Paris, 1894. 10 pp.

206. Chrisman, O.: Secret Language of Children. *Science* (New York). Vol. XXII. (1893), pp. 303–305.

207. Christmas with the Poets. London, n.d. x, 202 pp.

208. Cleveland, Duchess of: The True Story of Kaspar Hauser. From Official Documents. London and New York, 1893. 122 pp. Sm. 8vo.

209. Coffignon, A.: L'Enfant à Paris. Paris, 1890. xxii, 440 pp.

210. Coriveau, A.: La Santé de nos Enfants. Paris, 1890. 288 pp. 8vo.

211. Cuir, A. F.: Les Petits Écoliers. Lectures morales sur les Défauts et les Qualités des Enfants. Paris, 1893. 12mo.

212. Culin, S.: Street Games of Brooklyn. *Journ. Amer. Folk-Lore.* Vol. IV. (1891), pp. 221–236.

213. Culin, S.: Exhibit of Games in the Columbian Exposition. *Ibid.* Vol. VI. (1893), pp. 205–227.

214. Daniels, A. H.: The New Life: A Study of Regeneration (Repr. from *Amer. Journ. Psych.*, Vol. VI., 1893, pp. 61–106). Worcester, Mass., 1893. 48 pp. 8vo.

215. Deneus, Clément: De la Réserve héréditaire des Enfants (Art. 913 du code civil). Étude historique, philosophique et économique. Gand, Paris, 1894. xvii, 231 pp. 8vo.

216. DONALDSON, H. H.: Education of the Nervous System. *Educ. Rev.* (New York). Vol. IX. (1895), pp. 105–121.

217. DORSEY, J. O.: Games of the Teton-Dakota Children. *Amer. Anthr.* Vol. IV. (1891), pp. 329–345.

218. DRAGOMANO, M.: Slavonic Folk-Tales about the Sacrifice of One's Own Children. (Transl. O. Wardrop). *Journ. Anthr. Inst.* (London). Vol. XXI. (1892), pp. 456–469.

219. DREYLING, G.: Die Ausdrucksweise der übertriebenen Verkleinerung im altfränzösichen Karlepos. Marburg, 1888.

220. DÜRINGSFELD, J. V., und O. v. REINSBERG-DÜRINGSFELD: Sprichwörter-sammlung. 6 Bde. (Das Sprichwort als Kosmopolit. 3 Bde. Intern. Titulaturen. 2 Bde. Das Kind im Sprichwort). Leipzig, 1863–1864. 8vo.

221. EARLE, ALICE M.: Customs and Fashions in Old New England. [Chapter I., pp. 1–35, Child-Life.] New York, 1893. iii, 387 pp. 8vo.

222. EASTMAN, C. A.: Recollections of Wild-Life. III. Games and Sports. *St. Nicholas* (New York). Vol. XXI. (1893–4), pp. 306–308.

223. EELLS, M.: Twins among Indians of Puget Sound. *Science* (New York). Vol. XX. (1892), p. 192.

224. ELIOT, S.: Poetry for Children. Boston, [1879]. xii, 327 pp. Sm. 8vo.

225. Enfant (L') chez les sauvages et chez les civilisés. *Revue Britannique,* Nov., 1880.

226. FEWKES, J. W.: Dolls of the Tusayan Indians (Repr. fr. *Intern. Arch. f. Ethnogr.,* VII. Bd., 1894, pp. 45–73). Leiden, 1894. 30 pp. 4to. Five coloured plates.

226 a. FIELD, EUGENE: Love Songs of Childhood. Chicago, 1895.

227. FLETCHER, ALICE C.: Glimpses of Child-Life among the Omaha Indians. *Journ. Amer. Folk-Lore.* Vol. I. (1888), pp. 115–123.

228. FLOWER, B. O.: Lust Fostered by Legislation. *Arena* (Boston). Vol. XI. (1895), pp. 167–175.

229. FLOWER, W. H.: Fashion in Deformity. London, 1881. 85 pp. 8vo.

230. FORD, R.: Ballads of Bairnhood. Selected and edited with notes by Robert Ford. Paisley, 1894. xix, 348 pp. 8vo.

231. FOSTER, MARY J. C.: The Kindergarten of the Church. New York, 1894. 227 pp. 8vo.

232. FRACASETTI, L.: I giovani nella vita pubblica. Conferenza. Udine, 1893.

233. FROEBEL, F.: Mother's Songs, Games, and Stories. Froebel. Mutter- und Kose-Lieder rendered in English by Frances and Emily Lord. New and revised edition. London, 1890. xxxvi, 212 + 75 (music) pp. 8vo.

234. FURNIVALL, F. J.: Child-Marriages, Divorces, Ratifications, etc. In the Diocese of Chester, A.D. 1561–6. Depositions in Trials in the Bishop's Court, Chester, concerning: 1. Child-Marriages, Divorces,

2 E

and Ratifications. 2. Trothplights. 3. Adulteries. 4. Affiliations.
5. Libels. 6. Wills. 7. Miscellaneous Matters. 8. Clandestine
Marriages. Also Entries from the Mayors' Books, Chester, A.D.
1558–1600. Edited from the MS. written in court while the wit-
nesses made their depositions, and from the Mayors' Books. London, 1897 [1894]. lxxxviii, 256 pp. 8vo.

235. GAIDOZ, H.: Un vieux rite médical. Paris, 1892. ii, 85 pp. Sm. 8vo.

236. GAIDOZ, H.: Ransom by Weight. *Am Ur-Quell.* II. Bd. (1891), S.
39–42, 59–61, 74–75.

237. GAIDOZ, H., et M. PERDRIZET: La Mesure du Cou. *Mélusine* (Paris).
Tome VI. (1893), No. 10. See also *Amer. Anthr.*, VI. (1893), p. 408.

238. GARBINI, A.: Evoluzione della Voce nella Infanzia. Verona, 1892.
53 pp. 8vo.

239. GATSCHET, A. S.: A Mythic Tale of the Isleta Indians: The Race of
the Antelope and the Hawk around the Horizon. *Proc. Amer.
Philos. Soc.* (Philadelphia). Vol. XXIX., pp. 208–218.

240. GESSMANN, G. W.: Die Kinderhand und ihre Bedeutung für Erziehung
und Berufswahl. Eine physiognomische Studie. Berlin, 1894.
88 S. 8vo. 31 Abbild.

241. GILL, W. W.: Child-Birth Customs of the Loyalty Islands. *Journ.
Anthr. Inst.* (London). Vol. XIX. (1890), pp. 503–505.

242. GOMME, ALICE B.: Children's Singing Games with the Tunes to which
they are sung. Collected and edited by Alice B. Gomme. London
and New York, 1894.

243. GOMME, ALICE B.: The International Games of England, Scotland, and
Ireland, with Tunes, Singing Rhymes, and Method of Playing
according to the variants extant and recorded in different parts of
the Kingdom. Vol. I. According . . . Nuts in May. London,
1894. xix, 453 pp. 8vo.

244. GORE, J. H.: The Go-Backs. *Journ. Amer. Folk-Lore.* Vol. V.
(1892), pp. 107–109.

245. GRIFFIS, W. E.: Japanese Fairy World. Schenectady, N.Y., 1880.
vii, 304 pp. 12mo.

246. GREGOR, W.: Notes on the Folk-Lore of the North-East of Scotland.
London, 1881. xii, 238 pp. 8vo. [Chap. I., pp. 4–6, Birth; II.,
7–10, The Child; III., 11–13, Baptism; IV., 14–20, Nursery; V.,
21–24, "Boy Code of Honour."]

247. GÜLL, F.: Kinderheimat in Liedern. Volksausgabe. Gütersloh, 1875.
225 S. 8vo.

247 a. HAAS, A.: Das Kind im Glauben und Brauch der Pommern. *Am
Ur-Quell.* V. Bd. (1894), 179–180, 252–255, 278–279 ; VI., 22–24.

248. HABERLANDT, M.: Ueber tulâpurusha der Inder. *Mitt. d. anthr.
Gesellsch.* (Wien), n. F. IX. Bd. (1889), S. 160–164.

249. HALE, HORATIO: The Origin of Languages and the Antiquity of Speaking Man. Cambridge, 1886 (Repr. fr. *Proc. Am. Ass. Adv. Sci.*).
47 pp. 8vo.

250. HALE, HORATIO: The Development of Language. *Proc. Canad. Inst.* (Toronto), 3 s. Vol. VI. (1888), pp. 92–134.

251. HALE, HORATIO: Language as a Test of Mental Capacity. *Trans. Roy. Soc. Canada.* Vol. IX. (1891), Sect. II., pp. 77–112.

252. HALL, G. S.: The Contents of Children's Minds on Entering School. *Pedag. Sem.* Vol. I. (1891), pp. 139–172.

252 a. HALL, G. S.: Children's Lies. *Ibid.*, pp. 211–218.

253. HALL, G. S.: The Moral and Religious Training of Children and Adolescents. *Ibid.*, pp. 196–210.

254. HALL, G. S.: Child-Study: The Basis of Exact Education. *Forum* (New York). Vol. XVI. (1893–4), pp. 429–441.

255. HALL, G. S.: The Story of a Sand-Pile. *Scribner's Mag.* (New York). Vol. III. (1888), pp. 690–695.

256. HARQUEVAUX, E., et L. PELLETIER: 200 jeux d'enfants en plein air et à la maison. Paris, 1893.

257. HARRIS, W. T.: Eighth Annual Report of the Commissioner of Education, 1892. Industrial Education. Washington, 1892. 707 pp. 8vo.

257 a. HARRISON, ELIZABETH: A Study of Child-Nature from the Kindergarten Standpoint. 3d. edition. Chicago, 1891. 207 pp. 8vo.

258. HARTLAND, E. S.: The Science of Fairy Tales. An Inquiry into Fairy Mythology. London, 1891. viii, 372 pp. 8vo.

259. HARTMANN, B.: Die Analyse des kindlichen Gedankenkreises als die naturgemässige Grundlage des ersten Schulunterrichts. Zweite verm. Aufl. Annaberg i. Erzgeb., 1890. 116 S.

260. HASKELL, ELLEN M.: Imitation in Children. *Pedag. Sem.* Vol. III. (1894–5), pp. 30–47.

261. HERVEY, T. K.: The Book of Christmas. Boston, 1888. vi, 356 pp.

262. HIGGINSON, T. W.: Concerning All of Us. New York, 1893. vi, 210 pp. 12mo. [Pp. 103–109, "A Home Made Dialect."]

263. HÖFLER, M.: Die Lösung des Zungenbändchens. *Am Ur-Quell.* V. Bd. (1894), S. 191, 281.

264. HOYT, W. A.: The Love of Nature as the Root of Teaching and Learning the Sciences. *Pedag. Sem.* Vol. III. (1894–5), pp. 61–86.

265. HUGHES, J. L.: The Educational Value of Play, and the Recent Play-Movement in Germany. *Educ. Rev.* (New York). Vol. VIII., pp. 327–336.

266. HURLL, ESTELLE M.: Child-Life in Art. New York, 1894.

267. IM THURN, E. F.: Games of Guiana Indians. *Timehri* (Georgetown). Vol. III. (1889), pp. 270–307.

268. JOCELYN, E.: The Mother's Legacy to her Unborn Child. New York, 1894.

269. JOHNSON, G. E.: Education by Plays and Games. *Pedag. Sem.* Vol. III., pp. 97–133.

270. JOHNSON, J. H.: Rudimentary Society amongst Boys. *Overl. Mo.*, 1883.

271. JOHNSON, J. H. : Judicial Procedure amongst Boys. *Ibid.*, 1884.

272. JOHNSON, J. H.: Rudimentary Society among Boys (J. H. Univ. Studies . . . , No. XI., 2d ser.). Baltimore, 1884. 56 pp. 8vo.

273. JOHNSON, J., JR.: The Savagery of Boyhood. *Pop. Sci. Mo.* (New York). Vol. XXXI. (1881), pp. 796-800.

274. KALMANY, L.: Kinderschrecker und Kinderräuber im magyarischen Volksglauben. *Ethnol. Mitt. aus Ungarn* (Buda-Pest). III. Bd. (1893), S. 188-193.

275. KEBER, A.: Zur Philosophie der Kindersprache. Gereimtes und Ungereimtes. Zweite verm. Aufl. Leipzig, 1890. 96 S. 8vo.

276. KIPLING, R.: The Jungle Book. New York, 1894. xvii, 303 pp. 8vo.

277. KISS, A.: Magyar gyermekjáték gyütemény [Collection of Hungarian Children's Games, etc.]. Buda-Pest, 1891. viii, 518 pp. 8vo.

278. KLEINPAUL, R.: Menschenopfer und Ritualmorde. Leipzig, 1892. 80 S. 8vo.

279. KRAUSS, F. S.: Serbischer Zauber und Brauch Kinder halber. *Am Ur-Quell.* III. Bd. (1892). S. 160-161, 276-279.

280. KRAUSS, F. S.: Haarschurgodschaft bei den Südslaven (Sep. Abdr. aus: *Intern. Arch. f. Ethnogr.* VII. Bd. S. 161-198). Leiden, 1894. 38 S. 4to.

281. KRAUSS, F. S.: Geheime Sprachweisen. *Am Ur-Quell.* II. Bd. (1891). S. 21-23, 48-49, 65, 79-80 ; 98-99, 111-112, 127-128 ; 143-144, 187-189 ; III. Bd. (1892), 43-44, 106-107, 135-136, 167, 225-226, 328 ; IV. Bd. (1893), S. 76-78, 147 ; V. Bd. (1894), 74-78 ; VI. Bd. (1895), 37-40.

282. KRUSCHE, G.: Litteratur der weiblichen Eiziehung und Bildung in Deutschland von 1700 bis 1886. Langensalza, 1887. 43 S. 8vo.

283. KULISCHER, M.: Die Behandlung der Kinder und der Jugend auf den primitiven Kulturstufen. *Ztschr. f. Ethnol.* (Berlin), 1883. S. 191-203.

283 a. KULISCHER, M.: Eine Geschichte des Umgangs mit Kindern [in Russian]. Sslowo, 1878, H. 11.

284. KÜSTER, E.: Abergläubisches aus Schlesien [Superstitions about Childhood, Birth, Death]. *Am Urdhs-Brunnen.* IV. Bd. (1886). S. 190-191.

285. LAIBLE, H.: Jesus Christus im Thalmud. Berlin, 1891. 122 S. 8vo.

286. LALLEMAND, L.: Histoire des Enfants abandonnés et délaissés. Études sur la protection de l'enfance aux diverses époques de la civilisation. Paris, 1885. vii, 791 pp. 8vo.

287. LALLEMAND, L.: La question des Enfants abandonnés et délaissés au XIXième Siècle. Paris, 1885. vi, 238 pp.

288. LANGE, HELENE: Higher Education of Women in Europe. New York, 1890. 186 pp. 8vo.

289. LAURIE, S. S.: Lectures on the Rise and Early Constitution of Universities, with a Survey of Mediæval Education, A.D. 200-300. London, 1886. 293 pp. 8vo.

290-296. Laurie, S. S.: The History of Early Education. [Several Articles in the *School Review* (Ithaca, N. Y.), Vol. I. and II., 1893-1894, dealing with Egyptian, Semitic, Assyro-Babylonian, Indo-Aryan (Hindu, Persian, Medo-Persian), Hellenic and Roman Education].

297. Laurie, S. S.: Historical Survey of Pre-Christian Education. New York, 1895.

298. Leipziger, H. M.: The Education of the Jews (Educ. Monogr. Publ. by the N. Y. Coll. for the Training of Teachers. Vol. III., No. 6. Nov., 1890). New York, 1890. 39 pp. 8vo.

299. Letourneau, M.: Les Mensurations du Cou en Bretagne et en Kabylie. *Bull. Soc. d'Anthr.* (Paris). IIIe série. Tome XI. (1888), pp. 458-461, 472-473.

300. Lombroso, C.: The Man of Genius. London and New York, 1895. xvi, 370 pp.

301. Lombroso, Paola: Saggi di Psicologia del Bambino. Torino-Roma, 1894. xii, 284 pp. 12mo.

302. Lummis, C. F.: The Man who Married the Moon, and other Pueblo Indian Folk-Stories. New York, 1894. x, 239 pp. 8vo.

303. MacDonald, A.: Abnormal Man, being Essays on Education and Crime, and Related Subjects, with Digests of Literature and a Bibliography (Bureau of Education, Circ. of Inform., No. 4, 1893). Washington, 1893. 445 pp. 8vo.

304. Magnus, Lady: The Boys of the Bible. London, 1894.

305. Marenholz-Bülow, Baroness: The Child and Child-Nature. 5th ed. London, 1890. x, 186 pp. 8vo.

306. Mason, O. T.: Cradles of the American Aborigines. *Rep. U. S. Nat. Mus.*, 1886-87, pp. 161-212.

307. Maupaté, L.: Recherches d'anthropologie criminelle chez l'enfant; criminalité et dégénérescence. Lyon, 1893. 228 pp. 8vo.

308. McLean, J. E.: Psychic View of Infant Prodigies. *Metaphys. Rev.* (New York). Vol. I. (1895), pp. 156-164.

309. Mehnert, A.: Ein indischer Kaspar Hauser. Eine Erzählung aus dem anglo-indischen Volksleben. Dresden-Leipzig, 1893. 108 S. Kl. 8vo.

310. Miles, Caroline: A Study of Individual Psychology. *Amer. Journ. Psych.* Vol. VI. (1895), pp. 534-558.

311. Moreno, H. de: La festa del natale in Sicilia. Palermo, 1893.

312. Moutier, A.: Contribution à l'étude de la protection de l'enfance à Rome. Paris, 1884.

313. Newell, W. W.: Games and Songs of American Children. New York, 1884. xii, 242 pp. Sm. 4to.

314. Nicolay, F.: Les enfants mal élevés. Paris, 1890.

315. Ortwein, F.: Deutsche Weihnachten. Der Weihnachtsfestkreis nach seiner Entstehung, seinen Sitten und Bräuchen deutscher Völker. Gotha, 1892. 133 S. 8vo.

316. OWENS, J. G.: Natal Ceremonies of the Hopi Indians. *Journ. Amer. Ethn. and Arch.* Vol. II. (1892), pp. 161–175.

317. Papers Relating to Infant Marriage and Enforced Widowhood in India. Calcutta, 1886.

318. Pedagogical Seminary (The). An International Record of Educational Institutions, Literature and Progress. Edited by G. Stanley Hall. Worcester, Mass. Vols. I.–III. (1891–1895).

319. PEREZ, B.: Le Caractère de l'Enfant à l'Homme. Paris, 1892.

320. PEREZ, B.: L'Art et la Poésie chez l'Enfant. Paris, 1888. 308 pp.

321. PITRÉ, G.: Usi e Credenze dei Fanciulli in Sicilia. Palermo, 1889. 16 pp. Sm. 8vo.

322. PITRÉ, G.: Mirabile facoltà di alcune famiglie di guarire certe malattie. Palermo, 1889. 13 pp. Gr. 8vo.

323. PITRÉ, G.: Folk-lore giuridico dei Fanciulli in Sicilia. Palermo, 1890. 6 pp.

324. PITRÉ, G.: Il pesce d'Aprile. V. Ed. con moltiss. giunte. Palermo, 1891. 25 pp. Gr. 8vo.

325. PLOSS, H.: Das kleine Kind vom Tragbett bis zum ersten Schritt. Ueber das Legen, Tragen und Wiegen, Gehen, Stehen und Sitzen der kleinen Kinder bei verschiedenen Völkern der Erde. Leipzig, 1881. xii, 121 S. 8vo.

326. PLOSS, H.: Das Kind in Brauch und Sitte der Völker. Anthropologische Studien von Dr. H. Ploss. Zweite, neu durchges. u. stark vermehrte Aufl. Neue Ausgabe. Leipzig, 1884. 2 Bd. x, 394 ; iv, 478 S. 8vo.

327. POKROVSKI, E. A.: Fizicheskoe vospitanie detei u. raznich narodov preimutshestvenno Rossii ; materiali dlja medico-antropologicheskago izsledovanija [Physical Education of Children in Different Nations, especially in Russia ; materials for medico-anthropological Research]. Moskva, 1884. iv, 379 pp. Fol.

328. POKROVSKI, E. A.: Pervonachalnoe fizicheskoe vospitanie dietei (populjarnoe nukovodsto dlja materei). [The Early Physical Education of Children (popular manual for mothers)]. Moskva, 1888. 261 pp. 8vo.

329. POKROVSKI, E. A.: Ob ucho die za malymi dietmi [on the care of little children]. Moskva, 1889. viii, 100 pp. 16mo.

330. POKROVSKI, E. A.: Detskija igry preimushestvenno russkija (V. svjazi s istorei, etnografei, pedagogiei, i gigienoi [Children's Games, especially Russian] (from an historical, pedagogical, and hygienic point of view). Moskva, 1887. vi, 368 pp. 8vo.

331. PORTER, J. H.: Notes on the Artificial Deformation of Children among Savage and Civilized Peoples. *Rep. U. S. Nat. Mus.*, 1886–87, pp. 213–235.

332. POST, A. H.: Mittheilungen aus dem bremischen Volkleben [Zungenübungen]. *Am Ur-Quell.* V. Bd. (1894). S. 176–179.

332 a. POULSSON, E.: Finger-Plays for Nursery and Kindergarten. Boston, 1893.

333. RAND, K. E.: The Childhood of an Affinity. New York, 1893. vi, 304 pp. 8vo.

334. RASSIER, M: Valeur du témoignage des enfants en justice. Lyons, 1893. 88 pp.

335. RAUBER, A.: Homo Sapiens Ferus oder die Zustände der Verwilderten in ihrer Bedeutung für Wissenschaft, Politik und Schule. Biologische Untersuchung. Zweite Aufl. Leipzig, 1888. 134 S. 8vo.

336. RICCARDI, A.: Antropologia e Pedagogia. Introduzione ad una Scienza della Educazione (Osservazioni psicologiche; ricerche statistiche; misure antropologiche, ecc.). Parte Prima. Osservazioni psicologiche; ricerche statistiche e sociologiche. Modena, 1892. 172 pp. 4to.

336 a. RILEY, J. W.: Rhymes of Childhood. Indianapolis, 1894. 186 pp. 8vo.

337. ROBERTSON, E. S.: The Children of the Poets. An Anthology from English and American Writers of Three Centuries. Edited with Introduction by Eric S. Robertson. London and Newcastle-on-Tyne, 1886. xxxviii, 273 pp. 12mo.

337 a. ROBINSON, L.: The Primitive Child. *N. Amer. Rev.* (N. Y.), 1895.

338. ROMANES, G. J.: Mental Evolution in Man. New York, 1883.

338 a. ROY, RAJ COOMAR: Child Marriage in India. *N. Amer. Rev.*, Oct., 1888, pp. 415–423.

339. [RUNKLE, K. B.]: A Collection for Christmas. The New Year. Easter. Boston, 1884. xii, 388 pp.

340. SAUBERT, DR.: Maikäfer, Frau Holle's Bote. *Am Urdhs-Brunnen.* VI. Bd. (1888–1889). S. 22–24.

341. SCHALLENBERGER, MARGARET E.: A Study of Children's Rights as seen by themselves. *Pedag. Sem.* Vol. III. (1894–1895), pp. 87–96.

342. SCHECHTER, S.: The Child in Jewish Literature. *Jewish Quarterly* (London). Vol. II. (1889).

343. SCHELL, O.: Woher kommen die Kinder? *Am Ur-Quell.* IV. Bd. (1893), S. 224–226; V. Bd. (1894), S. 80–81, 102, 254, 255, 287.

344. SCOTT, C. N.: The Child-God in Art. *Contemp. Rev.* (London). Vol. L. (1886), pp. 97–111.

345. SCRIPTURE, E. W.: Arithmetical Prodigies. *Amer. Journ. Psychol.* Vol. IV., pp. 1–59.

346. SCUDDER, H. M.: Childhood in Greek and Roman Literature. *Atlantic Mo.* (Boston). Vol. LV., pp. 13–23.

347. SCUDDER, H. M.: Childhood in Early Christianity. *Ibid.*, pp. 617–625.

348. SCUDDER, H. M.: Childhood in Mediæval Art. *Ibid.*, LVI. (1885), pp. 24–31.

349. SCUDDER, H. M.: Childhood in English Literature and Art. *Ibid.*, pp. 369–380, 471–484.

349 a. SCUDDER, H. M.: Childhood in Modern Literature and Art. *Ibid.*, pp. 751–767.

350. SCUDDER, H. E.: Childhood in Literature and Art, with Some Observations on Literature for Children. Boston, 1894. Cr. 8vo.

351. Sessions, F.: The Younger Son (Folk-Lore Topics, No. 5). Repr. from *Gloucester Journal*, March 3d, 1894. Gloucester (Engld.), 1894. 8 pp.

352. Sessions, F.: Beating the Bounds (Folk-Lore Topics, No. 4). Repr. from *Gloucester Journ.*, Feb. 17, 1894.

353. Shinn, Millicent W.: Some Comments on Babies [of Various Races]. *Overl. Mo.* (San Francisco). Vol. XXIII (1894), pp. 2–19.

354. Sohnrey, H.: Geburt und Taufe in der Gegend des Sollinger Waldes. *Am Ur-Quell.* II. Bd. (1894), S. 197–202.

355. Starr, F.: A Page of Child-Lore. *Journ. Amer. Folk-Lore.* Vol. IV. (1891), pp. 55–56.

356. Steel, F. A., and R. C. Temple: Wide Awake Stories. A Collection of Tales told by Little Children between Sunset and Sunrise, in the Panjab and Kashmir. Bombay, 1884.

357. Steinmetz, S. R.: De "Fosterage" of Opvoeding in Vreemde Families [Repr. from *Tijdschr. v. h. koninkl. Nederl. Aardrijksk. Genootsch.*]. Leiden, 1893. 92 pp. 8vo.

358. Stevenson, Mrs. T. E.: The Religious Life of a Zuñi Child. *Fifth Ann. Rep. Bur. of Ethnol.* (Washington), pp. 533–555.

359. Stevenson, R. L.: A Child's Garden of Verse, 1885.

360. Stork, T.: The Children of the New Testament. Philadelphia, 1856. xi, 185 pp. 8vo.

361. Strack, H. C.: Der Blutaberglaube in der Menschheit, Blutmorde und Blutritus. Vierte neu bearb. Aufl. München, 1892. xii, 156 S. 8vo.

361 a. Straszburger, B.: Geschichte der Erziehung und des Unterrichts bei den Israeliten. Von der vortalmudischen Zeit bis auf die Gegenwart. Mit einem Anhang.: Bibliographie der jüdischen Pädagogie. Stuttgart, 1885. xv, 210 S.

362. Strettell, Alma: Lullabies of Many Lands. New York, 1894.

363. Strong, G. D.: Child-Life in Many Lands. Boston, 1870. iv, 210 pp. 8vo.

364. Studentensprache und Studentenlied in Halle von 100 Jahren. Neudruck des Idiotikon der Burschensprache von 1795 und der Studentenlieder von 1781. Halle, 189–. xliii, 118 S.; viii. 127 S.

365. Sully, J.: Studies of Childhood. [Numerous articles in *Pop. Sci. Mo.* (New York). Vols. XLVI. and XLVII.].

366. Sundermann, F.: Woher kommen die Kinder? Eine Beantwortung dieser Frage aus Ostfriesland. *Am Urdhs-Brunnen.* I. Bd. (1881), Heft II., S. 14–18; Heft V., S. 14.

367. "Sylvanus Urban": Infant-Marriages. *Gentlm. Mag.* (Lond.) Vol. 277 (1894), pp. 322–324, 427–428.

368. The Feeble-Minded Child and Adult. A Report on an Investigation of the Physical and Mental Condition of 50,000 School Children, with Suggestions for the Better Education and Care of Feeble-Minded Children and Adults. (Charity Organization). London, 1893. xii, 159 pp. 8vo.

369. The Epileptic and Crippled Child and Adult. London, 1893. xxi, 132 pp. 8vo.

370. TILTE, M. : Die Geschichte der deutschen Weihnacht. Leipzig, 1804.

371. TRACY, F. : The Psychology of Childhood. Sec. Ed. Boston, 1894. xiii, 107 pp. 8vo.

372. TREICHEL, A.: Provinzielle Sprache zu und von Thieren und ihre Namen. *Alt-Preuss. Monatsschr.* XXIX. Bd., Hefte I., II.

373. TREICHEL, A.: Zungenübungen aus Preussen. *Am Ur-Quell.* V. Bd. (1894), S. 122-126, 144-148, 180-182, 222-224.

374. TUCKER, ELIZABETH S. : Children of Colonial Days. New York, 1894.

375. TUCKWELL, Mrs. G. M.: The State and its Children. London, 1894.

376. TYLOR, E. B. : Wild Men and Beast Children. *Anthrop. Rev.* (London). Vol. I. (1863), pp. 21-32.

377. TYLOR, E. B. : Remarks on the Geographical Distribution of Games. *Journ. Anthr. Inst.* (London). Vol. IX. (1879), pp. 23-30.

378. VOSTROVSKY, CLARA: A Study of Children's Imaginary Companions. *Education* (Boston). Vol. XV. (1895), pp. 393-398.

379. WHITTIER, J. G.: Child-Life. A Collection of Poems. Edited by J. G. Whittier. Boston, n.d. xii, 263 pp. Gr. 8vo.

380. WHITTIER, J. G.: Child-Life in Prose. Boston, n.d.

381. WIEDEMANN, A.: Kinderehe bei den alten Ægyptern. *Am Ur-Quell.* VI. Bd. (1895), S. 3-4.

382. WIGGIN, KATE D.: Children's Rights. A Book of Nursery Logic. Boston and New York, 1893. 235 pp. 16mo.

383. Wild Babies. *Harper's Monthly* (New York). Vol. LVII. (1878), pp. 829-838.

384. WILTSE, SARAH E. : The Place of the Story in Early Education, and Other Essays. Boston, 1892. vi, 137 pp. 8vo.

385. WINTERNITZ, M. : Das Kind bei den Juden. *Am Ur-Quell.* II. Bd. (1891), S. 5-7, 34-36.

386. WOSSIDLO, R. : Volksthümliches aus Mecklenburg. De Jung [Proverbial Sayings of Children]. *Plattd. Sünndagsbl.* (Bielefeld). III. Bd. (1890), S. 75-77.

387. YODER, A. H. : The Study of the Boyhood of Great Men. *Pedag. Sem.* Vol. III. (1894-5), pp. 134-156.

Following is a subject-index of titles under Section B : —

C. GENERAL.

388. D'Alviella, Count Goblet: Lectures on the Origin and Growth of the Conception of God as illustrated by Anthropology and History. (Hibbert Lectures, 1891.) London, 1892. xvi, 296 pp. 8vo.

389. American Anthropologist (Washington): Vols. I.–VIII. (1888–1895).

390. American Notes and Queries (Phila.) Vols. I.–VI. (1888–1891).

391. Am Urdhs-Brunnen (Dahrenwurth bei Lunden, Holstein). I.–VII. Bde. (1881–1890).

392. Am Ur-Quell (Lunden). I.–VI. Bde. (1890–1895). Continuation of No. 391.

393. ANDERSEN, HANS C.: Fairy Tales and Stories. (Transl. Dr. H. W. Dulcken). N.Y., n.d. iv, 377 pp. 8vo.

394. ASTON, W. G.: Japanese Onomatopes and the Origin of Language. *Jour. Anthr. Inst.* (London). Vol. XXIII. (1894), pp. 332–362.

395. BAGEHOT, W.: Physics and Politics. New York, 1887.

396. BANCROFT, H. H.: The Native Races of the Pacific Coast. 5 vols. New York, 1874–1876. 8vo.

397. BARTELS, M.: Die Medicin der Naturvölker: Ethnologische Beiträge zur Urgeschichte der Medicin. Leipzig, 1893. 361 S. 8vo.

398. BASTIAN, A.: Zur naturwissenschaftlichen Behandlungsweise der Psychologie durch und für die Völkerkunde. Berlin, 1883. xxxviii, 230 S. 8vo.

399. BASTIAN, A.: Die Seele indischer und hellenischer Philosophie in den Gespenstern moderner Geisterseherei. Berlin, 1886. xlviii, 223 S. 8vo.

400. BERGEN, FANNY D.: Popular American Plant-Names. *Jour. Amer. Folk-Lore.* Vol. V. (1872), pp. 88–106; VI. (1893), pp. 135–142; VII. (1894), pp. 89–104.

401. BLACK, W. G.: Folk-Medicine: A Chapter in the History of Culture. London, 1883. iii, 228 pp. 8vo.

402. BOAS, F.: The Central Eskimo. *Sixth Ann. Rep. Bur. Ethnol.* (Washington). pp. 399–669.

403. BOAS, F.: British Association for the Advancement of Science. Newcastle-upon-Tyne Meeting, 1889. Fifth Report of the Committee appointed for the purpose of investigating and publishing Reports on the Physical Characters, Languages, and Industrial and Social Condition of the North-Western Tribes of the Dominion of Canada. First General Report on the Indians of British Columbia. By Dr. Franz Boas. London, 1889. 104 pp. 8vo.

404. BOAS, F.: Sixth Report, etc. Second General Report on the Indians of British Columbia. By Dr. Franz Boas. London, 1890. 163 pp. 8vo.

405. BOAS, F.: Seventh Report, etc. London, 1891. 43 pp. 8vo.

405 a. BOLTON, T. L.: Rhythm. *Amer. Jour. Psychol.* Vol. VI., pp. 145–238.

406. BOURKE, J. G.: The Medicine-Men of the Apaches. *Ninth Ann. Rep. Bur. of Ethnol.* (1887–88). Washington, 1892 [1893]. pp. 443–603.

407. BOURKE, J. G.: Popular Medicine, Customs and Superstitions of the Rio Grande. *Jour. Amer. Folk-Lore.* Vol. VII. (1894), pp. 119–146.

408. BRAND, J.: Observations on the Popular Antiquities of Great Britain. Ed. Sir H. Ellis. 3 vols. London, 1882–1888.

409. BRINTON, D. G.: The Myths of the New World. A Treatise on the Symbolism and Mythology of the Red Race of America. 2d ed. New York, 1876. 331 pp. 8vo.

410. BRINTON, D. G. : American Hero-Myths. A Study in the Native Religions of the Western Continent. Philadelphia, 1882. 261 pp. 8vo.

411. BRINTON, D. G. : Essays of an Americanist. Philadelphia, 1890.
489 pp. 8vo.

412. BRINTON, D. G. : The American Race. A Linguistic Classification and
Description of the Native Tribes of North and South America.
New York, 1891. 392 pp. 8vo.

413. BRINTON, D. G. : Nagualism. A Study in Native American Folk-Lore
and History. Philadelphia, 1894. 65 pp. 8vo.

414. BRINTON, D. G. : Ancient Nahuatl Poetry. Philadelphia, 1887. viii,
9-177 pp. 8vo.

415. BUSK, R. H. : The Folk-Lore of Rome. London, 1874.

416. BUSK, R. H. : The Valleys of Tirol, Their Traditions, etc. London,
1869.

417. CALLAWAY, Rev. Canon : Religious System of the Amazulu. London,
1870. viii, 448 pp. 8vo.

418. CHAMBERLAIN, A. F. : The Prehistoric Naturalist. *University Quarterly Rev.* (Toronto). Vol. I. (1890), pp. 179-197.

419. CHAMBERLAIN, A. F. : Nanibozhu among the Otchipwē, Mississagas,
and other Algonkian Tribes. *Journ. Amer. Folk-Lore.* Vol. IV.
(1891), pp. 193-213.

420. CLARK, W. P. : The Indian Sign-Language, etc. Philadelphia, 1885.
443 pp. 8vo.

421. CLODD, E. : The Childhood of Religions. New York, 1883. 51 pp. 8vo.

422. CLOUSTON, W. A. : Popular Tales and Fictions ; Their Migrations and
Transformations. 2 vols. London, 1887. xvii, 485 ; vii, 515 pp. 8vo.

423. CRAWFORD, J. M. : The Kalevala. New York, 1888. 2 vols. 8vo.

423 a. CULIN, S. : Notes of Palmistry in China and Japan. *Overl. Mo.*,
1894. pp. 476-480.

424. CUSHING, F. H. : Zuñi Fetiches. *Sec. Ann. Rep. Bur. of Ethnol.*
(1880-81), Washington, 1883, pp. 3-45.

425. DAWSON, G. M. : Notes on the Shushwap People of British Columbia.
Trans. Roy. Soc. Canada, 1891, Sect. II., pp. 3-44.

426. DAY, LAL BEHARI : Folk-Tales of Bengal. London, 1880. VII.,
284 pp. 8vo.

427. DE GUBERNATIS, A. : Zoölogical Mythology, or the Legends of Animals. 2 vols. London, 1872. xxvii, 432 ; viii, 442 pp. 8vo.

428. DE GUBERNATIS, A. : La Mythologie des Plantes, ou Légendes du
Règne Végétal. Paris. Tome I., 1878 ; Tome II., 1882.

429. DAVIDS, W. R. : Buddhist Birth-Stories (Ed. Fausboll). London, 18—.

430. Dialect Notes (Amer. Dialect Soc.). Cambridge, Mass., 1890-1894.
Parts I.-VII., pp. 1-355.

431. DIRKSEN, C. : Ostfriesische Sprichwörter und sprichwörtliche Redens-
arten mit historischen und sprachlichen Anmerkungen. I. Heft
(Zweite Aufl.). Ruhrort, 1889. 109 S. 8vo. ; II. Heft. Ruhrort,
1891. 95 S. 8vo.

432. DODGE, R. I.: Our Wild Indians. Hartford, Conn., 1890. xxxix, 653 pp. 8vo.

433. DORSEY, J. O.: A Study of Siouan Cults. *Eleventh Ann. Rep. Bur. of Ethnol.* (1889-90). Washington, 1894. pp. 351-544.

434. DOUGLAS, R. K.: Confucianism and Taouism. London (S. P. C. K.), n.d. 287 pp. 12mo.

435. DYER, T. F. T.: The Folk-Lore of Plants. New York, 1889. 328 pp. 8vo.

436. DYER, T. F. T.: Church-Lore Gleanings. London, 1891. vi, 352 pp. 8vo.

437. EELLS, Rev. M.: The Twana Indians of the Skokomish Reservation in Washington Territory. *Bull. U. S. Geol. and Geogr. Surv. of Territ.* III. (1877), pp. 57-114.

438. ELLIS, A. B.: The Tshi-speaking Peoples of the Gold Coast of West Africa. Their Religion, Manners, Customs, Laws, Language, etc. London, 1887. vii, 343 pp. 8vo.

439. ELLIS, HAVELOCK: The Criminal. London, 1890. viii, 337 pp. 8vo.

440. EMERSON, ELLEN R.: Indian Myths, or Legends, Traditions, and Symbols of the Aborigines of America, compared with those of other Countries. Boston, 1884. xviii, 667 pp. 8vo.

441. ERMAN, A.: Aegypten und aegyptisches Leben im Altertum. 2 Bde. Tübingen, 1885. xvi, 350 S.; viii, 351-742 S. Kl. 4to.

442. FARRAR, F. W.: The Life of Christ as Represented in Art. New York, 1894.

443. FEWKES, J. W.: A Summer Ceremonial at the Tusayan Pueblos. *Journ. Amer. Arch. and Ethnol.* I. (1891), pp. 1-62; II. (1892), pp. 1-160.

444. FEWKES, J. W.: The Nā-ác-nai-ya: A Tusayan Initiation Ceremony. *Journ. Amer. Folk-Lore.* Vol. V. (1892), pp. 189-221.

445. FLETCHER, ALICE C.: Indian Songs. Personal Studies of Indian Life. *Century* (New York). Vol. XLVII. (1893-4), pp. 421-431.

446. FLETCHER, ALICE C.: A Study of Omaha Music, etc. *Archæol. and Ethnol. Papers of Peab. Mus.* (Cambridge, Mass.). Vol. I., No. 5, 1893, pp. vi, 152. 8vo.

447. FLETCHER, R.: Myths of the Robin Redbreast in Early English Poetry. *Amer. Anthrop.* Vol. II. (1889), pp. 97-118.

448. FOLKARD, RICHARD, Jr.: Plant Lore, Legends, and Lyrics, embracing the Myths, Traditions, Superstitions, and Folk-Lore of the Plant-Kingdom. London, 1884. xxiv, 610 pp. 8vo.

449. Folk-Lore Journal (London). Vol. VII. (1889).

450. FRAZER, J. G.: The Golden Bough. A Study in Comparative Religion. 2 vols. London and New York, 1890.

451. FRAZER, J. G.: Totemism. Edinburgh, 1887. viii, 96 pp.

451 a. FRAZER, J. G.: Primitive Theories of the Soul. *Journ. Anthr. Inst.* (London). Vol. XV. pp. 64-104.

452. FREYTAG, L.: Pflanzen-Aberglauben in den Alpen. *Am Urdhs-Brunnen*, 1888-9. S. 33-41, 49-52.

453. FRIEND, H.: Flowers and Flower-Lore. 2 vols. London, 1884. xvi, 352, 353–704 pp. 8vo.

454. FRISCHBIER, H.: Volksglauben aus Preussen. I. Kindheit. *Am Ur-Quell.* I. Bd. (1890), S. 132–134, 151–152, 164–165.

455. GATSCHET, A. S.: The Klamath Indians of South-Western Oregon (Dept. of Int. U. S. Geogr. and Geol. Surv., etc.). (*Contrib. to North Amer. Ethnol.* Vol. II., Washington, 1890.) Pt. I., cvi, 711 pp.; Pt. II., 711 pp. 4to.

456. GATSCHET, A. S.: The Karankawa Indians. (*Arch. and Ethnol. Papers, Peab. Mus.,* Vol. I., No. 2). Cambridge, Mass., 1891. viii, 9–103 pp. 8vo.

456 a. GERBER, A.: Great Russian Animal Tales. *Public Mod. Lang. Assoc. Amer.* Vol. VI. (1891), No. 2.

457. GIBBS, G.: Tribes of Western Washington and Northwestern Oregon. *Contrib. to North Amer. Ethnol.* (U. S. Geogr. and Geol. Surv., etc.). Vol. I. (1877), pp. 157–361.

458. GILL, W. W.: Myths and Songs of the South Pacific. London, 1876. xxiv, 328 pp. 8vo.

459. GILL, W. W.: The South Pacific and New Guinea, Past and Present. Sydney (N. S. W. Govt.), 1892. 38 pp. 8vo.

460. GOMME, G. L.: Ethnology in Folk-Lore. New York, 1892. vii, 203 pp.

461. GOMME, G. L.: The Village Community. London, 1890. xi, 299 pp.

462. GRIMM, J.: Teutonic Mythology. Transl. J. S. Stallybrass. 4 vols. London, 1880–1888.

463. GRIMM, GEBR.: Kinder- und Haus-Märchen gesammelt durch die Gebr. Grimm, Stuttgart-Wien. 189–. v, 466. S. 4to.

464. GRINNELL, G. B.: Blackfoot Lodge Tales. The Story of a Prairie People. New York, 1892. xv, 310 pp. 8vo.

465. GRINNELL, G. B.: Pawnee Hero-Stories and Folk-Tales, with Notes on the Origin, Customs, and Character of the Pawnee People. New York, 1889. Cr. 8vo.

466. GUPPY, H. B.: The Solomon Islands and their Natives. London, 1887. xvi, 384 pp. 8vo.

466 a. HAAS, A.: Rügensche Sagen und Märchen. Greifswald, 1891.

467. HALE, HORATIO: The Aryans in Science and History. *Pop. Sci. Mo.* (New York), March, 1889, pp. 677–686.

468. HARLEY, T.: Moon-Lore. London, 1885. xvi, 296 pp. 8vo.

469. HENDERSON, W.: Notes on the Folk-Lore of the Northern Counties of England and the Borders. New ed. London, 1879. xviii, 391 pp. 8vo.

470. HENNE AM RHYN, O.: Die Kultur der Vergangenheit, Gegenwart und Zukunft in vergleichender Darstellung. 2 Bde. Danzig-Leipzig-Wien, 1890.

471. HITCHCOCK, R.: The Ainos of Yesso, Japan. *Rep. U. S. Nat. Mus.* (Washington), 1890, pp. 429–502.

472. Höfler, M. : Wald- und Baumkultus in Beziehung zur Volksmedizin. München, 1892. viii, 170 S. 8vo.

473. Hoffman, W. J. : The Midē'wiwin, or " Grand Medicine Society " of the Ojibwa. *Seventh Ann. Rep. Bur. of Ethnol.* (1885-86), Washington, 1891, pp. 143-300.

474. Hopf, L. : Thierorakel und Orakelthiere in alter und neuer Zeit. Eine ethnol.-zool. Studie. Stuttgart, 1888. xi, 271 S. 8vo.

475. Hose, C. A. : Journey up the Baranu River to Mount Dulit and the Highlands of Borneo. *Geogr. Journ.* (London), Vol. I. (1893), pp. 193-208.

476. Ihering, J. von: Die künstliche Deformirung der Zähne. *Ztschr. f. Ethnol.* XIV. Bd. (1882), S. 213-262.

477. Im Thurn, E. F. : Among the Indians of Guiana. London, 1883. xvi, 445 pp. 8vo.

478. Irving, J. T. : Indian Sketches. New York and London, 1888.

479. Joest, W. : Tatöwiren, Narbenzeichnen und Körperbemalung. Ein Beitrag zur vergleichenden Ethnologie. Berlin, 1890. x, 112 S.

480. Journal of American Folk-Lore (Cambridge, Mass.). Vols. I.-VIII. (1888-1895).

481. Journal of the Anthropological Institute of Great Britain and Ireland (London). Vols. I.-XXIV. (1872-1895).

482. Klemm, G.: Allgemeine Culturgeschichte der Menschheit. 10 Bde. Leipzig, 1843-52.

483. Köhler, C. S. : Das Thierleben im Sprichwort der Griechen und Römer. Nach Quellen und Stellen in Parallele mit den deutschen Sprichwörtern. Leipzig, 1881.

484. Lang, A. : Custom and Myth. 2d ed. London, 1885. 312 pp. 8vo.

485. Lang, A. : Myth, Ritual, and Religion. 2 vols. London, 1887. xvi, 340; vii, 370 pp. 8vo.

486. Lefèvre, A. : Mythologie du monde minéral; leçon professée à l'école d'anthropologie. *Rev. de Trad. Pop.* Nov. 1889.

487. Legge, J. : The Life and Works of Mencius. Philadelphia, 1875. vii, 402 pp. 8vo.

488. Leland, C. G. : The Algonquin Legends of New England. 2d ed. Boston, 1885. xviii, 379 pp. 8vo.

489. Letourneau, Ch.: The Origin of Literary Form. *Pop. Sci. Mo.* (New York). Vol. XLIII. (1893), pp. 673-682.

490. Letourneau, Ch. : L'Évolution Littéraire dans les diverses Races humaines. Paris, 1894. 582 pp. 8vo.

491. Letourneau, Ch.: L'Évolution Religieuse dans les diverses Races humaines. Paris, 1892.

492. Lippert, J.: Die Religionen der europäischen Kulturvölker, der Litauer, Slaven, Germanen, Griechen und Römer, in ihrem geschichtlichen Ursprunge. Berlin, 1881. xvi, 496 S. 8vo.

493. Lippert, J.: Allgemeine Geschichte des Priestertums. 2 Bde. Berlin, 1884.

494. LUBBOCK, J.: The Pleasures of Life. Philadelphia, 1894. xiv, 332 pp. 12mo.

495. LUMHOLTZ, C.: Among Cannibals. London, 1889. 395 pp. 8vo.

496. MacCAULEY, C.: The Seminole Indians of Florida. *Fifth Ann. Rep. Bur. of Ethnol.* (Washington), pp. 469–535.

496 a. MACKAY, CHARLES: Memoirs of Extraordinary Popular Delusions. 3 vols. London, 1841.

497. MACKENZIE, A.: Descriptive Notes on Certain Implements, Weapons, etc., from Graham Island, Queen Charlotte Islands, B.C. *Trans. Roy. Soc. Canada*, 1891, Sect. II., pp. 45–59.

497 a. MALLERY, G.: Sign-Language among North American Indians compared with that among other Peoples and Deaf Mutes. *First Ann. Rep. Bur. Ethnol.* (1879–80). Washington, 1881. pp. 263–552.

498. MANN, H.: On the Aboriginal Inhabitants of the Andaman Islands. London, 1884. xxviii, 224, and 73 pp. 8vo.

499. MANTEGAZZA, P.: Physiognomy and Expression. London, 1890. x, 327 pp. 8vo.

500. MARTINENGO-CESARESCO, COUNTESS E.: Essays in the Study of Folk-Song. London, 1886. 8vo.

501. MATTHEWS, W.: The Human Bones of the Hemenway Collection in the U. S. Army Medical Museum at Washington. *Nat. Acad. of Sci.*, Vol. VI., Seventh Memoir, pp. 139–286.

502–503. McGEE, W. J.: The Earth the Home of Man (Anthrop. Soc. of Washington, Special Papers, No. 2). Washington, 1894. 28 pp. 8vo.

504. MIKHAILOVSKII, V. M.: Shamanism in Siberia and European Russia. *Journ. Anthr. Inst.* (London). Vol. XXIV. (1894–5), pp. 62–110.

505. MONTEIRO MARIANA: Legends and Popular Tales of the Basque People. New York, 1887. vii, 274 pp. 8vo.

506. MOONEY, J.: Myths of the Cherokees. *Jour. Amer. Folk-Lore.* Vol. I. (1888), pp. 97–108.

507. MOONEY, J.: Sacred Formulas of the Cherokees. *Seventh Ann. Rep. Bur. of Ethnol.* (Washington, 1891.) pp. 306–395.

508. MÜLLENHOFF, K.: Sagen, Märchen und Lieder der Herzogthümer Schleswig-Holstein und Lauenburg. Kiel, 1845. 8vo.

509. MÜLLER, J. G.: Geschichte der amerikanischen Urreligionen. Basel, 1867. viii, 706 S. 8vo.

510. MÜLLER, F. MAX: Natural Religion (Gifford Lectures, 1888). London, 1889. xix, 608 pp. 8vo.

511. MÜLLER, F. MAX: Anthropological Religion. London, 1892. 486 pp. 8vo.

512. MÜLLER, F. MAX: Physical Religion. London, 1891.

513. MÜLLER, F. MAX: Theosophical Religion. London, 1892.

514–515. MURDOCH, J.: Ethnological Results of the Point Barrow Expedition. *Ninth Ann. Rep. Bur. Ethnol.*, pp. 3–441.

516. NELSON, W.: The Indians of New Jersey. Paterson, N.J., 1894. 168 pp. 8vo.

517. POLLE, F.: Wie denkt das Volk über die Sprache? Leipzig, 1889.
518. Popular Science Monthly (The). New York. Vols. I.–XLVI. (1871–1895).
519. POWERS, S.: Tribes of California (*Contrib. to North Amer. Ethnol.*, Vol. III.). Washington, 1877. 635 pp. 4to.
520. RALSTON, W. R.: Russian Folk-Tales. New York, 1873. 388 pp. 8vo.
521. RAND, S. T.: Legends of the Micmacs. New York and London, 1894. xlvi, 452 pp. 8vo.
522. RAU, C.: Von Martius on Some Points of South American Ethnology. *Journ. Anthrop. Inst.* (New York). Vol. I. (1871–72), pp. 43–46.
523. RECLUS, E.: Primitive Folk. Studies in Comparative Ethnology. London, 1890. xiv, 339 pp. 8vo.
524. RIGGS, S. R.: Dakota Grammar, Texts, and Ethnography (Contrib. to North Amer. Ethnol., Vol. IX.). Washington, 1893. 239 pp. 4to.
525. RINK, H.: Tales and Traditions of the Eskimo. London, 1874. xiii, 472 pp. 8vo.
526. ROLLAND, E.: Faune Populaire de la France. 6 vols. Paris, 1877–1883.
527. ROSKOFF, G.: Das Religionswesen der rohesten Naturvölker. Leipzig, 1880. xiv, 179 S. 8vo.
528. SARTORI, P.: Sondersprachen. *Am Ur-Quell.* V. Bd. (1894), S. 72–78, 99–100.
529. SCHULTZE, F.: Fetichism. A Contribution to Anthropology and the History of Religion. Trans. J. Fitzgerald. New York, 1885. 112 pp. 8vo.
530. SCHURTZ, H.: Grundzüge einer Philosophie der Tracht. Stuttgart, 1891, 148 S. 8vo.
531. SESSIONS, F.: Three Epics of Heroes (Folk-Lore Topics, No. 1). Repr. from *Gloucester* (England) *Journal*, Jan. 6, 1894. 8 pp.
532. SIMROCK, K.: Deutsche Mythologie. Sechste durchgeseh. Aufl. Bonn, 1887. xii, 643 S. 8vo.
533. SIMSON, A.: Notes on the Jívaros and Cañelos Indians. *Journ. Anthr. Inst.* (London), 1879, pp. 385–394.
534. SMITH, MRS. E. A.: Myths of the Iroquois. *Sec. Ann. Rep. Bur. of Ethn.* (1880–81), Washington, 1883, pp. 47–116.
535. SMITH, W. R.: Lectures on the Religion of the Semites. First Series. Fundamental Institutions. New York, 1889. xii, 488 pp. 8vo.
536. STEINEN, K. V. DEN: Unter den Naturvölkern Zentral-Brasiliens. Berlin, 1894.
537. STEINMETZ, S. R.: Ethnologische Studien zur ersten Entwickelung der Strafe, nebst einer psychologischen Abhandlung über Grausamkeit und Rachsucht. 2 Bde. Leiden, 1894. xlv, 486; vii, 425 S. Gr. 8vo.
538. STEVENSON, MATILDA C.: The Sia. *Eleventh Ann. Rep. Bur. of Ethnol.*, pp. 3–157.

2 F

539. Swainson, C.: The Folk-Lore and Provincial Names of British Birds. London, 1886. viii, 243 pp. 8vo.

540. Symonds, J. A.: Popular Songs of Tuscany. *Fortn. Rev.* (London). Vol. XX. (1873), pp. 596–613.

541. Tarde, G.: Les lois de l'Imitation. Étude Sociologique. ' Paris, 1890. viii, 431 pp. 8vo.

542. Temple, R. C.: The Legends of the Panjâb. 2 vols. London, n.d. xxvii, 546; xxii, 580 pp. 8vo.

543. Theal, G. McC.: Kaffir Folk-Tales. London, 1886. xii, 226 pp. 8vo.

544. Turner, L. M. Ethnology of the Ungava District, Hudson Bay Territory. *Eleventh Ann. Rep. Bur. of Ethnol.* (Washington), pp. 159–350.

545. Tylor, E. B.: Primitive Culture. Researches into the Development of Mythology, Philosophy, Religion, Language, Art, and Custom. Third Amer. ed., 2 vols. New York, 1878.

545 a. Vance, L. J.: The Meaning of Folk-Dance. *Open Court* (Chicago). Vol. VIII. (1894), pp. 4069–4070.

546. Wallaschek, R.: Primitive Music. London, 1893. xi, 326 + 8 pp. 8vo.

547. Weil, G.: The Bible, the Koran, and the Talmud; or Biblical Legends of the Mussulmans. New York, 1846. xvi, 264 pp. 8vo.

548. Yarrow, H. C.: Introduction to the Study of Mortuary Customs among the North American Indians. Washington, 1880. ix, 114 pp. 4to.

549. Yarrow, H. C.: A Further Contribution to the Study of the Mortuary Customs of the North American Indians. *First Ann. Rep. Bur. of Ethnol.* (1879–1880), Washington, 1881, pp. 87–203.

INDEX I.

INDEX II.

PLACES, PEOPLES, TRIBES, LANGUAGES, ETC.

———◆———

441

INDEX III.

SUBJECTS.

———•◦•———

www.ingramcontent.com/pod-product-compliance
Lightning Source LLC
Chambersburg PA
CBHW031819270326
41932CB00008B/469